Caring for Children
A Textbook for Nursery Nurses

Second Edition

Patricia Geraghty
M.A. (Educ.), Cert. Ed., Cert. Ed. Psych., Dip. School Hygiene, F. Coll. P.

Head of Department of Health and Community Studies,
Stevenson College of Further Education, Edinburgh;
Former Examiner, Scottish Nursery Nurse Examination Board

Baillière Tindall
London Philadelphia Toronto
Sydney Tokyo

Baillière Tindall   24–28 Oval Road
London NW1 7DX, England

West Washington Square
Philadelphia, PA 19105, USA

1 Goldthorne Avenue
Toronto, Ontario M8Z 5T9, Canada

ABP Australia Ltd, 44 Waterloo Road
North Ryde, NSW 2064, Australia

Harcourt Brace Jovanovich Japan, Inc.
Ichibancho Central Building, 22–1 Ichibancho
Chiyoda-ku, Tokyo 102, Japan

First published 1981
Reprinted 1984, 1986
Second Edition 1988

Printed and bound in Great Britain by the Alden Press, Osney Mead, Oxford

British Library Cataloguing in Publication Data

Geraghty, Patricia
  Caring for children.—2nd ed.
  1. Children. Home care – For nursery nursing
  I. Title
  649′.1

ISBN 0–7020–1242–4

Cover painting by Stefan, aged 5, Inchview Primary School, Edinburgh.

Contents

Preface

'Caring for Children' has been written primarily for nursery nurses following courses laid down by the Examination Boards in the British Isles. There are many similarities in the different courses and this textbook aims to meet the various needs.

The book will also be of value to many other people who care for children, including parents, nurses, teachers, social workers and all those concerned with the development and needs of the young child. The text covers sections on health and childhood ailments, physical and intellectual development and the importance of play and family life. Running a nursery and providing a learning environment for the child is discussed and there is a chapter devoted to children with special needs. This second edition contains updated material in each section. The importance of family life in development is emphasized in the new format, which also looks at all-round development without separating into four aspects as previously. Stressful situations within the family and their effect on children are introduced, as is child sexual abuse/incest, to reflect some of the major problems of life in Western societies today.

The term 'care-giver' is often used in this text to cover all the roles mentioned and 'nursery' can be interpreted as day nursery, nursery class or playgroup. Social Services departments are called Social Work departments in Scotland so the two names are used here.

No attempt has been made to describe the qualities necessary in a good nursery nurse as, like natural parents, every individual has qualities which could be regarded as necessary. Love for children is not enough as many criminal or inadequate parents love their children but nevertheless may jeopardise their development. Knowledge and understanding of child development are essential but theory without practical ability is insufficient. Even the most highly qualified child psychologist must have love for children while seeking to establish a successful, therapeutic relationship with them.

Many young people have caring abilities which can be fully developed by training, a process similar to the cutting and polishing that a diamond needs before its full potential is realized.

This book aims to provide a sound theoretical background which, combined with caring attitudes and practical experience, will provide the basis of care for the growing child in any environment.

Acknowledgements

I am indebted to many colleagues, past and present, for valuable help and constructive criticisms; to Health Visitor Mrs Joan Sneb for reading the Health chapters from a viewpoint of present practice; to Dr Ian Hamilton of the Royal Edinburgh Hospital Poisons Unit for the latest treatments in first aid; to Joe Reynolds, Head of Social Studies at Stevenson College, for reading the chapter on the child in the family and providing valuable help in sociological aspects; to Mrs Margaret Paton for valuable assistance; to Sarah V. Smith, Nursing Editor, Baillière Tindall for help in latter production of this edition; to the BBC Hulton Picture Library for permission to reproduce Figures 1.2 and 1.3; to Audio Visual Aids, University of Newcastle upon Tyne for their kind permission to reproduce Figure 10.2; and to all my students, wherever they are.

Patricia Geraghty

Introduction to the Care of Children

Children are cared for by parents, foster parents or parental substitutes, teachers, nursery assistants (nursery nurses), playgroup workers, childminders, day care-givers, residential social workers, health visitors and voluntary agencies. The present division between day care as provided by Social Services department staff and nursery school or nursery class provisions provided by Local Authority Education departments with the voluntary agencies operating sometimes independently, sometimes within Social Services Department's jurisdiction leads to confusion and discrepancies.

Many mothers who want full or part-time day care for their children are unable to have it because of lack of provision in many areas, others are unable to afford it. Firms (and sadly hospitals, colleges and schools) who employ women frequently ignore their family responsibilities and neglect to provide crèche and day care facilities on the premises. Nursery education is usually most sought after because of the greater opportunities it offers for children but it is usually only part-time provision which is not free. Even full-time provision finishes at 3 p.m., far too early for working mothers. Many working mothers have to resort to childminders who do not always provide satisfactory care though those who are registered and have undergone training courses are a safer proposition. Many scandals about childminders have tended to blight their image unfairly, as in many areas their form of day care, which usually provides a more intimate relationship than in the nursery, is regarded as ideal for some children.

Day Nurseries

Day nurseries, or children's centres as they are called in some areas, are responsible for day care for children from six weeks to five years of age. The majority of children will be from homes where both parents are working, but it is just as likely that they will be given a place on the recommendation of a health visitor or social worker, who considers the child 'at risk' or 'disadvantaged' because of adverse home circumstances, including mothers who find it difficult to cope with child-rearing on their own. Day nurseries may be staffed by nursery nurses with an Officer-in-charge/Matron/Superintendent, who may be an experienced nursery nurse with an additional qualification such as the C.S.S. (Certificate in Social Services); C.P.Q.S. (Certificate in Post Qualifying Studies — England); or the P.C.N.N. (Post Cert. Nursery Nursing—Scotland). The emphasis on 'physical care' attributed to day nurseries may be due to the presence of nursing rather than educational staff. Nurses should only work with children if they have taken an additional course in childplay and development (such as those mounted in Further Education colleges for playgroup staff), as it is now recognized that all child care-givers need training in the knowledge and ways of furthering learning abilities in children.

Differences in status and interpretation of roles may still cause conflict in day nursery staff unless each person sees themselves as a valuable member of a team with the welfare of the children paramount. Many nursery nurses also feel that their title no longer depicts their role, which involves care of the child intellectually, emotionally, and socially as well as physically. Some Social Services Departments now call nursery nurses 'nursery assistants' (but this does not distinguish the unqualified from the qualified) or 'nursery officers' which has the unfortunate military connotations, alien to the warmth required in these care-givers. A new title would have to describe the role of the nursery nurse in the school as well as in the day nursery, but it may prevent misunderstandings about the job, which calls for maturity as well as academic ability in applicants if they are to be care-givers in the fullest sense.

Perhaps a completely new form of training with social work, education and nursing input, would be appropriate. A number of Canadian provinces have two and three year training programmes in child development for those who work in statutory and voluntary child care agencies, including day care establishments. Of course, children do not start primary school (elementary school) until six years of age in Canada and America, and at seven years in some European countries, so many attend Kindergarten (literally child-garden) schools, which are the equivalent of our nursery schools, from three years of age, if the teachers consider they are able to benefit from substitute care. Mothers who are working leave their children in day care establishments which operate under the jurisdiction of the Ministry of Community and Social Services in Ontario and other states. Private nurseries are also operated for children of working mothers and mothers who want a break from full-time care, and these may be found on the ground floor of a large apartment building, which means that the mothers living off the ground can feel assured of their children's safety and well-being, while children know Mummy is near. Childminders are frequently the sole providers of substitute care in a number of Canadian cities but they are known as 'babysitters' there.

Education authorities provide nursery schools and classes but these are not found in every area where there is a demand for them, and unfortunately most provision is only for half-day sessions, which means that working mothers often have to use other forms of provision for their pre-school children. Many researchers have testified to the fact that nursery schools see their roles as primarily social, and several studies show that children who attend nursery school are better adjusted, happier, more self-confident and outgoing, and better able to adjust to primary school than children who do not attend.

The 1972 Government White Paper, 'A Framework for Expansion' based on the recommenda-tions of the Plowden Report, proposed that full-time nursery education should be available for 15% of three and four year olds, part-time for 35% of three year olds and 75% of four years olds with additional places in educational priority areas. Statistics show that provisions are still a long way from these recommendations. Nursery teachers undergo a three year (four year in Scotland) training in colleges of education, where they study all aspects of child development and learn how to devise programmes to meet the needs of children under five, provide for greater stability, security, new experiences, praise and recognition, responsibility and to give love through these provisions. In the nursery school or class, the teacher plans and directs the programme and usually has most inter-action with the parents, while the nursery nurse assists her in implementing the programme and organizing activities. At present there is little opportunity for advancement in the nursery school field, although some courses are available for nursery nurses with three years post-qualifying experience.

Pre-school Playgroups

These have spread rapidly since their inception in the 1960s, sometimes filling gaps left by lack of nursery school places, sometimes providing an additional service for parents whose children only require morning care, those who see it as enhancing children's social development and those who want to participate in this form of provision with other parents for their own children. The Pre-School Playgroups Association emphasizes parental participation, but not all playgroups are run by parents of the children who attend.

Most playgroup supervisors undertake a basic training course. A number of Further Education colleges operate training courses for playgroup workers, and some have advanced courses for those who wish to act as tutors to small groups of mother-helpers. These courses are usually conducted by staff with playgroup experience and tutors of nursery nurse courses. Playgroup staff often operate in difficult circumstances, having to clear away equipment after use in church halls, but many have excellent standards of play despite this. Social Services departments usually oversee playgroups, but some are private and can run without statutory approval.

Childminders and Day Caregivers

These are often found in areas where mothers have to work full-time and there are no other provisions available. Some mothers choose a childminder in preference to day nursery provision as they feel their child can benefit more from the closer relationship with the adult, but this depends on the number of children 'minded'. Social Service departments register childminders who have approved premises and requisite qualities. Day caregivers are paid by a Social Work department to look after a maximum of three children (including their own), in their own homes. Children referred to day caregivers are thought to be more appropriately placed with one person, than in a day nursery.

Some basic training courses for childminders and day caregivers are run by Social Work departments and in a few Further Education colleges but crèche provisions are necessary in order that the childminders can attend. The majority of childminders are still untrained, but they have formed associations for self-help and support.

Children's Centres

A number of day nurseries provide support services for childminders in their area and like to be regarded as Children's Centres, where health visitors, social workers, parents, nursery staff and others can meet and exchange information and advice. Mother and toddler groups for mothers with children under two years may also meet in a Children's Centre, and isolated mothers with a child in the nursery welcome the opportunity to meet together informally. Some groups ask a professional speaker along on occasions to talk to them on topics of interest.

Educational Home Visitors

These are trained nursery teachers who visit mothers at home to help them extend their own abilities in stimulating their pre-school age children at home. They often operate from Children's Centres, where there is usually a nursery teacher on the staff. The DES Educational Priority Report (1972) and the Bullock Report 'A Language for Life' (1975) recommended more educational home visitors. They are particularly needed in rural areas where there are isolated mothers and children and for children with special needs. These include not only physically and mentally handicapped children, but also those from one parent families; those socially deprived through overcrowding, lack of household amenities, lack of play space, financial hardship; those enduring long-term separation from parents in hospital or residential care; those at risk from battering parents; those in high rise flats and many others.

Toy Libraries

These are now part of pre-school provision in many areas. Toys suitable for different ages and stages and constructed from sturdy materials, may be kept in a children's centre, day nursery, nursery school or even in a local health centre. The library has to be situated centrally so that mothers caring for children at home will be encouraged to use it, as well as playgroup workers, childminders and others. Toys must be well made and the Toy Libraries Association circulates lists of ideas and suitable items. Books can also be borrowed, but local children's libraries often provide this service. The Children's Librarian may visit playgroups and nurseries to read to the children and introduce staff to suitable books which can be borrowed free of charge.

A number of voluntary organizations, e.g. the WRVS operate toy libraries, and often mothers find a visit to the toy library a useful outing for herself as well as for the children. She may welcome the chance to meet with other mothers and other care-givers. Exchange of ideas and information over a cup of tea, while the children 'test' the items available, make the weekly visits enjoyable and worthwhile. Many toy libraries have a selection of toys especially for handicapped children, and some were initiated specifically for this group, but this is a provision which mothers and care-givers were quick to appreciate, and they could rightly argue that all their children had 'special individual needs' as individuals. These needs can be partially met through access to toy libraries, where children from homes which are materially poor can enjoy a treasure trove of toys otherwise unavailable to them.

1

The Child in the Family

As most children grow up in a family setting, it is important that any study of child development, education or health should begin with a look at the role and function of the family.

The 'family' as the foundation of society is a concept which has long been accepted. Even other societies – perhaps less complex than ours – operate on the basis of a male and female offering allegiance for life to care for their offspring. Nature, too, provides examples of animals mating and then remaining with one partner to share the rearing of offspring. The family is said to be 'universal' because it can be found in all societies, even non-human kinds.

Proponents of family life tend to see it as a haven of peace away from public life and its demands – a place where the individual finds security among other individuals, where different roles converge in an integrated whole. But is this in fact true? The psychiatrist R.D. Laing has expressed the view that the stresses and strains within the family are often causative factors in mental illness and unsatisfactory relationships in later life. However, it has to be acknowledged that adverse environmental factors can affect even the most cohesive, affectionate family group.

The future of the family as the basis of Western society is the subject of continuous debate: there are those who see the role of the family as declining in society, but there are also those who see the family as adapting to a society which is changing. Currently, there seems to be a trend towards the latter view, and there is now more choice and variety in ways of family living, and an overall desire to make the family less constraining or oppressive as an institution. However, the gradual erosion of the welfare state means that the ultimate responsibility for the care of children and old or disabled people is mainly thrust back at the family, whereas, once, certain provisions were provided by the community. Here, women tend to be the carers, and although voluntary agencies (often dependent upon public charity) have come to replace the institutions set up as part of the welfare provisions, the modern family often finds the burden of caring too great, and the continuous strain caused by caring for a handicapped or ill child or an elderly relative can bring about great stress and breakdown in family life.

Types of Family Structure

The Nuclear Family

The nuclear family comprises man, wife and their children, and is the most common family structure in industrialized societies. The typical British nuclear family has 2.4 children (average of all children in UK families). Relatives no longer play an integral part in maintenance of the family, and the affiliation is expected to be monogamous – perhaps because of religious beliefs or the economic difficulty of one man supporting more than one family.

The functions of the nuclear family have specialized as a result of transferring previous functions (economic, educational, recreational) to state structures. Thus the essential functions of the family (procreation, socialization, economic maintenance, person-orientated relationships) have more meaning than previously. Many modern parents not only use schools, social, religious, and recreational provisions to assist them in the upbringing of their children, but tend to transfer all the responsibility to them. There is a tendency to forget the truism that the 'whole' child can best be cared for only by his or her parents. However, it is argued by some sociologists that provision of non-essential family functions by the wider community should promote greater satisfaction of essential family functions.

The small nuclear family tends to be child-centred, but this can sometimes mean that parents' expectations of their children are too

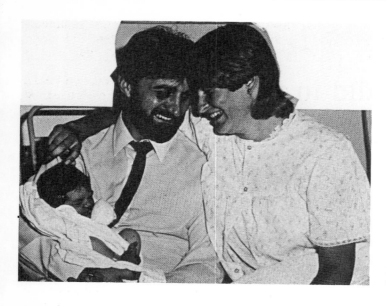

Figure 1.1 A baby transforms the couple into a family.

great. Lack of relatives within easy reach often means that children in nuclear families have a limited range of social experiences.

The Extended Family

This is described as a 'group of relatives who live in one, two, or more households, usually in a similar locality and who see each other every day, or nearly every day'. While common in tribal societies, this family structure is now rare in industrialized societies, although it can still be seen in areas of large cities where the rundown tenement or terraced housing has been replaced by high-rise flats or modern council houses with young families just around the corner from their parents or other relatives. Families who came from the West Indies, India and Pakistan one or two generations ago also tend to live near their relatives, with grandmothers retaining a matriarchal role, advising on pregnancy, birth and women's health problems. In the extended family concept of some Eastern cultures, the man is the breadwinner and taxpayer, while the wife is in charge of all home affairs, and the relatives are interdependent socially, culturally and financially.

Changed Roles in the Familiy

In the Victorian era, wives and children belonged to the husbands and fathers. All the wife's property belonged to her husband and if she separated from him he could legally cast her out without a penny. Divorce was virtually unheard of, since all the wife's possessions became her husband's on marriage, and she would not be welcomed as an impoverished, disgraced woman who had blotted the family name were she to return to her parents.

The introduction of the contraceptive pill in the 1960's gave women the freedom to choose whether to reproduce or not and this has had an impact on the family structure. Altered family roles are mainly due to a reduction in family size. This has also relieved mothers of the need to remain at home for the length of their child-rearing years, and enabled them to envisage broader horizons. Economic recessions, the silicon chip revolution and redundancies have also meant that women have become the major breadwinners in some families, while the men undertake household tasks.

Apart from those women who have to work to ensure a reasonable family income, there are considerable numbers who choose to work rather than remain at home because of the need for social stimulation, intellectual satisfaction or the pursuit of a non-family-orientated career. Many women in the UK working outside the family are married, and the reduction in family size has resulted in an increase in working women. Modern houses reflect the average size of family in that they rarely have more than three bedrooms, so larger families have problems.

Nowadays, one finds different perceptions of the roles in family life, often determined by social status and gender. Middle class and professional couples tend to see the wife's main responsibility as assisting the husband in the furtherance of his career, although the concept of 'dual-career' for both husband and wife is also frequently held in these groups. The growing reassessment of fatherhood in the context of a changing economy, with great numbers of men who may never find work outside the home, and changing conceptions of work, has, in some cases, led to the 'house-husband' idea, but, as one study shows, men do not necessarily spend more time in domestic or child-caring activities. Some politicians maintain that a return to 'Victorian values and family life' would bring about a change in society 'devoutely to be wished'! However, such narrow and retrograde thinking ignores the hardship suffered by many women and children who had to work long hours in appalling conditions, and who only had the workhouse – a notorious institution where death due to malnutrition and childhood disease was a daily occurrence – to look forward to when they were too old and frail to work.

Working Mothers

The Sex Discrimination Act of 1974 made it illegal for women to be discriminated against on the grounds of sex, and the Equal Opportunities Act was intended to remove barriers of single sex entry into a number of traditional 'male' and 'female' jobs. However, still comparatively fewer women train to become engineers, and more boys than girls tend to take advantage of further and higher education. There will probably always be those traditionalists who insist that a woman's place is in the home, but it is useful to look at the research concerning the effects on children of working mothers before opinions are formed. There is little research evidence to show that maternal employment in itself has a detrimental effect on a child's development – and there are some instances where it is positively advantageous. But not all research studies have taken account of variables such as whether the mother works full- or part-time, the quality and availability of substitute care, the age of the child, and the attitudes of both parents. Only a small percentage of

children under five have working mothers and, for these, a secure, consistent and stimulating environment in substitute day care is essential.

The effects of full-time day care on young children would be greatest in the earliest period of a child's life when there is a crucial need to form attachments to one or two people. 'Socially disadvantaged' children have often suffered from a lack of parental interaction, and many parents may not feel like playing with their children after a heavy working day. Older preschool children appear to benefit from a few hours away from their mothers as this enables them to gain independence and enjoy social relationships with other children. The mother herself often feels the benefit of this, too, and is able to devote herself to the child afresh after a short respite. Research carried out by the National Children's Bureau showed that children whose mothers had started work after the children had begun school were slightly less well adjusted at 7 years of age than children whose mothers had started to work during the pre-school period. However, a follow-up study of children in one-parent families found that at the age of 11 years there was a tendency for those whose mothers worked full-time to be better adjusted.

Research has also revealed that there is only a slight difference in educational attainment between children of working and non-working mothers. Working class children – particularly boys – show higher attainment when their mothers work, while the reverse is true of middle class children. The mother's own attitude to her working is important in that a mother who likes working will react positively to her child, but a satisfied mother – whether working or not – will be more adequate as a mother. Some studies show that the anxiety and guilt felt by working mothers of young children often lead to overcompensation and many mothers suffer from the strain of combining the two roles. The increased involvement of the father with his children, which often happens as a result of the mother working, is obviously beneficial to the child's development and also to family life.

Unfortunately, day care provision in nurseries and play groups is far from adequate, with usually only half-day care, which is not helpful for full-time working mothers. Full-time day care provision has not increased to match the increase in numbers of working mothers. Hence, many mothers have to rely on child-minders where grandparents and relatives are not able to help.

Teenage Parents

In 1982, almost one child in ten in Britain was born to a teenage mother. Most of these were unmarried, although a number of them were living with the father of the child.

Teenage pregnancies are associated with a number of physical problems for the mother, low birthweight of the child, and high rates of fetal, perinatal and maternal mortality. Many of these ill-effects are related to unemployment, low socioeconomic status, poor housing and disadvantaged environment, low educational achievements, lack of support and stable relationships, inexperience, isolation, depression and poor levels of attendance at antenatal and other clinics. Teenage marriages are particularly at risk of breakdown: a bride in her teens is twice as likely to become divorced as one aged 20–24 years. A national study of teenage couples points out that it is unrealistic to expect such marriages to survive if immaturity is combined with early parenthood, and adverse social and economic conditions. Teenage parenthood is also associated with child abuse. One study found that 50% of abusing mothers were under 20 years of age at the birth of their first child compared with 16% in a control group. Children of teenage parents appear to have more hospital admissions, more accidents and a higher incidence of Sudden Infant Death Syndrome. Studies have also suggested an association between maternal depression and child behaviour problems, with significantly more mothers who married before the age of 21 becoming depressed compared with those mothers who married later. There are few provisions for young teenage parents, although some family centres, community centres and youth clubs now welcome them into Young Couples' and Young Mums' clubs.

Single Teenage Mothers

Unmarried teenage mothers now tend to keep their babies rather than give them up for adoption, as much of the stigma which once marked a young single mother has disappeared. In this time of large-scale unemployment among school leavers, some doctors, youth workers and others have suggested that teenage girls are choosing to become pregnant as an escape from the boredom of tedious unskilled jobs. The financial and social problems faced by these young mothers would seem to be so great that it is difficult to see why they would volunteer for such an action. There are cultural differences in teenage parenthood too: while very few are from Asian backgrounds, those from Afro-Caribbean backgrounds are actually increasing. Many of these young teenage mothers will feel isolated from their peer groups, may have had inadequate parenting themselves and therefore need help in the acquisition of parenting skills. Some youth counsellors hold sessions of group work with teenage mothers which may help to prevent potential child abuse. Few single mothers will find supportive residential facilities since there has been a decline in the number of hostels run by religious or voluntary agencies for mothers and babies. There are, however, some family units set up by local social services departments where the personal and educational needs of the young mothers can be met. Those who wish to continue their education in colleges of further or higher education will find lack of finances and shortage of crèche and day-care facilities serious (and regrettable) obstacles to be overcome.

Teenage pregnancies can lead to considerable problems in all aspects of the child's development. A child health and education study carried out in 1982 showed that children born to teenage mothers and living with them for the first 5 years were more liable to hospital admissions – especially after accidents or for gastroenteritis – than children born to, and living with, older mothers. Since hospital admissions in early life may have adverse effects on children, this could mean another long-term disadvantage for these children. Infant mortality is higher in these groups, and children of young mothers have been found to suffer more physical, emotional and intellectual handicaps. They are also liable to behavioural disturbances and poorer educational attainment. The outcome of these problems could be child abuse and there is the risk that the cycle of disadvantage is likely to spiral onwards through subsequent generations.

One-Parent Families

There are about 1 million one-parent families in

Britain involving about 1 600 000 children – about one eighth of all families with children. Since 33% of new marriages end in divorce (as do 40% of remarriages) and 60% of divorcing couples have dependent children, the number of one-parent families is likely to increase. Poverty is present in many instances in one-parent families: half of all homeless families have one parent, and half of all one-parent families live on supplementary benefit. In the 3½ million people registered as unemployed in Britain today (and there are others not registered), single parents figure significantly as present government policies have reduced day and nursery care facilities, particularly full-time, to a minimum.

Health and social problems combined with poverty lead to mental and physical ill-health in both the parent and the child. Professor Morris of the London School of Hygiene and Tropical Medicine has pointed out that the ratio of infant mortality in social classes 1–5 is the same as it was before the introduction of the National Health Service and the Welfare State. Community medical workers now agree that they have to go to women with greatest need rather than expect the women to attend health centres which may require a bus journey.

Government policies of penalizing councils that 'over-spend' by increasing support to health and social services discriminate against inner-city populations which contain many single-parent families. Supplementary benefit, drastically insufficient for the provision of decent shelter, warmth and food for children, is denied to those women who are deemed to be cohabiting when a male visitor is observed on an overnight stay. This ridiculous and indefensible ruling by DHSS officials almost amounts to a morality check on single female parents, as a male parent is never assumed to be financially dependent on a woman who stays overnight with him!

One-parent families are not always the result of divorce: death of a parent or a parent's desertion, unmarried mothers, and single foster parents or guardians all make up one-parent families. The proportion of fatherless families to motherless families is 6 : 1. In the fatherless families, just over half were broken by divorce, in one-third of the families the father had died, and the remainder were children of unmarried mothers. In the motherless families half had been caused by divorce or separation and half by death. The 'broken home' is often blamed for numerous problems in childhood, possibly because of the stresses faced by the single parent in earning a living, caring for the children, and coping with their own emotional reactions to the absence of a partner and having sole responsibility for the family.

Single parents may feel rejected and unable to lead a normal social life in a society geared to couples. The effects on children of one-parent families depends on whether the single parent is the same sex as the child, the age at which the child lost his parent, and whether it was due to desertion, divorce or death. The bereaved child may have had a secure environment before the parent's death, but a child whose home is upset by separation or divorce is likely to have suffered a long period of emotional stress before the break finally took place. Fathers coping single-handed receive more support from female relatives than do single mothers, and usually earn more than single women parents. Housing problems often accompany financial difficulty, and single parents need full day care for their children if they want to work.

Divorce

The rate of divorce has increased by 500% since the Divorce Reform Act became law in 1971. However, this does not appear to reflect the unpopularity of marriage, since many divorced people remarry. There are many reasons for the increasing rate of divorce and some sociologists believe that the changes in Western society – unemployment being a major reality in communities once closely knit, and the subsequent necessity for men as the traditional bread-winners to seek jobs elsewhere – could be a factor. Many young people demonstrate their lack of faith in marriage as a life-long institution by living together unmarried. Others marry at an early age despite unemployment, possibly as an escape from an unhappy home life. It could be argued that they are the only sufferers in their transition from immaturity to stable relationship but, if pregnancy occurs, the effect on the child must be considered. Some children of divorced parents have difficulty in intimate relationships when they grow up, while others have good and happy marriages.

Whereas selfishness in either partner or in

both, when they put their own needs before that of their offspring, can destroy a loving relationship, children are more often affected by the continuous wrangling and tension which frequently precedes divorce. The majority of divorces occur in the first 10 years of marriage which means that a considerable number of young children are affected. Rutter found that children of two and three are particularly vulnerable psychologically to the loss of a parent of the same sex, and many studies show a higher risk of later emotional disturbance in boys, and of unmarried mothers in girls, whose parents divorced before they were 6 years old.

As divorce represents a bereavement, children often experience reactions of loss, fear and guilt since they may see themselves as responsible for the breakup of the marriage. Disturbed behaviour has been found to be more common in children of divorced parents. They may become accident prone, withdrawn or hostile, with outbursts of aggression, and boys, for some reason, tend to demonstrate this more often than girls. However, it is the antisocial behaviour from destructive and stormy parental relationships which is usually to blame for the adverse effects, rather than the divorce itself. The child can actually benefit from separation of parents who live in an atmosphere of constant conflict.

In the long term, some children of divorced parents do not achieve the same educational standards as those from undivorced families. Parental hostility may make access to the separated parent difficult, and lack of a father or subsequent male figure can affect both boys and girls. Despite recommendations from major governmental committees, the establishment of Family Courts where custodial, financial and welfare arrangements could be worked out in an informal setting has not yet taken place.

Stepchildren

As stated above, remarriage after divorce is common nowadays, which means that many children having experienced some time as part of a one-parent family face another transition as stepchildren of their parent's new partner. Since there are more children left in the mother's custody after divorce, the majority of children have stepfathers. A recent study on stepchildren by the National Children's Bureau revealed that there was little difference in the material circum-stances of children with stepmothers and those with both natural parents. The father's remarriage had largely overcome the economic disadvantage of the motherless family. Similarly, children with stepfathers were better off than those living with lone mothers as the mother's remarriage lifted many fatherless families out of the low income bracket.

Children in stepfather families tend to be somewhat disadvantaged in material terms when compared to children in undivorced families. This could, however, be related to the relatively large number of children in these families from possibly two previous marriages. This could also be the reason for the overcrowded living conditions of these families, as the father may have found himself with two families to support on one income, unless his new wife is employed outside the home. While the economic disadvantages are small, they may be exacerbated by the stress in personal relationships between children and the step-parent.

The legendary wicked step-parent in traditional children's stories is unlikely to figure in step-families today, but the problems experienced by stepchildren and step-parents are greater when the original family was broken by divorce rather than bereavement. There is a tendency for girls in step-families to marry early, under the age of 20 years, with all the subsequent problems associated with early marriage mentioned previously. Boys in stepfather families reveal less aspiration for further education and training than those in natural families, and the attitudes of both parents in these families echo that of the lone mother families.

As the number of children in step-families will increase with the rate of divorce and remarriage, nursery staff must exercise tact, discretion and understanding when caring for children who may carry a different surname from their step-brothers and sisters elsewhere in the school. Obviously, the choice of stories read and told in the nursery or primary class will also relate to the differing backgrounds of the children, and adaptations should be made where necessary. However, it is important to remember that a major difficulty in step-families is that they are judged by the norm of the nuclear family. This is unrealistic: the step-parent's role is ill-defined and critical attitudes can lead to unnecessary problems in terms of authority, responsibility, guidance and affection.

The Family in Other Countries

Israel

In Israel, families occasionally choose to live together in small communities known as *kibbutzim*. Here they live intimately: work is divided equally and child-rearing shared. There are schools for the children, known as 'children's houses', which are placed between residential houses with a house for each age group. The philosophy is that children are the centre of life and women are the carers. Some women will have children in different houses from the one in which they work. There is 'open house' all day so that parents working on the farms, or elsewhere, can look in for a short time at certain intervals during their working day. The younger children play as do children in Western countries, but their toys are realistic, and the objects used are similar to the practical ideas of Maria Montessori, i.e. boards with tie laces, materials with zips and buttons. Older children have teachers in the morning for more formal work, then play in the afternoon. Nowadays, some Israeli parents feel that they would like to see more of their children than the kibbutz system allows and that there is not enough emphasis on the father's role in parenting.

USSR

As the majority of mothers work outside the home in Russia, there are many crèches or day nurseries in the huge industrial complexes which are the places of work. Forty per cent of city children attend day nursery from the age of 2 months to 3 years. The 'collective' ideal, which was translated into Soviet farming and factory systems, is also seen in the playpens where children of the same age are grouped together. Babies are watched over in long rows of cots, and the child-care workers are usually nurses. By 3 years of age, 90% of children in towns are in pre-school provision. Here again, women do the caring, and the emphasis is on strengthening character through a programme of planned lessons and play. This rather formal approach to children of nursery or kindergarten age might seem strange when compared to the ideas of 'free' and 'child-led' play seen in most British pre-school provision, although this is also the trend in Canada and America where kinder-garten is the main provision for children up to the age of 6 years when they enter primary school. 'Dramatic' play in Russian nurseries is more like role-practising or role-acting than play, and tends to be based on real-life situations rather than make-believe. By 3 years, children are expected to recognize shapes and colours and to be able to catch and return a ball thrown by the teacher.

China

There have been changes in philosophy and ideals since the Chinese Socialist Revolution of 1949. The child is now regarded as an integral part of the commune and as making a valuable contribution to society in general. Ninety per cent of Chinese women work outside the home, and about 50% of children are cared for by their grandparents. Thus, in China, the extended family still survives though often in crowded two-roomed dwellings. Another 50% of children are, from the age of 2 months, in group care units situated alongside the mother's workplace. There are 'collective' nursing rooms, and nursing mothers, i.e. mothers who are breast feeding, are given time off from work to feed their babies. From 3 to 7 years, the children are in kindergarten in the care of women who clearly believe in the Socialist ethic. For 30–50 minutes each day, children are made to work for the common benefit. Perhaps sorting out seeds before they are packed, or finishing off some simple factory process (such as fixing lids on boxes), they are encouraged to be productive members of society. The fact that this is real work rather than a play activity does not appear to bother the children at all, perhaps because they have been taught to see it as worthwhile, and encouraged in their efforts. Their games, however, are rather less salutary and often involve the acting out of aggressive military combat, while the use of real guns is taught as part of their curriculum. Western observers may find the sight of 50 six-year-olds wielding machine guns horrific, yet Western children enjoy this type of play too.

Sweden

Sweden is a small country with a population of about 5 million – similar to Scotland. Seventy per cent of Swedish women work outside the home, and day nurseries or kindergarten are provided. There is full daytime provision from the age of 6 months to 6 years, until primary school. In day centres, each group has its own room with 'children's nurses' (all women) in the ratio of 10 children to 1 adult, and here they practise skills appropriate to their development stage. The 5- and 6-year-old children attend 'child centres' and have trained nursery teachers and children's nurses who are similar to the nursery nurses in the UK. The children can enjoy domestic play in 'Wendy' houses and their play is unstructured, giving scope for creativity and imagination. However, full day care means that children are away from their parents from 6.30 a.m. to 6 p.m., which is a long time, especially since the child cannot be left alone at any one time and, as nursery nurses are aware, this can be a deprivation for some children.

There is also a Family Day Care scheme – rather like child-minding. The 'day mother' caters for four children, including her own, in a family home which may or may not be her own. She cooks meals but is not expected to do house-work. Children of all ages help to prepare and serve the meal, and so learn to hold potentially harmful utensils, like knives, properly. The home environment is held to be better than that of the day centre since older children mix and play with the younger ones and there is much greater verbal interraction. Nevertheless, the Swedes feel that there is still a lack of day centres in Sweden.

Although crèches in workplaces feature largely in Israel, China, and Russia, they are also beginning to appear in Western countries. Some firms who rely heavily on female workers have had the foresight to install crèches with trained nursery staff in charge. Some hospitals and colleges are also providing this, although the numbers of such child-care facilities are notoriously inadequate. Some large stores have finally realized that parents prefer to shop, and will shop for longer periods (and spend more) if they know that their children are being looked after by trained staff and are playing happily away from the hustle and bustle of shopping.

A Swedish expert of child-rearing, Professor Urie Brofenbrenner has reservations about the Russian and Chinese methods of child rearing, and queries whether the subjugation of the individual to societal needs and the loss of individual freedom is too much to pay.

The Role of Parents in Development

The contribution of the family to a child's social, personal and cognitive development has been demonstrated by numerous studies. Parents whose formal schooling was brief or turbulent have difficulty in convincing their children that education is worthwhile. Good care from a child's parents involves not only the provision of material needs such as food, clothing, shelter, warmth and protection from infection and other noxious agents, but also satisfaction of emotional and intellectual needs through the establishment of early parental–child bonding and enjoyment of the love, security and stimulation which can result from it. This security gives children the impetus to develop social relationships outside the family with other adults and children. The relationship with the child's mother is traditionally stressed in child-rearing theories as it is usually the mother who has the most day-to-day contact and responsibility for the child. However, the importance of the role of the father apart from material provision is increasingly recognized.

Traditional theories of child-rearing have tended to stress the importance of the exclusive maternal role in sound development. Recent studies indicate that while bonding relationships are important, good parenting can be provided by other than the child's biological parents, and that children can relate to more than one or two people from the early months. A continual change of early care-givers is, however, not satisfactory. Constancy and consistency are essential for the formation of stable relationships even though it is the quality of care given, rather than the amount of time, which is most important.

Fathers, grandparents and older siblings are all capable of providing as much 'mothering' as the natural mother if she decides to continue with her job after the baby's birth, and often professional care-givers have to provide mothering for babies of 6 weeks onwards. Some people find it difficult to express motherly love spontaneously. Western cultures tend to have taboos about touch which can affect even intimate relationships between sexual partners. One often finds young couples who are reluctant to fondle and caress their baby in front of other people. Cuddling is enjoyed by all babies and children, and adults too, if they are exposed to it from birth and laid naked to the mother's breast while she and the father gently caress the baby.

Touch is the most developed sense at birth, and enlightened parents and care-givers utilize this to establish closeness and feelings of protection, warmth and security. When a baby cries, she is often demanding attention, and instead of ignoring this, parents should try cuddling to reinforce the feeling that an aspect of caring is the comfortable security of touching another's warm body, being held in supporting arms with the accompaniment of a soothing tone of voice.

Physical Development

The progress made through the stages of development whereby the child gains increasing control of her body from crawling to walking, running and jumping, and from being fed to the competent use of knife, fork and spoon, is dependent on the attitudes of parents and care-givers who must be aware of the child's needs. One of these is the opportunity to practise and develop growing skills. The confidence gained from an understanding, caring environment enables children to express themselves in movement, find joy in running, invent new 'stunts', and move on to further exploration as they feel more secure.

Space is necessary both indoors and out to allow maximum opportunity for movement. As far as possible, rooms should be adapted so that damage to furniture and accidents are avoided, and the children given their own room, or at least their own area. In small, cramped flats this is difficult, and the child may have to wait for a visit to the park or playground before giving free rein to physical expression.

Exercise in fresh air and sunlight is essential if the benefits of a well balanced diet are to be enjoyed. The provision of adequate food containing all the essential nutrients – proteins, vitamins and minerals essential for growth, and carbohydrates and fats for energy and protection – is at first available in breast milk (or modified cows' milk) and later replaced by a more substantial diet of solids and liquids.

Accommodation in damp-proof dwellings, free from vermin and insect vectors of disease, is also necessary to prevent serious curtailment of development through illness. Clothing, too, is important, and should provide warmth, protection from the elements and injury, but also room for growth and movement. It may sometimes be difficult for a mother to provide clean clothes every day, particularly if she has no washing machine or several children to clothe, but professional care-givers should not be judgemental. The 'mothering' of a good care-giver embraces all the children in her care, regardless of appearance or manner.

Emotional Development

The role of parents in emotional development is closely linked to physical care. The way in which a baby is fed, for example, is extremely important, and her emotional development is enhanced if the preparation is punctual and feeding unhurried and free from anxiety. Frustration is often felt by the baby if she is kept waiting, having been roused by the preliminary feeding sounds which she can recognize as early as 3 months of age. Furthermore, if the mother is tense or anxious this is all too easily conveyed to the baby who will then not feed well and so upset the mother even more.

While it is not easy to control one's emotions for the sake of the baby, it is important to remember that babies are sensitive to even the most subtle of cues. Insecurity, even in the early months, can affect the course of childhood and even later life. Holding the baby confidently and concentrating solely on her during feeding time makes her feel loved and secure. This is essential whether breast or bottle feeding.

Later, the child will progress from the egocentric stage to the recognition of others' rights and feelings. This is not always an easy transition, particularly if the child is insecure and resents attention directed at other children. Similarly, a relaxed approach and an understanding attitude through the toilet-training period also ensures that the child can progress gradually to maturity without upset.

The provision of space for play is integral to the child's emotional development as it provides an outlet for anger and frustration. Clothes, too, are important, as pride in appearance gives self-confidence. But while the mother of a 4-year-old can perhaps make a special 'treat' out of shopping for clothes, with a 6- to 8-year-old she must be prepared to hear the objections to her choice as children then prefer to follow the fashions of their school friends and like to be seen as part of the peer group. Obviously, sound parenting involves the ability to accept that the child changes as he grows up and the adult's attitude towards him must also adapt. Baby-hood eventually gives way to childhood but the child's emotional growth must not be stunted because it is easier to cope with a docile baby than with an argumentative 8-year-old child!

Intellectual Development

Intellectual development is dependent on a sound physical and emotional basis comple-mented by adequate stimulation. Sound parent-ing involves an understanding of the needs of the child at different ages and stages and a know-ledge of individual variations so that the child is not pushed beyond his or her capacities. This understanding also enables the parents of a handicapped child to realize when he or she is not attaining the expected goals for his or her age, and when to seek advice or help. Provision of play materials, suited to the child at each stage, is part of the stimulaton all children need. Parents and professional carers should not be afraid of devoting too much time to the child, and playing with him or her is also important as children learn much through play.

Social Development

A child who has enjoyed a good relationship with both parents in the first three years will soon be mature enough to join in with others at play. Nevertheless, the first day at nursery may be a daunting experience and the child often cries to express his feelings of strangeness and fear. However, the security of good 'mothering' relationships helps the child to settle in and many parents feel that mixing with other adults and children around the age of 3 years is con-ducive to healthy social development.

Children in Poverty

The number of families living in poverty or on the margins of poverty increased by over 50% in the early 1980s mainly due to economic recession and cutbacks in the welfare state provisions. Few children brought up between the 1960s and 1970s will have had to stay away from school because they had no clothes to wear, but, as the 1990s approach, absence from school may become as common for this reason as it was in the 1930s, 1940s and 1950s! Despite the 1982 Government Family Expenditure Survey which showed that the average weekly expenditure of a two-child family (excluding housing costs) was £134.00, many families on Supplementary Benefit (which is taken as the 'poverty line') have only £1.30 per day for each child's needs. Studies have shown that deprivation increases markedly if income falls below 140–150% of the Supplementary Benefit level; hence many families live in considerable deprivation on the margins of poverty. There are nearly 4 million children living in the UK out of a total of some 13 million people living on, or near, the poverty line. While, in many cases, unemployment is to blame for this, there is also an increase in the number of families living just above the poverty line where the parent is in full-time work. But the problem of poverty is not restricted to single-parent families since over 3–4 million children in two-parent families live in or on the margins of poverty compared with under 1 million single-parent families.

Studies carried out by the Child Poverty Action Group and the Family Service Unit showed that parents did all they could to protect their children from the effects of poverty. Despite their efforts, children in four out of ten families have to go without meals for lack of money. There may not be death as a result of this hunger, but the effects of malnutrition prevail into adulthood. Lack of fuel for heating houses which are often damp inevitably lowers the children's resistance to infection, and many will suffer from chronic ill-health with long periods of absence from school. Meanwhile, lack of clothing and footwear is a constant problem as children quickly outgrow these items and most families have to resort to second-hand clothes and shoes sold at jumble sales. This can have a depressing effect on children who begin to resent their lack of possessions. Attendance at school can become a problem. Even if school uniform is not required, 'free' education still involves extra expenditure for school outings and bus trips, etc. Many parents avoid this by keeping their children away from school on these days. Free school meals are a relief for worried parents during the school term but, when the holidays come around, they find it difficult to provide more than one meal each day. Family outings, trips to the park or swimming pool, inviting friends home for tea or birthday parties are all impossible.

A large survey carried out by London

Figure 1.2 Children in poverty – still not a thing of the past.

Weekend Television for their Breadline Britain programmes in 1983 asked more than a thousand people for their views on poverty and their own standard of living. The following items were listed as essential for a minimum standard of living by two-thirds of those interviewed: heating, an indoor toilet, a damp-free home, a bath (not shared with another family), enough money for public transport, a warm waterproof coat, three meals a day for children, self-contained accommodation, two pairs of all-weather shoes, no overcrowding, with enough bedrooms for children, a refrigerator, toys for children, carpets, celebrations for special occasions, such as Christmas, a roast joint or its equivalent once a week, and a washing machine. Almost three-quarters of those interviewed said they would be prepared to pay 1 penny more in the £ in income tax to ensure that everyone could afford at least these items.

Social Security Benefits

In 1984, the DHSS approached the National Children's Bureau to help them with their enquiry into Social Security Benefits. The NCB welcomed this as they thought that the state financial provision for children had deteriorated in comparison with other groups in society.

They laid down three major principles as the basis for their recommendations:

1 Every child must be treated as an individual in his or her own right.
2 Every child, by definition vulnerable and thereby dependent on society, has the right to at least a guaranteed minimum level of subsistence. It is the responsibility of the government to guarantee this right.
3 The protection of children must be placed above all other government priorities.

On Child Benefit, the overall recommendation of the NCB was that a universal child benefit should be paid in the name of every child, regardless of family circumstances, and should be set annually at an adjustable rate to take account of inflation and rises in living costs. This would correspond to the minimum amount required to supply the basic needs of a child. The NCB also recommended that One-Parent Benefit (index-linked to cost of living) combined with an enhanced Child Benefit should be paid to all single-parent families. This uniform rate of benefit would replace the wide range of benefit levels under the existing system. The underlying principle of this is that the One-Parent Benefit addition for single-parent families is needed because their average income is substantially lower than that of the average two-parent family and they are much more likely to be poor. They maintain that a uniform benefit for all one-parent families is justified on the grounds that a child-support policy should aim at achieving both adequate and equal treatment for all children. The NCB also recommended that the Maternity Benefit should be increased to a more relevant sum (£125) to be paid to all women during and after pregnancy. The underlying principle of this is that the babies of today are the adults of tomorrow, therefore policies that promote the health of children today also serve to enhance the potential productivity of the next generation. Also, the needs of babies begin before birth and should not depend on the employment status of their mothers.

On Family Credit the NCB recommended that the existing combination of Child Benefit and means-tested additions be replaced with the uniform higher rates of Child Benefit, and that the prescribed income levels at which FIS is payable should be raised to take account of increased costs in ordinary living

expenses. They maintain that these measures would reverse the trend of rising poverty amongst the children of the low paid. The NCB also recommended that the basic rates of Supplementary Benefit and National Insurance Benefit for the short-term unemployed or sick should be raised. Long-term unemployed people with dependent children should have the long-term rate extended to them and the present Children's Additions to Supplementary Benefit and Child Dependency Additions to National Insurance Benefits should be replaced by extension of the enhanced Child Benefit to all unemployed families. This is based on the principle that there should be a close correspondence between benefit levels and the needs of children. The needs of the children of the unemployed are no fewer than those of children whose parent(s) work. It is the duty of the government to protect the rights of all children to have their basic needs met because of their total dependency on society, and this priority must prevail over other labour market concerns. The NCB suggested that the primary source of funding for these benefits could be the Married Man's Tax Allowance which, if abolished, would yield approximately £3.4 billion. In addition, it maintained that there would be substantial savings resulting from greatly reduced demand for expensive means-tested supplement to benefits; significant reductions in numbers of children in care; the abolition of means testing for many benefits; and a reduction in the indirect social costs of ill-health, family breakdown, drug addiction, violence and vandalism.

In conclusion to their recommendations the NCB stated that 'in the interests of our own and future generations the resources must be found to lay the groundwork for building a society that genuinely treasures and builds upon the inherent and potential worth of its children'.

Deprivation and Disadvantage

Children of one-parent families, divorced parents and working mothers are often described as 'deprived' or 'disadvantaged', but this is frequently *not* the case. It is important to recognize the difference between privation and deprivation. Michael Rutter in *Maternal Deprivation Reassessed* (1972), criticized the literature on maternal deprivation which had gained considerable attention after John Bowlby's *Child Care and the Growth of Love* (1953). Those who misinterpreted Bowlby's findings condemned day care because it involved separation from the mother, and insisted that children suffering from parental abuse should be returned to their parents rather than taken into care. According to Rutter, privation is the *lack* of something necessary for development, whereas deprivation refers to the *loss* of some necessity for development. It is interesting to note that Bowlby referred only to maternal deprivation, yet the role of the father is now considered very important to the healthy development of children.

Children who are separated from their mothers may be adversely affected, but this depends on a host of variables, such as the age of the child, temperamental make-up, previous adjustments, continuity of other care-givers, duration of separation, and presence of family members in a separation situation. There is no evidence that children *inevitably* suffer ill-effects emotionally, socially or intellectually through separation from their mothers, but a homely environment and quality of care are essential factors in the adjustment to situations outside the family home. Attachments are made in the first 2 years of life which are important for future development, but these may not be to biological parents.

Long-stay residential institutions are no longer considered suitable for children since permanent one-to-one or one-to-two relationships are difficult to maintain with changing staff and children brought up in impersonal residential institutions may have difficulty in parenting their own children.

Medical research shows that Bowlby's theories on emotional deprivation can still be applied in cases of failure to thrive where the cause is non-organic. *Non-organic failure to thrive* is defined as growth retardation, with or without associated developmental defect, and the absence of organic disorders sufficient to account for such retardation. It is considered very likely that a combination of emotional deprivation, which is associated with diminished production of growth hormone, together with inadequate provision of food, is the cause of this condition.

In non-organic failure to thrive, careful evaluation of the family's social situation, their child-rearing practices, attitudes to the particular child, and their relationship to community supportive agencies is essential. Much is known about these factors but it is still uncertain what happens to these children in later years and which is the best way of dealing with their problem initially. A profile of 24 children who showed failure to thrive revealed that after 2 years, half had grown to normal size but one-third had delayed development and three-quarters had abnormal results in personality tests. After 6 years, two of the original group had died of injuries inflicted by an adult, and two others were admitted to hospital with fractured bones and another with bruising. The school performance of the 22 survivors was poor, reading ages below average, and half had abnormal profile scores on personality tests completed by teachers. When the mothers completed the same questionnaire 90% provided answers which gave their children an abnormal personality score. This seems to indicate that abnormal maternal perception of these children leads to emotional and then nutritional deprivation. The importance of the first days and weeks of life in creating a strong mother–child bond is now well known, as indeed are factors which can impair such bonding, such as complication of pregnancy, a prolonged labour, postnatal depression, early separation (e.g. from a premature or sick baby in an incubator), and everyday social stresses.

Most parents who are confronted with such problems still manage to relate satisfactorily to their children. Parents at risk are usually those who themselves suffered from maternal or paternal deprivation and are therefore more likely to have difficulty in establishing strong bonds with their own children. Real or imagined, unrewarding features in the child (e.g. insomnia, hyperactivity, etc.) also interfere with bonding. Furthermore, professional care is likely to reinforce the mother's sense of inadequacy, and part of the management of non-organic failure to thrive must be an attempt to involve the mother in the programme of daily care. Praise for effort, credit for progress in the child, and warm support must be given to the mother in hospital, nursery, and at home. Emphasis on supporting the mother and the child together can do much to prevent the developmental consequences outlined above.

Housing

The Housing Condition Survey (1981) revealed that over 4 million properties lacked basic amenities, were unfit for habitation and/or in a state of disrepair. In 1982 figures from the Central Statistical Office revealed that the number of houses exceeded the number of households by about 1 million, but there are still 2 million children who are homeless or living in crowded inadequate and unsuitable houses. Many 'surplus' houses are in areas where there is massive unemployment and so no purchasing power or money for renovation or even heating. Older houses, especially, may be damp and draughty with lofty ceilings, large rooms and big windows demanding massive expenditure on heating. Even houses built in the 1960s now show signs of wear and tear because of poor quality construction materials, and many of those built by local councils have had to be demolished since reconstruction and repair were deemed too costly. Not only were housing estates badly designed and built, but the lack of grassed areas and play space for children has made life in these concrete jungles depressing and monotonous. It is hardly surprising that adolescents in these areas resort to the excitement of drug taking and other illegal activities.

Young children confined in the small space of modern houses and further restricted by high wire fencing round the concrete playgrounds of their inner city schools react as young animals do when cooped up: they become distressed, turn to squabbling and fighting, form 'gangs' as their older brothers and sisters do, and carry on vendettas against any child or children who appear(s) different by colour, religion, customs or language. This is true of many parts of Britain and many local authorities have had to resort to waiting lists for housing and a points system based on such factors as the length of residence in the area, the size of the household, and any health problems.

The 1977 Housing (Homeless Persons) Act defined homelessness as 'being without accommodation' but the voluntary organization Shelter broadens the definitions to include people who have accommodation which is insecure, overcrowded, dangerous, damp or lacking in basic amenities. Overcrowding is defined as more than 1.5 persons per room, which means that two parents and four children in four rooms would not be 'overcrowded' officially, but very much so in reality. The National Dwelling and Household Survey of 1977 found 253 000 households living in other people's homes. In 1982 those accepted as homeless under the narrower definition numbered only 35 700 but the provision of hostel or bed and breakfast facilities for these families proved very expensive for local authorities.

Many studies have shown a clear relationship between poor living conditions and overcrowding, and below average educational performance, respiratory disease and even delinquency.

At 7 years of age, children in overcrowded homes were, on average, 3 months behind in reading, and children lacking basic amenities were 9 months behind. Truancy at 16 years of age is more common in children living in overcrowded homes.

Disadvantaged children who had experienced bad housing had more accidents than other children and missed more school through illness. Bad housing also exacerbates tense family situations. An NSPCC study of children who had been battered by their parents found that many of the families lived in particularly bad housing, most of it privately rented, and concluded that these conditions contributed to physical abuse.

Furthermore, children in overcrowded homes are more than twice as likely as other children to be delinquent or aggressive. There does not seem to be any direct causal relationship between crime and housing, but American research has shown that the design of an estate and lack of personal space and space for play encourages vandalism. Home Office research in the UK has found that the main predictor of vandalism is the number of children per household in the block. Design is less important, although vandalism does increase with the size and height of the building, with semi-public unsupervised areas and with little or no landscaping.

Children in flats

Since the 1960s which saw a boom in high-rise flat blocks, many studies have shown the adverse effects that living in high-rise housing can have on young children. Small rooms limit play space, mothers are afraid to let younger children play out on the balconies and neighbours complain of noise if the children play in the inside corridors or lift halls. In a flat on the fifth floor, with no lift, a young family may be isolated in their own home with a lack of stimulation and opportunities for mixing with other children. Surveys have shown that attempts made by mothers to keep small children quiet in flats are likely to impair normal personality development. Jephcott's Glasgow study concluded that the small child in a flat failed to acquire a sense of security, and had his curiosity and later ability to explore and experiment stultified. Even the development of neuromuscular skills needed for climbing stairs was impeded in children from 2 to 5 years who were accustomed to travelling in lifts. School-age children who live three or more floors up play outside both less and for shorter periods of time than those living near the ground.

Scottish teachers found these children reluctant talkers, oddly incurious, unusually quiet in class and short on general information. It has also been suggested that the distance between the flat and the ground may force some children, boys especially, into extra toughness and aggressive self-defence. The most vulnerable of those children living in high-rise flats were pre-school children in large, young families, especially when the parents were poor or socially disadvantaged. Strain imposed on mothers by the isolation forced on them by difficulties with prams, shopping and frequently defective lifts spreads throughout the family. Research suggests that social workers should recognize such families as potentially at risk. In Canadian cities like Ottawa or Toronto where there are many high-rise apartment blocks, the basement floor contains all the utilities such as washing and drying machines, indoor and outdoor swimming pools and, in some cases, nurseries run by trained Child Development workers for pre-school children. Mothers are welcome as helpers and, in turn, welcome the opportunity to meet with other mothers.

Although high-rise flats are no longer popular, studies show that even young families in lower-rise flats still have many problems – especially where there are children under five. Many mothers are worried by the lack of play facilities and isolation and the potential danger of balconies, lifts, stairs, windows and play areas near roads. A Newcastle study found that although the majority of mothers who had been rehoused from slum clearance found their new flats an improvement, 64% with more than one young child felt that the move had had a deleterious effect. Even where play facilities were provided these were unsupervised and 30% of the under-fives never used them. Most children had to play in the bedroom or living room, with the consequent risk of disturbing neighbours with their noise.

Depression, loneliness and dissatisfaction affect a high proportion of mothers and young children in both high- and low-rise flats.

Nurseries

The necessity for nurseries as 'compensatory environments' becomes vitally important if social disadvantage is not to become a major handicap for future generations.

Generally, the nursery should include a daily routine to provide predictability of events and security, but also flexibility to allow for changes of timetable, such as an outing to a farm or to the seaside. The provision of space for physical freedom and running about without fear of bumping into anyone or anything is essential. Equally important is a pleasant environment inside the playroom – even in an old school building – and pets and indoor gardens (if there are no grassed areas available) can do much to raise spirits and provide a useful calendar of the seasons. Lessons outside in Summer can be a delight, especially if the school is in an industrial area, and removing children to the nearest green area (fields if possible, although parks may have to suffice) should be done as often as possible. Meanwhile, a few large tubs and old sinks with brightly coloured plants and flowers can help to transform a concrete playground. Utilization of the environmental trappings such as buses and cars, which may restrict the child's play space on the streets but which can be converted into exciting play vehicles when contained in the playground, is also a good idea. Visits to a farm and the seaside should precede those to zoos and botanic gardens, as it is more relevant that the child should recognize domestic animals and their relative sizes than exotic animals and plants.

Cultural Variations

There are many cultural differences between ethnic groups and nursery nurses in schools or private homes need to be aware of some to avoid embarrassment and possible hurt feelings of the children in their care.

Figure 1.3   Children in an Asian family.

Pre-conceptual Care

This is a relatively recent development and the idea behind it is that parents should plan in advance when they would like to conceive a child and in the intervening period take positive steps for improving their general health and wellbeing so as to maximize the chances of conception and ensure that the fetus is conceived and nurtured in the healthiest possible environment – particularly during the first critical 12 weeks, often before pregnancy can be felt or even diagnosed. In practice, this often means adopting a more healthy lifestyle: taking more exercise, both to lose excess weight and control stress, giving up cigarettes, and drastically reducing alcohol intake, eating more nutritious foods to build up vitamin and mineral stores and, in some cases where there is a family history of disease, seeking genetic counselling. These measures should ideally involve both male and female partners as sperm morphology and production as well as the viability of the fertilized egg have been shown to be sensitive (if not vulnerable) to everyday lifestyle habits. However, the woman will also have to check that she is immune to rubella and, if not, organize immunization some 2–3 months before she plans to conceive, and stop taking the contraceptive pill well in advance to allow hormone levels to return to normal and use barrier methods of contraception (e.g. sheath or diaphragm) in the interim.

Good antenatal care still remains an essential ingredient for a happy, healthy and successful pregnancy, and pre-conceptual care is the ideal precursor.

Nature versus Nurture

'Nature versus nurture' refers to the argument that, regardless of environment, the child's genetic inheritance will determine his development. The reverse argument has been used politically to show that a healthy environment enables every child to reach his potential – the utmost development of which he is capable – and that those deprived of this for economic reasons will have stunted development. Typically, the perinatal mortality rates in different social classes reveal that mothers from the lower, unskilled groups have a much greater incidence of neonatal death than do mothers from professional groups. This indicates that socioeconomic factors play an important role in fetal life (cf. pre-conceptual care) as well as determining the progress towards healthy development throughout childhood in every aspect. It is, however, as wrong solely to blame lack of opportunity and environmental deficits

Table 1.1 Some common terms used in genetics

Genetic	Refers to the genes which are inherited from parents. Genetic factors may (or may not) be responsible for *congenital* abnormalities. Some types of visual handicap in babies (notably colour blindness) are caused by genetic factors.
Congenital	Means 'present at birth' and is not synonymous with 'genetic'. A viral infection such as rubella contracted by the mother in early pregnancy can cause congenital abnormalities.
Hereditary	Refers to those factors or features which are inherited through the genes.
Familial	Used in connection with disorders that occur frequently within families, but may not have a genetic basis, e.g. diabetes.

for poor academic achievement as it is to expect all children in the same family to be of the same height as their father. Genes and environmental factors are both responsible.

Conception

Conception takes place when a mature spermatazoon (male cell) carrying 23 chromosomes, of which one is a sex chromosome, fuses with an ovum (female cell) carrying 23 chromosomes, including one sex chromosome. As the normal human cell contains 46 chromosomes, or 23 pairs, both sperm and ovum go through a process of reduction and division during maturation so that each contains only 23, and fusion gives the normal complement of 46 chromosomes. The sex chromosomes in the father's sperm may be Y, which means that the offspring will be male, or it may be X, in which case the offspring will be female. The mother's ovum can contribute only X chromosomes as female cells carry two X chromosomes whereas male cells have X or Y chromosomes. Thus it is the father who is responsible for the sex of the child.

Genetic Counselling

Either family history may reveal familial genetic disorders, malformations, or unexplained stillbirths. Certain genetic disorders are related to certain ethnic groups (e.g. Tay–Sachs disease in

Jewish groups) as well as metabolic diseases, such as diabetes mellitus. Multiple sclerosis is more common in Europeans, sickle-cell anaemia predominates in Afro-Caribbeans who also have a genetic predisposition to hypertension, and these conditions could be found in children of mixed parentage.

Certain hereditary conditions such as colour blindness and haemophilia (see page 183) are said to be X-linked as they are carried on the female X chromosome. A woman can carry the affected X chromosome without having the condition herself as her other X chromosome will suppress the effect of the abnormal one, and this means that she will be a carrier of the abnormality. Her normal X chromosome is dominant, whereas the affected X chromosome is recessive.

As a male baby has the Y chromosome from his father he cannot inherit the condition from him, but if he has the affected X chromosome from his mother he will be affected, and his daughters will be carriers. Recessive genes on the X chromosome are revealed in daughters only when the father is an affected male and the mother is a carrier – hence the incidence of colour blindness is much greater in men than in women.

Each chromosome is an assembly of hundreds of genes which are units of deoxyribonucleic acid (DNA) and these transmit characteristics such as eye and hair colour, height and body type. Some may be potentially harmful and cause physical and mental handicaps but many congenital defects are the result of genetic and environmental factors, which makes the work of genetic counsellors difficult. Often the birth of one handicapped baby leads parents to seek advice as to the possibility of a recurrence but some conditions arise as the result of a mutant gene. This means that a gene undergoes some change, possibly through exposure to external influences, e.g. radiation, and neither parent has the harmful gene and both are clinically normal. The affected child could, however, have a one in two chance of passing on the condition to his offspring. It has recently been stated that one in 20 of all newborn babies has a congenital malformation, chromosome abnormality or genetically determined disorder. The malformations may be major or minor, and the genetically determined disorders mild or severe. Some, such as Huntington's chorea, may not be present until later life when the victim has already reproduced and possibly passed on the condition to their offspring. Cousins who have a common ancestor with a genetic disorder may be at risk of having a handicapped child with a one in four risk to any subsequent children.

Prenatal Existence

The prenatal period begins at the moment of conception and ends when the umbilical cord is cut at birth. This period lasts approximately 280 days and can be divided into the ovarian period, the embryonic period and the fetal period.

The Ovarian Period

This lasts about 2 weeks from the time of fertilization. After fertilization takes place the fusion of the sperm and ovum makes a *zygote*. The zygote begins to divide into two, four, eight and so on as it travels along the Fallopian tube until there is a clump of cells known as the *blastocyst*. This is minute (about 0.5 mm in diameter) and, having shed the wall of the ovum, becomes implanted in the wall of the uterus (endometrium) by enzyme action. A thin layer of endometrial cells covers the blastocyst and already it shows differentiation into the *inner cell mass* (which will become the embryo and umbilical cord) and *a wall* which will develop into the *chorion* and *amnion*. The part of the chorion next to the wall of the uterus becomes the placenta. Amniotic fluid fills the amnion and acts as a shock absorber for the blastocyst as a temperature regulator. The journey along the Fallopian tube to the uterus takes about 1 week. Once the blastocyst has been successfully implanted the woman is said to be pregnant, and soon after placental hormones – the basis of pregnancy tests – can be detected in the blood.

The Embryonic Period

This refers to the time between the second week and the end of the second month. Many rapid developments take place at this stage. The mass of cells becomes differentiated into the major internal organs, the central nervous system is established, the heart beats, and the liver and kidneys are formed. At 5–6 weeks the limb buds are developing and the hands and feet are forming. The first trimester of pregnancy which lasts up to the 12th week is the most vulnerable

time for the developing baby since any disturbance of the normal growth pattern, either through drugs – including nicotine or alcohol – or disease can have serious deleterious effects. If the mother contracts rubella in the first trimester (3 months) the baby could be born with heart defects, deafness, vision defects, hare lip, cleft palate and dental problems, and even mental handicap. Hence the need for mothers to have pre-conception check-ups to establish their immunity to rubella. Environmental factors within the uterus can also affect the growth of limbs since the limb buds continue developing until the seventh week, and congenital limb malformations or even missing limbs are thought to be due to disease or drug taking in pregnancy even before the mother is aware that she is pregnant.

Development in the human being takes place from head to tail. The brain is an outgrowth of the neural tube and spinal nerves are formed after the brain. The tail of the central nervous system is seen in the cauda equina ('horse's tail') which is a group of nerves in the coccygeal region at the base of the spinal cord enclosed in the bony, protective vertebral column.

The Placenta

As the embryo becomes firmly implanted in the uterine wall, a hormone (human chorionic gonadotrophin or HCG) is secreted to ensure that the lining of the uterus stays in place. It is the presence of this hormone in the mother's blood, and later urine, which forms the basis of pregnancy tests. Without this hormone the lining would break down – as it does during menstruation – and the embryo would not survive. The trophoblast cells form the placenta which acts as an exchange medium for oxygen, dissolved food and waste matter between mother and baby. Despite this there is no direct connection between the two circulations of mother and baby. The placenta has two sets of blood vessels but the walls of these are permeable and allow the passage of food and oxygen supplies, and the majority of drugs can pass through the placental barrier. The umbilical cord, which is connected to the placenta at one end and the abdominal wall of the embryo at the other, transports the essential oxygen and nutrients from the placenta to the baby, and waste products from the baby

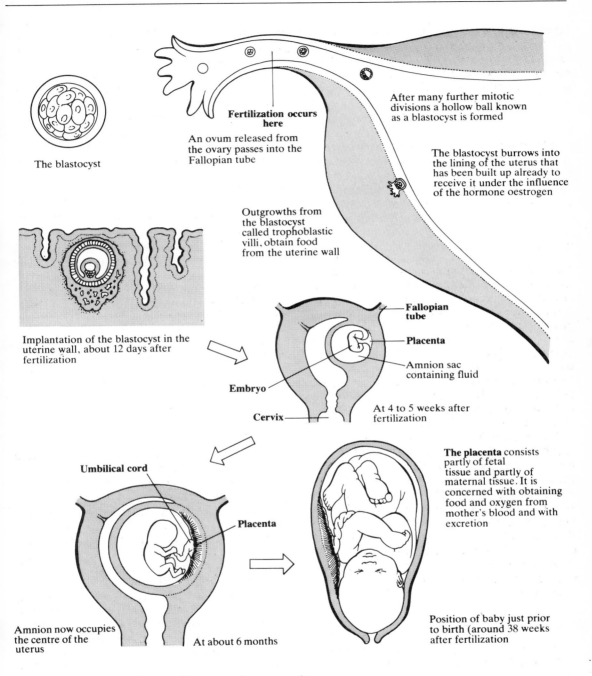

The blastocyst

Fertilization occurs here

An ovum released from the ovary passes into the Fallopian tube

After many further mitotic divisions a hollow ball known as a blastocyst is formed

The blastocyst burrows into the lining of the uterus that has been built up already to receive it under the influence of the hormone oestrogen

Outgrowths from the blastocyst called trophoblastic villi, obtain food from the uterine wall

Implantation of the blastocyst in the uterine wall, about 12 days after fertilization

Fallopian tube

Placenta

Amnion sac containing fluid

Embryo

Cervix

At 4 to 5 weeks after fertilization

The placenta consists partly of fetal tissue and partly of maternal tissue. It is concerned with obtaining food and oxygen from mother's blood and with excretion

Umbilical cord

Placenta

Amnion now occupies the centre of the uterus

At about 6 months

Position of baby just prior to birth (around 38 weeks after fertilization

Figure 1.4   Developmental stages of pregnancy from conception.

to the placenta. It takes only an hour or two for the intake of the mother to reach the embryo.

The placenta also acts as protection against infection by producing antibodies and keeping out bacteria. Certain viral infections, such as rubella, can unfortunately slip through the barrier to cause damage. Further protection for the baby is in the antibodies which give him immunity from various infections. The effect of these lasts about 6 months after which the immunization schedule begins. A bag attached to the placenta, known as the amniotic sac, provides external protection for the developing baby, as it is a bag of amniotic fluid in which the baby floats. Some obstetricians and midwives believe that the modern baby derives comfort from immersion in warm water and others actually help the mother to deliver the baby under water. It is true that when young babies are put into a bath they will exhibit an ability to roll on their backs and float without risk of drowning.

The Fetal Period

This lasts from the end of the 8th week to birth, which is usually at 38–40 weeks. At 8 weeks the fetus is about 1.25 inches long. Hands and feet (from which legs and arms will develop) are formed and the head already appears larger than the rest of the body, as it grows faster than other parts of the body. At 12 weeks the fetus is about 3 inches long, the external genitalia are formed, fingers and toes develop nails, but the nose, ears and eyes are still rudimentary. The eyelids remain closed until the 28th week to protect the developing eye. As the completion of major body parts is still taking place, the fetus is still vulnerable. For example, the antibiotic tetracycline can cause yellow discoloration of teeth in young children if it is taken by the mother during weeks 12–16 when milk and permanent teeth are forming in the gums of the developing fetus. At 16 weeks the hands can grasp and the movements within the amniotic sac can be felt. This sensation is known as *quickening*. By 20 weeks the fetus is about 12 inches long, has a strong heart beat which can be heard through a stethoscope, and is covered with soft, downy body hair, as well as the usual outgrowths of scalp hair, eyebrows and eyelashes. At 24 weeks the fetus is about 14 inches long and weighs about 600–700 g. The fetus becomes viable, i.e. capable of independent existence outside the uterus, during the 6th and 7th month of pregnancy. Modern technology has contributed to the viability of premature babies and even those who weigh only 500 g can now survive if placed in the compensatory environment of incubators in the special baby units of maternity hospitals.

In the third trimester, or last 3 months of pregnancy, the baby has a period of growth which is essential if he is to adapt successfully to extrauterine life. The developing brain undergoes a period of rapid development between 30 weeks and 18 months, hence fetal growth failure can also result in intellectual retardation. Maternal nutritional intake is no less important during the last trimester than in early pregnancy and can still influence fetal growth and birthweight. Deposits of brown and also subcutaneous fat are laid down in the last trimester and play an important part in fetal regulation of body temperature. This is one reason why low birthweight and preterm babies have to be nursed in incubators at a temperature of 36–36.5 °C. Impairment of motor function, as in some types of cerebral palsy, is also seen in babies who do not have the benefits of this growth period in the final trimester. Reflex actions such as sucking which are normally present before birth may also be impaired and the baby may therefore be fed with small volumes of breast milk through a nasogastric tube. The neonatal mortality rate is much greater in these babies due to deficits in circulatory, respiratory and digestive systems.

As the prenatal period is the period of most rapid growth and basic development, it follows that antenatal care is most important.

Antenatal Care

Ideally, antenatal care begins before conception so that the pregnancy can be given the healthiest possible start. However, for the vast majority of mothers, pregnancy is not always deliberately and conscientiously planned – which makes the early confirmation of the pregnancy and the prompt initiation of antenatal care all the more important.

The first and earliest signs of pregnancy include a missed period, enlargement and increased sensitivity of the breasts, Montgomery's tubercles in the areolae, frequency (the desire to pass urine often), nausea and/or vomiting, and going off certain foods. The mother may have all or none of these symptoms and each pregnancy is different so that she may feel very nauseous during one pregnancy but hardly at all during another. There are some women who know instinctively the moment they have conceived, but the surest sign of pregnancy is detecting the fetal heart beat.

Confirmation of pregnancy is by hormonal assay until about 12 weeks when this becomes unreliable, but the pregnant uterus can then be palpated on internal examination. However, most women are eager or anxious to know whether they are pregnant or not long before this time, and the usual method of testing for pregnancy is to test for the presence of the placental hormone HCG (human chorionic gonadotrophin) in the urine. This test, which is also the basis of the home-testing kits, is accurate from about 6 weeks of pregnancy – that is, 2 weeks after the missed period. This test is available through GPs, family planning clinics, some chemists, and private clinics. A recent and more accurate test is the β-HCG blood test which can detect HCG in the mother's blood as early as 2 weeks after conception (i.e. the week of the missed period). However, this test is not yet routinely available on the NHS.

Definite confirmation of pregnancy is by seeing the fetus on ultrasound scan and picking up the fetal heart beat.

The Purpose of Antenatal Care

The systemized care of women in pregnancy was introduced shortly after the First World War in a serious attempt to curb the maternal mortality rate, which was still high despite the general improvements in the standard of living and a decline in infant deaths.

The purpose of antenatal care is to survey and document the course of the pregnancy and to anticipate, if not prevent, problems which might jeopardize the life of both mother and child. The scope of antenatal care is therefore very wide as many factors prevail – from the mother's physical height, blood group and nutritional status to her marital relationship, financial and work situation – all can affect the course and outcome of the pregnancy.

The Needs of the Pregnant Woman

The needs of a woman in pregnancy are very special and unique. It is important to remember that she is not (in the normal course of events) ill,

Table 1.2 Infant and perinatal mortality 1983

Perinatal deaths (stillbirths & deaths in first week)		
England	6143	(10.3 per 1000 total births)
Wales	404	(11.3 per 1000 total births)
Neonatal deaths (deaths in first 28 days)		
England	3405	(5.7 per 1000 live births)
Wales	237	(6.7 per 1000 live births)
Infant deaths (deaths ages under 1 year)		
England	5890	(9.9 per 1000 live births)
Wales	380	(10.7 per 1000 live births)

Source: OPCS *Monitor* DH3 85/2

and therefore should not be regarded as a patient who is sick. However, whereas pregnancy is natural, it is not a normal state, and from the moment of conception unusual and sometimes taxing demands will be made on the mother's body – and mind. The physiological changes of pregnancy are enormous and wonderful. There is no greater strain placed on the body than on a woman during labour and childbirth.

Many women, particularly during their first pregnancy, feel ambivalent at some point, or are besieged by doubts, fears and anxiety about the future. This is a natural response, but explanation of what is happening, education about alleviating some of the symptoms, and emotional as well as practical support are all of paramount importance.

As the birth rate is falling and people are having smaller families, many women have no idea what pregnancy entails, as they were too young to remember or not around to witness their mother's or a sibling's pregnancy. Similarly, as families are becoming more 'nuclear', grandmothers, mothers, or even sisters are not available to support and help the pregnant woman. It is the duty, therefore, of every health professional who has contact with women during pregnancy to be particularly sensitive to their needs.

Dating the Pregnancy

The length of the pregnancy and the estimated date of delivery are calculated from the date of the mother's last menstrual period. Although the vast majority of women will have conceived some 10–14 days later (i.e. around the time of ovulation), this convention for dating the pregnancy remains. Midwives can also measure the distance between the uterine fundus (the top of the uterus) and the pubic bone and this, in centimetres, will give the age of the fetus in weeks.

However, nowadays, ultrasound scanning is the most accurate way of assessing the duration of the pregnancy and the fetal age.

Investigations and Diagnostic Techniques

Ultrasound

Ultrasonic radiation is used as a diagnostic tool by visually displaying echoes received from the fetus when an ultrasonic beam is directed at it through the mother's abdomen. No complications have yet been reported in human fetuses from the use of ultrasound, though currently there is debate about possible risks and routine use.

Measurements are usually taken between 16 and 30 weeks to assess fetal growth rate. Growth is important as poor growth implies poor fetal health and the risk of problems at birth.

An increasing number of disorders can now be diagnosed by ultrasound but, as this requires great expertise, mothers may be referred to a regional centre. Abnormalities detected by ultrasound include hydrocephalus, spina bifida, microcephaly and short-limbed dwarfism, but as yet, all women cannot be screened for every type of congenital malformation. Fetal breathing movements can be detected through ultrasound as early as 11 weeks gestational age, and the absence of these can indicate fetal distress. Recording fetal heart rates is done through ultrasound or electrocardiography and this helps to predict fetal asphyxia or the possibility of asphyxia at birth.

X-Ray

While radiation can have damaging effects on human tissues, obstetricians consider that the hazards of exposing the mother and fetus to a single radiograph are occasionally outweighed by the diagnostic information obtained. However, a radiograph should be delayed until 30–32 weeks, after which it will be less harmful to the fetus.

The appearance and size of the ossification centres of the fetus reflect the maturity of the fetus as a whole. Ossification centres are seen at the ends of long bones, such as the femur (the thigh bone) and the humerus ('funny bone' in the upper arm). Delayed bone maturation may be related to the cause of growth retardation and is seen in some babies described as 'light for dates', which means that even if they have completed a gestation period of 38 or 39 weeks they are still under the usual weight of babies at that stage. Diabetes mellitus in the mother may cause bone maturity to be in advance of gestational age and these babies are often very large for dates, and suffer from hypoglycaemia (low blood sugar) which can affect the brain cells.

X-rays are also sometimes used to assess the size of the mother's pelvic outlet if there is any suspicion that she may be too narrow to deliver the baby vaginally. This is called X-ray pelvimetry.

Amniocentesis

This is the withdrawal of amniotic fluid (the fluid in which the fetus 'floats') by inserting a needle into the uterus through the mother's abdomen. This is carried out under ultrasonic guidance to avoid the placenta. Amniocentesis is offered if two blood tests have shown a high level of alpha-fetoprotein in the mother's blood. This protein is normally present in pregnancy, but high levels are associated with failure of the neural tube to close – i.e. spina bifida.

There is a slight (1%) risk of spontaneous abortion or premature labour occurring after amniocentesis. In general, amniocentesis will detect only a chromosomal abnormality (e.g. Down's syndrome) or an open neural tube defect.

Most women over the age of 38 will be offered amniocentesis, and those between 35 and 38 may have it if they wish. Psychologically, it is quite a stressful procedure and amniocentesis is not offered to parents who would never accept a termination even if the fetus was affected e.g. Roman Catholics.

Fetoscopy

This involves using an endoscope to look at the fetus in the uterus. It helps in the diagnosis of some malformations which cannot be detected by ultrasound and in fetal blood sampling for diagnosis of certain blood conditions, such as haemophilia in a male fetus.

Oestriol

Excretion of maternal oestriol in the urine helps in assessment of the state of the placenta. In normal pregnancy the level of maternal oestriol excretion rises as gestation proceeds.

Bilirubin content

If this is present in the amniotic fluid it indicates the severity of Rhesus negative haemolytic disease in the baby. If the baby becomes severely affected as the pregnancy advances, an intra-uterine transfusion may be performed to prevent prenatal or postnatal death.

Maternal Health in Pregnancy

Whether or not the news of pregnancy is a cause for joy, it is important that both parents adopt a positive and nurturing attitude. The health of the mother is important because the fetus derives all its nutritional and metabolic needs from the mother and so the healthier she is, the healthier will be the baby. In addition, a fit and healthy mother will cope with the ups and downs of pregnancy better, and also with labour and delivery. Furthermore, she will be stronger for the postnatal period and for breast feeding.

Emotional Health

Pregnancy can be a stressful time. The images of pregnancy and motherhood presented in glossy magazines have little bearing on reality and serve only to exacerbate the mother's natural doubts about her ability to cope with pregnancy and motherhood. The upheavals of nausea or vomiting, and tiredness in the early months, coupled with physical and more subtle psychological changes can tax the most level-headed of women, particularly if they are also in paid employment and have other children. Fathers, too, are often affected by pregnancy: they are expected to support their partners whose emotional lability, chronic tiredness and perhaps lack of interest in sex they may find difficult to cope with, particularly if the pregnancy is not yet obvious. They also have to adjust to the idea of a new person in the family, and, in a first pregnancy, this means their life-style being interrupted by a helpless and demanding third party.

The mother should endeavour to make her partner feel part of the whole process, encouraging him to hear the baby's heart beat, feel the movements and join with her in gently massaging the abdomen while they talk soothingly to their baby. This is by no means a fanciful, idyllic idea, since we now know that babies of six months' gestation can hear and respond to different types of sound in the uterus. Where the new baby is the second or third, obviously the mother will have less time to rest and communicate with her developing baby. Children can be made to feel part of the pregnancy by 'watching' and listening to the baby growing in Mummy's tummy. This preparation may help to alleviate some of the jealousy often seen in older children when a new baby arrives.

Many women nurture secret fears and anxiety during pregnancy: will the baby be all right? Will I be able to cope? Am I still attractive to my partner? Can we really afford to move house? etc. It is important that these feelings are communicated and that the mother is given an opportunity to express herself fully. Sometimes firm reassurance is all that is needed; at other times, more constructive and practical support is required and even referral to a social worker or counsellor indicated.

Work

Many women in paid employment continue to work during pregnancy, because they want to, or have to, or both. The interest, stimulation and satisfaction afforded by working outside the home is beneficial in helping the mother maintain her sense of self and perspective on life. The financial independence is important too. As long as both mother and baby are in good health, there is no reason why a woman cannot continue to work up until the birth. However, the conditions of work are important and there are statutory guidelines. Contact with toxic substances, chemicals and radiation should all be avoided.

All pregnant women are entitled to time off work for antenatal care, and to maternity leave, maternity benefit and maternity pay (see Appendix).

Appearance

A woman's appearance is as important in

pregnancy as at any other time and reflects how she feels about her body, herself and the way in which she presents herself to the world. Many women find that their complexion 'glows' but this is by no means true of everyone. Attention to diet and exercise, attractive clothes and imaginative dressing can do much to boost morale and so enhance appearance.

Diet

Attention to diet is very important in pregnancy as the mother has to nourish not only herself, but also the growing baby. While there is little extra demand for calories *per se*, there is an increased requirement for vitamins and minerals – notably folic acid, calcium and iron. It is the quality rather than the quantity of food that counts. Foods which are high in calories but containing little else in the way of nutrients (e.g. biscuits, salted snacks, take-away hamburgers and milkshakes) should be avoided.

Daily menus should include portions of first class protein (red meat, fish, eggs) or second class protein (lentils, beans, peas), dairy products (milk, butter, cheese, yoghurt) for fats, protein and calcium content. Vitamins and minerals in fresh or dried fruit and vegetables are preferable to those taken in pills or capsules, since the fibrous parts stimulate peristalsis and prevent constipation. Bread and cereals provide energy, some fibre, iron, B vitamins and calcium which are essential to replace the amounts given to the baby. Iron is found mainly in red meat, liver, kidneys, eggs and leafy green vegetables. (There is a tendency for many antenatal clinics to prescribe iron and folic acid supplements routinely.)

Adequate fluid intake is also important and can help alleviate constipation and urinary tract infections. Diluted, unsweetened fruit juices and herbal teas are preferable to squashes, colas, and tea and coffee – which in any case should be drunk only in moderation and without sugar. Alcohol should be avoided throughout pregnancy, particularly in the first trimester, as there is increasing evidence that it can be dangerous. Frequent drinking and drunkenness put both mother and baby at risk and are associated with fetal alcohol syndrome. Smoking in pregnancy should be discouraged as it has been shown to potentiate the harmful effects of alcohol and to affect fetal growth.

Diabetic women will require monitoring of

Table 1.3   Example of a good diet in pregnancy

Breakfast
Half a grapefruit or orange or fresh fruit juice (unsweetened)
Porridge, Shredded Wheat, Grapenuts or Muesli made with oats, wheat germ, bran, hazelnuts, raisins, sliced banana
One slice of wholemeal bread, lightly buttered
Cup of unsweetened tea: whole pasteurized milk with tea and cereal

Mid-morning snack
A cup of unsweetened milky coffee and a piece of fresh fruit, if hungry

Lunch
Pilchards or sardines in tomato sauce with salad made from raw chopped celery, raw carrot and watercress
One slice of wholemeal bread
A piece of fresh fruit
A glass of milk

Mid-afternoon
Ryvita or crispbread spread with Marmite or peanut butter, or fresh fruit
Cup of unsweetened tea, herb tea or fruit juice

Supper
Baked potato with cheese filling or lightly boiled potatoes (steam cooking in a pressure cooker is best to retain the little vitamin C they contain), with freshly cooked mince, beef or lamb
Brussel sprouts, cabbage or broccoli
Natural unsweetened yoghurt – preferably 'live' – with chopped apple or pear pieces for dessert

Snacks
Unsalted nuts, sunflower, sesame or pumpkin seeds, dried or fresh fruit, small glass of milk – warmed at bedtime, with carob

Foods to avoid
Tinned fruit in syrup, fruit drinks (other than fresh juices),
squashes, sugary drinks, e.g. Coca-cola (try sugar-free versions)
Most commercial breakfast cereals (they contain a lot of sugar: you can make your own 'muesli' easily and cheaply)
Sweet biscuits, chocolate, crisps and salted nuts, white bread, processed cheese and meats, tinned vegetables, cream, ice cream, pastries and sweets

their condition throughout pregnancy, and even prior to conception as there is an increased risk of congenital malformations in the first trimester.

Weight Gain

Weight gain is inevitable in pregnancy, but to a certain extent should be monitored. Some women notice a gain in weight within weeks of conception, others, perhaps because of nausea and/or vomiting, actually lose weight in the first trimester. Both poor and excess weight gain are associated with maternal and fetal complications.

A total weight gain of about 20–30 lbs (9–13.5 kg) is considered satisfactory. Weight gained consists of: baby, 7 lb; placenta and amniotic fluid, 3 lb; enlarged uterus and breasts, 2–3 lb; increased volume of fluid in body, 8–9 lb; extra volume of blood in circulation, 2–3 lb; extra fat stored in tissues for breast feeding, 4–5 lb.

Dental Care

Dental treatment is free during pregnancy and for 1 year after the birth so mothers are advised to avail themselves of this opportunity if they require it. The mother's dental health depends to a large extent on her diet as protein, calcium, phosphorus, vitamins A, D and C are particularly essential for healthy teeth. Vitamin C promotes healthy gums and, as gum disease is more common than dental caries in adults, citrus fruits and leafy green vegetables – preferably raw or with very little cooking to retain the vitamin C content – should form part of the pregnant woman's diet.

Exercise, Relaxation and Sleep

Sufficient exercise, the opportunity to relax, and good quality sleep are all equally important in pregnancy.

As pregnancy makes extra demands on the body, the need for relaxation and restful sleep is obvious. However, the benefits of exercise are probably undervalued, and certainly shrouded in many popular misconceptions – e.g. that exercise can cause miscarriage. Walking, swimming, cycling, even jogging, can all be undertaken in pregnancy, especially if the mother exercised before she became pregnant. While the first 3 months are *not* the time to *take up* jogging or cycling (this last should only be confined to quiet country lanes), there is no reason why the mother cannot continue with most sports in pregnancy, or start a daily plan of gently stretching exercises or swimming. Exercise not only gives the mother a psychological boost and is a good 'pick me up', but also helps tone her muscles and increase heart–lung stamina – factors which can contribute to a more comfortable and easier delivery.

Preparation for the Birth

Attendance at Parentcraft classes (which are usually held in the evening to allow expectant fathers to attend as well) will help reinforce the positive and healthy regimen adopted in the waiting months, and can be a good way of meeting other parents-to-be.

Some women are dissatisfied with these hospital-based classes, feeling that while dealing with the physiology of pregnancy and mechanics of birth quite adequately, many questions are left unanswered. One of the outcomes of women articulating their need for better care and support during pregnancy and labour are organizations like the National Childbirth Trust and the Association for Improvement in Maternity Services. The NCT has a special interest in preparation for childbirth and holds meetings and supportive classes in education for parenthood, antenatal classes and breast feeding.

The Birth

When the first baby is expected mothers are advised to have the birth in hospital, mainly because of the medical and nursing facilities which are readily available there if required. However, there are nowadays women who dislike the clinical atmosphere and policies of maternity ward staff which may prevent them from delivering the baby in the position of their choice. Many of these women feel that birth should be 'natural', allowing them to squat, kneel or stand with or without support, and to deliver without the use of instruments, such as forceps, unless the birth is a difficult one. The father of the child, a relative or friend should be allowed to participate in the birth and can provide valuable physical and emotional support for the mother.

The mother may be offered various methods of pain prevention, but some mothers refuse these if they have been attending natural childbirth classes and want to conduct the birth themselves, with only guidance from midwife or doctor. Other women will have an epidural injection (given only by an anaesthetist) which blocks the nerves at the base of the spinal cord and makes the delivery relatively painless, but the birth has to be monitored by the attendant doctor and midwife. The benefit of this procedure is that the mother remains fully conscious during the birth. The length of labour differs with each woman and first babies often take longer than subsequent babies.

Stages of Labour

Until labour begins, the cervix, or neck of the uterus, is tightly closed. The first stage of labour (the stage of dilatation) begins with the regular uterine contractions pushing the baby and the 'bag of waters' (the amniotic sac) down, and the uterus itself upwards until the cervix is widely dilated. The uterus, vagina and cervix are now one continuous birth canal. The 'waters' may burst at this stage but sometimes they burst at the start of labour and have little or no effect on its progress.

The second stage of labour (the stage of expulsion) extends from the end of the first stage until the baby is delivered. During this time, the mother has to combine her own contractions with those of her uterus, which are involuntary. The baby's head is slightly elongated in its passage through the birth canal, and the neck is twisted and arched back to slide under the pubic bone and get safely through the outlet of the pelvis. Every contraction brings the baby further forward and once the baby's head (the largest part of the body) is through, the rest of the body, one shoulder after the other, can be eased out. The umbilical cord is still pulsating and still connects the mother to the placenta and the baby. Some doctors believe that laying the newborn baby at a lower level than the cord while it is still attached enables extra amounts of blood with important contents, such as iron, to implement the baby's store. Others think that the immediate contact of mother and baby even before the vernix caseosa, (the white covering of the newborn) is removed, helps to establish bonding or attachment.

The third stage of labour (the placental stage) extends from the delivery of the baby until the placenta and membranes are expelled and contractions of the uterus are complete. The umbilical cord is tied in two places to prevent bleeding and then cut between the two ligatures. Expulsion of the placenta usually takes place about 10–15 minutes after the birth and it is always examined by the midwife to ensure that it is complete and that no part of it, the membranes or the cord remains in the uterus. The uterus continues to contract and diminish in size to control the bleeding left from the separation of the membranes and placenta. The hormone oxytocin helps the uterus gradually to revert to its former size, which is about the size of a clenched fist. As oxytocin production is stimulated by breast feeding, this is a major argument for the promotion of breast feeding over artificial feeding.

On average a first childbirth takes about 14 hours and a subsequent birth 8 hours. Some mothers state that the process of childbirth is much easier when the mother is in her twenties and certainly hospital staff support this, as any woman having her first baby after 30 is described as 'an elderly primigravida'!

Nowadays many fathers choose to remain with their partners during labour and confinement. During the first stage of labour the father can massage her back, sponge her face and explain her needs to busy maternity staff. When the baby is born the father can caress the baby as he lies on the mother's abdomen, enjoying the feel of her skin. The mother can also massage the baby and these precious first moments in which the trio are together in true communication with each other can begin even before the cord is cut. While the normal physiological changes which close off the blood supply from the placenta take place the baby makes his first attempts at breathing, feeling warm and reassured by hearing the rhythmical beat of his mother's heart through her abdominal wall. The initial communication can lay the foundation of loving attachment or bonding between parents and child. The baby's first breath may be taken when his head has emerged from the birth canal, before the rest of his body is out, and the lungs inflate to begin the process of independent respiration. Sometimes the mucus in the newborn baby's mouth and throat may inhibit normal breathing so a mucus extractor is used by the midwife to clear the upper respiratory tract.

Before birth the mother supplies oxygen to the baby through the umbilical cord and major changes in the heart and blood vessels have to take place to enable circulation to the lungs for oxygenation of blood. Room temperature is important at the time of birth as the baby's temperature-regulating mechanism is immature. If his body temperature falls too low (35°C or 95°F) then serious harm can result from hypothermia. As he is naked and wet after birth, heat loss through evaporation may be minimized by gently drying the baby.

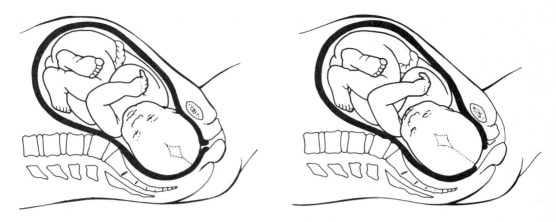

First, onset of contractions to full cervical dilatation (10 cm)

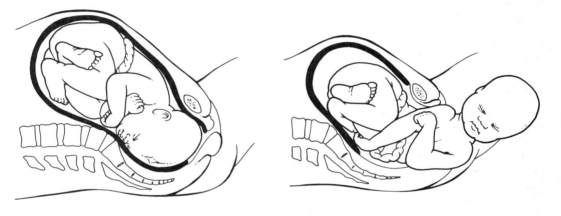

Second, full dilatation to delivery of infant

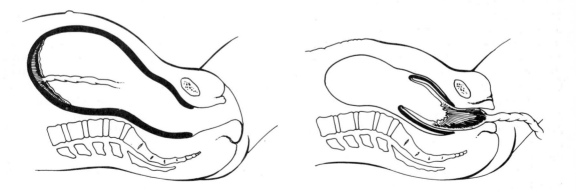

Third, delivery of the placenta or 'after birth'

Figure 1.5   The three stages of labour: first, onset of contractions to full cervical dilatation (10 cm); second, full dilatation to delivery of the infant; third, delivery of the placenta or 'after birth'.

Figure 1.6 The Apgar score

Sign*	Score		
	0	1	2
Heart rate	Absent	Slow (below 100)	Fast (above 100)
Respiratory effect	Absent	Slow	Good
		Irregular	Crying
Muscle tone	Limp	Some flexion of extremities	Active
Reflex irritability (stimulation of foot or oropharynx)	No response	Grimace	Cry, cough
Colour	Blue	Body pink	
	Pale	Extremities blue	Completely pink

*The first two, heart rate and respiratory effect, are the most important.

The umbilical cord will have been carefully tied or clipped and a dry sterile dressing may be applied or it may be left exposed to the air to hasten its drying and shrinking. The cord stump drops off within 7–10 days and cord dressings may be applied by the midwife on her visits when the mother returns home. After the 10th day the health visitor begins her visits and is able to advise the parents on various health problems concerned with rearing their family.

At birth the baby's skin is covered with a greasy film called *vernix* which is absorbed slowly through the skin and gives protection against skin infections. The baby's face tends to be puffy or red and wrinkled and there may be slight bruising if he has been delivered by forceps. The body will have some hairs which are shed in about 7 days; the skin may become flaky and also shed. Some babies have dark hair on the scalp which grows downwards on to the forehead. The first hair, whatever its colour, falls out and the new hair which grows backwards may be quite different in all respects.

At the time of birth whoever is attending the mother and baby will record his heart rate, muscle tone, breathing and colour. This is called the Apgar score, after the anaesthesiologist, Virginia Apgar, and serves as a permanent record of the baby's condition to be used later for reference if required.

Twins

One in 85 births results in twins. Triplets and quadruplets used to be very rare but the use of fertility drugs has given previously childless women multiple births and sextuplets are not unknown today. One-quarter of twins are identical and three-quarters are non-identical.

Identical twins develop from a single zygote (fertilized ovum). For unknown reasons the blastocyst separates into two separate growth centres, probably at the two-cell stage. Each baby has its own amnion and a single chorion surrounds both amnions, so they share the same placenta and the same genetic composition. Non-identical twins develop from two ova which are released from either one or two ovaries at the same time and are both fertilized. Both zygotes become implanted and develop their own amnion, chorion and placenta. All ova and all sperms are genetically different from each other, so the two zygotes which result from this double act of fertilization are as genetically dissimilar as if they were merely brothers and sisters and not twins.

Bonding

Various books published in the last 30 years have given rise to the doctrine that early separation of the natural mother and baby, or lack of skin contact at birth, can lead to numerous problems – including child abuse. The theory of maternal deprivation and its supposed drastic effects on children has been thoroughly investigated since it was first put forward by John Bowlby in the 1950s and 1960s. More recently, various child development experts have put forward different views and refute the idea of an exclusive bond between mother and baby. Dr Hugh Jolly, a paediatrician, always maintained that the idea of 'instant love' between mother and baby is a myth. He emphasizes the importance of sympathetic hospital staff and encourages mothers to object to a routine which removes their babies to the nursery instead of leaving them with the mother so that the two can become acquainted. He further states that mothers need to 'fall in love' with their babies.

Recent American and Swedish research shows that close contact after birth makes no difference in the long run to the quality of mothering or to maternal love. Theories of bonding as a phenomenon only possible between natural mother and baby are refuted too by many foster and adoptive parents who feel such a strong bond with the child that they are willing to raise court actions in order to keep them. The father's attachment to his baby is also belittled by these ideas of maternal exclusivity, and nowadays many unmarried fathers want to raise their child, and single-parent families where the father is the care-giver are no longer rare.

Differences in cultural customs also relate to bonding practices. An Asian baby is thought to be bonded to the family group rather than to the mother in particular. In some Asian communities mothers are considered unclean for the first 3 days after birth, so the baby is handled by close relatives of the parents during this period. The findings here, as elsewhere, are that there is no 'critical period' for bonding, and that maternal and paternal attachment, like any human relationship, develops surely but slowly.

Nursery nurses employed in the nursery units of maternity hospitals, or as nannies in private homes with full-time care of the newborn baby, can find reassurance in these findings. Sometimes parents will resent the nursery nurse or nanny and worry that their baby will become attached to the professional person rather than to themselves. Research shows that bonding is not a one-to-one process involving only the natural mother. Newborn infants will respond to a number of care-givers, not necessarily the natural parents, even if the care-giver is not the prime source of satisfaction, i.e. the basic need for food. The baby seems to recognize the mother's smell, and responds to her in different, often subtle, patterns of behaviour, especially if she breast feeds.

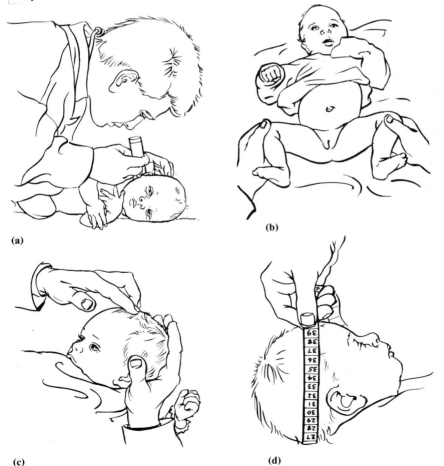

(a)

(b)

(c)

(d)

Figure 1.7 Examination of the newborn baby: (a) eyes and ears, (b) testing to exclude congenital dislocation of the hip, (c) feeling the anterior fontanelle, (d) measuring the circumference of the head.

The Neonatal Period

Immediately after birth, the doctor or midwife assesses the baby's condition rating colour, breathing, heart rate, muscle tone and reflexes according to the Apgar score. A doctor will usually examine the newborn baby within 24 hours following the birth to discover any congenital malformations, neurological disorders, intrauterine infections, haemolytic disease and effects of any birth asphyxia or injury.

Physical Checks

Basic measurements

Measurement of weight, length and head circumference form part of the assessment which can predict future problems in development. Birthweight is determined by antenatal factors including maternal health, age, smoking, alcohol, intrauterine care and heredity – tall parents tend to produce large babies. The average weight of the neonate is usually between 6 and 7 lbs (approximately 3.2 kg) and he is between 18 and 22 inches (45–55 cm) in length. His legs are short and his head, which is approximately half the adult size, appears very large in comparison to the rest of his body. There is usually a slight loss of weight in the first few days after birth and this is due to loss of body water. It is not normally more than one tenth of the birthweight, and by the tenth day after birth the birthweight has been regained. By the age of 6 months the birthweight has usually doubled and at 1 year it has trebled. The circumference of the baby's head usually measures about 13 inches (32 cm) at birth and grows to 18 inches (45 cm) by the first birthday. The birth height or length is usually about 30 inches (75 cm) by his first birthday. Thereafter the baby grows 2–3 inches each year and doubles birth height by the age of 4 years. The posterior fontanelle, which is the part at the back of the skull where the bones meet, usually closes at between 2 and 3 months after birth. The anterior fontanelle is larger than the posterior and it is a diamond-shaped space between the bones where the pulsating arteries of the brain can be felt. When the baby's head is passing through the birth canal these spaces between the bones allow the soft bones to fold over and decrease the head size. The anterior fontanelle closes at about 18 months but the hardening of the skull bones and the sutures or zigzag joints between them takes some years.

The face

Examination of the baby's face and mouth will reveal any abnormalities such as a cleft palate and harelip (caused by the failure of the palatal bones which form the roof of the mouth to unite before birth). These conditons can cause difficulty in feeding but they can be corrected – the harelip by 3 months of age and the cleft palate by 18 months. Children with these defects will need help with speech as the cleft palate makes articulation difficult.

Vision and hearing are checked for response to light and sounds.

The heart

The heart is checked for 'murmurs', which could indicate a congenital heart condition, and the colour of the baby's skin is noted. If it is blue this may be a sign of heart or respiratory problems; if yellowish, jaundice, which could be due to some defect in the production of bile. So-called 'blue babies' may have a 'hole in the heart' syndrome. This relates to the wall between either the upper chambers of the heart (the atria) or the lower chambers (the ventricles) which may not have closed properly before birth. The blood which normally goes from the right ventricle to the lungs for oxygenation does not receive adequate oxygen, hence the bluish colour of the baby. Sometimes the connection between the pulmonary and systemic circulation, which closes at birth when the baby's own circulation works independently of the mother's, remains open. This condition is known as a patent ductus arteriosus, but it can be corrected soon after birth.

The genitals

Inspection of the genitalia reveals any abnormalities such as undescended testes where the testes do not descend from the abdomen to lie in the scrotal sac outside the body, as is the normal process. This condition can usually be corrected by surgery if the testes have not descended by the age of 4 years.

Umbilical cord

The umbilical cord is checked to ensure that it is

drying out normally and not becoming infected. Sometimes a hernia develops around the area of the cord, which is a gap in the muscles through which the umbilical cord passed before birth. A loop of intestine in the area ruptures through and is known as an umbilical hernia. It is quite common and normally disappears without treatment before the age of five.

Congenital dislocation of the hip

Congenital hip dislocation is known to be associated with caesarean delivery, breech delivery, female babies, first-born babies and some foot deformities. The doctor will put both hip joints through a range of movements and if there is a definite click or jerk as the head of the femur (thigh bone) returns to the acetabulum of the hip bone, the baby is usually referred to an orthopaedic surgeon for correction of the dislocation.

Muscle tone

Muscle tone is checked by holding the baby over the hand, face downwards. An immature baby will be floppy. The back is examined for any marks or abnormal colouring, limb movements are checked, and hands and feet are inspected for extra or missing fingers or toes.

Reflexes

Neurological tests involve the testing of reflexes which are not voluntarily controlled and seem to be related to an earlier stage in the evolutionary process. The primitive reflexes seen in the neonate are simply responses to stimuli, and most disappear by the age of 1 month. The *'rooting' reflex* is seen when the baby's cheek is touched at one side of the mouth, when he will turn his head to the touch. In the same way, when placed with his cheek next to his mother's breast he roots around until he finds the nipple which he then begins to suck. This is the earliest and most essential reflex, to satisfy the basic need for food and drink. At 1 month the baby begins to associate sucking with satisfaction and comfort and the reflex becomes a voluntary action. If the newborn baby's hand is stroked along the palm with a finger or pencil he will close his fingers and grip it tightly. This *reflex grasp* is so strong that if both hands are grasping a pencil the baby can be lifted off the surface he is lying on and held suspended without falling off – rather like a trapeze artist. If the back of his foot is touched firmly he may bend his leg at the knee and hip and then straighten it out again. The baby can also be pulled from a lying to a sitting position when the doctor draws him forward by the wrists, and his feet have a greater ability to grasp in the newborn stage. This reflex has been attributed to the reflex grasp of baby monkeys who live in trees. The grasp reflexes of hand and foot are not related to the later ability to grasp, which does not develop until the age of 6 months. Neither can the *walking reflex* be described as the forerunner of walking since this is usually preceded by crawling and standing.

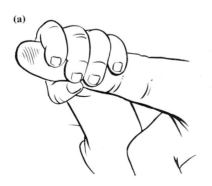

Figure 1.8   (a) The reflex grasp and (b) movements from lying to sitting of a newborn baby.

However, when held under the shoulders, the newborn baby will make stepping movements with the body held straight. This reflex is lost after 2 months and the muscular activities which precede walking, e.g. rolling over, do not usually begin until 6 months of age. When a sudden loud noise such as clapping the hands happens the baby responds with the *startle reflex*. The arms are flung outwards and then brought in towards the body which resembles the way a baby monkey would cling to his mother in times of fear. Another reflex which is useful is the ability to turn the head to one side when the baby is placed on his back.

Apart from these reflexes the newborn baby has a number of abilities which have not always been credited to him. In times past, various philosophers and thinkers stated that the mind of a newborn baby was like a blank paper on to which experiences were gradually drawn as he developed familiarity in his new environment, or that the baby's mind was a chaotic mess of new experiences. Much research has been done with newborn babies under 1 month old and we now know that they come into the world with a considerable repertoire.

Abilities of the Newborn Baby

Seeing

While the infant's sharp visual world is restricted to about 8 or 9 inches from his eyes, Dr Tom Bower's experiments at Edinburgh show that the newborn baby is actually capable of perceiving objects and people, rather than just looking or gazing at them. To establish his theory that infants see objects in a three-dimensional way he filmed the reaction of a number of babies, aged less than 2 weeks, when a large object was moved at different speeds towards them. He found that they pulled their heads back and put their hands between them and the object, which shows that they already have a defensive reaction as early as this and that they expect the object to be solid. Another Bower experiment involved the creation of an optical illusion of an object with the use of a polaroid light. The baby was sitting in a special supportive chair with his arms and hands free and he appeared to try to grasp the object as if it were solid, but was greatly disturbed when it did not materialize. The baby expected to feel the object he could see and thus revealed one aspect of eye–hand coordination.

The baby's visual field of 8 or 9 inches is appropriately the usual distance between the baby and his mother's face when he is feeding at breast or bottle. Daniel Stern found that mothers spend about 70% of the feeding time looking at the baby and he, in his turn, gazed back at the mother's eyes rather than her breast since the latter is too close to be in focus. The infant's ability to recognize a human face and, in particular, that of his mother, was tested by Robert Fanz and others who presented different drawings and shapes to the babies to find that they looked most at the oval shape with two large dots to represent the eyes. This suggests that babies are born with an innate preference for the human face. Genevieve Carpenter sat a number of 2-week-old babies in supportive chairs and presented their own mother's face to them followed by that of a strange mother. They spent a longer time looking at their own mother's face and looked away to show their aversion from the strange mother's face.

Hearing

Unlike the eyes, the baby's ears have been functioning before birth and the newborn infant arrives with a set of auditory reactions. As early as the 1960s tests indicated that babies went to sleep faster when played a recording of a human heart beat or a similarly rhythmical sound. More recent studies reveal that, by the time they are born, babies already prefer the female voice and, within a few weeks, they recognize the sound of their mother's speech. Any loud, sudden noise will cause a startled reaction, and newborn babies will turn their heads towards sounds and even look towards the source of the sound. However, sounds are somewhat dampened during the first few days after birth as the middle ear is still full of amniotic fluid. This gradually evaporates or is absorbed. Babies can also be taught to turn the head one way at the sound of a bell and the other way at the sound of a buzzer, if they are 'rewarded' when they get it right. Researchers have also discovered that infants can detect the relationship between the mouth movements they saw when films of faces saying 'ahh' and 'eee' were set beside a loudspeaker which could make either sound. American psychologist Andrew Meltzoff maintains that babies are essentially lip readers. Another psychologist, William Condon, observed many conversations between adults and found that a 'dance' involving movement and speech takes place when people are talking to each other. A later project revealed that babies between 12 hours and 2 days old seem to move 'in precise time' to human speech – and this was true whether the speech was in Chinese or English!

Smell and taste

These two senses are linked anatomically in that the olfactory lobes on the under surface of the brain lie close to the part that contains the taste centres. The sense of smell is not as well developed in man as in many animals yet infants only a few hours old exhibit preference for the smell of their mother's milk, although this is also mixed with the smell of her body. The sense of taste is present even when the baby is in the uterus. A piece of cotton soaked in banana or vanilla essence and waved under an infant's nose causes him to smile in pleasure, whereas the smell of fish and rotten eggs provokes an expression of distaste!

Touch and rhythm

Touch is highly developed at birth and even before when the baby in the uterus moves with gentle palpation. Many of the reflex responses occur as a result of touch – apart from the rooting reflex. If the baby is stroked firmly down the back of one side of the spinal column, he curves his back to that side. This is known as the salamander reflex. The touch of a hand on his tummy when he is crying usually makes him stop and blowing air at him will make him smile. The rhythm of the mother's heart beat heard by the baby in the uterus has a quietening effect on him when a recording is played after birth.

In 1969 Dr J.A. Ambrose tested various kinds of rhythm stimulation to discover the effect on crying babies. As a result of these findings a baby rocker, which is a strong nylon hammock fitted with a spring to produce vertical rocking at 60–70 rocks a minute on intermittent pushing by a parent, has been produced and found to be very effective in calming crying babies.

The Grenier manoeuvre

Dr Albert Grenier, a French paediatrician, has developed a new method for examination of the newborn infant which makes assessment of the neuromotor function (the action of nerves to muscles to bring about movement) possible before the usual age of 4 months. It has thus enabled the early diagnosis of a neuroma due to perinatal trauma.

The Grenier manoeuvre is achieved by holding the infant's neck and head stable, keeping his body upright and guiding the baby into upper limb movements normally seen in infants of 4–6 months. Observations of 220 infants, aged between 10 and 30 days, showed that 57% could communicate with their examiner, 43% could straighten the trunk and relax their arms, 39% could concentrate their attention on an object and reach out for it, and 19% managed to seize an object. Holding the baby in the Grenier way provides him with an anchor or point for balance and control and can rule out handicap in a large number of infants.

Special Care Babies

Babies who are of low birthweight, 'small for dates' or post-mature will usually require care in the Special Care Unit of maternity hospitals. For infants with birthweights between 2 lbs 3½ oz (1.0 kg) and 3 lbs 5 oz (1.5 kg) the present survival rate is approximately 90%, of whom 90% have normal intelligence and no physical handicap. Low birthweight usually means that the baby is under 5 lbs (2.3 kg) at birth and this may be due to prematurity (born before the usual 38–39 weeks gestation) or to problems during pregnancy which result in a full-term baby below the normal weight range and hence small or 'light for dates'. These babies may have breathing difficulties, no sucking reflex and be prone to infection. They are usually cared for in incubators with strict emphasis on a sterile environment and may be fed through a tube which goes from nose to stomach. As stated before, it is now possible to save babies who weigh as little as 1 lb 2 oz (500 g) providing the mother is able to obtain medical care when the baby is born. When the pre-term or small-for-dates baby weighs 4½ lbs (1.8 kg) he may be taken out of the incubator, but still requires constant medical care.

Staff in Special Care Units understand the problems of this early mother–child separation and the anxieties of parents about their child so they encourage visits to allow parents to help in feeding their baby and caressing him with their fingers if they cannot hold him yet. This helps to establish bonding and makes the baby feel good.

Figure 1.9   Parents are encouraged to visit their premature baby.

The inadequate temperature-regulating mechanism of the low birthweight baby can be compensated for by special neonatal thermal wraps and the incubator cradle is kept at a constant temperature. The baby is usually allowed to go home when he reaches 5½ lbs (2.2 kg), as long as his physical development is otherwise normal and his breathing problems have been resolved. The house should be kept at a constant temperature above 64°F and the baby must be protected from family members who have infections because of his immature defence mechanisms.

The post-mature baby is one who has been in the uterus for longer than the normal 38–40 weeks. However, as there may be confusion about the actual date of conception, the baby is not necessarily at risk. Nevertheless, the placenta loses its efficiency after the normal gestational period and lack of oxygen due to placental insufficiency can cause breathing problems and even brain damage. A test taken during pregnancy can reveal the likelihood of post-maturity, and labour is induced with oxytocin once an extra 1–2 weeks have elapsed. The incidence of post-maturity is higher in mothers over 40 years old.

The Postnatal Period

This is the period following labour and up to 6 weeks after the birth. It is characterized by three features: the uterus involutes and returns to its pre-pregnancy size, lactation begins, and recovery from the physical, emotional, metabolic and hormonal effects of pregnancy and the birth occurs. In caring for the new mother, health professionals should aim to advance her physical and mental wellbeing by offering support and advice on hygiene, diet and iron supplements, if necessary. Most mothers feel overwhelmed after birth and extremely tired. Supporting the mother by helping her to breast or bottle feed her baby, minimizing stress and allaying anxieties can do much to minimize postnatal 'blues'. The prevention of infection and other possible complications, encouraging the role of the father and parent–child bonding, and provision of babycare teaching are other essential aspects of postpartum management.

Immediate care after delivery involves the provision of comfort, refreshment, adequate pain relief as necessary, rest, sleep, and encouragement to nurse the baby. Nowadays, mothers are encouraged to be ambulant soon after delivery to discourage the risk of deep vein thrombosis. A bidet or shower with a mobile hand spray is often preferred to a bath after childbirth and enables the mother to wash and care for her perineum more easily and so encourage healing and reduce the risk of infection. Mothers who have had a forceps delivery where the perineum may have been cut, or an epidural anaesthetic, are always assessed as to the state of repair of the vulva. The mother's general health is also monitored: an eye is kept on bladder and bowel function to make sure that there are no problems like constipation (unlikely after delivery but may be secondary to a sore perineum) or urinary retention, and the haemoglobin is checked for anaemia. Breast feeding is established with the midwife teaching the basic techniques, and if the mother decides to bottle feed her baby she is taught how to prepare the feeds.

Postnatal exercises should be encouraged to help restore abdominal and pelvic floor muscle tone, and family planning should also be discussed with the mother.

If the birth was in hospital, the mother and her baby are usually discharged home after 2–3 days.

The Role of the Health Visitor

The mother is discharged home to the care of the community midwife, usually until the 10th day after delivery, although longer if this is deemed necessary by the midwife. Thereafter, care of the mother and baby is transferred to the health visitor and this may occur any time between the 10th and 28th day postpartum. The health visitor operates from the local health centre where she is a member of the primary care team, liaising with GPs. She visits the mother at home and offers advice on all aspects of child care, and encourages the mother to attend the child health clinic with her baby so that physical and developmental assessments can be carried out and vaccinations given. She also discusses family planning if this has not already been offered.

The health visitor is a trained nurse with post-qualifying experience in obstetrics and training in health visiting. Her responsibilities include:

1 The prevention of physical, mental and emotional ill-health and its consequences;
2 The early detection of ill-health and surveillance of those deemed to be 'at risk';
3 The recognition of need with initiation of appropriate measures and/or mobilization of resources, as necessary;
4 The provision of care, including support during periods of stress and advice and guidance during illness, as well as in the care and management of children;
5 Teaching on health matters.

Postnatal 'Blues'

The intense emotional and physical experience of childbirth does not end abruptly with the safe delivery of the baby into its mother's arms, but continues for many days – sometimes weeks – afterwards. Many women feel euphoric in this first week although often there is also the feeling of anticlimax, and a strange, inexplicable sadness. Tiredness, changing hormone levels, painful stitches or sore breasts can all too easily cause depression. Such mood swings are often helped by the mother asking for help from her mother or a compassionate GP, midwife or health visitor.

Postnatal *depression* is a relatively rare phenomenon. The mother not only *feels* unable to cope, but genuinely *cannot* cope, cannot sleep or eat properly, and cannot look after her baby. Postnatal depression should not be confused with the 'blues'. It is a serious condition demanding prompt and appropriate intervention.

When the Baby Cries

Mothers should not be afraid of asking for help – although media messages of the joys of motherhood only reinforce their guilt and feelings that they must be 'bad mothers' if they cannot cope alone. Neighbours are often only too willing to help by taking the baby for an hour or two while the mother goes shopping or catches up on some sleep, and this helps her to rest and relax. Many parents feel guilty when they find themselves becoming angry at the baby's crying, especially when this occurs during the night. This is a natural reaction, but it helps to establish the reason for the baby's crying. Most parents come to recognize and differentiate between the hunger cry, the tired cry, and the pain or discomfort cry. Often, the baby is just lonely or bored and needs a cuddle. Frequent cuddles and wrapping him or her up firmly in a shawl make the baby feel loved and secure.

Ignoring a baby's cries can have adverse effects: the baby panics, becomes frightened, continues to cry and feels insecure. He may become fussy and demanding because he gets panicky every time he needs help. It is nonsense to say that babies cry to 'exercise their lungs' or that it is 'spoiling' them to pick them up and cuddle them in response to their crying. Parents have to use trial and error methods to find out how to soothe their baby.

If a mother is unable to quieten the child she will become anxious and quickly reach breaking point. Learning to let off steam and recourse to neighbours while the mother recovers her equilibrium (through sleep or talking) will prove a valuable technique.

A survey by Sheila Kitzinger on crying babies revealed that 80% of mothers who went to antenatal classes said that the subject of unsettled babies was never discussed; nearly four out of 10 were unprepared for the baby crying a lot; 72% of babies started crying a lot during the first 6 weeks; and 86% of mothers said that their babies had stopped crying by the age of 6 months. Most mothers thought that their babies cried mainly through hunger or discomfort; two-thirds of the babies cried most during the evening; over half of the mothers felt desperate when the baby wouldn't stop crying and over a third felt depressed and angry; nine out of 10 mothers cuddled and rocked their baby to try and stop the crying; more fathers felt sorry for their crying babies than for the mothers; nearly two-thirds of fathers felt that the crying was a problem they wanted to share; and nearly half of the mothers sought help about the crying, usually from their health visitor.

Mrs Kitzinger recommends that mothers can learn to cope by:

1 trying to build up a network of support *before* the baby is born;
2 not being afraid to ask for help;
3 remembering they are not alone in this problem;
4 arranging some time away from the baby;
5 remembering it *will* stop – usually by the time the baby is 6 months old;
6 asking fathers to help – in some practical ways;
7 finding someone they can talk to about the problem.

Stroking and body massage are often effective with distressed babies, and cuddling and comforting by touch remain important to the child's stability and wellbeing throughout childhood and adolescence.

The National Childbirth Trust has postnatal support groups for parents who need help with crying babies and Cry-sis Support groups also offer help. Parents Anonymous offers a Lifeline – a number parents can ring when they feel desperate and worried in case they might harm their baby.

Feeding

Breast feeding

Changes in the breast take place from the earliest days of pregnancy as a result of hormone activity. The breasts enlarge, Montgomery's tubercles become more prominent (or, in a first pregnancy, appear for the first time), and the nipples and areolae darken. For some weeks before birth, a sticky secretion of colostrum is produced and this may form crusts around the nipple. If this happens, it should be washed off gently; handling the breasts and nipples in this way prepares them for the baby's suckling. Where nipples tend to be inverted, they can be grasped gently and raised, though sometimes a breast shield is helpful. It should be remembered that nipples can be large, small, light or dark in colour, and erect or inverted; all are normal variations – there is no common standard.

Colostrum is secreted for 2 or 3 days after the baby's birth and is then replaced by milk. Colostrum has a high protein content and contains vital antibodies which increase the baby's resistance to infections. The actual flow of milk is controlled by hormone activity and the baby's sucking – the mechanism is termed the 'let down' reflex.

Breast feeding techniques

These are usually taught by the midwife, either in hospital or at home.

1 It is important for the mother to be able to feed in a relaxed manner. She should be comfortable and perhaps even take the phone off the hook to avoid interruptions.

2 A baby feeds by *squeezing* rather than sucking, and this is why some breast-fed babies refuse a bottle teat. The baby holds on by suction, but feeds by moving her lower jaw up and down, thus squeezing on the milk reservoirs which lie behind the nipple. To do this, the baby must be properly 'fixed on'.

3 The baby should be put on the breast whenever he wants to, i.e. on demand. Time-tabling or strict routine will prevent successful breast feeding.

4 Wash the breasts daily and apply a little emollient or barrier cream if nipples are sore. Avoid plastic-lined breast shields.

5 Before feeding, wash hands and gently remove any cream from nipples with damp tissue.

6 Hold baby comfortably in a relaxed way. Support the breast and tempt the baby with the nipple held near his mouth.

7 When baby opens his mouth, let him take not only the nipple but the surrounding area as well. The baby should then close his mouth behind, not on, the nipple. If the baby is properly 'fixed', there should be no soreness and there-fore no damage to the nipple. Most babies need a little time to learn this – usually the first couple of days.

8 The mother should have trials of a few minutes only when the baby is learning to feed. Some babies take longer than others learning to feed. The mother needs to be patient and help will be available from the midwife or health visitor if she feels she needs it.

9 It is important to remember that the breasts produce milk on a supply and demand basis. Regardless of the size of the breasts, every mother can produce enough milk to feed her baby and whenever the baby wants to feed. The more often the baby is put to the breast (whether to feed or just suckle for comfort) the more milk the breast will produce.

10 Young babies may require six, ten or 12 feeds in 24 hours. As long as the nipples do not become sore or cracked, the mother can suckle the baby as often as the baby wants. The baby will get what he needs; there is absolutely *no need* to supplement or substitute the breast with a bottle feed.

11 The baby should empty both breasts at every feed to give them maximum stimulation. During unsettled days, excess milk should be expressed by hand to avoid engorgement.

12 If the baby is having sufficient milk once the supply is established, he should:

a fall asleep contentedly between feeds,

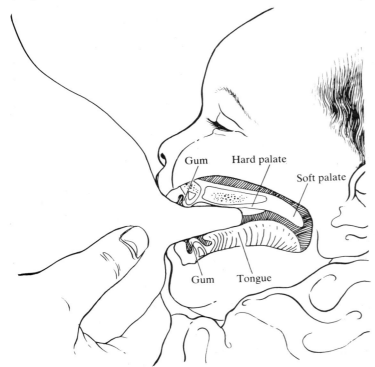

Figure 1.10 A baby breast feeding. Note that the nipple is well back in the baby's mouth.

b gain approximately 5–8 oz per week,
c pass soft, yellow motions – but not every day necessarily, and not before the end of the first week.

Breaking wind

Wind is air which the baby swallows while feeding. This may cause discomfort to some babies, but not to others. The baby should be given the opportunity to break wind during the feed and also for a short time at the end of a feed. If no wind is broken but the baby appears happy, he may be laid down in his cot without cause for concern.

Engorgement of the breasts

Breasts may become tense and uncomfortable, even painful, on the 3rd or 4th day. The longer the time between feeds, the greater the risk of engorgement. Treatment is by expressing the excess milk. The baby will not himself be able to do this by sucking as he will not be able to get a hold on the swollen areolae. Breasts should first be softened with warm water, then expressed by hand. If engorgement appears to be a recurrent problem, the application of a cool compress and even mild analgesia can provide relief.

Tender or cracked nipples

These are usually caused by the baby feeding on instead of behind the nipple. Treatment is by resting the nipple for 24–48 hours and feeding the baby from the other breast. A cracked nipple should be reported to the GP who can then prescribe a cream to encourage healing and prevent infection. The milk from the affected breast should be expressed by hand and discarded.

Diet during breast feeding

This should be particularly nourishing as the quality of the mother's diet is reflected in the quality of her milk. Breast feeding is both appetite and thirst stimulating for the mother. It is important therefore that she eats well, but sensibly, and that she drinks plenty of fluids. A diet rich in protein is advised – lean meat, fish, eggs, poultry, cheese and legumes (beans), together with plenty of fresh fruit and vege-

tables. However, while calorific needs are increased by breast feeding, the mother does have a good store of fat (laid down in pregnancy) for energy.

While breast feeding, it is important for the mother to remember that whatever she puts into her body will very probably also come out in the breast milk – and this includes drugs. Some drugs excreted in breast milk include alcohol, caffeine, nicotine, quinine, laxatives, valium and salicylates (e.g. aspirin).

Human versus Cows' Milk

Breast milk is the ideal food for babies, just as cows' milk is ideal for calves. It contains all the nutrients the baby needs, in the correct quantity, and in a form which can easily be digested by the immature digestive system:

1 *Protein*: There is 1.5% of protein in human milk compared to 3.5% in cows' milk. The protein is in the form of caseinogen and lactalbumin. Curds, which contain the caseinogen, are tough and rubbery in cows' milk while the curds in human milk are soft and more easily digested by the baby's stomach. Bottle-fed babies often produce undigested curds from cows' milk in their stools.
2 *Fat*: There is a little more fat in cows' milk but the fat in breast milk is more efficiently digested and absorbed due to the presence of the enzyme lipase.
3 *Lactose*: Human milk contains more lactose (milk sugar) than cows' milk and this means that breast milk gives a readily available source for the baby's large developing brain. Lactose also enhances the absorption of calcium and is thought to play a part in the prevention of rickets.
4 *Minerals*: The concentration of minerals in cows' milk is three times greater than in human milk. This can increase the work load for the bottle-fed baby's immature kidneys and may predispose to renal disease because the metabolism associated with the higher protein content of cows' milk also loads the kidneys. Retention of fluid may also occur due to high sodium content.
5 *Calcium*: There is more calcium in cows' milk than in human milk but it cannot be absorbed by the baby due to the higher fat content in cows' milk. The higher concentration of phosphorus in cows' milk leads to increased levels in the baby

but this is not useful because of the low calcium absorption. Calcium is required for the baby's developing bones and teeth.

6 *Iron*: Both human and cows' milk are low in iron but the iron in breast milk is more easily absorbed and, as more vitamin C is present to assist the absorption of iron, iron deficiency anaemia is uncommon in breast-fed babies. Most of the iron stored in the newborn baby has come from his mother during pregnancy. It has been established that the last 2 or 3 months of pregnancy are most significant for the transfer of iron from the maternal placenta to the baby and this is why premature babies are more likely to suffer from iron deficiency anaemia. The custom in Western societies of cutting the umbilical cord as soon as the baby is born has also been criticized, as it has been established that delay in clamping the cord with the baby lying at a lower level than the placenta can ensure a 40–60% increase in the baby's blood volume and in iron stores.

7 *Vitamins*: Breast milk contains more vitamins A, C and E than cows' milk. Vitamin C in cows' milk is destroyed in the preparatory process which involves heating and boiling. Vitamin supplements are usually given to pregnant and breast-feeding women and are particularly necessary where women are nutritionally at risk or in areas where climate or industrial pollution obscure the sunlight source of vitamin D.

Natural immunity

Apart from nutritional factors breast milk also contains anti-infective properties which are important as the baby's capacity to resist infection is immature. Lactoferrin is part of the protein in breast milk and prevents bacteria from growing. Lysozyme, an antiseptic substance (found also in tears), is effective against both bacteria and viruses, and interferon – derived from lymphocytes (white blood cells which have a protective function) – is known to be effective against viruses. Protection against respiratory and intestinal infections is also greater in breast-fed babies. Infective diarrhoea and gastroenteritis are serious and often fatal illnesses in newborn babies, and it is known that bottle-fed babies are more susceptible to these infections. Breast milk is known to give immunity against poliomyelitis, septicaemia and the herpes simplex virus.

Other benefits

Breast-fed babies also gain physically from the sucking process which is more vigorous than in bottle feeding and helps the development of jaws, gums and teeth. Milk from a bottle always flows at the same rate but breast milk has a rapid flow at first to satisfy the baby's hunger followed by a slower flow to allow him to enjoy sucking without taking too much. It is also thought that breast-fed babies are exposed to a wider variety of bodily stimuli than bottle-fed babies. A richer sensorimotor context in which learning can occur is said to be possible in breast feeding. Bodily contact with the mother also makes the baby feel more secure.

Economically, breast feeding is cheaper than bottle feeding (although the mother requires a good diet), requires minimal preparation and planning, and breast-fed babies are less likely to contract gastroenteritis.

Bottle Feeding

Cows' milk, ideally meant for calves, is not particularly suited to human babies and modifications therefore have to be made to make it more digestible for the baby's immature digestive system. Formula milk has been modified to make it as like human milk as possible, but it is still a substitute for breast milk. The protein content is greater in cows' milk and contains caseinogen which forms curds in the stomach. A baby finds these curds difficult to digest. Sugar is usually added to cows' milk as human milk contains more lactose or milk sugar. Fat droplets in cows' milk are larger and more difficult to digest than the fat in human milk. There are also major differences in the mineral salt content of human and cows' milk and overfeeding with cows' milk can cause serious upsets in the baby's salt balance. Vitamins A and B occur in both types of milk but there is insufficient vitamin D, which means that babies sometimes require supplements. The vitamin C content in cows' milk is destroyed by heating (for pasteurization or sterilization) but pure orange juice may be given to babies to compensate for this.

Between 1 and 5% of all bottle-fed babies develop allergies to cows' milk proteins and these are usually characterized by vomiting, diarrhoea, failure to thrive or eczema. Asthma and childhood eczema have been prevented by

Table 1.4   Some Weights and Measures

Metric equivalents (approx.)

Volume	1 fl oz	= 30 ml
Weight	1 oz	= 30 g
	2 lb	= 1 kg

Minimum daily fluid requirement
2½ fl oz/lb body weight
150 ml/kg body weight

Infant daily Calorie requirement
45 Cal/lb body weight
110 Cal/kg body weight

Calorie values
1 oz human milk   ⎫ all have the same
1 oz cows' milk   ⎬ Calorie value
1 measure humanized milk powder ⎭ = 20 Cal

the use of soya bean milk. Dried milk preparation for babies' feeds usually have vitamin D added and some have low lactose content for babies who show a reaction to lactose.

Cow and Gate Premium, SMA Gold Cap and Ostermilk Complete Formula are all low-solute, humanized milks and they have been modified so that they contain less protein, sodium and phosphate, which makes them less likely to cause chemical disturbance in babies who are bottle-fed.

There are a variety of reasons why mothers prefer to bottle feed: some mothers simply feel uncomfortable or shy about breast feeding: others are quickly disenchanted by early problems or sore breasts. As long as mothers are aware of the differences between human and cows' milk and the modifications which must be made, bottle feeding can be a satisfactory alternative to natural feeding. The preparation and care of feeding equipment and selection of a good brand are extra essentials for the mother who is bottle feeding her baby but she can utilize the feeding time to ensure healthy mother–child bonding and provide the baby with learning experiences.

Notes on bottle feeding

1 A brand of *modified* baby milk should be chosen.
2 When preparing a feed it is important to follow the instructions issued with the milk.
3 It is important to ensure that all feeding utensils have been correctly sterilized. A number of chemicals are available for sterilizing feeding equipment and instructions for making up solutions should be followed very carefully.

4 The scoop provided in the packet to measure the powdered milk should always be used, and *no more* than a (*level*) scoop used.
5 The scoop should be *lightly* filled and *levelled* with the blade of a knife.
6 An extra scoop of milk powder should *never* be added, and the scoop should not be packed too tightly, as this makes the feed too concentrated and may cause overload on the baby's kidneys.
7 Half a scoop should never be measured as this is not accurate.
8 Sugar must *not* be added to the feed.
9 If the baby is thirsty, give cooled, boiled water.
10 If the baby seems reluctant to take the bottle or becomes unsettled after the change, the health visitor or family doctor should be consulted.
11 Sweetened condensed milk should *not* be used for babies as it is too sweet (and will harm teeth before they even appear) and is lacking in nutrients.

Preparation of feeds

Most nurseries have a milk kitchen where milk preparations are stored and feeds are prepared. Strict cleanliness must be observed at all times and a clean gown kept available for use solely by staff in the milk kitchen. Tins of dried food must be carefully stored in dry, cool cupboards with lids replaced securely after use. Tinned milk is only sterile until opened. Afterwards, it should be stored in a refrigerator and used within 2 days. Bottled milk should be kept covered, stored within a refrigerator, and used within 2 days.

All equipment must be boiled (for at least 10 minutes) or sterilized before use. Milton, which is a solution of sodium hypochlorite, is available in solution or as sterilizing tablets. Bottles and teats must be completely submerged in the solution for at least 3 hours to ensure adequate sterilization. The bottle and teat should be rinsed in previously boiled water before use. As metal spoons and knives cannot be sterilized in Milton, they should be boiled. An enamel or stainless steel tray with two large jugs for boiling and cold water should be kept ready. It is easier to keep all feeding equipment separate from utensils for ordinary use. A plastic sterilizing unit large enough to hold six bottles and teats can be obtained quite cheaply and other utensils can easily be kept separate in a small cupboard.

A knife with straight blade, a teaspoon, glass or plastic ounce measure, feeding bottle with sterilized teat, dried milk, boiled water and sugar are the usual requirements for making up one feed.

Some mothers and nurses in hospital units make up the day's feeds at one time. The milk is put into bottles and then sterilized. This is called terminal sterilization and helps to prevent cross-infection in a hospital. However, since this method destroys vitamins it is better for the mother to use aseptic techniques on a small scale before each feed.

There are difficulties involved in warming up feeds prepared beforehand. The milk should not be kept warm in a thermos flask as bacteria will thrive in the warmth. If there is a cool storage place (as in a refrigerator) a number of feeds can be made up at one time and heated to blood temperature by immersing in boiling water before feeding. Some babies do not object to cold feeds and it is unlikely that they would suffer adversely from them, but other babies refuse to take unheated milk.

The manufacturer's instructions should be followed. Pour the correct amount of boiled water into the glass measure and then add the powdered milk formula to give the correct concentration of feed. The feed should then be poured into the sterilized bottle and covered. The feed tray with jugs of hot and cold water for heating and cooling feed, and a dish with covered teats and covered bottle all covered with a clean white cloth are then placed beside the feeding chair on a table. After washing her hands the mother or nurse puts a bib (tied round the waist to avoid suffocation) on the baby and begins feeding. To ensure that the feed is given at the right temperature of 100°F, it can be tested by allowing a few drops to fall on the back of the adult's hand. It should not feel too hot or too cold. The tip of the teat must not be touched when it is put on the bottle. The bottle should be held up to avoid air getting into the teat and the infant sucking air. *Do not* feed a baby lying flat on his back as he may choke or suffer adverse effects if the milk runs back to the Eustachian tube which connects the throat to the ear. *Never* leave the baby to feed himself from a propped up bottle.

As with breast-fed babies, it is not necessary to wait until the baby has apparently 'got rid of the wind'. Holding him upright for a cuddle after the feed will probably encourage air to be expelled. If the baby is wet or soiled, his nappies should be changed before he is returned to the cot.

Sterilization and care of feeding equipment

Spoons, knives, scoops and jugs should be boiled for 10 minutes after the water has reached boiling point. Glass and plastic utensils can be sterilized in a 1:80 solution of Milton. (This means 1 oz of Milton to 4 pints of water.) Check instructions on Milton as there are two strengths available now. The solution should be changed every 24 hours. Tray covers, towels and cloths should all be boiled before use. Feeding bottles should always be rinsed in cold water after use, then in warm soapy water using a bottle brush (which should be boiled daily). Wide-necked plastic bottles are easier to clean as any scum or milk deposits can be clearly seen and removed. The teats of these bottles can be inverted to keep the tip clean and then covered with a plastic lid for storage or travelling.

After washing, the bottles can be sterilized by boiling or by immersion in Milton 1:80. They must be completely covered and can be left in the sterilizer until they are needed for the next feed. The sterilizing unit must also be covered. It is more hygienic for each baby to have a separate container for his bottles and teats when there are a number of babies, as in a hospital unit or nursery.

Teats should be cleaned immediately after feeding. The outside of bottles and teats should be rinsed in cold water before the teats are removed as this removes milk residues and film. Then after rinsing the teats wih cold water they should be washed inside and out in hot water which is then squirted through to ensure that they are clear. Only thoroughly cleaned bottles and teats should be sterilized. Teats should be fully immersed in the Milton solution by placing a plastic egg cup or bottle cap over them. Metal equipment cannot be sterilized in Milton.

Preparation of the baby

Newborn babies' appetites develop slowly. Breast feeding will be 'on demand' at first, but eventually mother and baby find a three- to four-hourly feeding routine satisfactory.

It is important to treat each child as an individual and give feeds accordingly. Relaxation, a peaceful atmosphere and physical comfort are just as important in bottle feeding as in breast feeding. The mother should be prepared to give undivided attention to the baby at feeding times. The mother or nursery nurse should have a low chair without arms (although some prefer a chair with arms to support their elbow when they are holding the baby). A footstool may help to raise the lap so that the baby is on a level with the breast as if he were to be breast-fed. This position usually means that the baby's head is raised sufficiently for satisfactory feeding.

Before feeding, the baby's nappies should be changed so that he is dry and comfortable. He should be held firmly and securely to give ultimate psychological benefit. This is particularly important with preterm babies who will also need to be wrapped snugly in a shawl to stimulate the close sheltered environment of the uterus. The baby should be allowed to feed at his own speed. Some babies finish the feed quickly before they have satisfied their desire to suck. The flow of milk depends on the baby's sucking and he may suck vigorously at first until he is satisfied and then pause and appear to lack interest in finishing. Usually the mother will urge him to finish his feed if she is worried in case she has not had sufficient but it is important to remember that babies do not have the same appetite or require the same amount at every meal. It is not good to keep the bottle warm for too long, as the bacteria present in milk breed rapidly at room temperature and the mother should be ready to accept that the baby has had enough for the time being and dispose of unwanted milk.

Equipment Needed for the New Baby

A pram, a carry cot or basket (for the first few weeks) and a cot (from 4 months) will all be required (see Choosing a pram, etc.).

Bedding

1 Two waterproof sheets: one for use while the other is washed and aired. They should not be in direct contact with baby's skin, and should fit snugly to the mattress.
2 Four draw sheets: these are strong cotton or flannelette sheets which cover the waterproof sheet and are firmly tucked in at the sides. These will need to be changed frequently.

3 Two underblankets are required, one large overblanket and one cellular blanket (to be used as required according to climate).

Toilet requirements

1 A bathtub or basin, soft facecloth, towel, soap and a waterproof container for soap, plus cotton wool, cotton buds, talcum powder, zinc and castor oil cream, soft hair brush and comb.
2 Two dozen towelling (or one dozen muslin and one dozen towelling) nappies, one-way nappy liners.
3 A plastic bucket with lid.
4 'Napisan' for sterilizing.

Bottle feeding equipment

Two or three bottles so that there is always a sterile one ready for use. A measuring jug, bottle brush, sterilizing unit and sterilizing chemical (in lotion or tablets) to keep bottles and teats sterile.

Layette

Three vests, three stretch suits or nightdresses, three dresses or short cotton suits, three pairs plastic pants, three matinee jackets, bonnets, gloves, bootees (three pairs of each), six bibs (two plastic pelican bibs from 6 months onwards). Nightdresses and dresses should allow freedom of movement and maintain body temperature. Jackets should not be of open lacy design with ribbons and loops as the baby's fingers could be caught in these. Gloves and bootees should provide room for movement of fingers and toes.

Notes on Buying Equipment for Baby

Carry cots

1 'Moses baskets' and quilted cradles can only be used when the baby is tiny, so are uneconomical.
2 Maximum safety is ensured if the carry cot has its own stand or transporter fitted to its measurement.
3 The weight must be suited to that of the adult who will have to carry it (most weigh between 3.5 and 6 kg).
4 The carry cot should be of sturdy, washable, matt fabric for ease in cleaning and comfort of

the baby (shiny, white, plastic linings may cause glare).

5 Handles should be of strong, cord material firmly fixed to the sides of carry cot to avoid difficulty and accidents in carrying.

6 The carry cot should have a restraint harness which can be securely fixed into the back of the car to ensure safety in travelling.

7 When the blankets are in place, the mattress should fill the carry cot, to ensure that the baby cannot slip in between the mattress and the sides of the carry cot.

8 A carry cot that folds flat for storage and travel is best.

9 Plastic-covered mattresses can be dangerous unless covered with fitted sheets.

Cots

1 The cot should be stable and sturdily constructed.

2 It should stand level (if one-sided the child could slip down the side and be caught between the mattress and the cotside).

3 The cot should preferably not have bars but if it does (and some experts say it makes life more interesting for a baby a few months old to look through the bars and observe activities of others) they should not be more than 2¾–3 inches wide in case the child pokes his head through.

4 The cot should be painted with non-toxic paint.

5 Safety catch on the sides of the cot (if present) must be child-proof to prevent the baby from falling out.

6 The mattress should fit the cot (when the bedding is tucked in) to ensure that the baby cannot become wedged between the mattress and the cot.

Prams and pushchairs

1 Ensure that it is easy for the mother to handle to prevent overtiredness.

2 Check that there is a brake on two wheels for safety – faulty brakes on prams can be dangerous on busy street.

3 Try to obtain a dark lining as this reduces glare which can be disturbing or painful for the baby.

4 Materials inside and out should be easily cleaned to reduce dust and bacteria.

5 Clips for harnessing should be fixed to the sides of pram to prevent an older baby falling out.

6 The handle should be at a correct height for the mother to prevent over-stretching of muscles and poor posture.

7 Ensure that the child is comfortable in it to prevent wriggling about.

8 There must be plenty of support for the baby's back.

2

The Child, the Family, and Stress

Understanding Stress

Dr Hans Seyle, perhaps the first person to examine and quantify stress, states that 'stress is essentially the wear and tear in the body caused by life at any one moment'.

The physiological response to stress is the 'fight or flight' reaction: the heart rate increases, adrenaline flows freely, the senses become more acute and the muscles are primed for action. This is the basic 'survival response' which in animals and early man was essential in order to escape from life-threatening situations. Today, many people feel perpetually stressed and their 'fight or flight' response is continually alerted – but with no means of escape! The net result of all the undischarged tension and energy is illness – lowered resistance to infection, high blood pressure and heart disease.

Not all stress is harmful. Too little stress produces feeling of apathy, depression, hopelessness, while too much gives rise to feelings of anxiety, confusion, panic and forgetfulness. Everyone reacts to potentially stressful situations differently, and the optimum level of stress for each of us has to be found. When we achieve this balance of stress, we work well, have increased self-confidence, are enthusiastic and energetic.

While it is difficult to have a universal definition of stress, there is no shortage of problems attributed to it. Doctors estimate that up to 80% of all disease has a psychosomatic component.

The Effects of Stress

A direct link between stress and the immunological function of the body has been demonstrated and it is thought that this relates to cancer and the reaction of the body after bereavement, which may explain the high rate of death in the newly widowed. Sometimes it helps

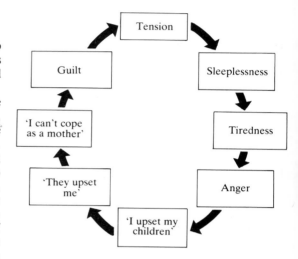

Figure 2.1 Vicious circle A: stress.

actually to draw the 'vicious circle' of psychosocial problems which cause stress (Fig. 2.1).

An example could be a mother of two boys aged eight and four who may find she cannot sleep at night because of the tensions and frustrations experienced during the day, exacerbated by guilt at shouting and screaming at the confused children. In this case the GP 'broke' the circle by aiding sleep – not necessarily with drugs but with relaxation techniques – until the family tension level was reduced and the children became less agitated, when the causative problems could be looked at more clearly.

'Tension headaches' are psychosomatic and can also be represented as a vicious circle (Fig. 2.2).

The Signs and Symptoms of Stress

These include increased heart rate and blood pressure, dryness of mouth, sweating, hot and

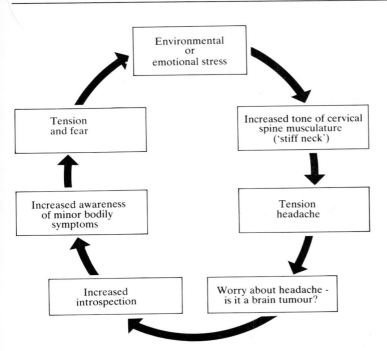

Figure 2.2   Vicious circle B: tension headache.

cold spells, a 'lump in the throat', numbness and 'butterflies in the tummy'. Stress can lead to asthma, allergies, chest and back pains, heart disease, diarrhoea, constipation, faintness and dizziness, dyspepsia, heartburn, frequent urination, headaches and migraines, nightmares, insomnia, menstrual disturbances, neuroses (nervous complaints), psychoses (organic nervous illnesses), ulcers, loss of interest in sex, and increased consumption of alcohol and tobacco.

Emotions and Stress

One aspect of stress that is often overlooked – particularly in Britain – stems from the belief that it is undignified or impolite to express emotions. The 'stiff upper lip' has long been advocated for men and boys who were afraid to be considered feminine if they gave vent to sorrow through tears. Many of us are inhibited even in expression of affection to members of the immediate family, and a common complaint of British wives is that their husbands rarely tell them of deep affection! The Mediterranean or North American father proudly shows photos of his wife and children and often says 'I love you' to them on the telephone in front of business colleagues. Family councils with even the youngest children are held in cases of problems and disputes which makes expression of feelings, negative and positive, a natural part of family life. This openness is admirable and worth imitation.

Unless we have been accustomed as children to voicing anger, resentment and frustration as well as joy, pride and happiness, it is very difficult to do so as adults. Hence the necessity for nursery and school staff to enable children to express their feelings without fear of censure in the safe compensatory environment of the playroom or classroom. Perhaps, too, we should be more physical as parents and teachers of young children – hugging and holding babies and little ones more, and even an embrace for the 7- to 8-year-olds when they have done well or are troubled by some event at home or school. Those who maintain that an 8-year-old boy would object to this as 'soppy' forget that their football heroes, usually hunky men, embrace each other unashamedly whenever a goal is scored! Tragically, the people we have to warn children against are usually recognized by their desire to touch, but most youngsters know the difference between a friendly hug and touching of the genitals or buttocks area, which makes them feel uncomfortable. If child carers feel unable to show physical affection for children they can still help to prevent inhibition and repression by enabling verbalization of emotions. Relaxation therapy and aerobics, which means exercising within one's own limits, can be beneficial in reducing stress. If done on a regular basis the mind and body will be able to cope better when a major devastating event occurs.

Coping with Stress

The present day emphasis on aerobic exercise, such as jogging, as being beneficial to desk-bound secretaries and executives alike – and most other occupations – is, in fact, very sound and sensible. Aerobic exercise is an effective and socially acceptable way of letting off steam; it strengthens the body, sharpens the mind, and helps counter many of the metabolic effects of stress.

For many people, any form of physical exercise is a boon as they find themselves able to concentrate only on the next few yards when running, or the next service when playing tennis. The woman who combines a full-time career outside the home with housekeeping may find housework invigorating as a complete change from her other occupation. Those who can forget the problems at work when they come home are less likely to become overstressed, and an engrossing hobby or leisure activity is useful here. Teachers and others whose work involves control and leadership are wise to adopt leisure activities where they are part of a group rather than the dominant person. A maxim handed on to groups of students for many years has been 'work hard and play hard'. It is still worthy of adoption since the different emphasis in each balances the stress factor.

Relaxation Techniques

First, check your tension! Shoulders hunched up, legs crossed tightly, hands clenched, jaw clenched, fingers twisting hair, bitten nails, irritability when spoken to – all are signs of tension and the physiological aspects of stress take over. A few minutes daily to practise the following exercises will prevent the problems of stress:

1 Stretch arms above the head as if reaching up to a high clothes-line.

2 Circle each arm to loosen the shoulders.
3 Shake your hands as if you were trying to dry them without a towel.
4 Pretend to be a floppy doll – bend knees, let arms swing about loosely.
5 Slowly and gently circle head each way or turn head from side to side slowly (only do this if not painful) to reduce neck tension.
6 Stroke firmly upwards under cheek bones and around the mouth to relieve face tension.
7 Lie on the floor or sit on a chair with good back support. Remove shoes or slippers and undo tight clothing.
8 Close eyes. Take two deep breaths slowly and clear mind of worries and anxieties.
9 Start with toes and work through each set of muscles in the body, tightening and relaxing until each part feels limp.
10 Relax facial muscles completely from furrowed brow to tight lips. Stay like this for a few minutes, enjoying the feeling of peace.

Stress at Work

Stress is frequently related to work and it is not just the high-powered executive who suffers. Many nurseries have members of staff who suffer from stress, possibly related to efforts to remain cheerful and energetic with children deprived of a happy home life. A neurotic, anxious senior person can often cause stress in junior staff, who find her moods unpredictable. Jealousies and frustrations at lack of opportunities for advancement may also cause an unhappy, stressful atmosphere. Teachers and nursery nurses in schools can also create a stressful environment if there is lack of professional team spirit or resentment of the teacher's role. When adults working with children either at home or in a nursery/playgroup find themselves using words and expressions like 'worried', 'too tired', 'depressed', 'irritable', 'frightened', 'I can't manage', 'no-one understands', then it's time to realize that they are overstressed and need to take some action to overcome it.

Premenstrual Stress

Some women experience the same reactions premenstrually and studies have shown that premenstrual tension (PMT) can cause increased accidents, marital squabbles, verbal and physical aggression. This is frequently a cause of great chagrin and guilt, and many women are at a loss as to what to do. Research has shown that PMT is related to aberrations in hormone levels and for some women progesterone supplement is helpful. For others, a low-salt, high-potassium, unrefined diet rich in minerals and trace elements has proved to be of value. Increased exercise premenstrually helps to ensure that any tensions are released without upset to the mother or her family.

Stress in Pregnancy

There is no doubt that pregnancy can be a stressful time for both parents – particularly if the baby is the first. The nausea, tiredness, aches and pains, the hours spent waiting in antenatal clinics, the frustration of not being able to communicate needs and secret fears to the doctor or midwife, the tests and investigations, fear of the birth itself, and the uncharted territory ahead can all contribute to a feeling of stress during what the media and everyone generally purports to be a wonderful time! Any stress in pregnancy will be exacerbated by tiredness, anaemia and an inadequate diet. There may be additional worries, too, if there has been a previous miscarriage or stillbirth, or if the couple have had to seek genetic counselling. Fathers may worry about the mother's health and the expense involved in starting – or increasing – the family. The father may also resent his partner's increased introspection in the later months and feel displaced or unloved.

Stress at Birth

When the baby is born the mother is usually anxious as to its welfare and health and this has been described as a normal part of the bonding or attachment process. However, the mother who does not feel this may worry that she is not normal and that her child will be a problem because of her inability to show affection or care. As seen in Bonding (p. 28) there are many myths about early mother–child attachments; it is not an all-or-none affair which must occur in the first few days of life or not at all, but a gradual process throughout the early years and is not dependent on care-giving or time spent

with the baby, nor is it exclusively maternal.

Childbirth which is the climax of the 9 months of pregnancy and which, for many parents, is an exhilarating experience, may be fraught with stress if the mother does not receive the care and attention she *needs* and *wants*. An induced labour against the mother's expressed wishes (and expectations), an uncomfortable delivery position, being left alone – even for 5–10 minutes – during labour, the presence of awkward, inexperienced medical students, inadequate or 'forced' pain relief, a bossy midwife or brusque obstetrician can all contribute to making the birth a stressful and miserable experience.

If the baby is premature or otherwise in need of specialized care, the parents may become very anxious and stressed when their child is taken from them and placed in a Special Care Baby Unit. However, some hospitals encourage the mother to live in and both parents are encouraged to touch and stroke the baby as much as possible.

A Handicapped Child

The birth of a handicapped child is a shock to both parents and often places great strain upon their relationship. There is frustration at the inability to cure or treat the condition, guilt that it was their fault, and many parents describe feelings related to bereavement, as if they had suffered the loss of a whole, healthy child. Fortunately, there are parent support groups for many handicapping conditions and ideally parents should be put in touch with these soon after the baby is born, as they feel better talking about their problems with other parents who have had similar experiences.

Miscarriage

Miscarriage is the spontaneous delivery of a fetus before it has reached a stage of independent viability (28 weeks). Thereafter, it becomes a stillbirth. Miscarriage or spontaneous abortion is far more common than is perhaps realized. The majority of miscarriages occur as a heavy period, which is usually slightly late, and the woman is unlikely to have realized that she was pregnant. However, approximately 150 000 fetuses are lost through spontaneous abortion each year and most occur during the first 12 weeks of pregnancy.

The causes of miscarriage are many; for

example, gross genetic or developmental defect (50% of cases), hormonal insufficiency, immunological factors, drugs, an inadequate placenta, a slightly gaping 'incompetent' cervix, or some unknown quantity like stress or upset. Exercise, incidentally, has been shown to have no effect on the risk of miscarriage. An incompetent cervix will usually cause a second trimester miscarriage but if noticed early enough can be remedied by a special stitch (rather like a purse string), which is later removed for the birth.

The first sign of miscarriage is vaginal bleeding, with very mild or no pain. This is known as a 'threatened abortion' and the mother is advised to go to bed and call her GP. She should avoid getting up, not drink any alcohol, and save evidence of blood lost to show the doctor. Surprisingly, perhaps, there is little that can be done to halt a miscarriage once it has started. Sometimes, though, the bleeding will stop spontaneously and then an ultrasound scan will be performed to check that the fetus is still alive. If, on the other hand, the bleeding continues and gets heavier, the miscarriage becomes an 'inevitable abortion'. The presence of cramping abdominal pain worsens the prognosis. To avoid haemorrhage and to check that no fragments of tissue have been left behind, the mother is usually admitted to hospital for an 'evacuation of retained products of conception'.

An often neglected factor in miscarriage is that the parents suffer grief, particularly if they had difficulty in conceiving. They may be told not to worry 'you'll soon have another' when this may not happen for some time, and result in increased anxiety when the mother does conceive again. The opportunity to grieve after a miscarriage is important and a future pregnancy can never replace a lost one.

Pre-conceptual care (p. 16) is essential to ensure a healthy and successful pregnancy, and should include a sensible diet, and abstention from alcohol and smoking; if a previous miscarriage has occurred, it may be advisable to abstain from sexual intercourse until after the stage at which it occured. Both parents should allow themselves to mourn the loss of a possible child and work through their grief before they try to conceive again.

Stillbirth

A stillbirth is when the baby dies after 28 weeks – before, during or shortly after it is born. The mother may have noticed an absence of fetal movements, or sensed that perhaps all was not well. The mother usually goes into spontaneous labour and this proceeds 'normally' although the mother's altered outlook may cause her to feel more pain. She should therefore be offered delivery by caesarian section if she so wishes.

Many parents want to see or touch their dead baby, and they should be given ample opportunity – alone – of doing so. This will help them come to terms with their loss, express their grief, and assist in the mourning process.

Postnatal Depression

Mood disorder after childbirth is very common. Postnatal 'blues' (p. 35) is experienced to some degree by almost every mother and often coincides with the start of her milk flow. Postnatal depression, however, is more serious, demanding prompt treatment with antidepressant drugs and/or referral to a psychiatrist. It is very likely that postnatal depression is under-reported, so all health care professionals should be particularly alert to clues from the mother that all is not well.

The Size of the Problem

Postnatal depression follows some 10–13% of all births with about 50–70 000 new cases per year in the UK. Surveys have shown that less than half these cases are known to their GPs, and can start at any time during the first postpartum (birth) year. The condition is not specific to any particular culture – there is a 9% incidence among the Bugunda women in Central Africa. It is thought that the reduction in perinatal and maternal mortality achieved by modern obstetric care may have resulted in postnatal depression becoming relatively prominent as one of the more untoward consequences of childbirth. Changes in society, such as the increase in the number of working women and the loss of the extended family, have tended to increase the isolation of women with small children. Postnatal depression today may therefore be more catastrophic than previously as mothers, sisters, aunts and grandparents are no longer around to help with baby care and provide company and support for the depressed mother.

Signs and Symptoms

These include:

Excessive tiredness
Listless, distraction, forgetfulness
Frequent tearfulness on slight provocation or
    for no reason
Loss of appetite
Nausea
Sleep disturbance and insomnia
Loss of weight
Anxiety about abilities as a mother
Inability to concentrate
Irritability
Headaches
Lack of pleasure in baby
Excessive anxieties about baby
Loss of libido (interest in sex) and marital
    deterioration
Guilt
Pessimism
Persistent depressed mood
Premenstrual exacerbation of symptoms

In psychotic depression (which means severe mental illness), a mother may express ideas about harming the baby and/or herself and in these cases she will be admitted to hospital at an early stage. A small number of these mothers may be emotionally labile (moods go up and down most of the time), forget to feed the baby, leave it unattended, treat it like a toy, and argue with those who try to help them. These women are not psychotically depressed, but their children could be at risk from abuse or neglect and social services will be involved by the GP or health visitor.

Causes of Postnatal Depression

As with other types of depression the cause is unknown but several factors appear to be involved. Some women have a previous or family history of depression so hereditary factors could be relevant. It is thought that biological factors could be involved and some doctors advocate hormonal therapy. There are also three social factors linked to postnatal depression: marital problems and the lack of a close confiding relationship, death of mother

before the age of 11, and accumulation of several recent life events (death of parent, husband's loss of job). It is not a disorder of large families and occurs in both poor and wealthy families. Unfortunately, there is a 20–30% chance that it will recur in subsequent pregnancies, but some doctors claim that hormone therapy can prevent these recurrences.

Treatment

Whenever someone, particularly a young mother, becomes depressed, there are always well-meaning relatives who try to 'jolly' her back into good mental health by telling her to 'pull yourself together and rejoice in the lovely baby'. This is a silly and harmful statement. Silly, because it is impossible for a depressed person to pull themselves together, and postnatal depression is characterized by lack of pleasure in the new baby, so it could be harmful, as it may add to negative feelings and loss of confidence. The day-to-day responsibility for a baby who cries incessantly (and, remember, many mothers are affected by this and have formed a 'Cry-sis' group to help them cope), who needs feeding and changing, is a long way from the rosy picture many women have of baby care. An impersonal, mechanical birth dulled by drugs often adds to the resentment especially when the mother assumed that she would receive unlimited and unquestioning love from her baby. If the mother has experienced lack of mothering herself she may further resent the baby's constant demands on her time and energy.

The mother should be advised to see her GP as quickly as possible – even before her 6 weeks postnatal check-up. She should try to have as much rest as possible during the day if she sleeps badly at night. Husbands and other relatives or neighbours should be asked to relieve the mother from time to time to enable her to go out on her own perhaps or to meet some friends who have young babies themselves. Postnatal diets for the mother to 'get her figure back' should be postponed as lack of blood sugar can make her feel even worse. There are a number of groups and organizations to help the mother and 21 mother and baby units in Britain, usually attached to psychiatric hospitals, where the mother learns to cope with her baby under supervision. Removal from the domestic situation, relief from the responsibility of total infant care without the pain of separation, and a good night's sleep can often relieve the depression in a few weeks. In some cases antidepressant drugs will also be required as the risk of relapse in the first year is high.

The Association for Post-Natal Illness has a countrywide network of 'phone volunteers' who have recovered from postnatal depression themselves. Sometimes, talking through a problem can be of considerable help to the mother who feels that no-one understands her predicament. MAMA (Meet-a-Mum Association) is a national network of self-help groups 'who would join together to help beat everything that can blight a mother's first months with a baby – from loneliness and depression to anxiety and fear'.

Single Parenthood

Most single parents are women and most, if not all, suffer from financial problems which necessitate employment. Unless adequate child care facilities and flexible working hours are available, this can place a great strain on both mother and child.

Keith and Schaffer (1980) noted different correlates of depression in single and married employed mothers. Longer hours at work protected single mothers from depression, both because of the extra income and also due to the increased involvement and satisfaction, while married mothers had higher rates of depression related to longer hours at work. The only factor associated with depression for both groups was low self-esteem. So employment for the single mother appears to be beneficial to her. The effects on children of working mothers have been mentioned before.

Working Mothers

The stress of combining occupational and parental roles is traditionally applied to mothers in full-time employment outside the home. The overload and conflict of her dual role – housekeeping, washing, ironing, preparation of meals, mostly carried out when she arrives home after a full day's work and travel in a crowded bus or train, coupled with the guilt she often carries because of her dual role – can at times become too stressful and illness may occur. Alternatively the full-time homemaker may

have stresses which could be lessened in outside employment. Not all mothers are content with full-time motherhood and some may desire some outside work and intellectual stimulation. She should ask her partner to help with household chores and child care, otherwise she has to ask herself whether she is not inviting more stress into her life. There are still many who hold the belief in the primacy of the maternal role or the 'motherhood mandate', a powerful social expectation that women should bear children, be a 'good mother' and stay at home to look after them. Employment is not excluded but, it is said, it must not interfere with what is seen as 'good mothering'. While the high commitment to professional work in middle class women can produce severe conflict, studies suggest that occupational commitment reduces stress for employed working class mothers and single mothers.

It is clear that the only solution to stress related to dual roles involves major changes in attitude and legislation to provide child-care facilities in the work place, job sharing, more part-time work, paternity leave and paid leave for child illness and revision of traditional sex role stereotyping.

Parental Disharmony and Divorce

All children need to experience stable relationships from an early age as these provide a model for their future social relationships. Those deprived of the opportunity to form firm emotional attachments in the first 3 years of life can suffer long-term detriment in later personal development. If parents set an example of conflict and disharmony, children will imitate their disturbed behaviour. Fighting parents are also likely to be inconsistent in their discipline and children become confused as to the correct response. Of course, every child reacts individually to family stress and some will copy more successfully than others. The child who has had experience of at least one stable, caring relationship will be able to cope better than the child who is brought into parental arguments every time.

One in three marriages now ends in divorce with a peak in the number of divorces in the first 5 years of marriage – when there are often young children. Many divorcees remarry, yet one in six divorces in Britain is a second divorce. Few divorces are not preceded by a period of anger, pain, bitterness and contempt which inevitably makes home life unbearable for all concerned. Parental disharmony does not always end in divorce, however. There may be periods of temporary separation or no separation at all, just continual rowing between the parents. Even where the parents do not argue in front of the children, the children will still pick up the body language of tension and feel torn between their parents.

Family discord has been shown to have more effect than divorce itself. A child from such a home may well be aggressive and attention-seeking at nursery, rejected by his peers because of his antisocial actions. After the divorce his behaviour may improve as there is less tension at home. When the decision is made to separate it is better if the parents gradually introduce the idea and deal with the child's worries and fears as they arise. Telling him at the last moment can be very traumatic. Most children feel guilty to some extent, as if their parents' separation was their fault. Some develop stress-related symptoms such as headaches, tummy aches, nightmares, sleep disturbances, bed wetting and depression. Behaviour at nursery or school deteriorates and the child may regress emotionally. Older children may play truant, steal or become aggressive and delinquent. Many children recover from this stressful period in their lives and eventually adapt to their new life as part of a one-parent family. A substantial minority, however, are permanently damaged and increasing numbers of children from broken homes require psychological help and may even be taken into the care of the local authority.

Nursery staff can offer comfort and stability to the child who is undergoing stress at home. If they are sensitive and know the child well they will be responsive to any changes in his behaviour. He may become anxious, withdrawn or aggressive as a reaction to his problems. The child should be encouraged to talk about his feelings – negative and positive. Nursery may provide the only safe environment for him to express his emotions verbally. Lots of opportunities to play with creative and imaginative materials – clay, water, bricks, wood – plus doll play in the house corner may provide a safe outlet for his troubled emotions. Stories which relate to his situaton but which emphasize the love of both parents for him can be made up, if not available in the nursery or children's library. Painting is a useful medium for children unable to verbalize their worries. Time alone should be allowed but social involvement with peers is also important to his adjustment. If the child shows no outward sign of inner conflict, it should not be assumed that he is free from it. He may not feel secure enough to work through his tensions. Parents should be kept informed of the child's behaviour in the nursery and re-establishment of good relationships can only be conducive to the child's welfare. Provision of security can be achieved by the nursery routine which has a comforting predictability but is, nevertheless, flexible to cater for outings and special activities. Nursery staff should not encourage unacceptable behaviour through mistaken sympathy, however – a kindly firmness is much better.

Sometimes a partner of a divorce or separation may take advantage of the child's presence in the nursery to gain access, and to avoid inclusion in domestic battles the nursery or school staff should make it clear to parents that legal visiting rights must not be exercised on nursery premises. A list of names of people the parent allows to collect the child should be requested to save embarrassment and upset.

Research shows that the main domestic tensions include: dissatisfaction with sexual relationships; one parent feeling that the other is inconsiderate; the inability to express emotions; the tendency not to discuss things openly; and one partner feeling that the other dominates them. Often, if *both* partners are willing, these problems can be greatly helped by resort to professionally trained counsellors, e.g. Marriage Guidance Council.

Violence in the Family

We have already noted that children tend to imitate parents. Where emotions cannot be expressed verbally, perhaps because the adult lacks the vocabulary and resorts to physical abuse instead, children too will be aggressive and behave antisocially. Often 'problem' children are in 'problem families' and unless intervention by attendance at nursery can be achieved many will enter primary school with a place in the records of social work departments, health visitors and even police.

Prevention is Better than Cure

The prevention of family violence is essential because there may be no cure. Removal of children into care may exacerbate their problems. Staff in community homes can rarely give exclusive love and attention to children but the emphasis on foster care has proved successful in many cases when foster parents have become attached to the child. The problem then is to decide whether the natural parents should have their child returned to them. Many abused children are loyal to their parents and may wish to return home despite threats of future abuse, but even where the children are reluctant to return, the social worker may decide after consultation with senior staff that it is in the child's best interest that they should rejoin the parents. As fatalities have occurred as a result of these decisions many professionals and lay people query the criteria on which the decision is based. Sometimes it is the parents' needs which take precedence. Perhaps it is naive to expect that abusing parents who request their child's return will now treat the child properly. Now that theories on the drastic effect of separation from natural parents have been rejected, is there any good reason for a child's return which may end in death from injuries inflicted by parents? The maturity of social workers in their twenties has also been questioned – particularly when they are appointed to adoption and fostering matters and give opinions as to the suitability of prospective parents.

Violence between Husband and Wife

'Wife-battering' is now taken seriously and many big towns now have refuges for battered wives and their children run by local Women's Aid groups. Bystander apathy which appears to affect the neighbours and relatives of these couples and lead them to non-intervention relates to the Victorian ideal that a man's wife and children are his possession and as such he has a right to inflict violence on them as he wishes. Nowadays one still hears the old adage 'never interfere in husband–wife matters' and there are many women emotionally and physically scarred for life because of this attitude. Some battered women themselves have a conspiracy of silence since they feel ashamed and guilty that they may, in some way, be responsible. Certain theories suggest that some women subconsciously seek out a violent man (possibly because they were physically abused as children), and not infrequently these women prefer to go back into the violent relationship even after discussing divorce and separation. There is also the fear that leaving home will be taken as surrendering rights to possession and therefore loss of entitlement to compensation.

Marital Problems

Lack of communication is often the basis of marital failure with the frustration resulting in attendant violence. Sex has been removed from the taboo subjects as far as the media are concerned, but true, open discussion of sexual feelings in a loving relationship is still rare, even in young couples who live together before marriage. Articles and stories in newspapers and books present a fantasy world of sex with a frequency and intensity of orgasms few would recognize as their experience. Expectations may increase only to give way to disillusion, lack of confidence in the male, and disappointment and resentment in the female partner. Marriage guidance counsellors can be of immense use to some couples but if one partner refuses to participate the advantage is minimal. Friends and relatives who are treated as confidantes of either partner can sympathize and possibly suggest remedies, but must not be disheartened when they are rejected or used as a substitute for effective counselling or therapy. The effects on the child of violent parents can be devastating, whether the subject is the mother or themselves, and they may present with behaviour problems which, in some cases, require psychiatric help.

Child Abuse or Non-accidental Injury to Children

Professor C.H. Kempe first used the term 'battered baby syndrome' in 1962 to describe the unexplained injuries presented by many children which were observed by teachers, nursery nurses and hospital casualty staff when the child was finally brought in for medical treatment. Often X-rays revealed older injuries such as fractures which had not been treated and had caused slight deformities. The parents' explanations were

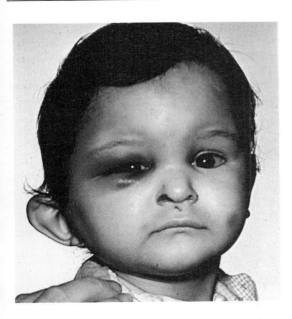

Figure 2.3   The reality of child abuse.

usually inadequate: 'he fell downstairs' or 'he slipped into the bath' when the child had been badly scalded.

In 1968 the NSPCC set up a special research unit to study the problem. The study showed that battered children are nearly always under the age of 4 years and more than half are under 12 months. Younger children have more serious injuries than others, perhaps because their pathetic vulnerability and cries of hunger and neglect provoke the assault. Some studies show a connection between prematurity and battering and it was suggested that lack of maternal–child bonding due to the baby's stay in a special care baby unit was to blame. The theory that failure, absence or disruption of bonding due to early separation experience was linked to child abuse has been strongly refuted. Often a sickly child is the victim of battering.

While the actual number of children involved is not accurately known, it is estimated that over 300 children are killed annually. Put another way, this means that one child is killed or maimed for life every day of the year. Over 4400 children have hospital treatment every year for non-accidental injuries.

More than half the number of children taken into temporary care by Social Services Departments following treatment for injuries are abused again after their return home, and younger children in the same family suffer the same fate.

Parents who abuse their children do not belong to any particular social class but child abuse is most common in families where the mother is young (under 30 years old) and two or three young children are born in rapid succession. Often the mother becomes pregnant or has another child soon after a battering episode, even when the battered child has been taken away into care. Fathers of abused children also tend to be young, unable to cope with responsibility and with a history of unemployment, illness or criminal activities. Often both parents have suffered emotional deprivation as children and some have been in care at some stage. The battering episodes often occur during periods of crisis based on housing, financial and social problems.

The abused child not only suffers from physical injuries, but also emotional trauma. He may show anxiety and timidity, only to later develop violent behaviour to other children (inside and outside the family) and to animals. Regression to earlier stages of behaviour with peiods of inhibition and aggressive outbursts is common. Many children are educationally backward, and a number develop speech problems. It has been demonstrated that there is a connection between battering and retarded growth.

Keen observation on the part of childminders, teachers, nursery nurses and others can lead to speedy diagnosis, and prompt intervention may help prevent further battering. Early warning signs may be a mother continually complaining about her new baby and her inability to cope. Every mother knows her natural reactions of anger and frustration with an insomniac baby when she is worn out herself, but most recognize this as part of motherhood and realize that their feelings are quite normal and common. The young mother who has never known what it is to be mothered may be completely insensitive to her baby's needs. Some neighbours and friends are afraid to be accused of 'nosiness' and even ignore the mother's cries for help which may manifest itself in her lack of fondling and interest in the child or in her expressed desire to 'shake him'. (It is now known that shaking a baby frequently and viciously can cause brain damage.) The mother should at this stage be encouraged to seek professional medical help. Improvement in her physical state, a few nights' sound rest and help from a social worker for financial and housing problems will help to reduce her stress and possibly avert another battering incident.

Professional Help

Obviously parents who batter their children often require psychiatric help and counselling for a number of years, but the child's needs and rights should be paramount. These rights of children were emphasized during the United Nations International Year of the Child in 1979.

Attitudes of professional workers to battering parents need to be mature and understanding, but this is often difficult. Many people tend to be judgemental: 'how could she do that to such a lovely baby? I couldn't' and many recriminations are levelled against social workers who decide to return a battered child home after a court case. Sentences for baby battering are often deemed to be too short, but punitive attitudes can be as disastrous to the parents as sentimentality.

Many local health and social services departments have combined with voluntary associations to set up Advisory Centres where families can receive professional help and parents have themselves helped to form Crisis Centres, to which any potential abuser can go for help from those who have experienced the same problems. Early identification is essential in order that postive help can be given. Social services departments now issue guidelines for nursery staff, child-minders, play group workers and day carers. They point out that most injuries to children are accidental but pinpoint a number of signs of possible non-accidental injury. Often the family doctor may be the first person called in for help as the mother calls for tranquillizers or at the suggestion of a worried relative or neighbour.

In some areas GPs have a district team parents can consult with representatives from social services, health visiting, psychiatry and paediatrics. Sometimes obstetricians are able to detect, in the antenatal period, mothers who will be at risk of abusing their children, but general practitioners who are concerned with the mother's personal and social history will have a good idea about the health and wellbeing of the mother's present children.

The Kempes suggested that battered children should be removed permanently from the small number of parents who are 'incurable'. They felt that prompt adoption and termination of parental rights was justified and emphasized that treatment of battered children and their brothers and sisters must begin as soon as possible after detection.

Factors Associated with Child Abuse

1 Youth of parents and childish, dependent personality types.
2 Family history of abuse or neglect.
3 Inadequate child spacing.
4 Marital maladjustment, separation, divorce.
5 Twins – one may be abused.
6 Unwanted pregnancy too far advanced for termination.
7 Disappointment over sex of infant.
8 Precarious financial situation.
9 Social isolation with poor support system.
10 Poor utilization of medical care.

Signs of Child Abuse

1 Small facial bruises, burns or abrasions, and 'black eyes'.
2 Injuries to the mouth.
3 Repeated minor injuries for which the reasons are not given or are unlikely.
4 Fractures, burns, scalds.
5 Bruises on the baby particularly when multiple and of different ages, together with scratches, cuts, bite marks, crescent marks of finger nails. Burns of peculiar shape and size, depicting various items used, e.g. cigarettes.
6 Swellings of joints or pain on moving a limb.
7 A child who flinches away from sudden movements of the adult's hand.
8 Failure to thrive, loss of weight or slowness in reaching developmental milestones.
9 Any injury at all to a young baby.
10 Depay in reporting an injury.
11 Unexplained absences from nursery or school.
12 Excessive tiredness, withdrawn or aggressive behaviour.
13 Periodic misery and tearfulness or unusually affection-seeking behaviour.
14 An unfeeling or mechanical way of handling a child by a parent.

Staff are warned not to *accuse* the parents, but to report to appropriate personnel. The NSPCC and RSSPCC have their own staff who will investigate any reported incident and the information can remain anonymous. Once a suspected case is reported, staff must be ready to attend a court hearing if required. If they do not report a case for fear of involvement or being proved wrong, they are being irresponsible and should remember that a child may die. Social services departments and health visitors often have records of families in which children are thought to be 'at risk' of abuse by parents.

Sexual Abuse and Incest

The Scale of the Problem

The repugnance experienced by professionals and lay people alike over child abuse of any kind is greatly deepened in cases of sexual abuse. It is one of the categories of child abuse recognized by the DHSS and although the actual injuries may be physical, sexual abuse can leave a child scarred emotionally for life, and often incapable of a natural, healthy, sexual relationship. Boys as well as girls are involved although more attention tends to be focussed on girls because most cases are of sexual molestation of girls. The NSPCC report on sexually abused children whose names were placed on child abuse registers by the society's special units between 1977 and 1982 showed that four out of five were girls, and more than half in the 10–14 years age group. A MORI survey of more than 2000 people indicates that more than 4 million adults in Britain experienced some form of sexual abuse as children and that more than a million of today's children could be abused by the age of 15. It is thought, however, that these figures are an *underestimation* since 13% of people refused to take part in the survey, possibly because they did not wish to recall painful or embarrassing memories. In North America, where more investigations have taken place into the problem, a study of 930 women in San Francisco found that one in four had had a sexual abuse experience by the age of 14, with most of the incidents involving parents or people known to them. The MORI survey confirms that the typical child abuser is not the lurking stranger but someone well known to the child. In about half the cases the offender was a close relative, friend of the

family like a baby sitter, or people in authority such as teachers or youth leaders. The MORI survey also indicates that far more *boys* suffer abuse than is generally supposed.

Defining Sexual Abuse

The late C. Henry Kempe, the American paediatrician, who made extensive studies of child abuse, defined sexual abuse as 'the involvement of developmentally immature children and adolescents in sexual activity they do not truly comprehend, to which they are unable to give informed consent, or that violates the social taboos of family roles'. A definition is useful because it enables everyone to be clear about how the young can be physically and emotionally damaged. It is important also because sexual abuse can lead to criminal charges and other actions such as the removal of a child from home. Also, it is helpful to establish clearly the thin line between what are desirable acts of affection and warmth between adults and children and what is unacceptable conduct.

The term 'sexual abuse' includes the following acts:

Rape
Sexual intercourse
Buggery (i.e. when the penis is inserted into the rectum)
Masturbation (manipulation of genitals)
Digital penetration (finger(s) inserted into vagina or rectum)
Fondling
Exhibitionism or flashing (showing parts of genitalia)
Involvement of pornographic activity (taking pictures or making the child participate in adult sexual activity)

Signs of Sexual Abuse

For a child to tell another adult about sexual abuse is very difficult. Children naturally defer to the authority figure and if that figure perpetrates the abuse, they are often afraid to reveal a horror made more horrific by the silence that has to surround it. These signs do not in themselves mean that sexual abuse is taking place but the possibility must be considered far more than in the past.

Behaviour signs include:

Lack of trust in adults
Fear of a particular person
Withdrawal and introversion
Running away from home
A girl taking over a mothering role
Sudden school problems, truanting and falling standards
Low self-esteem and low expectations of others
Stealing
Drug, alcohol or solvent abuse
Display of sexual knowledge beyond the child's years
Sexual drawings
Regression to younger behaviour e.g. thumb-sucking, acting like a baby
Aggression
Vulnerability to sexual and emotional exploitation
Revulsion towards sex portrayed on TV
Fear of school medical examinations

Physical/medical signs include:

Sleeplessness, nightmares and fear of the dark
Bruises, scratches, bite marks
Depression, suicide attempts
Eating disorders or change in eating habits
Difficulty in walking or sitting
Recurring urinary tract problems
Vaginal infections or genital damage
Sexually transmitted disease
Bed wetting
Vague pains and aches
Itching or soreness

Effects on Victims as Children

The problems caused by child sexual abuse can adversely affect personal relationships during the lifetime of the sufferer. Children abused within families are in emotional conflict – they want the parent to stop but are afraid that revelation could lead to break-up of the family. Their feelings are of guilt, shame and anger; the responsibility for their father's subsequent imprisonment and an end to their relationship with their mother weigh heavily on them. The offender reinforces their fears with threats such as: 'They'll put you in a home' or 'They'll break up the family' or 'If you tell, I'll kill myself'. The children come to believe that they are to blame and the low self-esteem which follows the offence makes them fearful that no-one will believe their story.

Effects on Victims as Adults

Emotional disturbance caused by sexual abuse can remain with a person throughout their adult life and affect their relationships with their own children and with their partners. A childhood experience could cause a mother to be prudish about the way her children behave, upset by their nudity or horrified at their sexual curiosity and infant masturbation. She may tend to avoid close physical contact with her husband and sexual relationships could be difficult.

Sexual abuse of boys may leave them worried and confused about their own sexual identity. Both men and women can suffer mental illness as a result of their childhood experience. If, however, they have a sympathetic, understanding partner it is possible for them to recover from their traumatic childhood experiences.

Mothers of Incest Victims

A mother may collude with a sexually abusive father because of fear of the consequences of disclosure. Imprisonment of the offender could mean loss of income, home and a child who would be taken into care. The mother may allow the situation to continue even when rivalry and change of roles occurs between daughter and mother. She may recognize that she is betraying her child but feels unable to face inevitable shame and break-up when the truth is disclosed. Hence the family holds its secret, sometimes for years, even when younger children replace the previous victim, who moves away from home.

The Abusers

The MORI survey shows that offenders come from all social classes and areas in Britain which dispels the idea that incest is mainly found in the lower classes living in rural areas. The age of offenders can vary from grandfather to adolescent and problems like alcoholism and mental disturbance can increase the likelihood of abuse. When interviewed by skilled and experienced police officers, many offenders confess. Some may attempt suicide, unable to face the shame and consequences of disclosure.

Legal Sanctions Against Offenders

Unfortunately, for the reasons described above,

only a tiny percentage of cases ever reaches the courts. Life imprisonment can be imposed for rape or incest by a man with a boy under 13, but 2 years imprisonment is the maximum for indecency towards girls in the same age group. Indecency against a girl under 16 years merits 5 years imprisonment, whereas against a boy under 16 the offender gets 10 years.

Treatment may involve counselling, group work and psychotherapy with the offender, individual members of the family and family therapy. If the case is very severe and the offender does not attend for treatment the case may be brought to court, but the aim of professionals involved is to look at the family circumstances, and the needs of the victim which must be paramount. Removal of the child from home into 'care' can be done under the Children and Young Persons' Act 1969 on the grounds of ill treatment or moral danger. This could reinforce the child's feeling of guilt and appear as if he or she were being punished, so more usually the offender has to leave home with the condition that they return or have contact with the children only under supervision.

Therapy for Incest Victims

Close cooperation is necessary between social services, health and education authorities and the police to ensure that the child is not subjected to an ordeal which may be worse than the offence. Obviously the psychotherapist has to be sensitive and never appear to disbelieve any part of the child's story since this will convince the child that his or her initial reluctance to tell because 'nobody will believe me' was correct. Often a collection of dolls (complete with sexual parts) representing the adults and children are useful in eliciting details from the child, and using the same terms for the genitalia as the child helps him to verbalize. The interviewer must not press the child in an inquisitorial manner or 'lead' him or her into answers. Interviewers must not reveal personal feelings to the child, however shocking the details may be. Apart from dolls, books are now available to help younger children talk about appropriate and inappropriate touching.

Professionals aim to:

1 stop the abuse of the child and arrange medical care where necessary,
2 reduce the traumatic effects on the child,
3 separate the offender from the family when necessary,
4 initiate short-term and long-term plans for the whole family, including medical, psychological and psychiatric treatment when necessary,
5 obtain forensic evidence when guilt is denied and the last offence was commited within the previous 48 hours,
6 coordinate with other services, including the establishment of a case conference to discuss legal and therapeutic intervention.

Prevention

A number of films, books and comics have been produced in North America, Canada and Britain to warn children of the very real danger of taking lifts in strangers' cars and accepting money from strangers, and policemen and policewomen now visit nursery and primary schools to reinforce the message.

Obviously sexual abuse by family, other relatives and family friends has to be approached in a different way, but just as urgently. Posters and comics have been distributed in Canadian schools pointing out that 'children have the right to trust their feelings and say 'no', yell for help, get away and tell someone' when they feel uncomfortable about someone touching them on certain parts of the body. A Spiderman comic is circulated in which he helps a young boy, molested sexually by his babysitter (a teenage girl) by recounting that he himself had been propositioned by an older youth when he was in his early teens. This is an excellent idea as it makes the victim realize that he is not the guilty party or alone in this predicament, and gives him confidence to tell an adult he can trust.

It is difficult for nursery and school staff to warn young children without frightening them but it is necessary to prevent occurrence or reoccurrence. Even where a child of 2 or 3 years is concerned, there are still some adults, particularly if they are parents of an abusing teenager, who will blame little girl victims as 'sexually provocative'. A few years ago, the *Vogue* magazine ran a series of illustrations for a famous jeweller in which a little girl about 4 or 5 years old was dressed in the style of 'a vamp', loaded with expensive jewellery and flaunting heavy make-up. This was accompanied by the words of songs like 'My heart belongs to Daddy'. No doubt this would appeal to

Table 2.1   Child Assault Prevention Programme*

When a child tells you, *stay calm and be reassuring.*
Say:
* That you are glad the child told you.

* That you believe what you are being told. Children very rarely lie about sexual abuse.

* That you are sorry that it happened and are angry with the offender, not with the child.

* That you know that it is not the child's fault.

* That you are ready to listen, but you will not press the child for information.

* That you will do your best to protect and support the child.

Some suggestions for parents and carers
* *Give children permission to say no to an adult when necessary.* Instead of teaching your children unquestioningly to listen to and obey all adults, tell them they have your permission and support to say no to protect themselves.

* *Discuss good vs bad secrets.* Teach your children to say no when asked to keep a secret that is bad or which makes them feel uncomfortable or confused. This can be taught from a very early age and is an extremely effective response in preventing child sexual assault. Offenders often begin by testing a child's willingness to keep a secret. No touch, kiss or hug should be kept a secret by a child.

* *Encourage children to tell.* Assure your children that no matter what happens you will not be angry with them and that you want them to tell you of any incident. Explain the difference between telling a tale to get someone into trouble and getting help when someone is threatening their safety. Believe your children; children do not lie about sexual abuse.

* *Do not define people as good or bad.* If children think only bad people hurt them, they will not be prepared for the person who approaches them in a manner which gains their trust. By teaching them the danger signs, you will be protecting them far better than by telling them to watch out for 'bad' people.

* *Teach children to keep safe.* The most important message you can teach your children is that they have the right to use any method to keep themselves safe. It is all right to bite, kick, lie, run, shout 'this is not my daddy', break a window, etc. Give them permission to break all rules to protect themselves.

*30 Windsor Court, Moscoe Road, London W2 4SN

paederasts (those who have an abnormal sexual attraction for children) but many normal people were shocked and disgusted at such a display, and informed the editor. The illustrations were changed shortly afterwards.

Nursery and school staff must exercise considerable vigilance – not only observation for signs of any type of child abuse, but also in a wider context – to ensure that the adult society we prepare children to enter successfully does not come to accept abnormal as normal, and takes pride in the formation of cultural traditions worthy to be our legacy for them. Addresses of organizations and groups to help in cases of child abuse are listed in the Appendix .

Death

Death is still a taboo subject in modern society which creates far more problems than it solves by reinforcing the feeling of denial and inhibiting the essential mourning process and the frank expression of emotion.

Death of a Parent or Sibling

Fewer children will have direct experience of death in the family nowadays since people live longer, but adult reticence and uncertainty as to the best approach may adversely affect the future emotional development of the child. Evasions in attempts to shield the child only exacerbate the anxiety, and an example of this is the popular use of euphemisms. 'Passing away' is a favourite which has little, if any, meaning for children when told this of a grandparent. Sometimes religious parents will tell the child that 'Granny has been taken by God', 'Granny is in heaven' or 'with Jesus' which can cause considerable confusion. When Vicky, aged 3, was told, she immediately asked where heaven was and afterwards told other relatives that her granny was in the sky so high up that she was invisible! She also queried why Jesus wanted her grandmother to play with when she would have liked her as a playmate – understandable reasoning from the information she was given. Using expressions like 'sleeping in the bosom of the Lord' may make the child acquaint sleep with death, with obvious problems to follow.

Children under five may have limited understanding but, if they view death as separation, they can react with deep grief. Indeed, Rutter's findings were that greater personality disturbances occurred when a parent had died during the child's third or fourth year – the period when parents are most needed as identification models. Those of 5–8 years with characteristic fantasies of magicians and fairies whose wishes always come true may be horrified that the parent died as a result of their expressed wish ('go away – I don't love you any more, I wish you were dead!'). At 9–10 years the reactions are similar to those of adults in that they become withdrawn with fits of weeping or anger and truculence. Initial reaction to death in most cases involves denial or refusal to accept the awful reality but *it is important for everyone concerned to go through the experience of mourning.* Families who are emotionally inhibited and endeavour to repress overt expressions of grief may find themselves entangled in a web of silence which persists in the adult relationships of the bereaved children. Where the marital relationship of parents was unhappy, the children are said to be more affected, and the death of a mother is more traumatic than that of the father at any age, possibly because the mother–child bond is stronger. However, there is no evidence that childhood bereavement causes depression or abnormal personality in later life.

Nursery pets often provide children with their first experience of death and nursery staff can help the children by frank, open discussion, structured if necessary, but not constrained to the language of a homily or presented as an event which can be tidily fitted into the daily timetable as the token talk on death. There is nothing morbid or unhealthy in children's curiosity about death and questions should be answered frankly, even when they relate to the subsequent fate of dead bodies. Cremation and burial may seem horrific to young children, and require careful, but always honest, answers. Some nursery staff find it easier when they utilize their own belief in God to explain that a very sick child or relative needed relief from pain and suffering so God decided she should have this relief and be taken to an after-life where she would be happy and without any illness. One could say, for example, that those who die after a short life, such as young children and animals,

were perhaps only intended to be on earth for that time to make children and parents happy. Once the subject has been broached openly children feel safe to talk about it again. Sometimes they will draw or paint images associated with death, like the 4-year-old boy who worried his teacher over a period of 2 weeks when he focussed on coffins and pictures of graves. Consultation with his parents resolved her fears – his granny had just died and was the main topic of interest at home. After 2 weeks the child reverted to happier subjects but had satisfied his curiosity and need to express an event which had deeply affected his parents and himself.

There is no 'right' way for nursery staff to deal with the subject of death – the guide as to appropriate level and length of discussion should be determined by the needs of individual children and their perception of dying and death. Consultation with bereaved parents by nursery staff is usually helpful to them and to the siblings who may still attend nursery.

Expressions of feelings, whether sad, happy, mournful, angry, joyful, proud, hostile, bad, should all be encouraged in school/nursery on a daily basis – perhaps through the medium of the class television set, made by themselves, to provide a modicum of separation from those listening, through the 'screen'. Children who are practised in verbalizing emotions will be less inclined to express them harmfully in physical ways. Parents should not feel embarrassed about showing sorrow – tears are not shameful in man or woman, they are a relief expressed in a natural way.

Death of a Child

When a child dies, the effect can be devastating as it is usually compounded by parental attitudes. If there is a baby in the family he could suffer emotional deprivation as the mother finds it difficult to give as much attention as before, and the toddler may interpret the parental preoccupation with grief as rejection and, literally, get lost. Older siblings may also resent the dead child who takes all the attention away from them, but then they feel guilty, and subsequent moods of melancholy and remorse may interfere with their progress at school and hinder emotional development. When the child has died as a result of illness which the parents did not recognize until too late for survival they will blame their own lack of insight, despite reassurances from medical and nursing staff.

Children who know they are dying often seem able to approach death with more equanimity than their parents. A father, writing of the death of his 8-year-old son from cystic fibrosis, a condition which requires painful treatment daily to drain the lungs of deadly mucus, told of the hospital nurses' account of the child's last stay. The boy knew he was dying and that this would be his final hospital visit, and he asked the nurses not to inform his parents of this as it would make them sad. His bravery led the father to write a book of the child's short but happy life, both to help other parents and also probably as catharsis (release) for his own grief.

Obviously no book can fully mitigate or lessen grief at the loss of a child, and the grief process has to be worked through, however long the period of mourning. Every birthday, every sunny Spring day, brings sadness as parents remind themselves of the dead child who is not here to enjoy the walks in the park or woods, or to welcome the Spring flowers in their rebirth after the cold of winter. A dead child can never be replaced and so the birth of another child who is intended to replace the dead one is rarely conducive to healthy development for him or appeasement of grief for the parents. In some families the parents refuse to admit that the child is dead and bind the other children in a numb silence of grief, while the personality of the dead child is 'kept alive' by susbequent references to him for years afterwards. Parents who have felt helpless in the face of fatal illness and death may subject their other children to angry outbursts related to their frustration at helplessness. Major events in the future lives of these children, such as birth or illness of their own children, often painfuly recall the death of a sibling.

Sudden Infant Death Syndrome (Cot Death)

This problem has come into focus as other causes of mortality in children between the ages of 1 week and 2 years have disappeared. The syndrome was defined in 1969 as 'the sudden death of any infant or young child which is unexpected by history and in which a thorough post mortem examination fails to demonstrate an adequate cause of death'. The incidence of cot deaths in the UK is about 2.1–4.0 per 1000 live births and it is found in other countries, such as the USA, Canada, Australia and New Zealand, with similar infant mortality rates. In countries with low infant mortality (Finland, the Netherlands, and Sweden) the rate is less than 1 per 1000 live births.

Most cot deaths occur in children between 4 and 20 weeks with a peak incidence in the 3rd month (8–12 weeks) and the majority of babies are found dead between the hours of 9 a.m. and 9 p.m. The incidence is higher amongst boys (who are known to be the weaker sex physiologically), twins, and babies of low birthweight. Families with a history of previous infant death seem to be more at risk of another occurrence. Cot deaths occur with greater frequency in areas of crowded living conditions, economic and social deprivation, in large families and where mothers neglect to keep postnatal clinic appointments. However, they are also seen in families of a higher social class, who live in comfortable homes.

Early studies showed a connection between cot deaths and bottle feeding, but the sudden infant death syndrome can occur in breast-fed babies who have never received cows' milk supplements or cereals at any time during their lives. It is still thought that incorrect bottle feeding can contribute to infant deaths from dehydration in conjunction with gastroenteritis and respiratory tract infection.

The cause of cot deaths

There appears to be a multiplicity of predisposing factors in cot deaths. These factors combine to produce fatality while the child is passing through a vulnerable period of development. Research has disproved many myths about the causes of cot deaths, e.g. overlaying, suffocation or inhalation of vomit. These account only for a very small proportion of unexpected infant deaths.

The following factors may be involved:

1 *Physiological factors.* These could be prolonged sleep apnoea (cessation of breathing) associated with age, low birthweight and infection, airway obstruction from a blocked nose or tongue and palate movement at a critical stage of development, a disturbance of heart rhythms caused by minor tissue abnormalities, or an abnormality in the lining of the lungs which prevents them from collapsing.

2 *Immunological response to infections.* Respiratory viruses are found in about 25% of cot

deaths and may cause a rapidly fatal infection or sudden apnoea.

3 *Sociological factors*. Parental reaction to symptoms of ill-health in their baby and their attitude to the medical services provided. Some doctors have implied a link between cot deaths and infanticide by the mother, but very few mothers of cot death babies resemble in any way the mothers who abuse or murder their babies.

Where extra health care attention is given by a paediatrician, and there is special health visiting and speedy access to hospital paediatric advice when the child is unwell, the numbers of unexpected deaths seem to have been decreased.

The effects on the family

These include shock, bewilderment and guilty feelings as they undergo the ordeal of the coroner's investigation and bereavement. Many parents suffer severely over a long period and hesitate to reproduce again. Family doctors, health visitors and paediatricians can add to the support given by relatives, friends and often social workers. Parents need reassurance, explanation of the cause of death and an opportunity to talk through their difficulties, anxieties and sense of loss. Nursery staff who know parents of children in their care who have suffered a cot death can also help by calm reassurance.

The Foundation for the Study of Infants Deaths was founded in 1970. Apart from promoting research into causes and prevention of cot deaths it also offers help and support to bereaved families, and provides information and leaflets. Local groups associated to the Foundation also offer help and advice where parents can share their experiences with other parents who have undergone similar tragedies to their own.

Sudden Infant Death – Patterns, Puzzles, and Problems, by Dr Jean Golding, Dr Aidan Macfarlane and Lady Limerick, was published in 1985 and offers advice which the authors maintain could prevent sudden infant deaths, or at least reduce them by 40%. They suggest that:

1 Mothers should not smoke either during the pregnancy or after the child is born.
2 Women should postpone childbearing until the age of 25 or so.
3 Family planning methods should be used to ensure that pregnancies do not follow each other too rapidly.
4 The dangers to their future children of drug addiction (whether nicotine, alcohol, cannabis, etc.) should be impressed upon young women.

The Foundation for the Study of Infant Deaths has also produced a set of recommendations for mothers of young babies. A doctor should be consulted if it is thought that the baby is ill – even without obvious symptoms – or if the baby has any of the following symptoms, especially if he has more than one:

Requiring urgent and immediate attention
1 a fit or convulsion, or blue or very pale colouring,
2 quick, difficult or grunting breathing,
3 exceptionally hard to wake, unusually drowsy, or does not seem to know the mother

Requires serious attention
4 croup, or a hoarse cough with noisy breathing,
5 inability to breathe freely through the nose,
6 crying in an unusual manner, or for an unusually long time, or seeming to be in severe pain,
7 repeated refusal of feeds, especially if unusually quiet,
8 repeated vomiting,
9 frequent loose stools, especially if watery/diarrhoea,
10 vomiting and diarrhoea,
11 unusually hot, cold or floppy,
12 even if a doctor, nurse or health visitor has been consulted and the baby is not improving or is getting worse, a doctor should be consulted again – the same day.

The authors point out the dangers of hypernatraemia (too much sodium), hyperthermia (too much heat) and hypothermia (too little warmth). While not proved to be the cause of sudden infant death, these situations should be avoided by careful mixing of feeds, and attention to clothing and climate for babies. Sweating is a major way a baby has of decreasing his or her temperature, and, since many modern synthetic materials are impervious to liquids and do not allow the normal evaporation of sweat from the surface of the baby's skin, the type of material used for baby clothes could be of significance. When a baby who is suitably wrapped for cold weather is brought into a heated room or conversely, put into a room without any wrappings or garments removed, the baby is at risk of both hypothermia and hyperthermia. As a general guideline, the authors recommend that the baby's room be kept at an even temperature of about 65°F (19°C) both day and night. Babies need to be well wrapped until about 1 month of age after which they become better at keeping themselves warm. It is sensible to protect the baby, including his head, from draughts, and the hood of the pram should be used if there is a chilly wind. In cold weather a baby can lose heat quickly, even in a cot or pram. To check whether the baby is warm enough, or too hot, one's hand should be put beneath the covers to feel the baby's skin. If the baby is too hot, he will feel hot and sweaty to the touch and may be thirsty.

Fresh air is good for a healthy baby, but not so important when he has a cold or when the weather is foggy or cold. In hot weather it is important that the baby should not get too hot; he should be kept out of direct sunlight with the pram hood down and a sun canopy.

The value of using apnoea alarms to prevent unexpected infant deaths is not yet established, as only a small proportion of babies who have died unexpectedly have had a proven history of apnoea (cessation of breathing).

3

Child Development

Development

Development involves four aspects, physical, intellectual, emotional and social, and each is dependent on the others. Thus, if a child is ill (physical) he will not want to participate in any learning activity (intellectual), he will be fretful and irritable (emotional) and will not respond to attempts to include him in interaction with his mother or others (social). While it is convenient to discuss individual aspects of development separately, it is important to remember that *a child is a whole person to whom all aspects are integrated*.

From birth, a baby is learning about his environment; trying to control it in whatever way he can. Learning is a life-long process which takes place in all aspects of development. Babies learn to grasp objects, learn hand-eye coordination, learn to stand, walk, speak, to control bowel and bladder, to relate to other people, to think and to understand. Growth in body and brain size is a natural process called maturation which proceeds naturally as long as the child is healthy and the body is not malformed. All aspects of development depend on the maturation of the brain and nervous system. Learning processes are different from maturational processes in that they are based on experience and the effects of environmental influences on the individual.

While all human beings follow the same order in development (or the same developmental pattern) there is a great variety in individual performance and children develop at different rates in different circumstances. Major developments in physical aspects of growth known as *milestones* usually occur at certain ages, e.g. focusing of eyes, recognition of sounds, use of pincer grasp, first words and first steps. Unfortunately some parents become concerned if their child's progress is not identical to that of others in the same age group. If a child is not ambulant by 1 year, they may fear that he is never going to walk. Recognition of the variety in ages at which different children reach developmental stages prevents these anxieties. Thus, ages given below are approximate.

Factors Influencing Development

Development of all kinds is dependent upon genetic and environmental factors. Genetic factors are sometimes referred to as 'inherent capacity' or 'innate abilities' as the child is born with them, and particular 'characteristics' are inherited from both parents – e.g. eye colour. Environmental factors include conditions in the uterus, the process of birth, and life stimuli. Malnutrition, diseases such as rubella, exposure to hazards such as radiation, effects of certain drugs, and even stress in pregnancy are known to affect babies (usually adversely) before birth. While genetic and physical factors may determine the limit of potential development, environmental factors – e.g. social conditions, the reactions of other human beings and education – are most important in determining actual development and subsequent behaviour.

Physical Development

Children today are, on the whole, taller and stronger than their parents' generation mainly because of improved diet, health services and living conditions, but many are still born into poverty and obliged to live in crowded areas usually bereft of outdoor playing space. Because these children are both economically and environmentally disadvantaged, they are more likely to suffer from ill-health and to be hindered in attaining their physical and developmental potential.

Nevertheless, much can be done both in nur-

Figure 3.1   Running is a good outlet for pent up frustrations.

series and primary schools to encourage physical development in the child. There should be ample opportunity for outdoor sports and recreation, including swimming, and while free school milk may no longer be available school snacks and lunches could be made far more nourishing than is currently the case. It is important to remember, too, that for a substantial number of children school lunch is the main meal of the day.

Intellectual Development

It is known that children reach half of their general attainment by the age of 9 years and that the capacity to respond to, and benefit from, education depends on the level of a child's intellectual and emotional maturity. Experience in the pre-school period has a vital influence on later scholastic progress and children removed from parental supervision and taken into care have lower educational attainment and more difficulties than other children.

As with physical growth, intellectual growth requires nourishment, and this primarily includes a rich speech environment where children are exposed to a wide vocabulary, are encouraged to participate in conversations, and are listened to instead of being the passive recipients only of television speech and instructions from parents and teachers. The importance of a stable, loving home and satisfactory emotional development has already been mentioned. Studies have shown a 'particularly close link between educational achievements, the home background and antisocial behaviour'.

Schools and child-care establishments can cause intellectual malnutrition by denying children the new experiences which are essential for their learning by continually undermining the child's confidence by disapproval and neglect of essential praise and encouragement; or by confining children to academic 'streams' from which they may never emerge. Children placed in the lowest streams often tend to work only to the norms or expected levels of those streams. In other words, they fulfil adults' expectations of them. Labelling children is usually harmful and unfair, yet professionals who should know better persist in it.

Emotional Development

A child's emotional needs are:

1 *Affection*: the feeling of being loved by parents, teachers, carers, playmates and the larger social community.
2 *Belonging*: the feeling of being wanted by the group. In the family this means that parents show that they are proud of the child and give her a significant share in family work and play. Peers provide companionship and offer a share in group activities. Teachers and other care

givers welcome the child in the school and give her a share in the activities of classroom and playground.

3 *Independence*: the feeling of managing and directing one's own life. Parents can help the child to 'stand on her own two feet' and provide opportunities for her to make decisions. Care givers can encourage initiative and participation in group discussions, guiding towards self-control and self-direction. Other children promote individual independence by giving turns and sharing leadership.

4 *Achievement*: the satisfaction derived from making and doing things. Parents who are interested in their child's schoolwork and who offer encouragement and opportunities for worthwhile tasks reinforce the efforts of teachers and care givers who provide opportunities for success in games, musical and other activities in which she has the support of playmates.

5 *Social approval*: the feeling that others approve of conduct and efforts. Obviously this has to be expressed by parents and others as praise for *efforts* rather than achievements, credit for good behaviour, and admiration for accomplishments from other children.

6 *Self-esteem*: the feeling of being worthwhile arises from a knowledge of confidence expressed by parents in the child and the efforts of other care givers to make the child feel worthwhile, while understanding her own strengths and weaknesses. Other children increase the child's self-esteem by their appreciation of her good qualities.

To this list can be added the need for new experiences which are found mainly through play and language but which are also essential for emotional development. In her *Ten Child Care Commandments (The Needs of Children)*, Dr M.K. Pringle includes the importance of treating each child as a unique person and of avoiding threats of rejection or withdrawal of affection. While general statements can be made about children's needs, the essential differences between them are most important and interpretation of needs is best appreciated through close observation of each child. A positive self-image in which the child sees himself as likeable, lovable and worthy of consideration by others is essential if satisfactory social relationships are to be made and maintained. Only

through interaction with others can we gain information about ourselves.

Social Development

Social development has been defined as 'the process by which an individual, born with potentialities of enormously wide range, is led to develop actual behaviour which is confined within a much narrower range – the range of what is customary and acceptable for him according to the standards of his group' (I.L. Child). Every child has to move from egocentrism, where he views the world as if it revolved around him and his desires and needs, to a state of socialization where he accepts the patterns of behaviour imposed on him by his family, culture and peer group, and learns to share and consider the needs of others.

The successful outcome of social development depends initially on parental attitudes. The security and love which comes from consistency of parental care is essential not only for healthy emotional development but also for social adjustment. While good parental care can be provided by other than the natural parents, consistency and constancy are essential. A series of care givers with differing attitudes and approaches to child-rearing may deny the child a secure emotional base from which he can venture into social relationships.

Stages of Development

These will be presented from four aspects – Physical, Intellectual, Emotional and Social (PIES is a mnemonic which helps us to remember this).

Piaget

Piaget, a Swiss biologist and psychologist, outlined stages of intellectual development based on years of research and observation of children at various ages (see Table 3.1). Piaget's work shows that before a child can progress from one stage to another both maturation (internal growth) and appropriate learning must take place and that special training is only temporarily effective as the child tends to revert to his developmental level. Intellectual development is not simply an accumulation of

Table 3.1   Piaget's stages of intellectual development

Stage	Approximate ages
1. *Sensorimotor period*	Birth to 2 years
Sub-stage I	Birth to 1 month
Sub-stage II	1–4 months
Sub-stage III	4–10 months
Sub-stage IV	10–12 months
Sub-stage V	12–18 months
Sub-stage VI	18 months to 2 years
2. *Pre-operational thought period*	2–7 years
Preconceptual phase	2–4 years
Intuitive phase	4–7 years
3. *Period of concrete operations*	7–11 years
4. *Period of formal operations*	11–15 years

changes but is restructured at certain periods and the child progresses through stages of increasing complexity to the level of 'formal operations' when he becomes capable of abstract thought. Piaget states that there is a constant interaction between emotional and intellectual aspects of development so that in times of stress a child may regress to an earlier level of thinking. Emotional difficulties can prevent progression to the next level of thinking and may render full logical functioning unattainable.

Erikson

While Piaget's major concern was with intellectual development, Erikson, another psychologist, has dealt primarily with social development. Erikson marks his eight developmental stages (Table 3.2) by the presence of a conflict stemming from the person's need to adapt to the social environment. Resolution of the conflict results in the development of a new competency. Erikson sees the first characteristic of infancy as 'trust versus mistrust'; that is, natural mistrust of a world about which they know nothing and yet the need to arrive at feelings of security and trust. Although confrontation and resolution of this and other conflicts continues throughout life, the safe and reliable environment parents provide for their child helps him or her overcome the early mistrust. As with Freud, the basic mistrust centres around bodily functions such as eating, and taking, and giving relationships with the parent.

Freud

Sigmund Freud founded a school of thought known as psychoanalysis which held that the

Table 3.3   Freud's stages of psychosexual development

Stage	Approximate age	Characteristics
Oral	0–8 months	Sources of pleasure include sucking, biting, swallowing, playing with lips; pre-occupation with immediate gratification of impulses
Anal	8–18 months	Sources of sexual gratification include expelling faeces and urinating, as well as retaining faeces
Phallic	18 months to 6 years	Child becomes concerned with genitals; source of sexual pleasure involves manipulating genitals; period of Oedipus or Electra complex
Latency	6–11 years	Loss of interest in sexual gratification; identification with same-sexed parent

Table 3.2   Erikson's developmental phases, 0–9 years

Approximate ages	Psychosocial crises	Radius of significant relations	Psychosocial modalities	Psychosexual stages
0–8 months	1 Trust versus mistrust	Maternal person	To get: to give in and return	Oral–respiratory sensory–kinesthetic
8–18 months	2 Autonomy versus shame and doubt	Parental persons	To hold on: to let go	Anal–urethral, muscular– (retentive–eliminative)
18 months to 6 years	3 Initiative versus guilt	Basic family	To make (going after): to make like (playing)	Infantile–genital locomotor
6–9 years	4 Industry versus inferiority	Neighbourhood, school	To make things (completing): to make things together	Latency

development of the child's personality is greatly influenced by his relationship with parents. According to Freud the infant's relationship with his mother develops as a secondary consequence of the way she provides relief from hunger and thirst. His emotional dependence on her grows out of his physical need to reduce the discomfort of his hunger. Freud also stated that the child's developmental progress could be seen in psychosexual stages (Table 3.3). These stages are characterized by certain sources of sexual gratification.

1–3 Months

Physical development

The newly born baby is endowed with primitive reflex actions which seem to be related to an earlier stage in the evolutionary process. A reflex action is not voluntarily controlled; it is simply a response to a stimulus. The earliest and most essential reflex is that of sucking. When placed with her cheek next to the breast the baby roots around until she finds the nipple which she then begins to suck. This is obviously a primitive reflex to satisfy the basic need for food and drink. At 1 month the child begins to associate

Figure 3.2   The neonate sleeps most of the time.

sucking with satisfaction and comfort and this reflex becomes a voluntary action. Most primitive reflexes disappear within 4 weeks of birth.

At 1 month the baby has lost some of her neonatal reflex actions but will still make reflex walking actions if held standing on a hard surface. When laid on her back or face downwards her head turns to one side. If her cheek is touched she will turn her head to the same side. The baby's head falls forward if she is held in a sitting position to form a C curve with the rest of her body. Grasping, rooting and random movements are seen in the first month.

At 3 months the baby shows anticipatory actions by moving her arms and legs. The grasp reflex, which is lost by 3 months of age, is one which illustrates the evolutionary process. When an adult's finger is placed on the palm of each hand of the newborn baby the response is to grasp it so tightly that the baby can be pulled from the lying to the sitting position. If a pencil or piece of rope is grasped by the baby and suspended above the cot she will hang without danger of falling on the strength of this grasp reflex. The newborn baby's feet also have more ability to grasp in their newborn stage. This reflex is seen at its most useful in baby monkeys who live in trees, but it is not related to the later ability to grasp objects which does not develop until the age of 6 months. Similarly, the walking reflex cannot be said to be the forerunner of walking as this is usually preceded by crawling and standing. However, when held under the shoulders the newborn baby will make stepping movements with the body held straight. This reflex is lost after 2 months, and the muscular activities which precede walking, e.g. rolling over, do not usually begin until 6 months of age. When a sudden loud noise, e.g. clapping the hands, happens the newborn baby responds with the startle reflex. The arms are flung outwards and then brought in toward the body. Another reflex which is useful is the ability to turn the head to one side when the baby is placed on her back.

Intellectual development

At 1 month of age, the baby responds to stimuli of light and movement. She turns her head and eyes towards the light and can follow a pencil light for a little when it is held about 12 inches away from her. She shuts her eyes tightly when the light is shone directly into them – a defence mechanism which persists throughout life. If a dangling toy or rattle is shaken about 6 or 8 inches away from her eyes, she will follow it as it is moved from the side to the front of her head in her line of vision. Contrary to myths that babies cannot see in the first few weeks of life, experiments have shown that they can respond not only to human faces but also to drawings resembling human faces. At 1 month, the baby is beginning to watch her mother's face as she feeds her.

Feeding presents valuable opportunities for learning, and in breast feeding the child explores taste, smell and touch as she sucks on the nipple and feels the soft breast. It is thought that the senses of touch, taste and smell are more acute at

birth than sight and hearing, although the new-born baby will turn her head at the sound of a human voice, and even pause during her sucking. Her heightened sensitivity to smell is shown in her ability to distinguish between the smell of breast milk and sugar-water.

Helping the child's intellectual development in the first 3 months involves extending the stimulation provided in everyday activities of feeding, bathing and changing nappies. Babies should be spoken to from birth as this enhances speech development and the child quickly comes to enjoy the auditory stimulation and communication. Adequate stimulation is essential for all aspects of development: babies left in sterile environments in cots, gazing up at white ceilings and walls, deprived of interaction with other human beings, fail to thrive. In studies

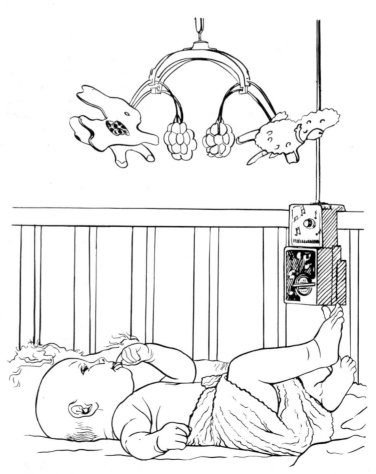

Figure 3.3   Mobiles provide an interesting and changing environment for the young baby.

undertaken on the long-term effects of stimulation in babies it was discovered that babies who had not been stimulated did not learn new tasks as quickly as those who had. Overstimulation does not accelerate development, however. If numerous coloured mobiles were hung above a baby's cot, which was placed in a room with patterned wallpaper and had flowered cot sheets, it could be too much and cause distress as the baby cannot respond to so much stimulation.

A single, colourful mobile which could be a shape cut out by the mother and suspended over the cot within reach of the baby is sufficient for the first 2 or 3 months, after which a more complex shape can be used. Obviously the object must be an attractive colour to gain the child's attention. At 1 month she will simply lie and look at it; at 2 months she will attempt to hit it, but without success as she does not achieve hand–eye coordination to enable her to make direct contact with the object until about 5 months.

Babbling often begins at 2 months of life and is repeated as 'play speech' rather than communication as the baby repeats sounds just for pleasure. Even babies of deaf parents babble contentedly although their parents cannot hear or respond to them. While babbling is not essential to the development of speech it does provide verbal practice which lays the foundation for developing the skilled movements required in speech. It is a good idea for the adult to encourage babbling by repeating the nonsense sounds. This delights the baby who then develops a range of noises.

Emotional development

The formation of secure attachments to one or two constant care givers in early infancy is crucial for satisfactory emotional development – as indeed is the satisfaction of the basic needs for food, security, warmth and protection. A feeling of trust, which is essential for human relationships, is engendered by consistency in provision of food and attention to other basic needs. Even at 1 month, babies respond to a soothing voice and a cuddle. Anxiety or tension can easily be transmitted to the baby through rough handling or a short temper. A mother who is upset and worried and complains that the baby is always crying may not realize how her own emotional distress can upset the baby.

Most mothers tend to position their babies on their left side. This means that the baby can hear the mother's heartbeat and studies show that babies find this very soothing – and reminiscent of their quiet intrauterine life. It has also been discovered that babies whose mothers continually listened to music in pregnancy slept happily with a radio or record player on in the first months of life.

Social development

While the child's first relationship is usually with his mother and father, he is also able to form attachments with others, and it is the quality of the interaction (rather than its length) which appears to be the mediating factor. Whether the primary care giver is the child's biological mother or not, there will exist from the earliest days a reciprocity of communication. The mother or primary care giver is sensitive to the baby's signals – smiles, cries or babbling – and her response establishes early socialization as a partnership. The basis for communication is laid in the dialogue between mother and baby: he responds to her by imitating or offering another initiative. This important interaction is observed in all the mutual experiences shared by mother and baby – feeding, bathing, playing, nappy changing and bedtime – and serves to reinforce and develop the relationship. Thus, as the baby learns about his social environment by initiating contact with, and responding to, his mother, her interest in him increases and so furthers the partnership. At 5 weeks, the baby may smile at his mother when she talks to him, and at 6 weeks may 'talk' back when he gurgles in response to her voice.

Observations of babies from birth to 1 month have shown that they will gaze for a longer period of time at the human face or drawings and cutout images most resembling it. By 6 weeks, most babies carry out detailed examination of the human face, with the eyes seeming to hold the greatest fascination.

3–6 Months

Physical development

At 3 months of age, the baby can keep his head erect for a few seconds when held in the sitting

Figure 3.4 A baby of 6 months can sit upright with support.

position. This is due to bone and muscle development in the cervical region of the verterbral column; it also enables the baby to move his head deliberately to look around. His limbs move more easily now, and when placed downwards on his tummy he lifts up his head and upper trunk using his forearms for support. When held standing with his feet on a hard surface, the legs now sag at the knees. At 3 months the reflex actions have usually disappeared and the baby has some voluntary movements which he likes to repeat. Finger play involves clasping and unclasping hands and the baby likes to watch the movement of his hands. At 5 months, the baby can reach out to grasp with both hands. One month later, his range of abilities extends as he develops the palmar grasp which enables him to use his whole hand as a scoop, and soon he will be happy to use just one, rather than both hands. Everything is taken to the mouth at this stage and oral exploration is the main sensory activity.

Intellectual development

This stage is characterized by the beginnings of intentional activity in that the baby repeats actions in order to make interesting events last. If some small bells are suspended across the cot and the baby discovers that the bells will ring if a cord is pulled he will continue to pull the cord although not in the sense of using a stimulus to bring about a response, as he is not yet able to link the activities and simply wants to make an interesting result persist. In the same way he will shake his rattle repeatedly. At the beginning of this stage babies still think that when an object is out of sight it is no longer in existence and when a toy falls out of his hand he forgets it or may search only vaguely round the cot with his eyes.

At 4–6 months the baby will reach out to take a partially covered object but is unable to obtain an object that has been completely covered by a cloth, as it has ceased to exist for him. Yet when the 5-month-old baby is presented with a stationary object that proceeds to move he can follow it wherever it goes. The child now seems able to realize that an object can go from place to place through movement, although his visual perception (or ability to translate and understand the information he receives through sight) seems to be ahead of his sensorimotor coordination.

Another result of the baby's playing at this stage is 'object attainment' which means that he comes to appreciate that an object seen in different ways is still the same object. Thus, when the baby is able to hold the bottle and suck from the teat he will attempt to suck the bottom if it is presented to him upside down. At a later stage, when he has come to recognize it as an enduring object, he will turn it round the right way before sucking.

During this period the child is able to distinguish between simple geometric forms such as circles, squares and triangles. These can be used as mobiles or plastic shapes which the baby can grasp – provided they are large enough not to be swallowed! Familiarity with the shapes through sight, touch, taste and movement can be developed in pictures or three-dimensional objects.

Emotional development

A firm but gentle way of handling contributes to

feelings of security and trust and is particularly necessary for bathtime when any hesitation on the adult's part can make the baby scream with terror. At 6 months, the baby is clearly able to distinguish between different emotional tones in his mother's voice. A quiet, but not flat, tone of voice, showing interest, care and even delight, will enhance the relationship with the child.

During these first 3 months, there are subtle, but no less definite, changes in the relationship between mother and child. These changes are partly due to the mother's growing self-confidence, but also occur in response to the maturational changes in the baby. He is now awake more, cries less, and spends more time smiling, vocalizing and looking at his mother's face. Meanwhile, the mother is gradually decreasing the amount of very close physical contact, spends more time near the infant, increases affectionate behaviour, provides more stimulation, and is more socially responsive towards him.

Social development

As early as 3 months a baby recognizes his mother's voice and shows delight in familiar happenings such as feeding, bathing and dressing, by smiling, cooing and moving his legs and arms. Studies with babies of 4–6 months of age have revealed that the younger infants respond happily to multiple images of the mother whereas older babies become agitated as they realize that this is unnatural and prefer one stable image. They do not distinguish between strangers and familiars at this stage. Around 6 months, the baby may show anxiety or slight shyness in the presence of strangers – especially if the mother is out of sight. The presence of the mother figure acts as a pivot on which an enlarging circle of relationships turns. The child gains confidence from the security of firm but gentle handling and the satisfaction of expectations in basic need areas, such as feeding.

6–9 Months

Physical development

The baby now holds his head erect with his back straight and although he may be able to sit alone for a few seconds his back should still be well supported. The baby can extend his forearms to raise his head and chest when placed face downwards, and is able to bear his own weight on his feet and bounce up and down when he is held standing. At this age he uses his arm and wrist muscles to pull objects he sees towards him and grasps them with the whole hand using a palmar grasp (hand–eye coordination). He also discovers his feet as useful playthings and even uses them for grasping although he prefers to put them in his mouth! As he is able to sit up with support now, the baby will turn his head from side to side with his eyes following all movement about him.

At 9 months, the child's exploration of his environment involves movement of his trunk in rolling as a preliminary to crawling, and standing with support. The child is very observant, manipulates objects by passing them from hand to hand and pokes at them with his index finger. He can sit alone for up to 15 minutes (on the floor), turn his body sideways and move about by rolling on his tummy. He also begins to crawl, although some babies miss out on this stage, preferring instead to shuffle along on their bottoms using one hand for support. He can stand holding on to support for a few minutes, but cannot lower himself to sit; when he is held standing he 'steps' on alternate feet and can now stretch out for objects he sees in front of him. When he picks up items with his finger and thumb they are crossed in a scissor fashion and he is less likely to put objects into his mouth. Instead, he will begin to explore objects tactually (by touch) or visually, or use the object for rhythmic banging.

Intellectual development

Toys may be offered if asked for, but as yet the child is unlikely to hand them over voluntarily. Meanwhile, his object attainment has now extended to a realization of permanence – he appreciates that an object, though hidden from sight, still exists and will look under a cup to find a toy. Another game he enjoys at this stage is 'peek-a-boo'. This involves temporarily hiding from the baby; providing the play partner reappears fairly soon, the baby can enjoy the game without feeling afraid. Often, laughter is mingled with fear as the child feels insecure when someone leaves him all alone; as yet he cannot appreciate the notion of time or the meaning of temporary.

He is now able to search in the correct place for toys he has dropped within reach and will look after toys which have fallen from his pram or chair. The baby's newly developed understanding of object permanence and ability to direct activity towards an end (e.g. removal of a cover before the toy can be discovered) is, according to Piaget, the precursor of adult problem-solving.

J. Bruner translates the range of activities enjoyed by the 6-month-old baby, after he has learned to hold on to an object and get it easily to his mouth, as early play. He terms it 'mastery play' as the baby's actions with the object demonstrate his developing abilities. First he looks at the object, shakes it, bangs it on his high chair, drops it over the edge and before long he manages to fit the object into every activity possible. Then all his newly acquired mastery is applied to every new object and Bruner found it surprising that at 6–8 months babies can carry on such varied activities for as long as half an hour.

Emotional development

Natural anxiety or fear of strangers is usually revealed at 7–8 months, much to the chagrin of acquaintances outside the family circle who are often nonplussed at a child beginning to scream when they approach, but if mother or a known adult is there the fear can be easily resolved. This fear of strangers combined with the ability to realize that unseen objects (e.g. a toy hidden under a cup or dropped over the pram side) still exist explains the delight in playing peek-a-boo games. Some minor fear can be thrilling. Like their parents who (probably) love the thrill of rides at fairgrounds and scream lustily, so, too, babies scream with delight when a known face suddenly reappears from behind a door or bobs up again in front of the pram. However, the child is distressed at any real separation from a familiar person at this stage.

Social development

At 9 months, the use of hearing and speech in social development is evident as the baby uses babbling, loud noises, 'mm', 'bah, bah' and 'duh duh' sounds to attract attention and communicate. This is highly successful as parents eagerly translate these meaningless sounds into 'mummy', 'mama', 'daddy' and 'baby', and they naturally respond with more attention, reassurance and reinforcement of acceptable behaviour. At this stage, the baby may respond negatively to strangers and will not accept them happily unless a known adult is present – when he may respond with a 'selective social smile'.

9–12 Months

Physical development

Between 10 and 12 months the baby begins to pull himself up to a standing position and can let himself down while holding on to furniture. At 12 months he may try walking round a low table sideways. Some babies can stand alone for a few minutes and even walk with one or both hands held. Others may not walk until they are 14–16 months of age but this is merely a variation in development pace. The first movements brought about by voluntary control of small muscles include the pincer grasp of thumb and index finger which is used to pick up small toys and sweets. He can click two blocks together after demonstration, and while both hands are still used a preference for one may be shown. At this stage the baby can drink from a cup with a little help and hold a spoon, but cannot use it properly without help. Hands are gleefully clapped in imitation of adults and also waved to say 'bye-bye'.

Exploration of the environment is furthered by the child's ability to crawl, which rapidly leads into standing, holding on to furniture, walking with one or both hands held, or stepping sideways around furniture. The child's self-confidence increases with the knowledge of his own name, the understanding of words related to his own world – e.g. cup, spoon, walk – and the understanding of simple commands and gestures. He may be experimenting with feeding himself at this stage, but the enormous opportunities for play in this situation may take precedence over the necessity to actually eat – although, if he is hungry, the food will eventually find its way into his mouth.

Intellectual development

The baby's developing ability to coordinate means and ends in activity is now evident: he grasps the bell by the handle and rings it in gleeful imitation of the adult; he is able to manipulate objects within his environment and will put wooden cubes in a cup or box and then lift them out again. To his delight he finds he is also able to manipulate adults, as he drops toys deliberately and watches them fall to the ground, only to be picked up by whoever is passing by and returned to the baby who promptly drops them again! The repetitive action strengthens his sense of control over events and demonstrates his understanding of object permanence as he looks in the correct place for toys which have rolled out of sight. He has learned how to point with his index finger and by the end of this stage he can pick up small objects with a pincer grasp of thumb and index finger. His behaviour indicates that he can discriminate differences in people and things and he moves from shyness and uneasiness with strangers to an acceptance, although he is still very dependent on a familiar adult. His understanding increases as his ability to perceive relationships between new and old situations increases. Relationships and meanings are more accurately seen if new material has something in common with past experiences. Aids to learning should involve this linking of ideas as it is through this that the child comes to develop concepts which help him to order his understanding of the world.

Emotional development

A number of mothers in Gordon Bronson's study (*Infants' Reactions to Unfamiliar Persons and Novel Objects*) reported that their babies developed a specific fear or dislike for a particular person at around the age of 9 months. He held that this fear was not just related to unfamiliarity but that some babies will develop particular fears based on particular associations. It seems that the 'fear of strangers' which we look for as a developmental milestone at 6–8 months depends on individual variation and the situation. Judy Dunn found that babies in real life outside of the laboratory situation never react to strangers in a way that could be called fearful. They show wariness and caution but not fearful reaction to strange people. Sroufe's study of 10-month-old babies showed that it was much more common for the babies to smile at the stranger and offer a toy than it was to cry. Judy Dunn warns that babies' reactions are complex and their emotional state is dependent

on a number of factors, including the setting, its familiarity, the presence of family figures and the behaviour of strange people to the baby and parent. While much of the behaviour seems geared to avoidance of danger, e.g. crying, which usually produces a powerful effect on the parent, babies seem to have a 'comforting system' of a group of ways with which they cope with upsetting or stressful events – turning away, crying, clinging – and, at this stage of emotional development, using a comfort object such as a bottle, blanket or thumb.

To test the visual perception of babies, babies of 9–12 months are placed on the 'visual cliff', a device which consists of a heavy sheet of glass raised about a foot from the floor. A sheet of patterned material (usually black and white squares) is placed underneath, flush with one half, while the other half is left bare, suspended above the floor but with the same patterned material below it. The entire surface of the apparatus is now solid but appears to end at the half-way point where vision would clearly tell adults that they are on the edge of a cliff. Only three out of 27 babies on Gibson and Walk's study ventured over the edge of the cliff – the others refused even when their mothers called to them from the other side. Some cried when their mother called since she seemed to be enticing them to fall over. This exercise shows that babies of this age have visual perception of depth and, since animals have this too, it is probably a safety mechanism.

As the child becomes ambulant his increasing independence must be fostered through an environment adapted to allow exploration. Homes or nurseries cluttered with too much furniture, ornaments or equipment can prove irritating and stultifying to the baby's attempts to (literally) stand on his own two feet.

Social development

As the child approaches the end of the first year he begins to realize that adults can be used to provide help in play with objects and that objects can be used to gain adult attention. E. Bates' study of one little girl, Carlotta, reveals this change in behaviour:

1 *First observation* (before 10 months). Carlotta's mother is holding a box in her arms. In an effort to get it Carlotta pulls at the arms, pushes her whole body against the floor and approaches the box from several angles. She never looks at her mother's face during this exercise.

2 *Second observation* (at 11 months 22 days). Carlotta cannot pull a toy cat out of the adult's hand so she sits, back up straight, looks at the adult's face intently and then tries once again to pull the cat. This pattern is repeated three times. The interruption of an object play sequence to look towards the adult permits us to infer that the child now understands the potential role of the adult. At this stage he can play alone quite happily but enjoys the presence of his parents, who should try to help his social development by spending as much time with him as they can.

He also needs space to test his burgeoning physical independence and will happily show off his standing/walking ability to family visitors. Confining him to a small playpen may inhibit him, and lack of space is one of the reasons for stunted development in children living in high-rise flats.

By 12 months, the child now begins to realize that he is a separate entity from his parents as he responds to the sound of his own name, but he still likes the comfort of an adult presence and shows affection for those in his family circle.

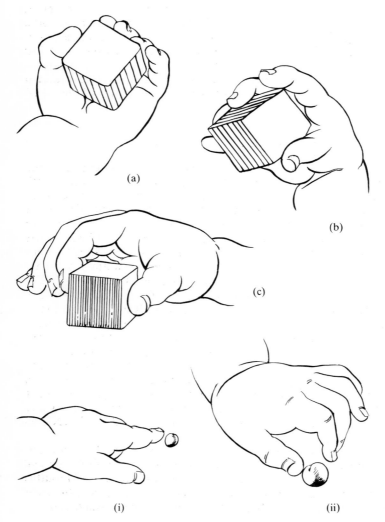

Figure 3.5 Fine motor movements (a) and (b) palmar grasp (6 months), (c) pincer grasp (12 months). Then (i) pointing with index finger (9 months), (ii) picking up small objects (15 months).

Figure 3.6   Small muscle control: (a) placing one cube on top of another (15 months), (b) arranging cubes horizontally (18 months).

15–18 Months

Physical development

At 15 months, the baby can now usually walk – but unsteadily and there may be frustrations and anger as she bumps into furniture. She can get to her feet alone, set off alone, sit down backwards (with a bump), or fall forward onto her hands and then sit. As she can crawl upstairs at this stage, safety measures should include a stair gate which is strong and stable enough to withstand her weight. Leg muscles may be sufficiently developed to enable her to bend and pick up toys from the floor. She is able to hold her cup and bring the spoon to her mouth, but just to lick it; she lacks sufficient control to hold it in one position. Large wheeled toys with handles are useful at this stage as the child loves to push them. Small muscle control is seen in the neat way she can pick up small objects and crumbs between thumb and finger. She can build a tower of two cubes after demonstration, grasp a large crayon and scribble.

By 18 months the child can usually walk well, start and stop safely, push and pull large toys and cardboard boxes around the floor, and carry a large bear while she is walking. She can run, but in an awkward manner, and stops in front of furniture. While she is able to back into a small chair, she usually climbs forward into an adult's chair, then turns round and sits. Balance is now sufficiently controlled to enable her to pick up her toys from the floor without falling. She can walk upstairs with the help of an adult and crawl downstairs backwards, although she may prefer bumping down on her bottom.

Fine movements involve spontaneous scribble with pencil (which should be chunky for easy holding) and paper using the hand of preference, building a tower of three cubes, turning the pages of a book two or three at a time, pointing at pictures, holding a cup in both hands and drinking without excess spilling, using a spoon to get food to her mouth and taking off her shoes, hat and socks.

Between 12 and 18 months, the *anterior fontanelle* which is at the front of the skull closes.

Intellectual development

The baby now shows even greater curiosity and experimentation through trial and error with different objects using different aspects of sensorimotor schemes. For example, if the baby is in the playpen, she may experiment with various movements or objects to bring a toy through the bars from its position outside. Thus she demonstrates increasing mastery over her environment. Greater exploration is possible as she is now able to crawl upstairs and walk a few steps, if unsteadily. Adult supervision is required to prevent her from possible dangers in this extended environment but this should not be obstructive or hinder natural curiosity. Valuable ornaments should be placed out of reach as she will want to handle everything she can take hold of at this stage. A large wheeled toy is a popular aid to independence in walking and picture books are appreciated as interesting sights.

She will delight in imitating adult expressions and actions. If shown how to scribble she will use a crayon and copy, and later, at 18 months, will scribble spontaneously. At 15 months, she is usually able to indicate when she has soiled her-

Figure 3.7 Fine muscle control is seen in the ability to draw with large crayons.

self, but neurologically, is not yet ready for toilet training.

Hand preference is becoming increasingly evident and should not be thwarted. Myths abound as to the merits and advantages of right-handedness. Left-handedness has long been considered wrong, perhaps because it was associated with evil. The Latin term for right is *dexter* and we admire anyone who is dextrous or has manual dexterity, whereas the word for left, *sinister*, has unfortunate connotations. Various theories exist as to the physiological basis for hand preference, but because of adverse effects in children forced to use the right hand in school they are now allowed to indulge their natural preference. Apart from learning to cope with furniture, utensils and machines designed for right-handed people, there are few disadvantages of left-handedness – and indeed there are advantages – notably in racquet sports!

15–18 Months

Emotional development

Even as he struggles towards independence, he is still emotionally labile and requires constant reassurance. Toilet training may begin at the same time as a child is expressing his identity conflict in temper tantrums. Numerous studies have shown that the adult's attitudes to evacuation and control of bowels and bladder can affect all aspects of development. A child will soon realize that the process of evacuation control is considered important to his parents if they continually make a fuss about it and he may use this to show non-compliance with their wishes, by either holding in the contents or soiling himself. This relates to Freud's anal phase, although most babies do not develop control until after 18 months. At 15 months the baby can only tell his mother when he has emptied his bowels (usually in his pants) whereas at 18 months he can indicate that he feels the urge before evacuation.

Social development

Although he is becoming more mobile and independent, the child is still dependent on the adult presence for reassurance. This emotional instability and striving for independence precedes the temper tantrum stage.

By 15–18 months, the baby will have developed a number of social relationships based on his early attachments. Babies seem to form relationships with those people who are particularly responsive to their signals for attention, and initiate exchanges with them. The amount of time the adult spends with the child is not the most important factor, and in one study a third of the sample of babies at 18 months showed that they were most attached to the father who is usually unable to spend as much time with them as their mother. (The Israeli kibbutzim is another example of this since the children do not form attachments to their caretakers who look after them all day but are intensely attached to their parents whom they see only for 2 hours each evening.)

18–24 Months

Physical development

The child's mobility in crawling, walking and running allows her independence as she moves around the home. She will enjoy running ahead of her mother on their way to the park, where she shows off new abilities in climbing the 'Jungle Jim' or balancing on parallel bars. She will join in a ball game with her father and siblings though her throwing ability is still not very good. She now has increased hand–eye coordination in reaching, grasping and manipulating objects by bringing them together and relating them to one another.

At 2 years of age the child can now run safely avoiding obstacles and stopping and starting easily. She is able to rise to her feet from a sitting position without using her hands, and likes to express independence through climbing on to furniture to look out of the window or open cupboard doors and handling whatever she can. When she walks upstairs and down she holds on to the rail or wall and puts two feet on each step before moving forward. A small ball can be thrown but she will walk into a large ball when trying to kick it. Meal times also give scope for independence as she is able to lift and drink from a cup, replace it on the table and spoon food without spilling. Small muscle control is seen in the way she removes sweet wrappers, builds a tower of six or seven cubes, turns pages singly, scribbles spontaneously in circles and makes dots, imitates a vertical line and sometimes a letter V, puts on her hat and shoes and turns door handles.

Intellectual development

The child is now passing from the sensorimotor to the preoperational period and intuitive thinking. At 18 months she is aware of practical relationships – where objects are, where they were previously and where they belong. She indicates her nose, eyes, hair, shoes and points to pictures of familiar objects – a clock, a car, a dog. This transition from the 'sensorimotor' to 'preoperational' period is characterized by symbolic games when the child imitates her own past actions in very simple, concrete ways which show that she has mental images of these actions, e.g. pretending to go to sleep, curling her body round and shutting her eyes. Her

Figure 3.8   Building a tower of seven pieces.

imagination develops as she learns to pretend to drink first from a cup, then another object unlike a cup. Possessed of a vocabulary of about 15 words, she can, in fact, understand many more and shows appreciation of speech by imitating certain words and trying to join in nursery rhymes. She can undress herself at bedtime now, and she begins to appreciate excreted products – faeces, urine – although does not distinguish between them and generally uses one word or expression to vocalize toilet needs. Bowel control begins to be developed at this stage; bladder control comes at around 2 years of age.

In spatial concepts, at 18 months, she is still at the vertical stage and will imitate a vertical stroke with a pencil and make a pile of three blocks. Her spatial and mechanical abilities are developing as she enjoys spontaneous scribble and can fit round and triangular shapes into a formboard. She can now recognize fine details in pictures she likes. Her tower of cubes is now made with six cubes which indicates a gain in attention span. Three shapes: round, triangular and rectangular can now be replaced in a form-board. Horizontal control which shows further progress in hand–eye coordination is seen in the ability to make a horizontal stroke and build a 'train' by placing three blocks in a horizontal fashion. Neurological growth (brain and nervous system) is required before the transition from vertical to horizontal can be made. Her intellectual abilities are also demonstrated in her behaviour with a chair. At 18 months she pushes

a chair and climbs into it in forward fashion to sit in it whereas at 2 years she uses the chair as a means to an end. It is pushed over to a shelf she cannot reach and she climbs on to it to achieve the desired object.

Her vocabulary has expanded to about 50 or more recognizable words although she may understand about 300. She now understands 'down', 'up', 'on', and 'in' and is able to express 'no' and 'not' verbally rather than by shaking her head. Single words are replaced by two- or three-word sentences, 'Sally run' or 'Daddy go car' and although she usually refers to herself in the third person her sense of possession is seen in her use of the word 'mine'. Everything still revolves around her in her world and she cannot understand what it is to share with other children and cannot play with them – although she is content to play alongside ('parallel play'). Her use of plurals and physical relationships 'under', 'on top' is related to further neurological development which enables her to utilize certain words. Simple sound patterns as in nursery rhymes and songs are enjoyed and repeated. Imitation is shown in her play as she copies her mother's domestic activities and she extends symbolic play to her toys as she pretends to put her horse to sleep. Piaget calls imaginative play 'the purest form of egocentric and symbolic thought'. While egocentric in that the child is lost in her own dramatization, symbolic play leads her away from egocentricity because it enables her to feel what it is like to be something or someone else apart from herself, e.g. a dog or an aeroplane. Egocentricity is a characteristic of the second major stage of intellectual development – the 'preoperational thought period'.

Toilet training

Toilet training must be a gradual process and never become a 'battleground' between adult and child. Habit formation should be started in babyhood, with regularity of meals, evacuation of bowels, bath and sleep times established to promote feelings of security. At 15 months some children can indicate when they are wet and at 18 months they may be able to indicate beforehand. The child should be able to sit comfortably on a potty and climb onto a chair before attempts are made to start toilet training. Until he can do this, he is not yet ready for toilet training, as the brain cells involved in this are not sufficiently mature until he is between 18 months or 2 to 3 years old. However, adverse parental reaction to his lack of control can affect his learning ability as guilty feelings or a desire to please may sap his independence. It will be helpful if the child is allowed to accompany the parent to the toilet in order that he realizes how natural it is. The mother or father may say 'I need to go to the toilet' (better than the use of expressions like 'wee-wee' or 'poo-poo' which usually come from parents not children) and a child of 2½ or 3 years also has a simple lesson in sex differences when he sees Daddy holding his penis while Mummy sits on the toilet seat. Some parents are naturally shy about performing toilet practices in front of their children, but it can be of considerable help. Bowel control is often achieved before bladder control as bowel actions are less often. Some children will be dry at night by 2½ years, but boys usually take longer and may not be dry until 3 years of age. Most children can keep dry with vigilance during the day at 2½–3 years. When an accident does occur it is best to mop up without comment rather than scolding the child. Instead praise him highly when he is able to warn you before the incident occurs, or even brings the potty to you. Patience and understanding are prerequisites for management of the eighteen-month-old child who is proceeding from the dependence of babyhood to the more independent toddler stages in some bewilderment, which is often expressed in temper tantrums and clinging behaviour.

Social development

The child's social development depends to a great extent on the environmental influences of her home (e.g. high-rise flat, apartment with no facilities for outdoor play, or a 'semi' with a small back garden), her family, her siblings, her proximity to other children to play with, and her relationships with the extended family – grandparents, cousins and even neighbours.

Emotional development

The child now experiences and exhibits a variety of emotions – pleasure, satisfaction, joy, anger, frustration, distress, as she struggles towards independence from her parents. As she is still dependent on them for comfort and security when strangers are at hand, conflict between independence and dependence occurs, often exploding into temper tantrums. The adult should not show anger during this phase as it is a developmental stage; but neither must the child's outburst be condoned. One way is for the adult to remove the child from the nursery or room at home (to avoid disturbing the other children) and to stay with the child until she recovers, giving the impression that they are involved in some activity, as attention could be interpreted as approval by the child. After the tantrum is over the child may be hugged tightly as she is rather frightened at her own anger. The hug makes her feel secure and ready to resume normal relations. Fear, anger and aggression may be represented in the child's fantasy play as she smacks her teddy for wetting himself – providing a safe outlet for pent-up emotions and displacing her guilt.

The child now shows pleasure in possessions which she labels 'mine', and in her achievements, as when she enjoys looking at a picture book with a familiar adult, pointing and naming objects she recognizes, such as dog, car, bus, train. There is also the warm comfort of the adult's lap or knee which provides the perfect setting for exercising the imagination.

At 18 months the child may show negative reactions to an adult's suggestions. 'No' becomes a favourite word as she stands in defiance, refusing to obey simple commands. She gets very annoyed if her wishes are crossed and may scream with rage, often to the adult's chagrin, particularly if it happens in a shop! These outbursts become more frequent as she enters her second year. Now she struggles to be independent and is alternately self-willed and lovingly responsive. Her temper tantrums become more frequent and she may have nightmares and irrational fears. Consistent, loving understanding from the adult is essential to bring her through this phase without traumatic effects.

2½–3 Years

Physical development

At 2½ years of age, the child can now run (straight forward) well and climb simple apparatus. She jumps with her feet together, can stand on tiptoe and kick a large ball. She can walk upstairs on her own but holds a rail when walking downstairs, still with two feet to a step. Although she is now able to push and pull large toys easily, she cannot steer round obstacles. Fine movements include manual dexterity as she picks up pins and thread, builds a tower of seven cubes and arranges blocks to form a train, imitates a horizontal line, letters T and V and a circle, and paints strokes, dots and circular shapes on an easel. At table, she uses her spoon skilfully and may use a fork. She can pull down her pants to go to the toilet but finds it difficult to pull them up again. She enjoys filling jugs and tipping the contents into sand or water trays.

At 3 years the child can walk upstairs independently with alternating feet, downstairs with two feet to a step, and usually jumps from the bottom step. She is able to climb nursery apparatus, can turn round obstacles and corners while running or pushing and pulling large toys, and ride a tricycle and turn wide corners on it. She can stand on one foot (stork stand) and sit cross-legged. Small blocks can now be made into a tower of nine or deliberate patterns. She can scribble freely, imitate circles, a cross, letters V, H, T, draw a man (usually head and face with projections for arms and legs), cut with scissors, and paint pictures confidently with a large brush. A fork and spoon can now be used for eating, hands can be washed (but drying needs help) and pants can be pulled down and up, but help is required in putting on coats and fastening zips and buttons. She loves to pound clay and dough and is able to carry her own cup of milk or juice without spillage.

Intellectual development

Piaget identified a preoperational thought period as occurring between 2 and 7 years:

1 *pre-operational phase* – 2–4 years,
2 *intuitive phase* – 4–7 years.

The increasing bodily coordination from the first 2 to 4 years is important for the development of intelligence, as sensorimotor schemes concerned in body control form the base for intellectual achievements. For example, the ability to grasp one cube and place it on top of another leads to development of concepts 'under', 'on top', and how the movement of the lower object causes movement of the upper which is resting on it. Those who follow Piaget's theories insist that children at nursery and primary schools should be encouraged to explore and discover properties of play materials for themselves. Thus activities such as threading beads and movement to music develop the child's understanding of space and time, as well as helping his fine movements. Pre-reading and pre-number activities such as selection of clothes for dressing dolls and putting them on in the right sequence, setting the table with one plate and one mug for each child are more important than formal reading skills at 4 or 5 years of age.

At 2½ years of age the child engages in domestic play such as putting toys to bed and washing their clothes. She is very jealous of adult attention and while she may show interest in other children at play she still has no notion of sharing playthings or participation. Developing curiosity is seen in the frequency of questions beginning 'What?' and 'Where?' and her conversations with herself at play show that she has no idea of past tense. Everything happens in the present and the concept of time is not understood until later.

At three, the child's command of vocabulary gives her great confidence to extend her experiences. She now asks 'Who?' and is beginning to see herself as a person, having passed through the confusing 2-year-old stage where she alternated between dependence and independence. Her motor ability, always a reflection of brain development, enables her to build a tower of nine cubes, a train with a chimney and 'a bridge' (two blocks placed side by side with one placed in the middle on top of both). She can draw circles and when asked to draw

Figure 3.9   Push and pull toys are popular at 2–2½ years.

a man will produce a large circle for the head, sometimes with strokes or dots to represent other parts. Colour-making with yellow, red and blue shows ability to discriminate, and she is able to paint pictures with a large brush and to use scissors, which requires fine movements. Hand–eye coordination is dependent upon motor development and although she is able to match a circle, square and triangle into the form-board she still requires demonstration before she can build her 'bridge' or assemble her 'train'.

Her ability to cope with requests for little errands in the house, and pleasure at the satisfactory accomplishment of these indicates her transition from babyhood to childhood. She is even able to show affection for younger babies and begins to join in play activities with other children, although she still prefers solitary and 'parallel' play. Gradual appreciation of past and present is shown as she describes experiences of 'last night', 'yesterday', 'last week'. Pretending to tell the time is a favourite game and she loves to ask 'what time is it?', 'When is lunchtime?'. Use of expressions such as 'all the time' and 'all day' shows that she is beginnning to understand the concept of duration.

As this stage is egocentric the child is unable to take the viewpoint or role of another person. However, as the child progresses through a new developmental phase, the preoperational phase, new intellectual skills and knowledge are acquired which enable the child to predict other people's perceptions, thoughts and feelings. This spatial role-playing means that the child can imitate the behaviour of others, put herself into 'someone else's shoes' and say how she sees things. Although children will pretend to be mummy and daddy at this stage and even use the expressions and words that their parents use, only about 79% of 3-year-olds can take an adult perspective. More often than not, when mummy is ill, for example, she will be offered a doll or teddy as comforter, and a toy car may be suggested as a Christmas present for daddy.

Spatial role playing means that the child must also be able to suspend her own visual field while she chooses the scene that the other person sees, and she is beginning to achieve this by 3 years. However, perceptions have most influence in the child's thinking at this stage. She believes whatever she sees, hears or experiences at a given moment and is not able to apply what she has learnt in previous situations to the present. Thus pre-school children enjoy a magician's tricks because they really believe everything they see, including rabbits coming out of tall hats!

During the first half of the *preoperational period*, which Piaget called the *preconceptual thought stage*, the child is organizing his experiences into concepts of classes; time, space, number and causality. In the second or *intuitive phase* he becomes able to think in terms of classes but may be unaware of his classificaton. *Class concepts* refer to the child's ability to group like objects together; for example, an apple, an orange and a banana are all fruit but orange also refers to a colour and could be put into another class of orange-coloured objects. Often children will use one word to indicate a group of associated objects, e.g. 'gog' for dog was used by Claire, aged two, to refer to horses, dogs, cows and other four-legged animals. Likewise some children use the term 'Daddy' to refer to any man. Another child used 'quack' to mean duck, water, milk and orange juice. Sometimes objects are put into 'families', as when Jonathan, aged three, sorted out the tablespoon, dessert spoon and teaspoon into 'Daddy, Mummy and baby'.

Concepts of quantity refer to words like 'more,' 'less', 'all', 'some' and 'none', which children use before they can count meaningfully. Even before they know the meanings of the words 'more' or 'less' they will choose a dish with more sweets in preference to one with less! If asked whether they would like 'another biscuit' children of 2 years will hold out the empty hand to accept it but they cannot understand whether objects seen one after another are the same or a series of objects.

Concepts of number are determined from concrete experience at first and the child who 'counts' from 1 to 10 at 3 years of age is probably enjoying the jingle without understanding the concept of five or ten objects in a numerical sense. Counting on the fingers provides a useful practical aid and an experiment showed that the ability to articulate the fingers was evident in a group of retarded children with a high ability in number concepts.

Emotional development

At 2½ years the child is still emotionally labile – that is, she swings between positive and negative reactions. Sometimes she is rebellious, uncooperative and naughty; other times, dependent and clinging. Six months later she can seem remarkably different as she reacts in a cooperative, friendly and loving manner to adult suggestions – appearing to model herself on adult behaviour. However, the 2½-year-old child can also appear very aggressive: she may quarrel noisily with one of her peers who has perhaps a favourite toy. Children of this age do not always distinguish clearly between people and things, hence the importance with which she considers her possessions. She is also interested by other children and likes to regard them as curiosities by poking, pushing and even tasting!

Usually, the child's imagination begins to develop at around 2 years, and games of make-believe are enjoyed. She will also be having dreams and nightmares and sometimes finds it difficult to distinguish between reality and fantasy.

At 3 years of age, many children experience sibling jealousy and rivalry for the first time in the shape of a new addition to the family. Jealousy arises when the child is frustrated in his desire to be loved best, whereas rivalry is the angry feeling that results when a person is frustrated in his desire to do best or to win. The new baby makes the youngest child jealous as he is now displaced from his position and rivalry may be felt towards an older brother who is stronger and more able. Such feelings are quite natural but can be made less painful with understanding parents and care givers who prepare the child for the new arrival through stories, pictures, pointing out other babies, stressing their dependency but always reassuring the child of his parent's undiminished continuing affection for him. Emphasis on the individuality of each child in the family and avoidance of competition or comparisons also help. These plus the provision of acceptable outlets in dramatic and imaginative play will help the child to accept the new baby without emotional trauma. Those who look after the child in nursery should be told of the impending event to enable them to understand the child's difficulties at this time and help him towards resolution of them by appropriate care and activities.

Social development

Many mothers feel that the socialization process should begin at 2½–3 years with nursery school or playgroup to extend the child's range of relationships. When a child begins nursery school, as some do at this age, he may be seen to offer sympathy and help to other children although he does not play with them. One may, for example, see two children crying when the problem is peculiar to one. In order to avoid the trauma of what is often the first separation of mother and child as he enters nursery, it is a good idea for her to stay with him for the first morning and gradually ease off the amount of time she spends with him until he seems able to be parted from her without much fuss. Often his interest will remove tearful protests as he sees the wonderful treasure trove the nursery can offer. Not all children find this separation from mother painful and sometimes it seems that the child cries to fulfil his mother's fond expectations that he will miss her dreadfully!

3–4 Years

Physical development

Large muscle control is seen in the ability to walk up stairs with alternating feet, march, run ten steps with coordinated alternating arm movement, pedal a tricycle, somersault forward, kick a large ball when rolled to him, swing when started in motion, climb up and slide down a 4–6 ft slide, jump from height of 8 inches, catch a ball with two hands and walk on tiptoe. The ability to use scissors, cut along an 8-inch straight line within ¼ inch of the line, trace templates and put together a three-piece formboard or puzzle, use a knife, fork and spoon skilfully, brush his teeth, put on mittens, button and unbutton large buttons, put his coat on a hanger, dress and undress himself with help on fasteners; all these indicate fine muscle movements and small muscle control.

Intellectual development

The child now utilizes his large vocabulary (about 900 words, with understanding of many more) to talk to himself and others. His favourite words are 'Who?' 'What?' 'Where?' as he eagerly seeks information about all the exciting aspects of his new world in the nursery. He also uses plurals 'mine dogs' but in Scotland he may make 'mine' plural as in 'mines' – a common expression to Scottish children! His senses add greatly to his knowledge of his environment as he observes the actions of other children in play, joins in sometimes, takes part in music-making sessions and extends his play repertoire. His liking for imaginative play is seen in dressing up and role-taking in the house corner, and his appetite for fantasy play can be satisfied through stories, picture books, puppets, finger plays and songs. He is now approaching the 'intuitive' phase and beginning to form concepts as he plays with sand and water.

Time is first experienced in infancy as a series of events linked to body rhythms and the patterns imposed by the environment on functions such as eating and sleeping. Later, actions which deal with a succession of objects such as filling a cup with cubes at 18 months of age, pushing and pulling a wheeled toy which starts and stops, all form the basis of time perception. Apart from the succession in time involved in these actions, the repetition of stimuli such as in music, dance or even rhythmically patting a baby in arms provide another kind of experience necessary for time concepts. An understanding of duration or appreciation of the intervals between events is also required for a mature concept of time. Piaget states that the young child sees duration in terms of content rather than speed, which is the same idea we all share when it appears that pleasant events such as a party pass very quickly while painful experiences like examinations seem to go on for ever! We have noted that a child of 3 years appreciates past and present and can talk about 'all day' but at 3½ he can use past and future tenses correctly and is able to use complicated expressions of duration such as 'for a long time', 'for a whole week'. He can tell his mother that he goes to playgroup 'on Fridays' and that he played for 'only a short time' in the sandpit, but he may still confuse yesterday and today: 'I'm going for a walk yesterday'. Tomorrow and future events are well understood by the 4-year-old child. He is able to recount recent events and experiences although his stories are frequently a mixture of fact and fantasy.

It is important to realize that children under 4 cannot 'look forward' to events or even appreciate 'later this afternoon'. One often hears adults trying to comfort a 3-year-old child on his first morning at nursery with an expression like 'Mummy will come back soon' or even 'at three o'clock', when children of this age have no concept of 'later'. Naturally they respond to the adults kindly but misinformed efforts by crying even louder as they see their Mother disappear through the door in what is to them finality. Similarly, when a young child has to go into hospital, he cannot 'look forward' to visits from his parents or appreciate morning, afternoon and evening before the 4-year-old stage.

At 4 years of age he fluently reveals his vocabulary of some 1500 words, talks in sentences and continually asks questions – 'How?', 'Why?', 'When?', 'What?'. The adult should answer truthfully as the child responds reasonably if treated so. He now joins in

Figure 3.10   Learning to share toys with other children is not always easy.

enthusiastically with more advanced books, stories, songs and dramatic play.

Space concepts are derived from bodily experiences also. In the sensorimotor period the child looks, touches, grasps, feels, mouths and moves arms, legs, fingers, toes and trunk to gain concepts of his body and other objects. In the preoperational thought period, his concept of space is still egocentric, i.e. related to his body movements and perceptions. The distance between the child and an object will influence his judgement of its size and his own size also affects this. He tends to judge a close object as larger than it actually is and distant objects as smaller. Playing with blocks, trucks, tricycles and mobile toys helps him to perceive short distances accurately but he cannot judge longer distances unrelated to his own body size. Concepts of relative size enable children between the ages of three and four to select the biggest and smallest of a small selection of sweets.

Between the ages of 4 and 5 years children can build a tower or pyramid of ten blocks after demonstration and any number of 'bridges' of three when requested. Building vertically is easier at this stage than making horizontal rows.

Figure 3.11   At 3 years, the activity is important, at 4 years the product is treasured.

Even in experiments where a frame was supplied to make addition to the rows from one side only, children still found it difficult to make a horizontal row of blocks. It has been suggested that this may be due to the vertical space orientation of the body itself which remains constant in an up and down sense whereas the environment of left and right side changes constantly. Experiments with retarded children showed that given a vertical and a horizontal arrangement of blocks and asked to choose a certain coloured one from these rows, correct responses were greater in selection from the vertical row. Children's use of spatial terms also seems to be linked with a vertical orientation. Experiments have shown that they can usually say which is the biggest when shown toy models of a horse and a dog (if made to scale) but if the dog is placed on top of a box while the child watches, at 4–5 years of age he will point to the dog as the 'big one' rather than the horse. When he is shown the animals with the horse on the table and the dog already on top of the box he gives the right answer. This seems to indicate that the movement upwards makes the child think vertically and hence 'big' means 'tall' or 'high'.

The concept of causality refers to the child's ability to explain events of the outer world. At the egocentric stage he naturally explains everything in personal terms as he perceives them. Sometimes he will involve people close to him or if his parents have told him about God as the all-powerful being, he may quote God as the cause of a number of events. Siobhan illustrated this at four when she pointed to the darkness outside and said 'God has put the lights out 'cos it's bedtime'. He then progresses to understanding causes for natural events as forces within the events or by the useful term used ubiquitously by adults to explain adverse circumstances – 'they', the mysterious universal agents of disaster and misfortune.

Emotional development

At 3 years of age, the child now emerges from his identity conflicts as a trusting, generally friendly person, who will now join in play with other children, show affection for younger brothers and sisters and even be willing to share some of his toys. Now he likes to help around the house and garden and reveals his feelings in make-believe play. His self-confidence increases and at 4 years he may show reluctance to follow adult's wishes, and give cheeky answers when reproved. While he prefers to play with other children he may show aggression towards them at times. However, he does understand that he cannot always be first, he has to take turns with other children and share adult attention. He can be seen showing compassion for others at this stage, e.g. comforting a crying baby or a newcomer to the nursery. This compassion develops further as he moves to primary school.

The 4-year-old child becomes more confident and assured and indeed may be the 'senior' in the nursery or play group. He shows friendly, kindly interest in younger children and likes to be regarded as 'sensible' by adults on whom he will model his behaviour. If the adults present a confusing, inconsistent environment the child feels insecure and finds it difficult to trust them. He may still turn to the adult for comfort when he is tired, hurt, afraid or ill.

Social development

Three years has traditionally been considered an appropriate age for entry to playgroup or nursery school as the child is said to be ready to extend his social relationships at this age. However, it is the stage rather than the age which is important. Some children may be ready at 2½ years, others not until 5 years.

At the 4-year-old stage children tend to play in groups but with the focus of interest on activity rather than one child. These are not permanent groups: they will play together over some project, e.g. construction of a spaceship, then fade away to a newer activity and come together again as the interest moves on to another topic. The 4-year-old typically tells long stories, most of which are purely imaginary, but some adults become annoyed when they give credence to the stories only to be told later that they are not true. On the other hand parents sometimes worry in case the child is lying when he indulges in fantastical tales. However, a lively imagination is of great benefit in that it enables the child to solve problems of loneliness and jealousy. Often he does this with an imaginary companion. This may be in the 'form' of another child, a pet or even an adult. Parents and siblings are expected to accept the newcomer to the family who is conveniently blamed for naughty deeds and often used to draw attention to the child, who feels he is being neglected. The playmate may express the child's own wishes to be grown up and powerful or alternatively naughty and babyish. Wise parents usually allow the child to 'outgrow' his playmate but it may be necessary to set definite limits if it is not to disrupt family life.

The socialization process by which a child accepts the customs, manners and traditions of his family, culture and peer group, and becomes accepted as a member of society, involves two aspects which remain controversial. Sex-typing refers to the theory that boys and girls are expected to behave differently, have appro-priate toys, activities, dress and even emotional reactions. Thus at 3–4 years children are said to have definite sex-appropriate preferences as in boys choosing guns, soldiers, trucks and aero-planes, while girls choose dolls, kitchen utensils and nurses' uniforms. Certain characteristics such as aggression are said to be 'masculine' and are encouraged in boys while girls who try to assert themselves are described as 'tomboys' to emphasize the non-feminine nature of their behaviour. Tom Bower has revealed that the recognition of sex differences occurs to children much earlier than 3 or 4 years of age – babies

Figure 3.12 Dressing up and cookery activities provide opportunities for developing manual dexterity (4–5 years).

under a year old seem able to identify others of the same sex even when seen only in silhouette. The clues for discrimination appear to be in the way male and female babies move. However, the child of three is able to observe physical differences – particularly if he shares bathtime with brothers or sisters. It is silly to regard dolls as girls' toys with trains and cars for boys. Children usually choose toys from interest and only pressure from parents and nursery staff (which could just be non-provision of other than sex-stereotypical toys) makes them go for 'appropriate toys'. Small boys enjoy doll play just as much as girls given the chance without horrified reactions from parents, and which little girl could resist imitating Mummy as she drives her car or bus?

4–5 Years

Physical development

At this stage the skills already acquired are developed and extended. Balance, seen when she walked on tiptoe at $3\frac{1}{2}$–4 years, is now developed further as she stands on one foot without aid for 4–8 seconds, walks a balance beam, hops on one foot five successive times, jumps backwards six times and jumps forward ten times without falling. Large muscle control is demonstrated as she runs, changing direction, jumps over a string 2 inches from the floor, bounces and catches a large ball, walks downstairs with alternating feet and pedals a tricycle, turning corners. Manual dexterity is seen in her ability to make clay shapes, put together with two to three parts, cut along a curved line, cut out a 2-inch circle, cut out and paste simple shapes, and draw simple recognizable pictures such as a house, man and tree. She can wash and dry her face and hands, dress and undress alone, count fingers on one hand with the index finger of the other, use correct utensils for food, carry out toilet activities unaided, lace and tie shoes and help set the table for meals.

Intellectual development

Most children will transfer from nursery to primary school at 5 years of age. This should be a natural sequence without trauma, and the child should be previously prepared by visits with his parents. If he has not had the oppor-

tunity to attend nursery school or playgroup he may find the transition difficult and traumatic. Some of the pre-reading and pre-number activities in the Primary or First School may be similar to those in the nursery school, as it is important that children should approach 'formal' lessons in an informal play-oriented way. This play is indeed work to the 5-year-old child and should not be dismissed as 'only playing all day'.

Nowadays children of $4\frac{1}{2}$ years are accepted into some Primary or First schools but, since the needs of a 5-year-old are different from those of the $4\frac{1}{2}$-year-old, it is not a good practice. The Primary 1 teacher often has 20–30 children or more to teach and most primary schools as yet do not employ nursery nurses in these classes. Various reports have shown that children are spoken to individually by the Primary 1 teacher on very few occasions and not for long, which can lessen the effect of good language development gained in the nursery. At this stage the child usually has a vocabulary of some 3000 words and asks many questions. She likes to show off her oral abilities and tests the adult's reaction to 'bad language'. Parents usually react with horror and insist that 'she never heard that at home'. Yet the child learns to talk by trying to imitate the adults around them, and often picks up words and expressions the adults use in front of her without realizing her ability to remember them! It is unfair of parents to punish younger children for using 'swear words' heard at home. The best approach is to ignore them as far as possible (without meaningful glances and sniggers), as to comment on them gives the child the attention she craves and acts as a reinforcement for the unacceptable language. If she persists, talking to her quietly and sensibly about the effects her language could have on the teacher and her friends may work.

Emotional development

At 5 years of age she is kind and protective towards younger children and pets and able to join in group activities with rules which she appreciates. Peer approval now begins to assume importance as she adapts to the primary school modes.

Social development

Between 4 and 5 years of age the child often

changes from a stable, friendly nursery 'senior' to a noisy, rude, boastful extrovert. This is usually a defensive reaction to the major change she undergoes as she enters First or Primary school where she could be afraid of older children. The nursery staff have to be able to extend the play of 4½-year-olds who may have experienced all the activities in their nursery and disrupt other children in an effort to overcome their boredom. While she wants to be seen as 'big' and independent of adults, she is, nevertheless, still anxious as she contemplates starting the 'big school'. Parents and nursery staff have to be prepared to continue giving support and approval when required. Play with other children, particularly in constructive and imagi-

Figure 3.13   The 4-year-old child shows interest in young children.

native play, is enjoyed but at times she may play alone, concentrating on a particular project. Group games tend to be competitive rather than teams and the adult may need to act as referee!

At this stage she enjoys stories about strong and powerful people, such as Spiderman and the boy who overcomes the threat of monsters in *Where the Wild Things Are*.

5–6 Years

Physical development

Now he is in primary school and a sample of children at this age (or any) will reveal the wide variety in developmental stages. While the majority may have mastered all the skills mentioned above, others will need help to take off coats and boots and to dress themselves for outdoor activities. Some children appear to be ahead of others in learning activities, e.g. they may be able to read, but behind in manual skills, needing help in dressing, and may become emotionally distressed at their inability. A sensitive adult will understand and appreciate these developmental differences and give the child encouragement and help unobtrusively, leading him towards self-help by praising his efforts, however slow the progress. Most children at this age have motor skills which enables them to walk a balance board forwards, backwards and sideways, skip, swing on a swing initiating and sustaining motion, climb step ladders or steps 10 ft high to the slide, dribble a ball, kick a favourite football, skate forward 10 ft, ride a bicycle, slide on a sledge, jump a rope by himself, steer a wagon propelling with one foot, walk or play in water waist high in the swimming pool, jump up and pivot on one foot, jump from a height of 12 inches and land on balls of feet, stand on one foot without support and eyes closed for 10 seconds, and hang for 10 seconds from horizontal bar bearing his own weight on his arms.

Small muscle control enables most children at this age to spread fingers, touching thumb to each finger, copy small letters, print large, single capital letters anywhere on paper, hit a nail with the hammer, colour in an outline staying within the lines 95% of the time, cut pictures from magazines or catalogue without being more than ¼ inch from edge, use a pencil sharpener, copy complex drawings, tear simple shapes from paper, fold paper square twice on the diagonal in

imitation, catch a soft ball or bean bag with one hand, hit a ball with a bat or stick, print his name on lined paper, open a carton of milk, buckle his own car seat belt, and prepare and serve himself and others with breakfast cereal.

Intellectual development

The intellectual needs of the 5-year-old child are promoted with the start of Primary or First school life. Here he learns to adapt skills practised at home such as eating, drinking, dressing, undressing, going to the lavatory, washing his hands. As with all aspects of development intellectual growth progresses with the maturation of the central nervous system (CNS). This 5–6 year stage marks a period of rapid growth, both physical and mental. Maturation is sometimes described as 'readiness' and as with all developmental stages, the child cannot be forced through any unless their brain cells have matured sufficiently. The maturation process is fostered or restricted by the wealth or poverty of intellectual stimulation in that environment during the formative years. Education is one of the factors in the growth of intelligence and, although the original potential is an inherited quality, the growth of that capacity depends upon the total experiences of the child, and in this the quality of education is the most important. However, it is necessary to recognize differences of ability and to accept that there is no educational process that can bring all children up the same level. The effective nursery nurse, teacher or parent appreciates the differing ages, stages, interests and needs of each child in order that they can benefit from schooling.

Intuitive phase: As egocentrism decreases the child begins to see causes as impersonal and as with thought, understanding progresses from the concrete towards an appreciation of the abstract. However, children cannot understand the concept of impersonal causes as explanation for every event as this requires formal and logical thought (period of formal operations 11–15 years). Instead they either explain events by a mere description or give a number of different causes.

Piaget described the tendency of children to attribute living qualities to inanimate objects as 'animistic thinking'. Adults often encourage children in this and television too encourages animistic thinking as children see stories of

Figure 3.14 A child can show off his physical prowess in front of younger children (5–6 years).

animated toys, trains and even furniture.

A thought problem which Piaget used to illustrate intellectual development in the intuitive phase is that of the conservation principle. Adults accept that the mass or amount of a substance remains unchanged even when its shape is changed or when it is divided into parts. Studies with children from 4 to 7 years show that attainment of this concept takes years of intellectual growth. To demonstrate the child's concept of conservation of mass, a 4-year-old child is given some plasticine or clay and asked to make it into a ball of the same size as a given ball. He is then asked whether they are the same and will reply 'Yes'. One ball is then rolled into a long sausage shape and the child now states that this contains more clay than the other ball, because it is longer (therefore 'bigger' or 'more'). Piaget showed that the child cannot appreciate the conservation of mass until he is 5 years old.

Emotional development

The entry to First or Primary school can be traumatic for the child who has no previous experience of daily separation from parents in nursery or play group. Reception class teachers are prepared for the tearful farewells, and have obtained relevant information about the child's choice of name (he may be known as Bobby rather than Robert), his specific likes and dislikes at break and lunch ('he won't drink milk but loves yoghurt – oh, and we're Muslim, so can he have Halal meat [some Education authorities allow this in schools with a large Asian intake – it's a particular method of slaughtering sheep and lambs] and of course no beef stew, mince, sausages or burgers'). The child is still bewildered as he is taken by the nursery nurse or teacher to a group of children who appear to be playing with various types of calculators, including the brightly coloured abacus and some which actually speak! Curiosity soon overtakes his reluctance but he may still be content to watch other children until he feels comfortable. An informal learning atmosphere pertains in the reception class but the introduction to formal learning also begins here, and if the child has the confidence of good relationships as part of his pre-school experience he will react in a sensible manner. Outbursts at this stage are rare and may coincide with problems at home. More common is the transition of trusted, secure relationships at home to the school where teacher/nursery nurse soon comes to be literally *in loco parentis*. After a few months parents become accustomed to hearing what the teacher has pronounced on every subject from pets to wearing wellies in the rain! Eventually the real friends are introduced to parents but dramatic play is still used as an outlet for his fears, hopes, frustrations and enjoyment.

As he progresses to Primary II his self-confidence is evident as he avidly joins in games with his companions or rough and tumble, or simply skipping, running and jumping with joy! He is kindly and helps younger children who appear troubled.

Social development

Those who come to Primary school from nursery or playgroup may be more accustomed to playing with other children for some time during the day away from his parents (unless they were helpers in a playgroup). However, some of these children do not always adapt easily to primary school. There is a more controlled approach to the pre-number and pre-reading activities but there is often the excitement of new apparatus such as electronic aids and, if he's lucky enough,

computers. It is of course impossible for the teacher of a class of 20–30 children to provide one-to-one contact and nursery experience may have increased their expectations in this respect. Surveys have found that only 9% of teacher time is available for individual verbal contact with each child. Teachers also have a considerable amount of management and directive function which may make them even more remote from the individual needs of their pupils. The child who has been the 'senior' in the nursery may become bored if he has already experienced the apparatus and equipment available in the reception class, and frustrated if he can no longer monopolize an adult in conversation. His independence may enable him to overcome this as he extends his circle of companions and throws himself eagerly into games which, at this stage, have rules held sacrosanct, and 'that's fair' or 'not fair' become frequent expressions in the playground. Now that adults view him as 'a big boy' in primary school he begins to gain some self-identity through his social relationships. The limits which adults apply to children's behaviour are now interpreted as sensible rules and are usually observed as such.

6–7 Years

Physical development

At 6 years the average height is 3½ ft (1.07 m) and weight 40 lb (18.14 kg). This is a period of rapid growth and 'filling out'; a similar process occurs again in early adolescence. The development of motor skills during this stage depends less upon informal, spontaneous learning, and more upon the learning of rules for formalized and standardized activities. There is now a change in the classroom setting and programme so that children are able to sit for longer periods than in their first primary year and concentrate on the acquisition of literacy, numeracy, oral skills and aesthetic appreciation. However, their muscle coordination and balance continues to improve as physical exercise is enjoyed for its own sake rather than as competition with other peers. Team games, e.g. football and rounders, are popular at this stage. Usually boys' games are different from those of girls, who may join in rounders but prefer ball play in small groups, skipping and traditional games, e.g. hopscotch. This sex difference is often imposed by the cultural ethos of the school which reflects a society in which girls are not generally accepted as footballers!

Intellectual development

The concept of conservation of weight and volume is more difficult than that of mass, and most children cannot grasp this until they are 6 years of age or older. In the volume experiment the two clay balls are placed one at a time in a graduated cylinder filled with water. The child observes that each raises the water level by the same amount but cannot agree that the sausage shape would do likewise as he believes that its volume is greater. This concept is first grasped at around 7 years.

Children between the ages of 6 and 7 can accurately answer questions to the questions related to conservation shown in Table 3.4.

Table 3.4

1 *Conservation of substance*	
A	B
The adult presents two identical clay balls. The child agrees that they are equal amounts of clay.	One of the balls is rolled out to form another shape. The child is asked whether they still contain equal amounts.
2 *Conservation of length*	
A Two sticks are aligned in front of the child. The child agrees they are equal.	B One of the sticks is moved to the right. The child is asked whether they are still the same.
3 *Conservation of number*	
A	B
Two rows of counters are placed in one-to-one correspondence. The child admits they are equal.	One of the rows is spread out or brought closer together. The child is asked whether each row still has the same number.

Emotional development

At 6 years the child seems less stable than at five. He can be very irritable, self-centred and aggressively refuse to share his toys and books. At times he may rebel against the rules and limits set on his behaviour in the Primary 2 class. He loves to tackle new skills like computer programs but can become frustrated when they prove difficult to master.

Social development

This is Erikson's stage of 'industry versus inferiority' which lasts from 6 to 9 years, and the radius of significant relations becomes the neighbourhood and school.

During this phase the child discovers not only that he is a distinct person but that he is also able to do things by himself and with others. Now he avails himself of every opportunity to learn, to become 'someone' in his imagination – perhaps a pop star, astronaut, footballer, doctor, nurse or policeman (preferably mounted on a fine horse or zooming around on a very big motorbike). They become very keen on the world around them and in gaining approval of adults. It is interesting to note that children in Canada, the USA and most European countries start school at this age. Some may have been at nursery school or kindergarten beforehand but British children are apparently deemed ready for formal schooling a year or two earlier. There are even efforts to bring children of 4½ years into the first Primary class with 5-year-olds, which is not a good idea since children's needs change between 4½ and 5 years.

The advantage of later school entry can mean that there is a longer period of time for informal pre-number and pre-reading activities, perhaps more opportunity for greater exploration of the environment, unperturbed by the anxious ambition of parents who want to hurry their children on. Some children experience feelings of inferiority as they cannot be sure that they are people of importance. They eventually resolve this conflict by continued industry before they pass on to the next stage of puberty at 9 years.

Nursery nurses who intend to work as nannies in any of the countries mentioned above will find that they have to adjust their ideas of 'normal' skills acquisition (such as reading ability) at 6 or 7 years.

7–8 Years

Physical development

Physical growth continues but not as rapidly as in the earlier stages. Physical skills increase through informal play and more formal games with rules and teamwork. This is a time when cooperation rather than competition should be encouraged in games. Rough and tumble play in adventure playgrounds should also be provided at this stage as an outlet for frustration and aggression.

Intellectual development

The stage from 7 to 11 years is Piaget's period of 'concrete operations' when the acquisition of concepts shows progression from the preoperational thought period. Now the child is able to classify (group objects or events with similar properties) and from this to understand the meaning of numbers and symbols. She is, however, still unable to think of hypothetical numbers, hence the use of the label 'concrete' since at this stage she is tied to the 'real'.

Concepts of colour are usually grasped more easily than concepts of form. Experiences in which children were asked to choose from a group of red triangles and green circles the items that were like another item (which was either a green triangle or red circle) showed that children of less than 4 years and 8 months chose colour for matching, whereas those over this age chose form or shape to match. Learning to read and write demands attention to form, which may be the explanation for this change to form preference. Sub-grouping (that is, sorting by form or shape and then by colour within this group) is not usually possible until the child is 6 years old, as children of 3 and 4 years find it difficult to change from one classification to another. This ability means that she has to be able to perceive form, colour and size in an abstract way. Experiments have shown that no child under eight can do this without help. Sorting activities are often used in play through which experiences and cognitive or intellectual abilities are organized and adapted in various ways to enable the child to gain control over her environment as she perceives it. It is thought that sorting into shapes, colours and sizes is a useful pre-number activity and helps develop mathematical concepts.

Concepts of direction are still difficult for children under 8 years of age. When asked where their home or school is they may be able to give the address, but actual directions may only be 'over there' or 'near the bus stop'. One girl of four was convinced that London was at the top of her street as she last saw her uncle there when she had been told he was returning home to London. Children do not usually gain a clear concept of direction until they are at the next stage of development (that of concrete operations).

Concepts of the size of different shaped objects such as a circle or a square are not usually developed until the child is 5 or 6 years and although she can copy a triangle and diamond shape at this age, she cannot see objects three-dimensionally. She is able to point to her right and left arm or leg but cannot apply the concept of right and left to other objects until she is 7 or 8 years old.

Emotional development

In the third year of primary school the child becomes increasingly confident as she masters new skills such as reading and writing, tying knots and bows, climbing trees, and swinging and balancing on ropes and apparatus in the adventure playground. The wonders of myths and magic become hers through stories of wizards and modern heroes of fables. Now she enjoys dramatic interpretation and may need to be restrained from too literal a translation of her idol's pursuits, such as flying through the air! This stage should be a time of great joy and enthusiasm for life, from the discovery of frog-spawn in February and visits to the nearest park, to the collection of leaves and fruits in October and the recognition of some evergreen trees in winter – all have special meaning.

At 7 years children are said to become aware of morality, i.e. they know the difference between right and wrong, and according to some authorities are now moulded into a pattern of behaviour which will remain with them through puberty, adolescence and adulthood. Others would argue that personality and character are irreparably moulded in the first 5 years, hence the importance of good nursery nurses and other professional child carers.

Social development

Team activities with scope for rough and tumble play are entered into with gusto. Both girls and boys have football heroes and can often reel off the names of current football stars. Children of 7 to 8 equally seem to enjoy imitating the gyrations of pop singers and are often way ahead of their older siblings in computer appreciation! One social accomplishment which will bring the child enjoyment and enable him to give pleasure to others is that of writing letters. At first they can be thank-you letters for Christmas and birthday presents, then a letter for Gran who may be a little lonely at times and would love to hear what her grandchild does at school. Children quickly learn that this is a good form of communicating one's feelings and thoughts to others and also sharing pleasures.

Sex-typed activities such as 'crafts' for boys, sewing and knitting for girls, have no place in primary schools today, where all children have had experience of a wide range of activities in nursery and Primary 1 with teachers who are conscious of equality of opportunity. Nursery children today are the scientists and engineers of the new Century 2000 AD, and the aspirations of girls to join what are still regarded as male occupations must be encouraged.

Although some children appear to be 'natural' leaders, it is important that leadership is shared. It is still the custom in British schools to emphasize competition rather than cooperation. Other societies, such as the Communist USSR, teach their children to help each other in schools. Instead of tests and examinations aimed at distinction for a few and failure for many, Soviet children 'coach' their playmates who have difficulties in schoolwork. While Communist philosophy is unacceptable in its entirety to many British people, this practice is praiseworthy and would lead to all the members of the team learning to pull together, to the benefit of all. Each child, even the slowest, clumsiest and least clever, has the right to a positive self-image and this can only be obtained from the approval and esteem of peers. In social acceptance lies the key to emotional wellbeing, which inevitably affects other aspects of development.

Intelligence Tests

A variety of tests, some verbal, some using pictures and others manual skills, are used to assess the intelligence of children in the nursery years. The result is usually given as the child's IQ or Intelligence Quotient or Developmental Quotient, and a high IQ or DQ is supposed to predict superior intellect, although the child may not necessarily score as highly in attainment tests if for any reason his schooling has been adversely affected. IQ is calculated in the following way: $100 \times$ Mental Age (MA) divided by

Chronological Age (CA). The mental age is obtained by comparing the child's test performance with the average performance of a large number of children. Binet, who was a pioneer of intelligence tests, gave a large number of tests to a large number of children, found the ages at which most children passed each test, and arranged the tests in order of difficulty. If a child of 8 years passes the test for that age, his mental age is eight which is the same as his chronological age, so he is like the average child of his age. If he is only 6 years old when he passes this test, he is above average and if he is 10 years old he will be below average. The first child will have an IQ of 100, i.e. $100 \times 8(MA) \div 8(CA)$, the second child an IQ of 133 and the third child an IQ of 80. The Intelligence Quotient can change as the child grows older and environmental factors can produce radical change.

Language Development

The acquisition of language is essential for adequate functioning in a world which relies on communication through the spoken or written word. As with other aspects of development, the acquisition of language is dependent upon a conducive atmosphere. This will first be in a stable home environment with caring adults, and later in nursery and school with adults who utilize the child's play experience to extend her use and understanding of language. Language is not, however, the only means of communication that humans possess and there are many effective non-verbal ways of communicating. Cries, screams, smiles, frowns and grimaces indicate a baby's moods and needs adequately enough in infancy, but ideas and feelings can be expressed much more precisely in language.

Birth to 6 months

Two-way communication begins at birth and Schaffer's studies of mothers and babies demonstrates how the basis of non-verbal dialogue is established as the child sucks at the breast. Some adults feel embarrassment in talking to a baby who at first reveals little reaction, but reward comes quickly as the baby quietens down after a fit of crying to the soothing tone of her mother or primary care giver. At 4 weeks she has her own language of coos and gurgles to show pleasure, and loud crying to indicate discomfort or hunger. The adult can carry out a conversation by repetition of the sounds vocalized by the baby. Gradually the baby begins to show by movements that she is exploring her environment – she tries to grasp moving objects in the mobile on cot or pram, particularly if they make a noise. The adult has to keep up a continual commentary to provide meaningful symbols for the objects baby finds attractive and gradually she will be able to repeat these sounds.

Listening is just as important as talking since the adult has to know how much the child is capable of understanding at various stages and conversation cannot take place when one person talks all the time. A meaningful relationship between the adult and the child will only develop the two-way communication. Security and self-confidence are strengthened in the child who receives verbal proof of adult attention and intellectual development flourishes. Those who are deprived of the stimulation of spoken language will eventually feel neglected and rejected as their efforts to communicate are ignored.

At 6 months

The 6-month-old baby provides a reward for the adult who has constantly persisted with the spoken word as she vocalizes in single and double syllables which sound very like 'mum', 'dada' and are eagerly translated as such by delighted parents. Familiar noises such as mother's voice, preparation of feeds, running water in the bath are greeted with laughs, chuckles and delighted squeals but screams of annoyance fill the air if her expectations are not fulfilled. The adult cannot ignore these overtures and responds with reinforcement of desired words. The baby quickly realizes that certain sounds provoke a pleased response from the adult and she provides her own reinforcement as she shouts at them to attract attention. She also pauses to listen for the response and, if it is not forthcoming, shouts again. Her powers of imitation are evident as she imitates the coughing, smackings of lips and other sounds she hears around her.

At 1 year old

Now the baby recognizes her own name and turns round when she hears it. Apart from continual babbling, made even more joyful by the adult's imitation, the baby shows that she understands simple demands accompanied by gestures, e.g. 'Give the spoon to Mummy', 'Wave bye-bye', 'Clap your hands'. She also indicates by movement and welcoming behaviour that she understands a considerable amount of simple words such as names of family members, cup, spoon, dinner, walk, ball, car. The adult helps to extend the baby's language by continual repetition and explanation of daily activities.

18 months of age

By this age the child talks to herself in her own tuneful babble continuously. She can use about 20 simple words but understands many more. Her demands are made known by shouting, pointing or simple words. The adult helps by singing or reciting nursery rhymes which the baby likes and attempts to join in; naming various parts of the baby (hair, nose, foot) and encouraging the baby's efforts to demonstrate these. Simple picture books are now enjoyed as the baby points out familiar objects and the adult talks or tells a story about them.

Language is, of course, much more than speech since it involves cognitive development. Piaget maintained that the development of certain logical concepts frequently precedes the understanding of words corresponding to those concepts. Words such as 'bigger', 'smaller', 'longer', 'further', are not understood until the logical properties themselves are understood. Vygotsky contended that language and thinking have separate roots and develop independently. The evidence of thought before language in the preverbal child is unquestionable, and it can also be seen in mentally handicapped children who are able to answer questions about the content of their reading by pointing out the written word answer, despite their inability to verbalize more than two or three words. Some people can 'think' music or imagine physical activity without any accompanying verbalization. Vygotsky maintains that thought becomes verbal about the age of two, and at the same time, speech becomes rational (sensible).

At 2 years

Now the child has a vocabulary of about 50

words and can understand many more. She is able to put two or more words together to make simple sentences, e.g. 'Daddy go car', 'Annie (her name) want teddy'. Her curiosity seems insatiable as she continually asks the names of objects. As curiosity is a useful means of learning, the adult should answer the question in a meaningful way which can be understood by the child, otherwise her efforts will decrease and her intellectual development will be stultified. Nursery rhymes, finger play, songs and picture books are all useful aids at this stage.

Language growth is dependent upon a good learning environment (both in the home and at school), the affection and interest of parents, and also the quality and quantity of time spent with the child – talking about daily activities, sharing TV programmes, encouraging the perusal of books and outdoor play activities. Almost every part of the daily routine provides rich opportunities for language development, yet many 3-year-olds enter nursery with few words in their vocabulary. Rutter blames the failure of language growth on disruption of bonding and separation in the early years, and the effect of these on the child's emotional and intellectual development. The way parents speak to their children can also have an effect on language development. However, most children of 2½–3 years usually have a large vocabulary of over 200 words and, as they have struggled through the identity conflict stage referring to themselves in the third person, indicate their recognition of self as a separate entity now in the use of pronouns – 'I' being the most important, 'he', 'she', 'it', 'you', 'we', 'they', 'us'. They are usually able to give their full name, use plurals (although this may result in 'sheeps', 'mouses' at first) and relate some event or happening. Familiar objects can be identified in pictures and their function given, e.g. ball – throw, bounce.

Incorrect pronunciations should never be imitated, however appealing they may be to the adult. Infantile language often persists until 5 or 6 years because parents consider certain expressions attractive.

From 3 years of age onwards

Now language development relates to the total behaviour patterns of the child in the relative complexity or difficulty of the situations which can be dealt with verbally. Long sentences with compound structures are now common and the child can talk about situations in the past or future. Generalizations are still used, e.g. horses seen on television or in pictures may be called 'dogs' as a collective noun for all four-legged animals. Infantile substitutions for certain letters (usually p, t, th, f, s, r, l, w, y) are given as the child says 'I will wun' or 'I will go for a wide' (ride), 'Give me dat', 'Put it dere', but the child should not be corrected at this age as it may inhibit her free flowing conversations.

By the time children start nursery school, they have acquired many communication skills, but their level of competence depends, as with other aspects of development, on the level of maturity reached and experience gained. Fundamental to the development of skills in communication are the experiences that provide opportunities to use them. Block play, clay and dough play, woodwork, puzzles, domestic play and all the other activities in the nursery environment provide these. The nursery staff can ensure that children can practise the skills they already possess, acquire more skills, and understand what language can do for them. When children do what they are really interested in doing, they tend to use language more meaningfully than when they are placed in pre-arranged, structured activities.

The fourth year

This represents the 'flowering period' in language development as the child talks, plays with words, questions comments, makes simple responses into long narratives, criticizes, balances comparisons. All situations are likely to be verbalized, even block play and drawing. Language is now spreading out beyond his immediate situation and egocentrism. With an active vocabulary of about 2000 words, the child is able to blend sounds together – an ability which is important for learning how to read. She also uses complete sentences: 'Daddy's coming home soon', 'The tree is outside'. During the third, fourth and fifth years the adult can learn much from listening to children's conversations with other children. If the child is unable to communicate successfully with her peers, her self confidence is likely to suffer. Linguistic attention from a sympathetic understanding adult can help the child to overcome this obstacle to emotional, social and intellectual development.

The fifth year

The entry to primary school at five should be a natural transition otherwise the child may find it hard to adapt to a new system and regress to an earlier stage characterized by refusal to cooperate, infantilisms in language and even 'accidents' in bowel and bladder control. Adults who are disciplinarian and use language mainly for criticism and punitive purposes will find that children tend to 'cut off' and cease to listen, particularly if they have been exposed to this in earlier stages when they were trying to use language to attract attention. A vocabulary of 2500 words now serves to unify adaptive, motor and personal–social aspects of behaviour. Number concepts up to ten are established at this age, more familiar colour names are correctly used and names of objects are defined verbally in terms of use. The child gives her age and birthday when asked. She also knows her home address which proves useful if she ever gets separated from her parents on a shopping expedition.

Language Development Skills

Listening, speaking, reading and writing are all part of language development and skills essential to the child's understanding of people, things and processes in his world.

Listening

This involves more than hearing and we should not always assume that because a child is quiet she is listening. Real listening involves giving meaning to what is said, and interpreting this meaning in the light of one's own experience. A child's experiences contribute to her facility with language, and, in turn, language contributes to her experience. Children must be able to differentiate sounds before they can grasp the idea that patterns of sound convey meaning. They can play with the dynamics of sound (softness and loudness) while at a woodwork bench or pounding clay. Also, the environment is often cluttered with sounds, and children need to sort out and select those to which they will give their attention. Children enjoy playing with words and sounds, as in rhymes and nonsense poetry.

Poetry offers more experience with pattern and rhythm, and with repetition of favourites children become familiar with possible uses of sounds.

Speaking

Speaking or oral skills combined with listening or auditory skills are essential for reading and writing abilities. Adults in nursery and primary schools should develop habits of correct usage in clear and distinct speech, but they should hesitate to correct children as they excitedly recount some venture, since this interferes with the ideas they are trying to communicate. All the people in the child's environment at home and school act as models in communication skills. A few children do not like to talk, but most do, and it is useful to have a set time for this every day, when they have the opportunity to do so. The time for this could be when the day begins in the nursery, as the children are often keen to tell what happened last night or on their way to school. In Canada, and in some schools here now, there is a 'show and tell' session every morning which allows children to enter the limelight, if only for a brief period. The 'television set', i.e. one made from two large boxes designed to provide a front screen of cellophane paper and to hide the body of the child sitting behind, provides scope for this. Even the timid child finds this appealing, as she is not expected to stand up in front of her peers. Opportunities for talking and listening are frequent during the nursery day. When children take part in an activity, they like to talk about it, whether it is role-play (where they assign the roles and dictate what the person has to say and do), stories or puppets which stimulate creativity and conversation. A tape recorder is very useful here: sometimes the children tape their own stories, rhymes, songs and conversations. Hearing their own voices is a great incentive to listening and assimiliating new words, and for comments on the wrong pronunciations too!

Reading and writing

These skills are both based on symbols put together in patterns. A child has to be able to differentiate between shapes and sizes, decode patterns and translate them into meanings before she can read, e.g. matching and sorting activities with buttons, large beads, colour and picture cards using everyday objects such as fruits, flowers and animals. Children will sort and classify them as to size and shape as well as colour and similarity.

Reading ability requires that the child can move from concrete, three-dimensional objects to two-dimensional, pictorial representations, then onto two-dimensional symbols. Pictures are another useful preparation for reading, particularly when they are used in a sequence, and the children make up their own stories about the illustrations. Handling a book also calls for certain skills. Children learn to turn the pages from right to left, to follow the movement from left to right, top to bottom, and from front to back as they watch the adult from close proximity during story time. When they see the pictures which accompany the text, they are able to guess the meaning of the words which accompany them. Nursery and primary school staff are sometimes amazed when a child says she can read, and apparently does so, then makes one mistake in a word that has another meaning for her, and reveals that she is just good at remembering texts! There are many types of symbol in the child's environment, including street signs, numbers and names on doors in school, and their own name on the pictures they produce. Sometimes they will be asked to 'make up' a story, which the teacher will write down for them. This is a great thrill for the child, to realize that other people can interpret the symbols which represent her own words. Plenty of pre-reading activities will help the child to achieve a state of reading readiness rather than formal workbook exercises. Children's drawings and paintings contain the elements of writing, as they move from scribbles to representations of people, houses and trees. The skill involved in holding a brush transfers to holding a crayon or pencil. Hand–eye coordination achieved through posting and hammering play is refined in drawing and painting, straight lines and curves. In these are the basic shapes they will require for writing, and children experiment with spatial relationships and configurations as they position shapes on paper. Reading and writing are therefore closely related. Some teachers believe that children can learn to read through writing; others begin by teaching phonics (sounds) and then introduce writing; others still begin with the whole word approach; while some teach a combination of all of these. Good and poor handwriting may be inextricably linked with self-image, since writing is a form of communication. Successful communication gives a positive self-concept, and social development is fostered when children acquire language skills. Children with the most advanced language skills make the most social contacts, and are then able to lead others into cooperative play.

The nursery nurse's role in language development

In fostering language development, the nursery nurse has above all to be aware of the emotional factors. Unless rapport has been established with a child, based on caring and awareness of his needs, little progress will be made. His language can only develop if the adult listens as well as talks to him. Listening to children also enables the nursery nurse to gain some idea of their state of language development, grasp of concepts (if any), home background and parental support, scope of language, emotional development, and any obvious speech defect. Children are usually full of information when they come into the nursery each morning or afternoon. What the child says at this time should be noted and used as an opening conversational gambit later. It may also help the nursery nurse understand the child's mood that day and organize play activities accordingly. Apart from labelling objects or naming them, the nursery nurse should indicate what their purpose is and help the child to attain concepts of everyday import, e.g. properties of water, wetness, dryness, colours, sizes, shapes. Concept formation is assisted by sensory exploration of materials – touching, seeing, hearing, tasting and smelling. Questions put to children should be open-ended, i.e. requiring an extended response. Young children are often afraid to say 'No' to the adult authority figure, so they may reply 'Yes' inappropriately. Questions should require answers involving description (e.g. 'What is your Daddy's car like?'), memory ('Where did you go last Sunday after breakfast?' or 'What did we see at the farm?') or reasoning ('What do you think might happen if we don't water the seeds?') . Infantilisms should not be encouraged, no matter how appealing they may be. They should be ignored and the correct word used: 'I bringed it to you' becomes 'Oh, you brought it to me! Good boy, now I'll put it in the cupboard'.

Pre-reading activities which involve classifying, sorting by size, shape or colour, and sequencing with pictures and the child's own story line are necessary for the development of reading, writing and oral language. Stories, rhymes, songs and poems all help to extend vocabulary and enjoyment of language. Literature suited to the ages, stages, interests and needs of the children should be used and the nursery nurse should use her voice, facial expression, hands, feet and entire body to convey meanings. Visual aids should also be used, preferably those made by the nursery nurse, with an intimate knowledge of the children for whom the story is intended. Utilizing the everyday experiences of the children as a medium for language is more important than introduction of unfamiliar words. For example, outings to the zoo may enable the child to recognize and name a lion or camel, when they cannot recognize a cow or a horse. Experiences for children must be planned beforehand so that command of their own familiar language comes first. The calm, tension-free nursery environment is an important requisite for learning of any kind, and the way that nursery nurses talk to each other, the children and parents should reflect the image of the nursery as a pleasant, comfortable place.

Children from ethnic minority families sometimes have difficulty in language acquisition if they are exposed to a language other than English in their homes. It is essential that nursery and primary school staff should encourage the parents to visit the nursery or school when they will have the opportunity to meet the staff and discover how the child's day is spent. Sometimes parents will misunderstand certain activities and be unable to talk about these with the child at home. Barbara Tizard noted in one of her research studies of nursery schools that some Asian mothers had apparently believed water play was intended to teach children how to wash dishes, and sand play to remind them of happy times at the seaside. The nursery staff can ask the parents to inquire about play activities when the child comes home, and not be content with evasions like 'I just played' from a 4-year-old child who is full of chatter at play!

The family may watch videos made in their country of origin, such as India or China, so that the children are most often in a language environment different from that of school. It may be difficult to replace these videos with British television programmes, as many of these may not concord with the parents' views on life and morals, but even if children's programmes alone are watched by parents and children it is an advantage. In no way must children feel that it is somehow less advantageous to come from a family which is not 'British' in language and customs, since these families contribute to the multi-ethnic richness of our society. Instead, children should share the experiences of those whose parents or grandparents belong to 'ethnic minorities' by special days, when they are invited into school to show their exotic clothes and talk about their family customs, if they are different, and their food. Perhaps this could be followed up by cookery next day, involving some of the dishes the children associate with different countries, such as Indian curry or highly spiced food, Chinese stir-fry meals and Greek moussaka.

Now that there is an abundance of outstanding children's books, parents may ask which are most suitable for their child, and the nursery staff can show them which are used for storytelling and drama sessions. It is useful if the nursery or school library could have more than one copy of books currently in use, so that parents may borrow them, and when the child begins to read in school he should be allowed to take books home, and later to bring some in from home. Some parents may consider bedtime stories unnecessary or the remit of the mother, but fathers should be persuaded to realize that their role in the child's development is also important.

List of Books for Use
(See also Books and Storytelling, p. 229.)

Poetry

At 3 years of age, children enjoy the comforting reassurance of predictable, familiar rhymes, so these should be provided at first.

Mother Goose Nursery Rhymes, illus. by Brian Wildsmith
This Little Puffin, E. Matterson (Kestrel)
The Faber Book of Nursery Verse, ed. B. Ireson (Faber)
This Little Pig Went to Market, N. Montgomery (Bodley Head)

Sing Hey Diddle Diddle, B. Harrop (Black)

The Real Mother Goose (4 vols.), illus. B. Fisher Wright (Benn)

My Favourite Mother Goose Rhymes, G. Stomann (Lansdowne)

My Big Book of Nursery Rhymes, P. Stevenson (Ward Lock)

Rhymes Around the Day, ed. P. Thomson (Kestrel)

Leon Baxter's Book of Nonsense (Macdonald) This delights children from three to eight. The younger children will love favourites such as '1, 2, 3, Mother caught a flea', and 'Rat a tat tat; Who is that? Only Grandma's pussy cat', plus 'Miss Polly' and 'I'm a little teapot'. The 6- to 8-year-olds enjoy rhymes like 'Look at your hat. Just look at your hat. It's back to front and squashed quite flat'.

Jelly Belly, Dennis Lee (Blackie). This is more suitable for the 6- to 7-year-olds, who are familiar enough with words to appreciate the funny words. The name Jelly Belly refers to a character with a 'big fat bite' who fought 'with a big fat bite', and there's a delightful verse about dinosaurs: 'Allosaurus, Stegosaurus, Brontosaurus too. All went off for a dinner at the Dinosaur Zoo'.

Revolting Rhymes, Roald Dahl (. . .) This is best kept for those who are six and above because of his retelling of nursery stories like Red Riding Hood, where she admires the wolf's fur, shoots it, and returns home wearing a new fur coat! The 6-year-olds love the 'rude' bits, like 'The small girl smiles. One eyelid flickers. She whips a pistol from her knickers'.

The King's Breakfast, a selection of A.A. Milne (Methuen)

Snowman's Sniffles and Other Verses, N.M. Bodecker (Faber) Mostly about animals with peculiar habits, e.g. 'The rooster's crowing in the morning is just his silly way of yawning'.

Board books

These are useful with very small children, as they will withstand rough treatment from sticky hands and attempts at tearing and eating! Macdonald's series is particulary good: *My Family*, *My Toys*, *My Clothes*, *Myself*.

Animal Noises, Sally Kilroy (Kestrel) Gives 2-year-olds pictures of animals for the child to identify by their noises.

Baby Bodies, Sally Kilroy (Kestrel) Points out parts of the body.

Books to read to children*

The Read-Aloud Handbook by Jan Trelease (Penguin) provides a list of 300 suitable stories, picture books and poetry for this purpose.

The following guidelines should be used in reading aloud:

1 Start with picture books, which allow children to tell the story by looking at the pictures in sequence.

2 Vary the length (5 minutes is a long time for a baby under 2 years!) and subject matter, but remember the child's pleasure at repetition of familiar stories.

3 Let the children settle down before you begin. 'Are you sitting comfortably?' is quite a sensible question!

4 Choose books which have a lively pace, without lengthy descriptive passages.

5 It's a good idea to give stories which are a little beyond the children's knowledge to 'stretch' them from time to time.

6 Always *prepare* your story reading by becoming familiar with the plot, and being able to read fluently, without hesitation before a page is turned (as when you do not know the following word).

7 Reading the book yourself before reading it to children also helps you to know what to eliminate (e.g. distressing material), what to elaborate on (e.g. reading about a visit to a farm can be extended to cover the listeners' experience on a recent visit) and what to shorten, remembering the short attention span of under fives, or the impatience of older children who have so many exciting things to discover for themselves.

8 Try to link the stories to an activity which has recently taken place, or is about to, e.g. a visit by a policeman, and perhaps ask the children to draw a picture, while the older children could write their own story or poem about the subjects.

9 If there is not enough time to finish one whole story, decide beforehand where you will stop, and make it at an interesting point.

*When choosing books for children, remember to follow SAIN guidelines, i.e. Stages, Ages, Interests and Needs.

10 Ten minutes is long enough for most 3-year-olds, then 15 for those who are at the next stage, and can sit for longer, then 20 minutes for the 4- to 6-year-olds.

11 It is easier to be expressive when the story is being told, rather than read, but facial expression and vocal variety are still essential if the story is to retain interest for the listeners.

12 Interruptions may occur, as when one child just *has* to tell everyone his father has a big one when the book is about trucks! The adult should acknowledge the child's remark without anger, but still carry on with the story.

13 If the book's illustrations are inadequate, the adult should produce some of their own individual pictures to further stimulate the children's imagination.

Badgers Three, Jenny Koralek (Kaye and Ward) Good for the adult to read while the children follow the pictures.

The School Fair, Althea (Dinosaur) Deals with a theme which will be familiar to most children.

One Little Monkey, S. Calmenson (Hamish Hamilton) Very funny, and lets the children enjoy his naughtiness second-hand.

Paddington and the Knickerbocker Rainbow and *Paddington at the Zoo*, Michael Bond (Collins) Links up with television programmes.

Tariq learns to Swim, Hassina Khan (Bodley Head) Useful for schools with multicultural groups.

The Lazy Beaver, Giovanni Gallo (Collins)

Lucky Dip, Ruth Ainsworth

Little Pete Stories, Leila Berg

Time for a Story and *Tell me a Story*, Eileen Colwell

My Naughty Little Sister, Dorothy Edwards

Peter Rabbit and other Tales, Beatrix Potter

Wonder Tales, Kornic Chikousky

Ameliaranne Series, Constance Heward

Arthur's Aunt Stories, Helen East (Macdonald)

These will also be enjoyed by older children up to 7 years:

Mabel's Story, Jenny Koralek (Patrick Hardy) The child tells a story to her Grandpa, instead of the other way round.

The Day the Teacher Went Bananas, James Howe (Viking Kestrel) Funny, about a teacher who swings from trees and draws on walls.

Home in the Sky, Jeannie Baker (Julie MacRae Books) A pigeon's attempts to spread its wings make him appreciate his home.

For those beginning to read

My First Big Story Book, Richard Bamberger (Read Aloud Books/Puffin)

Professor Branestawm's Pocket Motor Car, Norman Hunter (Read Alone Books/Puffin)

Mouldy's Orphan, Gillian Avery (Story Books/Puffin)

Books can make you laugh:

The Hungry Caterpillar, Eric Carle (Hamish Hamilton)

Mrs Mopple's Washing Line, Anita Hewitt (Puffin)

The Tiger who came to Tea, and *Mog the Forgetful Cat*, J. Kerr

You Can't Catch Me!, John Prater (Bodley Head) Jack's bid for freedom when Dad calls him for a bath.

There's a Hippo in my Bath!, Kyoko Matsuoka (Dent)

Aunt Nina and her nephews and nieces, Franz Bradenburg (Bodley Head)

Books can show that we know and understand worries and problems:

Problem Solvers, Nigel Snell (Hamish Hamilton): *Danny is Afraid of the Dark, Jenny Learns to Swim, Sally Moves House, Sam's New Dad, Mark Gets Nits, Ruth Goes to Hospital*

Books can encourage sympathy:

Borka the Duck with No Feathers, John Burningham

Don't Forget Tom, Hanne Larsen

Desmond the Dinosaur, Althea (Red Label series)

Ben Finds a Friend, A.M. Chapouton and U. Wensell (Methuen) A boy in a high-rise block of flats longs for a pet to keep him happy.

Maria, Catherine Brighton (Faber and Faber) Maria is blind, and the book follows a day in her life.

Books can let the child enjoy naughtiness second-hand:

Peter Rabbit, Beatrix Potter

After Dark, Louis Baum (Andersen Press) A

little girl is supposed to go to sleep while her mother goes out to do late night shopping.

Ben Bakes a Cake, Eva Rice (Picture Lions) Ben bakes his birthday cake, but Ralph, the dog, eats it. Tragedy is narrowly averted, however.

Angry Arthur, Hiawyn Oram and Satoshi Kitamura (Puffin) The story of what happens when Arthur loses his temper – and he can't remember why!

Ameliaranne, Constance Heward

Harry the Dirty Dog, Zion and Graham

Albert Herbert Hawkins – the naughtiest boy in the world, Frank Dickens

My Naughty Little Sister, Dorothy Edwards

Books can let the child feel big and strong:

Little Toot, Hanlic Gramalky

An Evening at Alfie's, Shirley Hughes (Bodley Head) Little Alfie solves a babysitter's problems when every thing goes wrong.

Books can give imagination a treat:

A Lion in the Meadow, M. Mahy

Quangle Wangles Hat, Edward Lear

Here Comes the Bride, Emil Pacholek (Andre Deutsch) A little girl decides to marry a reluctant boy, so involves dressing up and role play.

Books can tell about special events:

Mummy goes into Hospital, Evelyn Elliott (Hamish Hamilton)

Sikh Wedding, Olivia Bennett (Hamish Hamilton)

Steve is Adopted, Nigel Snell (Hamish Hamilton)

Clare's New Baby Brother, Nigel Snell (Hamish Hamilton)

David's First Day At School, Nigel Snell (Hamish Hamilton)

Paul Gets Lost, Nigel Snell (Hamish Hamilton)

Peter Gets a Hearing Aid, Nigel Snell (Hamish Hamilton)

Kate Visits the Doctor, Nigel Snell (Hamish Hamilton)

Tom Visits the Dentist, Nigel Snell (Hamish Hamilton)

Books to look at and talk about:

The Very Busy Spider, Eric Carle (Hamish Hamilton) A picture book with pictures like the spider's web, to feel as well as see.

The Apple Bird, Brian Wildsmith (OUP) Pictures only: shows how a beautiful bird eats an apple, until he comes to look like it.

Old and new favourites of children:

Poem – Rice Pudding, A.A. Milne

Poem – The Three Little Kittens, Anon

Papa Small, Lois Lenski

Ben in the Kitchen, Pat Albeck

The Black Kitten, Eileen Ryder

Mr Joe Dingers, Dorothy Edwards

Mr Gumpy's Outing, John Burningham

Thomas Goes to the Doctors, Gunilla Wolde

The Enormous Turnip, Tolstoy

No Roses for Harry, Zion and Graham

A Dog Came to School, Lois Lenski

The Rabbit, John Buringham

Old Mother Hubbard and her Dog, illust. Paul Galdone

The Magic Porridge Pot, (Ladybird)

Knock Knock! Who's There?, Sally Grindley (Hamish Hamilton) A wicked witch, a creepy ghost, a fierce dragon and the world's tallest giant come knocking at the bedroom door. Then in comes Daddy with the cocoa and all's well.

Wishwhat, Alex Brychta (OUP) Do we always get everything we ask for?

Daisy, Brian Wildsmith (OUP) Daisy is a cow who finds out that the cow's grass on the other side is not always greener.

4

Child Health

Personal and Environmental Health

Health is 'a state of physical, mental, and social wellbeing and so not merely the absence of disease' (WHO). While there are many 'don'ts' in striving for good health, it is far more effective to concentrate on promoting the positive aspects of health. 'Prevention is better than cure' is an old cliché, but one that still pertains, and examples of good health practices should be demonstrated by all who have the responsibility for babies and young children, whether their own or those of other people. Health is still seen by many people as concerned only with hygiene, smoking, alcohol and the prevention of sexually transmitted disease, but there is much more to it than that.

The pattern of illness has changed considerably over the last 20 years. Instead of acute illnesses and deaths from childhood diseases, such as measles and scarlet fever, the major health problems affecting children today are increasing malformation, chronic illness, physical and mental handicap, psychiatric disorder, and ill-health arising from family stress and breakdown. Rather than admission to long-stay hospitals and institutions, children suffering from chronic illnesses and handicaps are now more frequently cared for in the community. As a result, professional staff should see their role as supporting parents in the care of their children rather than substituting for them. Community health provision should be based on a child and family centred service in which skilled help is readily available and accessible, which is integrated through seeing the child as a whole and as a continually developing person, and which ensures that paediatric skill and knowledge are applied in the care of every child, regardless of age, desirability or social circumstance.

Infant mortality rates in the UK (i.e. deaths per thousand of live babies under 1 year old) are still higher than in other Western countries, although they have fallen due to improved nutrition, living conditions and antenatal and postnatal care. Accidents, many of which are preventable, are still the most common cause of death between the ages of 1 and 15 years. There is room for improvements in the school health service, including more school nurses, screening of vision, hearing and growth, development of children's interest in personal health, and more effective preparation for parenthood.

The following factors are essential to the development of healthy children as defined by WHO declaration:

1 food and drink in sufficient quantity and nutritionally adequate,
2 warmth,
3 fresh air,
4 exercise,
5 rest and sleep,
6 good posture,
7 personal and communal health,
8 dental care,
9 sensible clothing,
10 prevention of illness and injury,
11 medical supervision.

To this list must also be added love, security, consistent and continuous affection, and opportunities for independence leading to a positive self-image.

Food and Drink

See p. 130.

Warmth

Human beings are homeostatic, i.e. their body temperature of 37°C (98.4°F) usually remains the same regardless of the environmental temperature. This is unlike some other animals who adopt the temperature of their surroundings.

The temperature-regulating centre is in the hypothalamus of the brain. In the newborn baby this mechanism is still immature, particularly if he is premature or small for dates, in which case he will not have an insulating layer of fat, either, so special provision has to be made and these babies are usually kept in incubators.

All babies should have a temperature of 21°C (70°F) in their first environment outside the uterus. Newborn babies cannot sweat and they are totally reliant on their mother or care giver to ensure that they are kept warm but not too warm. The baby has deposits of brown fat between the shoulder blades and around the kidneys and adrenal glands which can be used as fuel to maintain normal body temperature. Babies' temperatures fluctuate a great deal, however, and doctors sometimes use a 'low-registering' thermometer with a range of 25–40 °C, so that they can recognize hypothermia in infants. A *low* body temperature in infants can indicate the presence of infection, whereas in older children and adults a high temperature indicates infection.

Hypothermia

This means a body temperature of below 36.4 °C (85°F) and the condition can be fatal. Babies under 1 year must be constantly observed to prevent this. They move very little and lose heat through their comparatively large surface area so the baby's daytime room temperature should be kept at 20–22°C (70–72°F) for the first 6 weeks. Premature babies require even higher temperatures.

Check that the baby's legs, arms and neck are warm. His hands and feet may be cold while the rest of the body is warm. Pink cheeks are not an indicator of warmth either, as they are often seen in babies suffering from hypothermia. Sufficient clothing, constant room temperatures and observation should prevent babies from slipping into the coma of hypothermia which is often mistaken for sleep.

Room temperatures of 18°C (60–65°F) should be maintained where older babies and children spend their day. Lack of warmth affects the ability to concentrate and unless they are involved in physical activity, children will soon become lethargic and miserable. Heating methods most commonly used are radiators which run off central heating systems, convector wall heaters, night-storage heaters, under-floor heating systems and fan heaters (which can also be used as air coolers in summer). Suitable clothing and food (not necessarily hot) also help to maintain warmth.

Sleep and Rest

Adequate sleep and rest is essential for all aspects of development.

Physically:

1 Sleep and rest promote healthy functioning of the circulatory and respiratory systems.
2 The brain and nervous tissues need sleep and periods of rest for development of the central nervous system.
3 Sleep builds up resistance to infection, and during bouts of infection or illness give the body's internal defence systems time to work as blood is not diverted to organs of metabolism or to the muscles.
4 Waste from muscle fatigue is removed during sleep.
5 After sleep and rest, the body has more energy available for activities.
6 Lack of sleep lowers resistance to infection.
7 A tired baby or child does not feed properly.

Emotionally:

1 Good quality sleep and adequate rest promote a feeling of wellbeing and enhances emotional stability.
2 Lack of sleep can lead to fretfulness and irritability.
3 The tired child (or adult) tends to feel particularly vulnerable or overly sensitive.

Socially: Tiredness leads to loss of motivation and lack of interest.

Intellectually: Development and recovery of the nervous system during sleep enhances the overall functioning of the body, promotes alertness, and allows for eagerness and enthusiasm to participate in all activities.

Checklist for baby's rest and sleep times

Babies under 1 year will be in a cot although some newborn babies will sleep in a Moses basket or cradle. Transition from a cradle to a large cot can be eased by placing the cradle in the cot for a few nights.

1 Check the safety of cot, mattress and coverings.
2 Ensure that the mattress cover cannot work loose to reveal the plastic inner cover.
3 'Hospital corners' ensure that sheets and blankets remain in place.
4 Remove hot-water bottle or other heating device and all large fluffy toys.
5 Check that the temperature of the bedroom/restroom is adequate.
6 Check the amount of clothing and coverings to ensure that the baby is not too warm and at risk of developing sweat rash, or that clothes can be thrown aside as the baby moves about, which could lead to chilling.
7 In the first months after birth, the baby should be wrapped firmly, but not tightly, in a lightweight, non-fluffy shawl to give a feeling of security.
8 Check that the baby is not hungry and has had his nappy changed.
9 Bathtime produces a soothing preparation for sleep.
10 Confident handling and cuddles predispose to restful sleep.
11 Place the baby face down his tummy, or on his side, to avoid inhalation of fluid, which can occur if he is laid on his back. Note that the baby turns his head to the side, to ensure safe breathing.
12 *No pillows* for safety reasons.
13 If the baby cries, he can be safely left until he sleeps, provided that all the above items have been considered. Some babies always cry a little before they fall asleep, so panic is unnecessary, but if the crying is prolonged attention must be given as to its cause.

Toddler's bedtime preparations

Most toddlers in the 1–2½ year age group wear all-in-one stretch suits which cover feet and toes, so that there is not much risk of chilling if bedclothes are kicked off during sleep. When the child grows out of these, pyjamas or a nightdress is worn, and these should be of non-flammable material. Most parents will still use bathtime as a preparation for bed, but sometimes bathtime frolics excite rather than subdue the child who may then find it difficult to settle to sleep. Simple stories (preferably 'special for bedtime') help to induce sleep. The best story at bedtime is of course the one that is told, rather than read, and related to the child's experiences. Bedtime

should be the child's special time. It may perhaps be the only time in the day when parents can share togetherness with their children, and worries and anxieties which may have perhaps marred his day can now be resolved in the warmth of parental cuddles while the familiar voice tells a favourite familiar story. The comfort of security expressed in the presence of the parent enables the child to relax and fall contentedly asleep. Many toddlers will want to have a favourite doll, teddy or other soft toy in bed with them. Very large toys, sometimes bigger than the child, are best kept out of the cot. Some children will be just as happy with an old doll or teddy which has been chewed, battered and torn, but much loved, nevertheless; others may like a 'comfort' item, such as a shawl or piece of blanket. These comforters may accompany the child throughout childhood, but no pressure should be brought to bear to end what is a self-limiting phase of development. If the child is afraid of the dark, it is important to understand the very real nature of this fear and to leave the bedside lamp or the landing light on until the child is fully asleep. Low-watt light bulbs can be used. Where there are children of different ages in the family, different bedtimes are often sensible. Some toddlers do not go to bed until very late, since working parents may see little of them during the day. Hence, some nurseries still offer the lunchtime nap.

Bedtime for the older child

The transition from cot to bed usually takes place at 3 years of age, perhaps because another baby has arrived to fill the cot! Parents and nannies should be careful not to base the transition on this fact alone, since the older child may resent the new arrival even more. It is better to greet his new status as 'older' and that therefore the 'grown-up' idea of a bed is more suitable for him. If there are older brothers and sisters in the family bunk beds can be great fun. Children can pretend they are on a ship or a train, and bedtime stories related to this theme can encourage imaginative ideas.

Children of 3–5 years will benefit from continuation of the nightly routine of their earlier years, i.e. bathtime followed by bedtime with a story and some reassuring cuddles from a parent as they settle down. If a babysitter takes over at some point, he or she should be familiar with the routine, as children will feel insecure with an unfamiliar person who does things in a different way. It is preferable for the babysitter to have met the child or children beforehand to prevent any distress or upset.

As children enter primary school and progress through the first years of 'the big school', they have so much to see, discover, experience and enjoy that the waking hours often seem inadequate. After days filled with triumphs and joys, as well as worries and anxieties linked to a new class or group, they are often apparently still full of energy at bedtime and very reluctant to calm down in preparation for sleep. In summer, when the days are long, the 6-year-old child will naturally object to bedtime at 8 o'clock when it is still light! Instead of becoming embroiled in long, unhappy arguments with the child, it is better to offer to read a chapter of some favourite story which can then be given to the child to continue himself, as reading before sleep is a good soporific.

Factors and procedures which promote good sleep

Sleeping clothes. All sleeping clothes should be light, warm (a night vest under cotton pyjamas is warmer than a thick interlock sleepsuit), comfortable, and allow movement. Pyjamas for boys and girls are more popular than nightdresses, but materials used must be nonflammable, and all fires and heaters guarded to prevent accidents.

Bedmaking has to be simple in families where both parents are out working and there are a number of young children. Bedclothes are usually made of easy-care synthetic materials nowadays, but some children are allergic to nylon, and smooth nylon sheets often cause blankets to slip off. Duvets are warm, light and take much of the work out of bed-making, but cheaper makes have inadequate filling and those filled with real goose down can cause allergies in some children. Loosely woven cellular blankets are lighter and warmer than heavy wool blankets. Where duvets are used instead of blankets, there is only one sheet to tuck in, and if the bottom sheets are fitted there is little time and energy involved. Many people now prefer duvets to blankets. Duvet covers will need to be changed weekly, with pillow slips. In colder weather, a blanket may be placed under the bottom sheet, or an electric underblanket used to heat the beds, but these require careful supervision to ensure that they are not left on when the child is in bed, and that he cannot reach the switch when in bed.

Pillows are not considered necessary for babies under 1 year, and safety pillows which do not have plastic covers, can be used for young children after that. Flat pillows are better as they promote correct development of the skull in relation to the spinal column. Hot water bottles, if used, must be removed before the child is put into the cot or bed. Babies should be laid on the tummy (not the back) for ease and safety in breathing (head turned to the side).

Newborn babies prefer to be wrapped firmly (but not too tightly) in a shawl or blanket before they are laid down to sleep. This makes them feel secure, stops them rolling about in the cot, and is more like the confined space of the uterus which they have recently experienced.

Ventilation. The bedroom should be ventilated, but free from draughts. If there is a sash window in the bedroom, it can be opened a little way at the top. If the windows are the swivel type, it is best to have them locked to avoid accidents and leave the bedroom door open. A fan heater/cooler can be used in hot weather to make the atmosphere pleasant but, of course, these are expensive to operate. A stuffy atmosphere causes irritation, headache, and is not conducive to satisfying sleep. If the child is sleeping in a nursery, cots or beds must be not less than 3 feet apart to lessen the risk of spreading droplet infection.

Light. A nightlight may be necessary in the nursery (or on the landing outside the bedroom door) to give comfort where a child is afraid of the dark. When the door is left open the child can hear reassuring household noises, and some experts state that it is better for babies to establish sleeping patterns without preventing the rest of the family from carrying out their usual activities. There should be no need for everyone to be told to 'keep quiet and tiptoe around' just because the baby has been put to bed! However, sudden or persistent noises, such as rattling of windows, doors and loud records, can easily disrupt a child's sleep so common sense should prevail.

Bedtime stories. A bedtime story can be read or told by the mother or the father (this is often an occasion when the father can devote some time to his young children, who may not see him during the day) and this comforts the child. Obviously, stories which do not excite or over-stimulate the child should be kept for bedtime. Most children like a soft toy to cuddle in bed but this should not be too large or fluffy in case it falls over the child's face when he is asleep.

Bedtime snacks. As children will not usually sleep if they are hungry, a feed or light snack (e.g. breakfast cereal) should be given, as a satisfied appetite induces sleep. However, care should be taken to avoid digestive upsets.

The younger child may like a biscuit or a piece of fruit with his cup of hot milk or cocoa, but, as at any age, teeth should be cleaned to remove any foodstuffs before sleep. Cocoa and malt drinks contain a substance known as tryptophan which is said to promote restful sleep. As many hot drink mixes contain sugar, there is no need to add extra sugar to the drink.

Some night-time problems

Bedtime should never be used as other than a pleasant normal part of everyday routine. Parents who use going to bed as a punishment for naughtiness will find it extremely difficult to persuade their children to go to bed without fuss at a reasonable hour. As this is the child's 'special time' of the day he should be given loving, individual attention from parents or child-carers. Deprived and disadvantaged children particularly need to have this care to ensure sound, healthy sleep.

Bedwetting (or nocturnal enuresis). While most children are dry at night by 2½ years of age, one in 15 is still bedwetting when he starts primary school at 5 years of age. Many parents worry that this is due to psychological complications, but although sudden shock such as separation from home or admission to hospital can produce this reaction the reason is often less dramatic. There is a wide variation in the age at which the sphincter muscles around the openings of bowel and bladder are able to control a full bladder during the night and sometimes bedwetting occurs in families. Boys have a greater tendency to bedwetting than girls but they have less sphincter control anyway. In these instances, it is merely a delay in normal development but if pain and fever accompany micturition (passing of urine) obviously the doctor must be consulted

as a bladder or, more rarely, kidney infection may be present.

Threadworms can also cause bedwetting during the period of infestation, mainly because of the irritation around the anus where the female worm emerges to lay her eggs. Some other illnesses, even the common cold, can lead to an occasional episode, but stress linked to attendance at a new school, a family upset and jealousy at the birth of a sibling can also cause periods of bedwetting. It is important that parents do not make the child anxious because of their own anxiety, as this could prolong the condition.

The child should be taken to the lavatory or given a potty before he goes to bed and again when his parents go to bed. Plastic covers can protect mattresses and a washing machine and dryer are necessities for coping with urine-soaked bedding. Drugs may be prescribed after the age of 4 years (these are an antidepressant in syrup form) but the child may relapse when the course is stopped. When the child is 6½ or 7 years of age, and the doctor is satisfied that there is no abnormal cause for the bedwetting, a buzzer may be used. This is an alarm device which goes off when the child wets the bed. The child is supposed to become conditioned to wake before the buzzer sounds but often it is ineffective. If the child is too young or his bedroom too far away for the mother to hear the buzzer, it is unlikely that the child will get up, empty his bladder, dry the bed and reset the alarm! However, persistence with older children in use of this device is often effective. Patience and understanding are the major requisites for parents of bedwetting children as rewards and punishments rarely help.

Sleepwalking. This is a very rare occurrence in children under 10 years of age. It is most frequently seen in those aged 10–14 years. However, it has been known to occur in pre-school age children who were subsequently referred to child guidance centres and found to be over-sensitive and suffering from a major upset such as the death of a parent or grand-parent. Parents can have a bell system fitted between the child's room and theirs so that they can be aware when the child gets out of bed. Sleepwalkers do not normally injure themselves in any way and provided safety measures are taken (removal of keys from outer doors, fitting stoppers to windows) the child can simply be gently guided back to bed without being woken.

Nightmares. These are not usually experienced by children under 4 years (when the imagination becomes more active) but sometimes babies wake up screaming in the middle of the night. Often a frightening bedtime story or television film can cause a bad dream, or it may be caused by a feeling of suffocation due to a stuffy nose in a respiratory infection. When the baby or child wakes up the adult should comfort, cuddle, reassure him, and stay with him until he has recovered and dropped off to sleep again.

Talking and grinding teeth. While talking and grinding the teeth in sleep are irritating habits to any other child or adult within hearing range, they are harmless. Sometimes children will express suppressed aggression by shouting out in their sleep but often it is incomprehensible one-sided conversation!

All the phenomena associated with sleep are known to be more common in boys, mainly due to a delay in normal development, and these are usually corrected without treatment.

Personal Cleanliness

Everyone is responsible for their own good health, but those who are responsible for the health of babies and children have additional responsibility. Basic cleanliness is one aspect of health care which *cannot be ignored*.

Care of the skin

Perfumed soaps are not necessary, and some skins are sensitive to them. Low-lather baby soaps can be used for babies and children: they do not sting if suds get into their eyes. Hands are a potent source of infection and need to be washed more frequently than the rest of the body, especially after using the toilet and before preparation, serving and eating of food. In hospital the hands are scrubbed with soap and then covered with sterile gloves for aseptic procedures to avoid the risk of infection. While clinical cleanliness is not always possible at home or in a busy nursery, adequate care can be taken to ensure that body defences against infection are maintained. Hot water is more pleasant and more effective than cold water as it lathers soap more easily.

Promotion of healthy skin, hair and nails

This depends not just on cleanliness (although this is important to remove dead skin cells, dried sebum, microorganisms and dirt) but also on a well balanced diet and sufficient rest, sleep and exercise. Much can be learnt about a child's state of health from his skin, hair and nails. The colour of the skin (paleness, redness) is often a sign of an illness and is distinguishable from the healthy glow of children who have been playing in the fresh air. Lank, greasy hair is often seen when prepubertal children are unwell, but even healthy looking hair can harbour head lice! Bitten nails are often a sign of anxiety.

Daily bathing

This is not only refreshing, but gives a sense of wellbeing. Younger children love bathtime if it is a time when they can relax, have fun and play with the water rather than a daily necessity for removal of dirt and microorganisms! A bag of bathtub toys can be kept in the bathroom to provide lots of fun.

A bubble bath is also a fun way of contributing to cleanliness, and dishwashing liquid is a good substitute. Safety measures must be remembered: cold water put into the bath before hot and the temperature tested with the elbow. Constant supervision is also required as children have been known to drown in a few inches of water. Showers are frequently used nowadays, but these are better kept for children of 7 or 8 years and the temperature of the water must be thermostatically controlled to avoid a spray of hot water which could scald. Some children are afraid of showers and it is often a good idea to let them join in with an older brother or sister or their parents, to help remove their fear. Care must be taken to wash all parts of the body thoroughly, not forgetting between the toes, the ears and underarms, genitals and bottom. Hair is often washed at the same time and non-sting shampoos are now available so fears of 'soap in the eyes' and dislike of the whole procedure should be rare. Scrub the nails with a soft nail brush (as microorganisms can lurk under the nails) and trim them regularly. Thorough drying with towels is important—creases of the body and between the toes should not be forgotten. A light dusting of talcum powder adds to a feeling of enjoyment after the bath. Tangled hair, the torment of many children in the past, is now unnecessary if 'conditioning' shampoos are used. These leave the hair easy to comb through after washing (a brush should not be used on wet hair as it tends to tear it). Once the hair is dry, a brush can be used. Brushing stimulates the sebaceous glands which secrete sebum in the scalp and make the hair shine.

Baby bathing procedure

Note: Hold baby firmly
      Never let him become chilled
      Never leave baby unattended even for a
      second

1 Wash your hands.
2 Put on a plastic apron.
3 Prepare the equipment.
a The bath can be placed on the floor on top of a plastic sheet or on a table against a wall. A low nursery chair is useful for the adult to sit on.
b The bath should be filled two-thirds full with water (cold water then hot), then test the temperature with an elbow.
c Place the bath on the left-hand side of the cot.
d Have baby soap and baby shampoo ready.
e Have clean linen set out.
f Have a receptacle (covered bucket to receive soiled napkin) ready.
g Cotton wool swabs.
4 Prepare the baby.
a Strip off the top covers, fold these and place them on the right-hand side of the cot.
b Remove baby's gown. Leave the nappy on.
c Wrap the baby in a towel, leaving the fold at the top on the outside of the towel lengthwise.
5 Baby bath.
a Lift baby out of the cot and tuck him firmly under your left arm, with the hand supporting his head. Using damp cotton wool swabs cleanse baby's face.
b Dry using the soft part of a towel.
c Lifting baby as before, shampoo and wash baby's hair. Wash the fontanelle well to prevent scurf forming.
d Rinse and dry the hair thoroughly.
e Remove the nappy and place it in the receptacle provided. Clean the bottom with a damp cotton wool swab wiping from front to back.
f Quickly soap baby from the neck down leaving the bottom until last. Ensure that all skin creases and folds are washed.
g Lift baby into the bath, holding his head and shoulders with the left arm and hand, and sup-

porting the lower extremities with the right hand. Rinse off soap thoroughly.
h Lift baby out of the bath, holding him as before, and wrap him in a warm towel in the cot.
6 Drying baby.
a Starting at his neck, dry the right side of the baby, then re-cover him with the towel.
b Dry the left side of the baby, roll him towards you and dry his back.
c Place the left sleeve of a clean gown on the baby.
d Place a clean sheet and nappy under his left side and roll the baby onto it.
e Remove wet linen.
f Place the right sleeve of the clean gown on the baby and tie. Straighten the sheet.
g Place the baby on his back on the clean nappy.
h In a newborn baby, clean the umbilicus with mediswabs (sterilized swabs). (If instructed, apply cord powder).
i Apply zinc and caster oil ointment to bottom and seal nappy.
j Make baby comfortable and place him on his front or side.
k Cover him with a baby blanket, used singly and tucked in.
l Apply the top cover.
m Clear away the equipment, dispose of used swabs and leave the cot tidy.
n Put soiled nappies into Napisan (or into the bin if it is a disposable nappy).

Clothing

Clothes fulfil the following functions:

1 Helps to maintain body temperature. Layers of lightweight clothing are more insulating than two bulky garments, as they allow air to circulate.
2 Helps in protection of the skin against accidents, exposure to strong weather or strong heat in hot weather, and illnesses which can result from these. Clothes should be chosen for the climate, not the season.
3 Feeling of wellbeing – comfortable, cool, clean materials, e.g. soft cotton towelling next to the skin helps to avoid sweat rash in babies.
4 Clothing for children under 1 year old should not hinder freedom of movement as the child needs to kick, stretch and crawl. At 8–9 months, rompers and baby stretch garments are useful to facilitate this. Dungarees in cord or denim are popular with children from 2 to 6 years old for ease of movement.

1.

Fold the nappy in half to make a triangle.

2.

Lay the baby on the nappy with his waist on the widest part. Then bring up one corner between his legs.

3.

Fold the sides over to the middle and hold with one hand.

4.

Secure the nappy with a safety pin.

1.

Fold the nappy into a kite shape.

2.

Lay the baby on the nappy at the level of his waistline.

3.

Fold a side corner over and bring the bottom flap up between his legs. Pin to the side corner.

4.

Do the same with the other side corner. Tuck it under the front flap, and secure with a safety pin at the corner.

5 Clothing which is suitably designed for the child to put on and remove himself fosters a sense of independence (especially if he is 2–3 years old and in the process of toilet training).

6 Clothing can promote pride in appearance and a sense of identity in older children (4- to 7-year-olds). Clothing gives a 4- or 5-year-old the chance to show that he can recognize colours he likes and choosing his favourite colours increases self-confidence. Clothing with details like Mother's or Father's (and children's fashions are increasingly like those of adults – a reversion to the Victorian idea of 'little men and women' but without the attendant result of denying children the right to be children).

7 Give the child pleasure and provide a realistic extension of role play which helps his psychological development.

Clothes for everyday wear should be attractive, comfortable and suitable for the demands of the day, e.g. attending a playgroup or nursery with the possibility of painting or glue play. Clothes for warm weather are relatively simple.

Most children are content to run around in T-shirts and cotton shorts, trousers or skirts in warm weather. A pullover or denim jacket is useful for cooler days. If the weather is very warm, and space permits, children should be allowed to play wearing as little clothing as possible – a swimsuit or trunks. When the sun is very strong, a cotton hat is advisable for protection. Sandals should preferably be leather as some children develop skin allergies to canvas and synthetic footwear when these are worn constantly. Vests are not worn in the summer and a wool/acrylic/cotton cardigan can be worn if it becomes cooler.

Clothing for colder weather should include:

1 A vest and underpants, to provide inner layer (more warmth from layers of clothing than from bulky items). These must be of woollen or cellular material to allow movement of air between body and clothes.

2 A warm shirt of wool/acrylic material to combine the benefits.

3 A pullover should be a wool and acrylic or nylon mixture to provide warmth and easy washing.

4 Stretch knee-length socks of a wool/nylon mixture big enough to allow toes to move. The wool mixture provides absorbency and keeps the toes and feet warm; it prevents shrinkage in washing.

5 Long trousers of the pull-up type (with elasticated waist and velcro fastenings, no buttons for children under 4 years). Courtelle, corduroy, denim, nylon and acrylic are useful for warmth, easy care and to withstand tough treatment in play.

6 Leather shoes: leather, rather than vinyl, allows the feet 'to breathe'. Unfortunately leather is expensive but leather shoes usually last longer than cheaper materials. Rubber wellingtons should be worn in wet weather, but rubber prevents ventilation. So these must be roomy and worn with a thick pair of socks.

7 A woollen hat and scarf need only be worn if it is very cold. (If a child is playing about vigorously, adjust clothing as necessary.)

8 Gloves should be a wool/nylon mixture to keep the hands and fingers warm. (These are easy to wash.) Knitted gloves can be attached to the inside of a jacket or to a coat lining by cords to prevent them from being lost.

9 Duffle coat, warm, loose, to cover layers. Usually made of wool/nylon or acrylic mixture. Their relative cheapness and easy toggle fastenings make these popular.

10 Nylon and polyester quilted jackets are brightly coloured, reasonably cheap, provide warmth and waterproof covering and are popular with children.

11 Snowsuits, all-in one nylon quilted trousers and top, are copied from Canadian and Swedish designs and are useful for outdoor play in the winter.

12 Sleeveless jackets in quilted nylon, worn with a thick sweater, are also useful and fashionable for cold weather.

Care of clothing

Regular washing, and ironing if necessary, makes clothes look better and protects from infection. Soiled clothes should be soaked or washed promptly.

Clothes should preferably be hung on child-size hangers to retain shape and texture and kept in the child's wardrobe or cupboard. Sweaters, underwear and socks can be folded and are best kept in separate drawers. A receptacle should be available for dirty clothes and a fresh T-shirt, blouse or sweater every day if possible makes clothes last longer and keeps the child feeling fresh and comfortable.

Holes in socks, trousers and sweaters soon get bigger and can be embarrassing. Simple repairs can be carried out without much expense or difficulty: a patch is easy to apply. Repairing clothes also teaches children that clothes must be cared for, as they are often expensive, and where there are younger children in the family will probably be passed on from elder to younger children. When the child is going away to camp or on holiday he should be shown how to pack clothes correctly and summer clothes should be folded and packed away in boxes or cupboards during the winter to protect against dust, moths and parasites.

Footwear

Width and length should be considered in fitting. The shoes should have enough room for growth and free movement of toes. A shallow-fronted shoe puts pressure on the toes from top and sides, so ample depth is required with straight side walls to eliminate pressure from the sides. A firm fit at the instep and the ankle is required to hold the foot gently in the correct position in the shoe whereas a loose fit allows the foot to slip forward, forcing the toes against the front of the shoes. There should be some room between the end of the longest toe and the tip of the shoe – at least ½ inch for growing toes.

The top of the shoe should not press down tightly on the foot, but if it is too deep a ridge will be seen in the upper of the shoe. Shoes should be closely fitting at the heel, without cutting into the ankle bone. If the child stands on tiptoe, the shoe should not slip off at the heel. The toes should be able to spread and grow and should never be cramped. Shoes which are too big can cause rubbing and blistering. They should follow the natural outline of the foot and be checked every 3 months for fitting. They should not have hard seams, but should be light and flexible with non-slip soles and a low broad heel for balance.

Materials

Leather is comfortable to wear, allows water vapour from sweat to escape and soaks up a lot of sweat. It also stretches with the foot. Leather is not very satisfactory for soles of shoes as it is slippery. Polyurethane 'leather' is less resistant to wear, but waterproof and cheaper than leather. Polyurethane soles are soft, light and generally durable.

Well fitting shoes:

1 prevent deformities and blisters of the feet,
2 promote good walking habits and posture,
3 help normal growth of the feet, promoting good bone development.

Socks

These are just as important as shoes. They should fit well to avoid bending soft young bones and squashing the cartilage pads between them, apart from restricting the blood supply. If the socks are too big, friction and sores may develop. Suitable materials are cotton and wool as these allow absorption of sweat. Wellingtons and gym shoes should be worn for short periods and only when necessary. Rubber is non-porous and does not provide proper ventilation for the feet so socks should be worn inside wellingtons.

Foot problems

Ingrowing toe nails. Incorrect cutting of toe nails (they should be cut straight across) and ill-fitting shoes can cause ingrowing toe nails. A shoe that is too narrow at the front presses the big toe against the second toe, which pushes up a ridge of flesh into which the nail may grow.

Corns and bunions. These may be caused by pressure from ill-fitting shoes. Once acquired they tend to remain.

Bursitis behind the heel. This is painful swelling caused by the pressure of a shoe that is too tight, or by the continual rubbing of one that is too loose. The bursa (the liquid-filled sac protecting a joint) swells and becomes inflamed under pressure. Sometimes an extra growth of bone called an *exostosis* may form.

Overlapping, crooked toes. Toes cramped by ill-fitting shoes may gradually and imperceptibly become deformed giving endless trouble in later life.

Care of feet

Foot problems can lead to swollen ankles, cramp in the toes, pain in the knees, backache, round shoulders, irritability, headaches and dizziness. Good foot care prevents this. Shoes should never be handed down from one child to another. Feet must be kept clean and should be washed at least once daily to keep the skin in good condition and dried thoroughly with special attention to the areas between the toes. Plantar warts or verrucae can occur on the soles of the feet, and may cause considerable discomfort through pressure. They are highly contagious, so children should be taught to step out of the shower, bath or swimming pool directly into their own shoes and should avoid communal bath mats. Wet skin encourages the spread of fungal infections such as Athlete's foot which is also picked up from swimming pool floors and causes intense irritation. It can be cured by use of fungicides in powders and creams. A light dusting of talcum powder will give smoothness and a feeling of wellbeing.

Nails should be cut regularly, straight across, not curved, to prevent ingrowing toe nails.

Daily exercise in bare feet encourages a good blood supply and strengthens the muscles.

Posture

Good posture is when the weight of the body is distributed evenly on either side of the centre of gravity. Stresses on the muscles, joints and skeleton are reduced if good posture is maintained. 'Muscle tone' is the term given to the slight contraction of muscles which maintains posture. A child's posture can often indicate his state of health to an observant mother/care giver. Sometimes one encounters a child who suffers from a congenital or, more rarely, inherited condition which affects their posture, e.g. scoliosis (curvature of the vertebral column), which may require medical treatment. Congenital dislocation of the hips is usually diagnosed soon after birth and can be corrected. Poor posture in children may be a sign that the child is tired, has inadequate clothing and footwear, or is emotionally upset.

Standing posture

This is correct when weight of the thoracic region is in front of the centre of gravity. (To visualize this, one should imagine a straight line running through the body vertically and a point of balance at the top front of the lumbar region.) The pelvic region behind the centre of gravity (point of balance) counterbalances the weight of the thorax.

When the shoulders are hunched and the chest hollowed or the abdomen pushed forward, there is too much weight in front of the centre of gravity. Muscles in the back and thighs have to be constantly contracted to maintain posture and this causes fatigue.

Sitting posture

This is good when the chair is broad enough from back to front to allow support for thighs, and designed to give support for the lumbar region, with a space to allow the pelvis to project, where the back and seat of the chair join. Chairs for children are usually designed to help maintenance of good posture but some modern, cheap, plastic chairs can be harmful. Bad sitting posture is seen when the chair has no support for under thighs, no lumbar support, and the pelvis pushed into the back of the chair. Children are often urged to sit up straight which means that they push their buttocks to the back of the chair, and without support for the lumbar region, soon become tired. The pelvic girdle has the sacrum bone (which ends in the coccyx or tail of the vertebral column) at the back and two ischium bones at each side of the front. When in the correct position, the ischial tuberosities (the 'bumps' on the bones which protrude) should be below the sacrum and the body literally sitting on these bones. If the buttocks are pushed into the chair, the child is in fact sitting on the sacrum bone.

Lifting posture

This is also important if backache and fatigue are to be avoided. Adults (to whom good posture is just as essential a part of health as to children), should demonstrate correct lifting posture to the children with them. The person should stand close to the object to be lifted with the vertebral column straight and nearly upright, the legs under the centre of gravity and used to lift. Here the weight of the body behind the centre of gravity acts as a counterbalance to the weight being picked up. The body should bend at the knees, not the waist. Incorrect lifting posture usually means that the muscles of the back, not the legs, are used to lift, which causes stress on the lumbar region and leads to backache, as most of the weight is in front of the centre of gravity and there is no counterbalance.

Factors which affect posture

1 *Diet*. Nutrients such as protein are essential to build good bones and muscles. Vitamins A, B,

C, D, calcium and phosphorus are also required in the daily diet for adequate growth and functioning.

2 *Exercise*. The use of large and small muscles improves muscle tone (which means that the muscles are always in a state of readiness for action) and helps development. Fresh air facilitates a good intake of oxygen which encourages all parts of the body to work better and helps to remove the accumulated waste.

3 *Rest and sleep*. These allow the lactic acid (which builds up in muscles as a result of exercise and causes fatigue) to be removed so that muscles can function efficiently when next required.

4 *Footwear*. Well-fitting shoes allow room for normal growth of bones and muscles and give good support. They also promote equal distribution of body weight.

5 *Clothing*. Lightweight and non-restrictive clothing allows freedom of movement, which encourages good muscle tone.

6 *Bed/bedding*. The correct size of bed to allow for stretching and movement, a firm mattress to provide good support, and lightweight bedding to promote ease in breathing all contribute to good posture as well as restful sleep.

Teeth

The foundations of both primary and secondary teeth are laid in the baby's gums during pregnancy. At birth the teeth buds are in the baby's gums and they usually start to erupt at 6–9 months of age, although the time of cutting teeth varies greatly. At 1 year the baby has 6–8 teeth and the first set of 20 is complete by 2–2½ years of age. The temporary or primary dentition has 20 teeth which are usually shed from the age of 6 years. Frequent sips of cool boiled water should be given if the gums are inflamed and swollen.

Care of the primary dentition is important as teeth lost cause the remaining teeth to move together and cause crowding when the permanent teeth come through. The weaning diet should include biting foods at 4 months such as hard crusts, a piece of apple or a piece of carrot. Later, when chewing starts at 6–8 months, a piece of orange and hard sugar-free biscuits or rusks are useful.

Sticky syrups should not be rubbed on the gums or given in feeds at bedtime. Vitamin C is better given in juice in correct dilution than in syrup. Sweets should be restricted and biscuits at bedtime avoided as this can initiate dental decay. Raw fruit and vegetables are naturally sweet, as they contain fructose, and although they help teeth to develop and gums to harden, they should not be given at bedtime.

Visits to the dentist can be started when the child begins primary school, although dentists and dental hygienists visit nursery schools to help allay any fears in pre-school children.

Cleaning teeth

Brushing stimulates the blood supply to the gums. A medium-soft toothbrush can be used and the children can be shown how dental floss should be used to remove particles between the teeth. When teeth cannot be cleaned after a meal or eating sweets during the day, children should be shown how to rinse their mouths out with water to remove sticky substances.

The benefits of good dental health

1 Sound teeth help mastication (chewing) which allows the enzyme ptyalin in saliva to begin the process of digestion by breaking down starch into a simpler form of sugar.

2 Well formed teeth and dental care in the primary dentition prevent overcrowding of the jaw and promote clarity of speech.

3 Good dental health means freedom from the pain of toothache and dental or gum abscesses.

4 Sound teeth prevent gum disease related to dental caries.

5 Prevention of tooth decay prevents loss of sleep and irritability through toothache.

6 Sound teeth and good dental health means that the secondary dentition has a better chance to develop naturally and lessens the risk of false teeth which is sadly a frequent occurrence in young children and adolescents today.

Tooth structure

See p. 123.

Environmental Aspects of Health

Fresh air

Fresh air is best enjoyed outdoors, where the ultraviolet rays of the sun can act on the skin to produce vitamin D. It:

1 helps the maintenance of normal temperature through evaporation of sweat,
2 stimulates circulation in superficial blood vessels of the skin,
3 ensures good ventilation of the lungs and therefore good oxygenation of the blood,
4 helps to produce restful sleep,
5 promotes a feeling of wellbeing and alertness as the brain is well oxygenated.

Lack of fresh air can lead to apathy, listlessness and lethargy. At one time it was thought that these reactions to a stuffy atmosphere were due to a build-up of carbon dioxide. However, experiments conducted with students at an American university showed that it was the amount of water vapour (a product of exhalation) which was the major factor. Overcrowding, too, whether in a nursery or at home, not only adversely affects physical health by encouraging the spread of infection, but has been shown to produce mental ill-health.

Ventilation

This is the substitution of stale air by fresh air. As pathogenic bacteria which cause airborne infections breed well in hot, moist air it is essential to ensure an adequate supply of fresh air at home or in the nursery. Overcrowding and group activities such as singing increase the number of droplets (from mouth and nose) in the air, but even a small number of children and adults excrete a large amount of water vapour in ordinary respiration. A number of children develop 'colds' if they are living in a centrally heated atmosphere at home and insufficiently clothed to combat chilling from lower temperatures outside or in nursery/school. In the home, ventilation is usually provided by windows. Where they are of the sash type it is recommended that they should be open at the top as hot air rises and open windows at child height could be dangerous. Some nurseries and schools have windows which have panes especially constructed to allow air to enter at the lower part (without enabling children to climb through) and at the top, for exit of stale air. New buildings, hospitals, most factories and offices nowadays have air conditioning systems which remove stale air, purify it and allow circulation of fresh air. It has been found that inadequate ventilation has adverse affects on work output. Unfortunately air ducts of some ventilation systems in hospitals harbour organisms which cause upper respiratory tract infections (URTI) in the dust which sometimes clogs part of the outlets. Cleansing procedures to avoid cross-infection now include cleaning these ventilation systems.

Many modern houses have single frame windows which swing out and in. While these are useful for cleaning they can prove a major hazard for young children, particularly if they are in bedrooms, and care should be exercised to ensure that these are kept locked or made child proof when children are around. They provide adequate ventilation but unfortunately this cannot be controlled and if left open at night may cause draughts. In these circumstances it is often better to open the window in the morning when beds are made (provided the children are supervised or elsewhere), and keep the door locked or have the door knob at adult height, until the room is well aired.

Extractor fans can be fitted to windows or outside walls in kitchens to remove cooking smells and steam. Most of these can be manually switched on or off, so it is important to ensure that children cannot reach them in case their fingers are caught in the fan blades.

Temperature of the environment

This is important and often a cause of anxiety particularly to parents of babies under 1 year of age. All humans have a temperature-regulating centre in the hypothalamus, a part of the brain. When the skin becomes too cold, information goes to the temperature-regulating centre which reduces heat loss from the skin by constriction (tightening) of the tiny capillaries in the skin. If the skin is too hot, the brain centre cools the body by dilatation of the capillaries, which increases the blood flow to the skin and reduces heat. Sweating also helps to cool the body through evaporation on the skin surface but newborn babies (especially if they are premature) cannot sweat – this mechanism does not begin to function until the baby is about 2 months old. Newborn babies also have a supply of 'brown fat' at the base of the neck and round the kidneys which can be 'burned up' to provide heat.

A newborn baby's temperature-regulating centre will be undeveloped if he is under 2.2 kg (approximately 5 lb) and because of this premature or small-for-dates babies may be nursed in incubators. Babies of average weight under 6 weeks are happy at a room temperature of 20–22°C (68–72°F) during the day and not less than 15°C (65°F) daily temperature is satisfactory for babies under a year and 15–18°C (60–65°F) comfortable for young children's playrooms.

As the temperatures of young babies fluctuate between high and low extremes, doctors use a special low-reading thermometer. However, underheating and overheating can be dangerous. Underheating can cause swollen hands and feet and if the temperature drops too low the child could suffer from hypothermia (body temperature below 85°F) which could be fatal. Overheating produces discomfort, heat rash and rarely convulsions.

Routine Medical Examinations

These are usually carried out in the pre-school years by health visitors or GPs.

0–2 months

1 Weighing the baby and comparing the weight with average weights of babies the same age.
2 Measuring the size of the baby's head and comparing with average measurements of babies of the same age.
3 Checking the anterior fontanelle (the soft spot in the centre of the head).
4 Checking that the eyes move normally in all directions.
5 Checking the soft palate in the mouth, to make sure there is no cleft.
6 Listening to the baby's heart.
7 Checking the baby's hips for any evidence that they might be dislocated.
8 Checking the movements and general tone of the arms and legs and making sure that the baby's head moves normally.
9 Checking, in boys, that both testes are descended into the scrotum.
10 Checking that in both boys and girls the genitalia are normal.
11 Checking the skin for birthmarks, rashes, etc.
12 Asking the parents whether they think the child can see and hear normally.

7–9 months

1 Weighing the baby and checking the weight against the average weights for babies the same age.
2 Measuring the size of the baby's head and checking it against the average head circumference of babies of the same age.
3 Checking the baby's eye movements.
4 Testing for squint.
5 Doing the 'distraction test' to see whether the baby hears normally.
6 Checking to see whether the baby says any understandable words.
7 Checking the baby's heart.
8 Checking the skin for skin rashes, bruises.
9 Checking the baby's hips for possible congenital dislocation of the hip.
10 Checking to see if the baby is sitting without support.
11 Seeing whether the baby picks up small objects between forefinger and thumb.

18 months

1 Weighing and checking weight against average for age.
2 Testing for a squint.
3 Hearing test.
4 Checking to see that the child is walking.
5 Checking the teeth for normal development.
6 Checking the skin for bruises, etc.
7 Checking language development.
8 Checking that the child can get from lying to standing without holding on to anything.

3 years

1 Measuring the child's height.
2 Checking the child's vision and hearing.
3 Checking the child's teeth.
4 Checking language development.

4½ years

1 Checking the child's height.
2 Listening to the heart for murmurs.
3 With boys, checking that both the testes are descended.
4 Checking language development.
5 Checking general coordination of muscles and bones and looking at the coordination of movement to make sure that the child is not clumsy.

Basic Anatomy and Physiology

Fundamental to all health care professions is at least a basic knowledge of the working of the human body. The outline given here is intended merely as groundwork and should be supplemented by reference to books and lectures.

Anatomy concerns the *structure* of the body. Physiology concerns the *functions* of the body parts.

The body consists of skull, neck, thorax, abdomen, pelvis, and upper and lower limbs. 'Anterior' refers to the front, 'posterior' to the back of the body.

There are three main cavities in the body:

1 *The thoracic cavity.* This is the chest region and contains right and left lung, the heart, blood vessels and nerves. The diaphragm which is the main muscle of respiration separates the thoracic from the abdominal cavity.

2 *The abdominal cavity.* This contains the liver (the largest organ in the body), stomach, gall bladder (on the undersurface of the liver), spleen, pancreas, kidneys, adrenal glands (on top of the kidneys), intestines, peritoneum, nerves and blood vessels.

3 *The pelvic cavity.* This contains the reproductive organs, rectum, urinary bladder, blood vessels and nerves.

The *systems of the body* are as follows:

1 The *skeletal system* consists of the bones of the body which form the skeleton.

2 The *muscular system* consists of muscles covering the skeleton and attached to bones.

3 The *respiratory system* consists of the lungs, pleura, trachea, bronchi, bronchioles and alveoli. The function of the respiratory system is to take in oxygen and give out carbon dioxide.

4 The *cardiovascular system* is the heart and blood vessels (arteries, veins and capillaries) whose function is to carry blood round the body.

5 The *lymphatic system* has capillaries, large vessels, ducts and glands which return lymphatic fluid to the circulation.

6 The *digestive system* consists of mouth, pharynx, oesophagus, stomach, small intestine, large intestine and rectum. Its function is ingestion, digestion and absorption of food.

7 The *urinary system* consists of kidneys, ureters, urinary bladder and urethra and has excretory functions.

8 The *endocrine system* consists of glands which produce hormones.

9 The *nervous system* consists of brain, spinal cord and nerves which control and coordinate the body.

10 The *reproductive system* consists of testes, vas deferens, seminal vesicles, prostate gland and urethra in the male; ovaries, uterine tubes, uterus and vagina in the female.

The Skeletal System

The skeleton forms the framework of the body (the bones are symmetrically arranged). It gives attachment to muscles, protection to delicate organs, flexibility and support, and manufactures blood cells. Bone is composed of cartilage or fibrous tissue with mineral salts – calcium carbonate and calcium phosphate. It occurs in two forms: compact bone is tough, solid and white; spongy bone is spongy and white.

Classification of bones

Long bones. These are long in shape (not always in length), have a wall of compact bone tissue and a hollow shaft. There is spongy bone at both ends, e.g. bones of the limbs.

Flat bones. These are flat in shape and have a wall of compact bone tissue covering spongy tissue, e.g. bones of the cranium.

Short and irregular bones. These are small and light. They consist of a mass of spongy cancellous tissue surrounded by a thin shell of compact tissue, e.g. the bones of the vertebral column.

The skull. This consists of 22 bones: eight forming the cranium and 14 forming the face. The cranium protects the brain, the orbital bones form sockets for the eyes, the malar bones are the cheekbones and the nasal bone forms the bony upper part of the nose (the rest is cartilaginous). The jaw bone (lower mandible) is the only movable bone in the skull and helps in mastication (chewing).

The vertebral column. This consists of 33 irregular bones: seven in the cervical (or neck) region, 12 in the dorsal or thoracic region, five in the lumber region, five in the sacrum and four in the coccyx or tail end. The vertebral column provides bony protection for the spinal cord.

The rib cage. The rib cage has 12 ribs attached to the thoracic vertebrae behind and to the sternum or breast bone in front. The ribs provide protection for heart and lungs.

The shoulder girdle. This consists of two clavicles or collar bones and two scapulae (shoulder blades).

The bones of the upper limb. These articulate with the clavicle and scapulae to bring about movement. The humerus ('funny bone') of the upper arm is joined at the elbow to the radius and ulna of the forearm. The radius is the outer bone when the hands are held palm upwards (it is on the same line as the thumb) and the radial pulse is felt over this bone at the wrist. The carpus or wrist, has eight carpal bones arranged in two rows. The metacarpal bones which form the palm of the hand are attached to the phalanges, the bones of the fingers.

The bones of the lower limb. These articulate with the bones of the pelvic girdle (two innominate bones) and the sacrum to bring about movement. The thigh bone (femur) articulates with the bones of the lower leg (the tibia and fibula). The ankle bones (tarsus) articulate with the bones of the foot (metatarsals). Phalanges form the bones of the toes.

Structure of the foot. The foot can be divided into *tarsus*, seven bones including os calcis (or calcaneum) which is the heel bone, *metatarsals* which are five in number, and *phalanges* – there are two for the big toe, three for each of the others. The limb buds are formed in the first few weeks of intrauterine life and deformities due to chromosomal defects, drugs or disease in the mother can be caused before she is even aware that she is pregnant. At 6 months of age, the bones of the toes (phalanges) are still not fully formed but are cartilaginous. Cartilage (or gristle) is soft and easily moulded into an incorrect shape if the baby's feet are pushed into an ill-fitting pair of shoes. Shoes are unnecessary until the child begins to walk which may be at any age from 12 to 18 months. The first pair of shoes should only be bought after the child's feet have been measured and will be of flexible material with plenty of room for growth.

At 2 years of age the bones are gradually lengthening while the area of cartilage grows less but the growth of feet bones is a long, slow process during which the young feet are easily damaged.

At 8 years the bones have grown a great deal but there are still distinct gaps between them where the gristle remains. In the late teens foot growth is usually complete and feet are more resistant to pressure from ill-fitting shoes. On average the foot grows rapidly in the first 4 years, increasing by two sizes a year, then slows down to only one size per year until the mid-teens (15–16 years) when growth in length usually ceases.

The Circulatory or Cardiovascular System

This consists of the heart, the blood vessels and blood. There are four main circulations:

1 the systemic circulation supplies the body in general,
2 the pulmonary circulation is to the lungs,
3 the cerebral circulation is to the brain,
4 the portal circulation is to the liver from the intestines.

Factors which influence the circulation of the blood are:

1 the volume of the blood,
2 the pumping action of the heart,
3 the size of the blood vessels,
4 the activity of the central nervous system.

The heart is a pear shaped, hollow, muscular organ the size of a closed fist. It weighs 8–10 oz (280 g approx.). It is situated in the thoracic cavity between the lungs in the mediastinal space.

Structure of the heart

The heart has four chambers. The right and left *atrium* at the top are receiving chambers. The right and left *ventricles* are distributing chambers below. Vessels entering the right atrium are the upper and lower vena cava (*inferior* and *superior vena cava*) which bring *deoxygenated* blood back to the heart from the head, body and limbs. The *pulmonary artery* carries deoxygenated blood from the right ventricle to the lungs for oxygenation. (It is called an artery because it carries blood away from the heart although it contains deoxygenated blood which is usually carried in veins.) The *pulmonary vein*, so called because it brings blood back to the heart, carries oxygenated blood from the lungs to the left atrium of the heart. The *aorta* which is the largest artery in the body carries oxygenated blood away from the left ventricle of the heart to different parts of the body. The coronary arteries supply blood to the heart itself.

Blood supply to the upper part of the body

The aorta branches to supply the brain (internal *carotid artery*) and face (external carotid artery). The *temporal artery* is placed on the side of the face above the ear and the pulse can be felt here in a sleeping child. From the *subclavian artery*, which lies behind the clavicle, the axillary arteries (in the armpit) become the *brachial arteries* which supply the upper arm. The *ulnar* and *radial arteries* supply the lower arm, wrist and hand. The radial pulse is felt over the radial artery at the wrist. Veins bring the blood supply from the upper part of the body back to the heart via the superior vena cava. Branches of the *jugular vein* enter the *subclavian vein* which drains into the superior vena cava, as do the brachial veins from the arms.

Blood supply to the lower part of the body

The descending *aorta* becomes the *abdominal aorta* which branches to supply the liver, kidneys, spleen and stomach. The *iliac artery* divides to become *two femoral arteries* in each leg. In the lower leg the anterior and posterior *tibial artery* extend downwards to the foot and the *dorsalis pedis artery*. The long and short *saphenous veins* bring blood from the foot and lower leg to the *femoral vein*, which joins the *common iliac vein*. The *inferior vena cava* finally drains into the right atrium with deoxygenated blood from the lower part of the body.

The portal vein

This carries absorbed food products – amino acids, glycerine and fatty acids, glucose and mineral salts – from the small intestine to the liver, which acts as a storehouse and sorting office for the body.

Differences between arteries and veins

Both arteries and veins have three coats, but whereas these keep the arteries open when cut, they are thinner in the veins so that the walls of a vein collapse when it is cut. The lining of the arteries can become thickened which means that the passage of blood through them becomes more difficult and this can increase blood pressure. Veins in the abdomen and lower limbs contain valves which prevent the blood from flowing back and enable its return to the heart. In varicose veins the valves do not work and the veins become distended with blood. Arteries carry oxygenated blood away from the heart whereas veins carry deoxygenated blood back to the heart.

Capillaries are tiny hair-like vessels which form a network and allow the passage of oxygen and carbon dioxide through their unicellular walls. Small cuts usually involve bleeding from capillaries in the skin, but severe bleeding (or haemorrhage) can occur when an artery or vein is severed.

Composition of blood

There are about 5–6 litres of blood in the body and it contains red cells, white cells, platelets and plasma.

Red cells (erythrocytes) number about 5 million/ mm³ of blood. They are manufactured in the marrow bone of all bones in infants and in the sternum, vertebrae and long bones in adults. Vitamin B_{12}, folic acid, iron, nicotinic acid, riboflavin, protein, copper and cobalt (traces) are all required for the maturation of red blood cells. When mature, they lose their nucleus. Red blood cells live for 3–4 months and are destroyed by the spleen which stores the iron from them. Haemoglobin, a protein substance containing iron and pigment, gives the colour to red cells and has a strong affinity for oxygen. Hence the function of red blood cells is to carry oxygen around the body. Lack of iron means that haemoglobin cannot be manufactured in sufficient quantities and anaemia results with characteristic paleness of skin and mucous membranes, and breathlessness on exertion due to lack of oxygen.

White cells (leucocytes) provide the body's internal defence against infection as they are able to change shape and engulf pathogenic microorganisms. There are usually 6000–8000 leucocytes/mm³ of blood, but the numbers are increased in the presence of infection.

Platelets number about 200 000/mm³ of blood and are required for blood clotting. Calcium, vitamin K, prothrombin and fibrinogen are also necessary for the clotting of blood.

Plasma contains 91% water, 7% protein (albumin, globulin, fibrinogen) and 2% of nutrients, metabolic wastes, inorganic elements, antibodies and hormones.

Functions of blood

1 To carry water, oxygen, nutrients and hormones to various parts of the body.
2 To remove metabolic wastes from the tissues and take them to the kidneys, lungs, skin and bowels, as appropriate, for excretion.

The Lymphatic System

This is a drainage system in that it removes water and waste products from cells and tissues, and transports them to the venous bloodstream. Thus it helps maintenance of normal water balance in the body. In the lymphatic system there are a number of lymphatic capillaries which are blind-ended tubes linked to a lymph gland. The lymph glands act as a filter for pathogenic microorganisms and produce lymphocytes, which are like white blood cells and form antibodies to specific organisms. As the lymphatic glands provide a body defence against infection, they often swell during infection. Lymph glands are found in the neck, tonsils, adenoids, axillae (armpits), groin and small intestine. Swollen neck glands are often seen in upper respiratory tract infections.

The Digestive System

Digestion is the process by which complex food substances are reduced to simpler forms in which they can be absorbed. It is a chemical process in that enzymes, which are chemical substances produced by living cells, act as catalysts in digestion. A catalyst is a substance which speeds up a reaction but is itself unchanged. Digestion is also a mechanical process in that the food is dissolved and reduced in size by the grinding and chewing action of the

teeth (mastication) and the muscular action of the alimentary canal.

Structure of the teeth

The teeth are covered with a hard outer layer called *enamel*. Below this is *dentine* which is similar to bone but not as hard as enamel. In the centre of the tooth there is soft connective tissue called the *pulp* which contains blood vessels and nerves. The *root* of the tooth is in the socket and embedded in the jawbone. *Cement* covers the dentine at the root of the tooth. The interior of a tooth is hollow and is called the *cavity*. It contains the small blood vessels and nerves which supply the tooth.

The following is the order in which a child cuts his teeth:

Lower central incisors } 6–9 months
Upper central incisors }
Upper lateral incisors } 7–12 months
Lower lateral incisors }
Upper first molars } 15–21 months
Lower first molars }
Lower canines } 16–24 months
Upper canines }
Lower second molars } 20–30 months
Upper second molars }

The alimentary canal or tract

This is a long continuous tube which stretches from the mouth to the anus and is convoluted in parts to fit inside the abdomen. It is about 9 m (30 ft) long and consists of layers of smooth, plain, involuntary muscle lined by a mucous membrane which secretes mucus to aid the passage of the food (see Fig. 4.2).

The mouth

In the mouth the food is masticated into small pieces by the teeth, and saliva from the salivary glands is mixed with it. A soft mass of food or *bolus* is formed by the muscular action of the jaws and the tongue. The surface of the tongue is covered with taste buds which enable sweet, salt, sour and bitter tastes to be distinguished. Taste-buds do not usually develop until about 6–8 months from birth. The *salivary glands* are placed below the tongue and in front of the ears on each side of the face. At the sight, smell or even thought of food they pour forth their secretion of saliva. There are three pairs of salivary

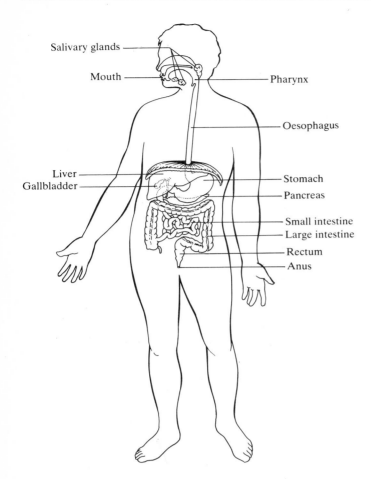

Salivary glands

Mouth

Pharynx

Oesophagus

Liver
Gallbladder

Stomach
Pancreas

Small intestine
Large intestine
Rectum
Anus

Figure 4.2   The alimentary canal.

glands: parotid, submandibular and sublingual. The parotid glands are situated in front of and below the ear. It is these glands which become swollen in mumps (infective parotitis), and affect the amount of saliva produced, which causes the difficulty in chewing often seen in the condition. The sublingual glands are below the tongue and the submandibular glands are just under the angle of the jaw.

The oesophagus

The bolus of food then passes into the *oesophagus*, a tube which leads straight into the stomach. Next to the oesophagus in the neck and *thorax* are the *trachea* and *bronchi*, tubes of the respiratory system. Usually a flap called the epiglottis covers the entrance to the trachea when food is eaten to prevent it going down 'the wrong way'. Sometimes talking and eating at the same time causes the food to be inhaled instead of ingested and the person appears to be choking as the food blocks the trachea. When this happens with a baby, it is best to turn the child upside down and hold him by the legs, slapping his back between the shoulders to dislodge the food.

Peristalsis is the muscular contraction which causes the food to move through the oesophagus and the intestines. It is an involuntary movement not under the control of the individual and is initiated by the food pressing on the sides of the oesophagus. A wave of relaxation in front of the food bolus is followed by a wave of contraction which pushes the food forward.

The stomach

This is in the upper part of the abdomen, although children will usually say they have a

V.S. Canine tooth

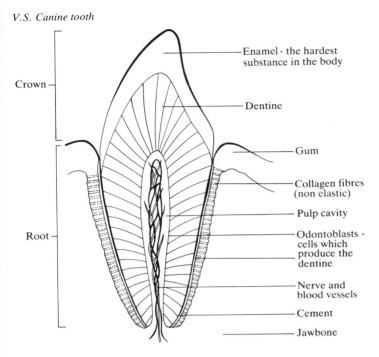

Crown

Root

Enamel - the hardest
substance in the body

Dentine

Gum

Collagen fibres
(non elastic)

Pulp cavity

Odontoblasts -
cells which
produce the
dentine

Nerve and
blood vessels

Cement

Jawbone

Figure 4.3   Section through a canine
tooth.

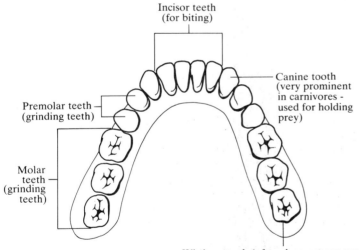

Incisor teeth
(for biting)

Canine tooth
(very prominent
in carnivores -
used for holding
prey)

Premolar teeth
(grinding teeth)

Molar
teeth
(grinding
teeth)

Wisdom tooth (often does not appear
until around twenty years of age)

Figure 4.4   Organization of teeth in the
mouth.

sore stomach and point to the lower abdomen or 'tummy'. A J-shaped organ, it is lined with mucous membrane which contains glands secreting gastric juices which are subject to stimulation like the salivary glands. The stomach also has a muscular layer which contracts to churn the food and turn it into *chyme*, a milky fluid, in which form it is passed through the pyloric sphincter at intervals into the duodenum. Apart from the psychological stimulus of the sight or smell of food, gastric juices are also secreted by the presence of food in the stomach. Gastric juice contains two enzymes – pepsin and rennin – which work in the presence of hydrochloric acid secreted by the stomach lining.

The small intestine

This is divided into three parts: the *duodenum*, the *jejunum* and the *ileum*. As the chyme from the stomach enters the duodenum, juices from the pancreas and bile from the gall bladder act upon it.

The main function of the small intestine is absorption of the digested food substances. As its surface is covered with small projections called *villi*, it has a large area over which absorption can take place. Each villus has a network of blood capillaries and a lymph vessel. Simple sugars, amino acids, water-soluble vitamins and mineral salts are absorbed directly into the blood while fatty acids, glycerol and fat-soluble vitamins pass into the lymph vessels and enter the bloodstream at the junction of the thoracic duct and left subclavian vein. Iron, vitamin B_{12} and calcium (in the presence of vitamin D) are also absorbed in the small intestine. Glucose and amino acids are transported via the portal vein from the small intestine to the liver for storage and distribution to all parts of the body.

Bile is produced in the liver and stored in the gall bladder. When fatty food is eaten the gall bladder contracts and bile flows into the duodenum. Bile salts emulsify fats. Pancreatic juice and bile are alkaline and they neutralize the acid chyme.

The large intestine

This prepares the undigested food or faeces for removal from the body. It has only one secretion, mucin, which lubricates the faeces and eases the passage through the rectum and anus. Water is absorbed in the large intestine so that the faeces are in a semi-solid form for defecation. Some glucose and salt and certain drugs are also absorbed in the rectum and rectal drips utilize this function, as do suppositories. A large number of bacteria are present in the large intestine to break down undigested food materials and to synthesize vitamins. Excess salts such as calcium and iron can be excreted in the faeces. Iron supplements taken by children turn the faeces black.

The food passes through the large intestine by peristalsis and adequate roughage (cellulose fibre of fruits and vegetables) is necessary for good evacuation. If faeces are passed through the large intestine too quickly there is not enough time for the water to be removed and watery stools are the result. If evacuation does not take place when the desire arises, constipation occurs, when the faeces become hard and solid as water is removed from them while in the rectum. When evacuation does occur the hard faeces can cause straining and pain. Defecation is entirely a reflex act in babies – the rectum empties when full – but between the ages of 18 months and 3½ years the control centre in the brain becomes active.

The Respiratory System

Respiration involves the taking in of oxygen required for all cell processes, and the giving out of carbon dioxide which is the end product of respiration. Oxygen is taken in through the nose and mouth. The nose is lined with cilia, tiny hairs which act as a filter for pathogenic micro-organisms. Behind the nose is the *nasopharynx*, which contains lymphoid tissue and is known as the adenoids. These may become swollen in an upper respiratory tract infection. The tonsils at the back of the mouth are also lymphoid tissue and become inflamed and swollen in infections such as tonsilitis and sore throat.

Below the nasopharynx is the *oropharynx* and this leads down to the *larynx* or voice box, which contains vocal cords. Air circulating through these cords causes sounds to be produced. The larynx leads to the *trachea*, which is a tube made up of horizontal C-shaped cartilaginous rings, lined with mucous membrane – as indeed is every part of the respiratory system. Two *bronchi* branch from the trachea. The left bronchus leads to the left lung where it branches further into *bronchioles*, which terminate in air sacs (*alveoli*). The right bronchus leads to the right lung. Inflammation of the bronchi is called bronchitis, whereas inflammation of the lungs is known as pneumonia. Alveoli are tiny air sacs and there are millions of these in each lung. Exchange of oxygen and carbon dioxide takes place through the capillaries which cover each alveolus.

Inspiration, the taking in of air, is brought about as a response to the activations of the respiratory centre in the medulla, part of the brain stem. The levels of carbon dioxide and oxygen act as stimuli for the respiratory centre. Nerves from the respiratory centre cause the intercostal muscles between the ribs to contract and raise the ribcage upwards and outwards. At the same time, the diaphragm, which is dome shaped at rest, contracts and flattens. The lungs expand to fill the thorax and become inflated with the air they draw in.

In expiration, the nerves from the respiratory centre stop sending out nervous impulses to the organs of respiration. The intercostal muscles relax, the ribcage returns to its former size, the diaphragm rises to its former resting position, the lungs are compressed, and air is forced out of them. Respiration takes place 18–20 times a minute in adults (from 14 years of age), 50–30 a minute at birth to 6 months; 45–30 per minute at 6 months; 30–25 per minute at 1 year and 2 years; 25 per minute from 3 to 6 years of age.

Apart from acting as the chief muscle of respiration, the diaphragm separates the thorax from the abdomen and has three openings for the passage of the inferior vena cava, the oesophagus and the aorta (see Artificial Respiration).

The Urinary System

The urinary system consists of two kidneys, two ureters, one urinary bladder and one urethra. The kidneys are bean-shaped organs which lie on the posterior abdominal wall, one on each side of the vertebral column. On top of each kidney is an adrenal gland. The right kidney is slightly lower than the left as it is related to the liver at the front. Each kidney contains millions of *nephrons*, microscopic units in which urine is formed. The blood reaches the kidneys via the renal arteries (branches of the aorta), and as it is under high pressure it is forced through the capsules of the nephrons where filtration takes place. Water, glucose, sodium chloride, urea and other salts are removed from the blood. As the blood goes through the Loop of Henle (part of the convoluted tubule attached to each capsule in the nephrons), some water, a little salt and glucose as required by the body pass into the capillaries surrounding the tubules. The fluid left in the tubule now contains mainly waste products, especially urea, the end-product of protein digestion, and uric acid. Blood free of waste products returns to the circulation via the renal veins. The urine from the tubules collects in the pelvis of the ureter (the expanded top part). The ureters are tubes leading from each kidney to the urinary bladder and they carry urine. Urine contains 96% water and 4% of solids. Functions of the urinary system include excretion of electrolytes and maintenance of blood alkalinity, and excretion of harmful waste substances.

The Skin

The skin is an important part of the body. It:

1 protects and covers the entire surface of the body forming a barrier to infection – it is also waterproof;
2 helps in temperature regulation of the body in that evaporation causes cooling with heat loss through skin pores;
3 excretes sweat containing water and salts;
4 is a sensory organ with nerve endings for heat, cold, deep and light touch, and pain;
5 acts as a source of vitamin D through the action of ultraviolet light on a substance in the skin.

Structure of the skin

The outer part of the skin is called the *epidermis* and is composed of layers of cells. As these cells die, they flake off, and can be seen in samples of dust. Under the epidermis is the dermis, a loose fibrous tissue containing fat cells for protection and insulation. The dermis contains blood vessels, sebaceous glands, sweat glands and hair follicles. The capillaries in the skin constrict and conserve heat and give the skin its characteristic paleness when its owner is cold or suffering from shock. 'Goose pimples' are caused by constriction of the tiny muscles attached to the hair follicles, which cause the hairs to stand on end. Dilatation of the capillaries in the skin causes a pink colour and blushing. Nerve endings in the dermis convey sensations of light and heavy touch, pain, heat and cold to the brain.

Sweat, produced in the sweat glands, evaporates from the skin surface and helps in the regulation of body temperature. In a hot climate the sweat glands are more active, so more sweat is produced and the capillaries dilate, enabling more heat to be lost from the body. About 500 ml of sweat are lost insensibly (i.e. not seen as glistening drops on face or body) every 24 hours. Control of heat gain, heat loss, and temperature is in the hypothalamus of the brain. It is through this that sweat glands, blood vessels in the skin, production of thyroxine (which speeds up metabolism and thus increases heat), and general metabolism are adjusted to keep the body

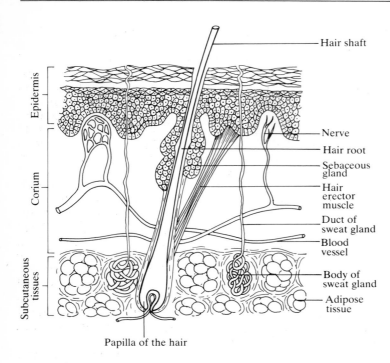

Hair shaft

Nerve

Hair root

Sebaceous gland

Hair erector muscle

Duct of sweat gland

Blood vessel

Body of sweat gland

Adipose tissue

Epidermis

Corium

Subcutaneous tissues

Papilla of the hair

Figure 4.5   Section through the skin.

temperature at 36.8°C. The sebaceous glands secrete sebum, a greasy substance which makes the hair shine.

The Endocrine System

This consists of a number of ductless glands, so called because they secrete their substances directly into the bloodstream. These glands produce *hormones*, or chemical messengers, which affect all bodily functions. Together with nerves, they control the body. The *pituitary gland* is situated at the base of the brain near the *hypothalamus*. It is called the 'master gland' because its secretions affect those of the other endocrine glands. The anterior lobe of the pituitary gland produces hormones which influence growth, the adrenal, thyroid and reproductive glands, while the posterior lobe influences blood vessels and the kidneys.

The *thyroid gland* is situated in the neck: two lobes on either side of the trachea, joined in front by an isthmus. It produces thyroxin which controls the rate of metabolism and affects physical and intellectual development. Under-secretion of thyroxine causes cretinism in children and myxoedema in adults. Children affected by this are undersized and mentally

subnormal. Cretinism is rarely seen nowadays as a diagnosis of hypothyroidism is quickly followed by administration of thyroxine. In hypothyroidism patients are always cold due to poor metabolism and may have dry, flaky skin and poor hair growth.

The *parathyroid glands* are situated behind the thyroid gland. They produce parathormone, which controls the amount of calcium and phosphorus in the blood and bones.

The *pancreas* is both an exocrine (it produces pancreatic juice which contains digestive enzymes and pours through the pancreatic duct) and an endocrine gland. It produces the hormone *insulin* which controls glucose metabolism. A rise in blood sugar causes a secretion of insulin which reduces the level, while a fall in blood sugar stops insulin secretion and mobilizes glucose from the glycogen stores in the liver and muscles. Lack of insulin causes diabetes mellitus.

The *adrenal glands* have an outer part (cortex) and inner part (medulla). The cortex produces several hormones which control the metabolism of salts, protein and, partly, carbohydrate. The medulla provides *adrenaline* which increases the activity of the sympathetic nervous system, raises the blood pressure, increases the heart beat, enables the body to cope with stress and increases blood supply to the muscles of the limbs away from the organs of digestion.

The *sex glands* are the *testes* in the male and *ovaries* in the female. The testes produce *testosterone* and the ovaries produce *oestrogen* and *progesterone*. Testosterone and oestrogen produce the secondary sexual characteristics in male and female: deep voice, hair on the face, axillae, and groins in the male; high-pitched voice, axillary and pubic hairs in the female. Oestrogen also repairs the uterus after menstruation and childbirth. Progesterone prepares the uterus for pregnancy, softens the inner lining of the uterus and suppresses the production of ova.

The Nervous System

The nervous system consists of the *brain, spinal cord, cranial* and *spinal nerves*. The brain contains grey matter made up of nerve cells, and white matter made up of nerve fibres. Grey matter forms the outer part known as the *cortex*. The *cerebrum*, the large 'forebrain', controls all thought processes and body movements. It is divided into halves or hemispheres and has a deeply folded and convoluted surface. Each *cerebral hemisphere* is responsible for the voluntary movements of the opposite side of the body. The *hypothalamus* is a region below the *thalamus* in the brain. With the *medulla oblongata*, which is part of the brain stem joining brain to the spinal cord, it controls internal functions such as breathing, digestion, circulation, vomiting, body temperature, sleep, water content of the body and adjustments for fear, anger and flight. The *cerebellum* or hind brain controls balance and is connected with the semicircular canals of the inner ear.

The *spinal cord* is made of nervous tissue and is not only the link between the brain and spinal cord, but also a reflex centre. From the spinal cord nerves branch out to the limbs and internal organs. Reflex actions involve a response to a stimulus. If someone stands barefooted on a sharp object, the sensation of pain is conveyed to the posterior part of the spinal cord. From here a signal is sent to the brain which causes the person to say 'ouch!' or a similar expression of pain. The motor response to the sensory stimulus is conveyed by a motor neurone from the anterior part of the cord to the foot, which enables it to be pulled away from the painful object. This all happens very quickly and involves more than the simple process described here.

The *autonomic nervous system* is concerned with the activity of the involuntary muscle in the walls of the organs and vessels. It has two separate parts, the *sympathetic* and *parasympathetic* nerves. 'Autonomic' means without conscious control. The sympathetic nerve supply prepares the body for flight or fight. It releases energy to the limbs, quickens the heart, increases respiration, dries up salivary secretions and makes the skin white and cold. This picture is seen in a person about to face a stressful situation, or on the defensive. The parasympathetic nerves usually have the opposite effect. They calm the person down by slowing the heartbeat and respiration, store energy and relax the muscles. Appetite and digestion are stimulated, pupils of the eyes constricted, and under normal conditions the person feels warm and comfortable again. Both sympathetic and parasympathetic nerves come from the spinal cord with a centre in the brain.

The *neurone* is the unit of the nervous system. Each neurone has a cell and fibres. There are millions of neurones in the nervous system; some have a motor, some a sensory function. Sensory neurone tracts run up the spinal cord while motor neurone tracts run down. Nervous impulses are like electrical impulses except that they are not continuously joined. Between the endings of the nerves is a space or gap called the synapse and the impulse leaps over this by chemical action. *Neuroglia* is the connective tissue which supports the neurones. The brain and spinal cord have three coverings and floating around these is the cerebrospinal fluid.

Cerebrospinal fluid is a colourless, clear, alkaline fluid containing water, protein, glucose and a small amount of salt. It is formed in the ventricles (cavities in the brain) and is finally absorbed by veins lining the skull. It acts as a protective cushion for the brain and spinal cord. Inflammation of the brain coverings (the *meninges*) is called meningitis and samples of cerebrospinal fluid may be taken from the lumbar region for examination of microorganisms present in this illness.

The Reproductive System

The male reproductive organs are:

1 Two testes (glands producing spermatozoa)

contained in the scrotum, a fleshy bag which lies outside the body, between the legs, as sperm require a cooler environment than is possible inside the body.

2 Two vas deferens – these are tubes which carry sperm in seminal fluid.

3 Two seminal vesicles – sacs to hold the sperm which are found behind the urinary bladder.

4 One ejaculatory duct which passes through the prostate gland.

5 One urethra in the penis.

One to two million sperm are ejaculated at one time from the seminal vesicles. The testes produce the hormone testosterone which causes secondary sexual characteristics to appear at puberty (11–14) in the male. The gonads are under the influence of the pituitary gland.

The female reproductive organs consist of:

1 Two ovaries, glands which produce ova and hormones.

2 Two uterine tubes, one attached to each side of the uterus – they receive ova and transport them from the ovaries to the uterus.

3 One uterus, a pear-shaped organ behind the urinary bladder. As its walls are very muscular, it can expand to hold a fully grown fetus. The uterus receives the fertilized ovum and allows for the growth and protection of the embryo and fetus.

4 One cervix. This is the neck of the uterus and leads into the vagina, which is lined with mucous membrane. The outer part of the vagina is surrounded by fleshy folds called the vulva. Oestrogen and progesterone are both produced by the ovaries. The production of ova and these hormones is under the control of the pituitary gland.

The menstrual cycle usually covers 28 days and occurs in females between the stages of puberty (12–14 years on average) and the menopause, which can take place from 45 years onwards. The menstrual flow usually lasts for 2–5 days and is followed by a 7-day period when the lining of the uterus builds up again under hormonal influence.

Ovulation occurs when an ovum is released from the ovary into the uterine tube. If fertilization of the ovum does not occur, the lining of the uterus breaks down and menstruation occurs. Ovulation usually occurs 14 days before the start of the next cycle. Many women experience premenstrual tension, which is caused by the imbalance of hormones at this time. Retention of water is also felt before a period, and some women complain of feeling swollen and fat. The family doctor may prescribe a drug to alleviate symptoms, and avoidance of over-tiredness helps. Menstruation should, however, always be regarded as a natural process and not as an illness.

Reproduction

Spermatozoa are ejaculated from the penis high into the vaginal vault at orgasm during sexual intercourse. Sperm swim up to the uterine tubes, and if an ovum is present one sperm unites with it to form a zygote. This moves along to become embedded in the uterus and, if conditions are favourable, develops into an embryo and then a fetus.

Vision and Hearing

All the senses – smell, taste, touch, hearing and sight – contribute to development. Taste, touch and smell are known to be highly developed at birth and the baby responds to the touch and feel of his mother's skin when he is placed on her abdomen immediately after birth. Vision and hearing play an important part in social and emotional development as they are the accepted means of communication in our society, although awareness of other means is essential for all who care for babies and children. Needs, conscious and unconscious, can be communicated through body movements or 'body language' as it is often called.

Vision

At birth the cone cells in the retina which are needed for colour vision are not fully developed, which means that the newly born baby is colour-blind. The rods of black and white vision are also less numerous at first so the child has only a blurred image and lacks the ability to focus both eyes on one object at the same time, due to inactivity of the eye muscles. For the first 4 weeks of life the baby will not be able to see his mother clearly but at 1 month old he is beginning to watch his mother's face closely and research shows that 38% of babies react positively to mothers at this age.

By the age of 3 months, the baby begins to

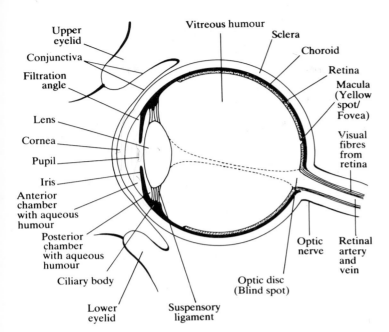

Upper eyelid

Conjunctiva

Filtration angle

Lens

Cornea

Pupil

Iris

Anterior chamber with aqueous humour

Posterior chamber with aqueous humour

Ciliary body

Lower eyelid

Suspensory ligament

Vitreous humour

Sclera

Choroid

Retina

Macula (Yellow spot/ Fovea)

Visual fibres from retina

Optic nerve

Retinal artery and vein

Optic disc (Blind spot)

Figure 4.6 Section through the human eye.

recognize the difference between his mother and strangers and at 15 weeks most cry when their mother leaves the room. At 6–8 months, babies become upset when left with strangers and the mother fully appreciates the loving relationship which exists between the baby and her, the most important relationship of all, as it will affect all others. For the first few months of life, the baby gazes around him and will fixate on moving objects for a few seconds. At 6 months he is able to see an object within 6–12 inches in front of him and achieves hand–eye coordination as he reaches out to grasp it. A squint is seen in the first 6 months as the baby's eyes often converge when an object is brought closer towards his face, but after this it is abnormal and the mother should seek medical advice if it persists.

Binocular vision when both eyes focus on the object of interest begins between 6–8 weeks of age. This enables the baby to judge distance and depth more accurately. From 6 to 10 months the baby examines objects held in his hand and eagerly watches the activities of adults and children within 10–12 ft of him. At 1 year, he can recognize familiar figures from 20 ft away and points at objects of interest. The retina which receives all the images that enter the eye is not completely developed until 6 years of age, and the eyeball does not reach adult size until 12 or 14 years of age.

Structure. Light waves enter the eye through the cornea, and pass through the anterior chamber, pupil, posterior chamber lens (which is a biconvex crystal-like disc), and vitreous humour to the retina. The retina is the lining of the eye and contains rods – cells which are sensitive to white light – and cones which are concentrated at one point, the *fovea*, or yellow spot, at the back of the eye, and are sensitive to colour. The retina also contains a substance called visual purple which requires vitamin A for synthesis. The nerve endings in the retina send elaborate patterns of signals to the optic nerve. These patterns finally reach the back of the cerebrum and give rise to the sensation of vision. The lens focuses the images of the objects upside down on the retina.

Interpretation of images is carried out in the back of the cerebrum where the sight centre is situated. The eye adapts to light by contraction and dilation of the pupils. When the light is dim, the pupil is large, and when the light is bright the pupil is small. Accommodation to distance takes place through thickening or flattening of the lens which is attached by suspensory ligaments to muscles. For viewing the objects in the distance the pupil dilates and the lens flattens. In near viewing, the pupil constricts and the lens thicken. The iris is the coloured muscular diaphragm surrounding the pupil which allows it to

The right eye

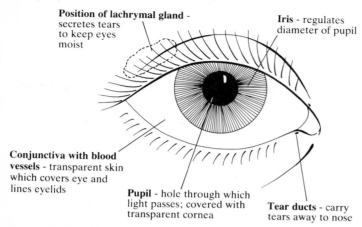

Position of lachrymal gland - secretes tears to keep eyes moist

Iris - regulates diameter of pupil

Conjunctiva with blood vessels - transparent skin which covers eye and lines eyelids

Pupil - hole through which light passes; covered with transparent cornea

Tear ducts - carry tears away to nose

Figure 4.7   Anterior aspect of the eye.

constrict and dilate. Colour of eyes is inherited from parents.

Hearing

Sound waves enter the outer ear through the pinna, the external auditory meatus and the auditory canal to the tympanic membrane. In the middle ear there are three tiny bones (ossicles) which form a bridge across it. At one end they are attached to the tympanic membrane, at the other to the oval window which is a small, thin, oval-shaped sheet of fibrous tissue joining the middle ear to the inner ear.

The inner ear contains a bony canal and a membranous canal which form the *cochlea*, the organ of hearing. *Perilymph* is a fluid which fills the bony canal, *endolymph* fills the membranous canal. Vibrations from the endolymph are transmitted to the organ of Corti in the cochlea and from here to the 8th auditory nerve and the temporal lobe of the brain where the hearing and speech centres are situated.

The Eustachian tube leads from the middle ear to the back of the throat which means that infection can easily spread from the throat to the ear. Inflammation of the middle ear is known as otitis media which can be a complication of measles.

Hearing is the least developed sense at birth but the fetus does respond to high levels of auditory stimulation, as do newborn babies. Difficulty in hearing low levels of sound may be due to amniotic fluid blocking the passage of sound waves from outer ear to inner ear, and the immaturity of the sense cells in the inner ear. Newborn infants respond to loud noises with the startle reflex and often cry. If there is any doubt about the child's hearing, he is referred to an audiology clinic for further tests. Audiometricians, who are trained to test hearing, visit primary schools to ensure that no child who is only partially hearing suffers educational setbacks because of missed diagnosis.

Nutrition

The nutrients present in food and essential for the functioning of the body are: proteins, fats, carbohydrates, vitamins, minerals, trace elements and water. A well balanced diet is one which supplies these nutrients in the proportions required for each aspect and stage of development and growth.

All foods supply the body with energy; all foods contain calories. An excess of calories causes weight gain as the surplus 'energy' is stored as fat. Insufficient calorie intake causes weight loss as the body then draws on its fat reserves to supply itself with energy.

1 g carbohydrate supplies	4 kcal of energy
1 g protein supplies	4 kcal of energy
1 g fat supplies	9 kcal of energy

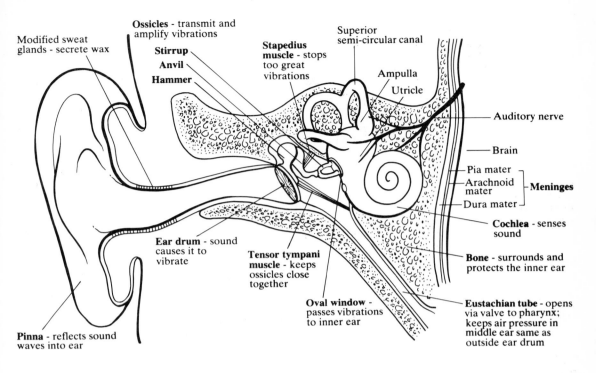

Figure 4.8   Diagram of the ear.

Nutrients and their Function

Carbohydrates

Carbohydrates are found mainly in bread, potatoes and sugar. They provide energy in the form of glucose for all body processes and this is stored in the liver and muscles. Excess is converted into fat. Carbohydrates exist in food as simple sugars and starches – glucose, fructose, sucrose, maltose, lactose are all simple sugars; starch, dextrin, glycogen, pectin and cellulose are all compound sugars.

Glucose. All carbohydrates are broken down into glucose before they are absorbed by the body. 'Blood sugar' refers to the amount of glucose which is present in the blood. This is controlled by the hormone insulin and is normally 70–120 mg/100 ml blood and is lowest before a meal. Glucose is not as sweet as sucrose but can be absorbed and utilized very rapidly by the body.

Fructose. This is 'fruit sugar' and occurs naturally in fruit, fruit juice and honey. It is metabolized more gradually by the body than glucose.

Sucrose. This is all forms of sugar cane and sugar beet. It is the commonest form of sugar in the diet. Brown and demerara sugars, commonly held to be more nutritious than white sugar, are in fact merely unrefined cane sugar, though containing mineral traces.

Lactose. This (milk sugar) is found in milk. Human milk contains more than cows' milk (6–7% compared with 4–5%). The enzyme lactase is required to break down lactose into glucose. Some children from certain ethnic groups, e.g. African, Chinese, Thai, often lack this enzyme and consequently are actually ill if they drink milk.

Starch. This is the main source of energy for most human beings and requires breakdown by enzymes into the simplest form of glucose before it can be absorbed. It provides a steady supply of energy, unlike the rapid burst which glucose and sucrose provide, but which is then rapidly depleted. Cereals are a popular source of starch, and as minerals such as calcium and some vitamins are now added to processed cereal products and flour many babies derive their main supply of their nutrients from these. Examples of cereals are: rice, oats, barley, maize/corn, rye and wheat.

Cellulose. This is found in the fibrous parts of fruits and vegetables but, apart from a few bacteria in the large intestine, the human alimentary tract lacks the digestive enzymes capable of converting it into glucose. It is thus useful only as bulk or roughage which stimulates peristalsis (bowel movements) and helps to prevent constipation.

Pectin. This is found in apples, plums and other fruit, turnips and root crops. It is used to make jam set and since it makes food attractive, which stimulates the appetite, it has some nutritional value.

Roughage

Cellulose has already been mentioned as a form of bulk required in the diet to stimulate peristalsis (bowel action) and prevent constipation. The stalks of cabbage and cauliflower, celery, skins of apples, pears, tomatoes and wholemeal bread all provide sufficient roughage in the normal diet.

Fats

Fats provide a concentrated source of energy in the diet and are generally considered to make food more palatable, e.g. bread and butter is preferable to dry bread. Fats are normally solid at room temperature whereas oils are fats which remain in the liquid state at room temperature. Oils and fats can be classified according to their origin as animal or vegetable.

Animal fats are found primarily in lard and butter and in meats and bacon. Eggs, milk and cheese also have a considerable proportion of fat. Fat provides a vehicle for vitamins A, D, E and K, which are all known as fat-soluble vitamins to be absorbed by the body. Fish oils are more beneficial to health than fat found in meat.

Vegetable oils are derived from soya beans (which are also a valuable source of protein and are often used as meat substitutes), ground nuts (monkey nuts), palm oil, olive oil, coconut oil and sunflower seeds. Nuts and cocoa beans are also good sources of fat.

Margarine is prepared from vegetable oils to which vitamins A and D are added. Saturated fat consumption is very high in rich countries and this has been related to the high incidence of heart attacks in these areas. Margarine has a higher unsaturated fat content than butter and is therefore considered a more healthy choice than butter.

Fats have a protective function in that they form adipose tissue which is found round organs like the kidneys, and is more extensive in women than in men. Excess fat has adverse effects on body systems.

Saturated fats include all meat and dairy products. *Polyunsaturated fats* include fish oil, sunflower, and most vegetable oils.

Proteins

Proteins, unlike fats and carbohydrates, contain nitrogen which is essential for growth and repair of cells. Protein has to be converted into amino acids, its simplest form, for absorption. There are ten essential amino acids, and proteins in food are termed 'first class' if they contain all of these in the right quantities and 'second class' if they just contain some or all in smaller amounts. Meat, fish, eggs, milk and cheese are all good animal sources of protein and termed 'first class'. Vegetable sources (second-class protein) include soya bean flour (which in fact contains more protein than any food mentioned in animal sources, but is deficient in tryptophan and methionine – two essential amino acids), peanuts and pulses – lentils, peas, beans, brazil nuts, walnuts. Fruit and vegetables contain small amounts of protein as do oatmeal and bread flours (gluten is the protein found in bread) and when the total dietary protein is calculated according to food source, it may be that bread will contribute more than eggs, as more bread is consumed. Excess protein, i.e. more than the body's requirements, is stored in the adipose tissues as fat.

Mineral elements

These are elements (other than carbon, hydrogen and oxygen) which form salts and are essential for all body functions, growth and development.

Sodium. This forms an essential part of plasma, sweat and tears and is required for the extra-cellular fluid in which body cells float. Maintenance of salt balance is essential for health. An excess of salt in the diet is usually excreted in the kidneys, but it can cause retention of water (when oedema will be seen) and have adverse effects on blood pressure. In these cases, a low-salt diet may be prescribed. Where vomiting, diarrhoea and excessive sweating cause serious loss of fluid and salt from the body, the dehydration which follows is relieved by giving saline which is a mixture of salt and water. Babies cannot tolerate high sodium intakes because of the immaturity of the kidney functioning and extra salt should not be added to their diet.

Calcium. This is often associated with phosphorus and 99% of the total calcium content of the body is found as calcium phosphate in bones and teeth. At birth a baby's bones are soft and require calcification before they become hard. Calcification requires the presence of calcium, phosphorus and vitamin D and a deficiency of any of these causes badly formed teeth and bones and poor growth. Calcium is also essential for the clotting of blood.

Vitamin D is essential for the absorption of calcium. Delayed dentition and rickets, a deficiency disease, can occur in a diet which lacks either calcium or vitamin D. Sources of calcium are yoghurt, cheese, milk, eggs and fish, particularly sardines and haddock. Brown and white bread are good sources as calcium is added to flour during manufacture. Milk, cheese and flour products provide most of the calcium content in British diets. Hard water, found in areas where there are deposits of calcium carbonate (chalk) contributes a small amount of calcium salts to the diet which compensates for its disadvantages in washing where it requires more soap or detergent to produce a lather than soft water.

Phosphorus. This is an essential constituent of body fluids and is required for cell structure. About 85% of the phosphorus in the body is found in the calcium phosphate of the bones and teeth. Phosphorus occurs in many foods but is found mainly in cheese, liver, sardines, eggs, haddock, brown bread, milk, rice, white bread, green cabbage, roasted peanuts and (a little) in oranges. High levels of potassium in the first few days of life can produce low levels of calcium in the blood and muscular spasm (tetany) may develop. There is a greater risk of this in babies fed on cows' milk which has a high ratio of phosphorus to calcium compared to human milk, and a combination of calcium and fat which may hinder calcium absorption.

Potassium. This is required for the fluids within the body cells and works closely with sodium. The main sources of potassium are potatoes, brussels sprouts, cauliflower, mushrooms, peas, dried prunes, bananas, oranges, canned peaches, beef, pork, liver, kidney, chicken, herrings, kippers and haddock. Milk chocolate and yeast extract are also rich in potassium. Diuretics and purgatives can cause excessive losses of potassium as can diarrhoea. Heart failure can occur in cases of severe depletion, unless potassium supplements are given. Potassium deficiency is rare in the UK.

Iron. This is an essential nutrient required for the formation of haemoglobin, the pigment of red blood cells, which carry oxygen from the lungs to the tissues where it is required for metabolism. Red blood cells live in the blood for about 120 days and when they die the iron in haemoglobin is stored in bone marrow, the liver and the tissues for further use. Where there is a deficiency of iron sufficient haemoglobin is not produced, and the body suffers from oxygen shortage which reveals itself as anaemia. The signs and symptoms of anaemia indicate the effect of oxygen shortage on a variety of cell processes: lassitude, giddiness, headache, sleeplessness, breathlessness on exertion, poor appetite, dim vision and stomach upsets.

Dietary deficiency of iron has caused such widespread ill-health and resultant loss of work that legislation in UK and USA was required to ensure the addition of iron to flour, since bread is a major staple in the diet. Now cereals provide about a third of the total iron intake, a quarter from meat and the rest from vegetables. Even foods which are rich in iron contain only small quantities. Cooking in iron pots and pans is said to increase the iron content of food.

Good sources of iron are black pudding, ox kidney, pigs' liver, sheep's kidney and liver, calf liver, corned beef, chicken liver and ox liver. Curry powder, once used mainly in Indian dishes and now used in a popular alternative to plain mince on many school menus, is amazingly rich in iron, and contains more than any other food mentioned here. Cocoa and treacle, which are also popular items in the diet of young children, are good sources of iron. Other sources are beef, lamb, chicken, pork, canned sardines, eggs, herrings, salmon, haddock, parsley, oatmeal, wholemeal flour, dried apricots, prunes, dates and blackcurrants. Vitamin C aids the absorption of iron in the body. Phytic acid, which occurs in the outer husks of cereals, interferes with the absorption of iron and may cause iron deficiency in people who have chapattis (flat cakes made from wholemeal cereals) as a major item in their diet. Chapattis are often eaten as an accompaniment to curry dishes but could negate the benefit of the iron-rich substance.

Requirements of iron differ according to age and sex. Women of reproductive age need more iron than men to replace the loss in menstruation. Pregnant and nursing women have a greater need of iron than other women, as do adolescents. Babies usually have stores of iron in their livers, if their mothers have had a sensible, nutritious diet during pregnancy and childbirth, and this suffices in the first few weeks of life when milk is their sole food. As milk is deficient in iron, it is useful to include egg yolk in the first weaning foods. It is easily taken in liquid form and can be absorbed by the baby's immature digestive system. Later, foods like sieved green vegetables and strained chopped liver can be given as iron sources. Some baby cereals have iron and vitamins added to their contents to increase their nutritional value.

Iodine and fluorine. These are sometimes described as trace elements. *Iodine* is an essential nutrient as it is required for thyroxine, the hormone secreted by the thyroid gland. Minute amounts of iodine are needed and it can be obtained from seafoods. Seaweed is rich in iodine and in some parts of the UK, cooked seaweed, known as laverbread, is regarded as nutritious food.

Fluorine is usually supplied in drinking water or in some toothpastes. It is known to prevent dental decay in children, but only during the period of teeth development.

Vitamins

Until the beginning of this century, it was assumed that a diet which contained adequate amounts of protein for growth, and fats and carbohydrates for warmth and energy, was sufficient. However, the prevalence of scurvy among sailors and its resolution upon obtaining citrus fruits in port led to the recognition of accessory food factors – vitamins.

Vitamins are now known to be essential for adequate growth and functioning of body systems. They may be water soluble or fat soluble.

Vitamin A. Vitamin A (chemical name *retinol*) is fat soluble and thus found in fish liver oils (halibut and cod), sheep and ox liver, butter, margarine (to which vitamin A is now added artificially), cheese and eggs. Carrots, tomatoes, spinach and cabbage (in that order) contain large amounts of carotene, which is converted into retinol and makes them good sources of vitamin A. Watercress, a popular sandwich filler which can be grown quite easily by the children in the nursery, is a very rich source of this vitamin. Dried apricots, often used as an accompaniment to semolina or rice pudding, are also an excellent source of carotene.

In the British diet, two-thirds of the intake of vitamin A comes from retinol (in animal sources) and one third from carotene (milk and vegetables).

Vitamin A is required for good vision, particularly the ability of the eye to adjust to dim light after exposure to bright light. This is a function of the retina, the light-sensitive organ at the back of the eye, hence the name of retinol given to vitamin A. Healthy skin and mucous membranes (tissues which line the mouth and alimentary tract and secrete a sticky protective substance called mucus) also require vitamin A for maintenance. When the teeth are formed in infancy, vitamin A is required for the formation of enamel, the hard outer covering of teeth. Resistance to infection is known to be promoted by vitamin A hence its title 'the anti-infective vitamin'.

Where the diet has been adequate, the liver should have a store of vitamin A to last up to 2 years, so it is usually only after this period that deficiency symptoms will appear. Rarely, an overdose of vitamin A can occur, particularly where mothers insist on exceeding the prescribed dosage of halibut liver oil, for example. Instead of drops, the child may be given spoonfuls. The extra vitamin A accumulates in the liver and may cause dry, itchy skin, vomiting and painful swelling of the limbs.

Vitamin B. The vitamin B group comprises several vitamins with a different chemical structure but similar functions in the body. They are all concerned with the release of energy from food and assist enzyme activity. As they are water soluble, they are not stored in the body and excess is excreted through the kidneys as urine. A regular and adequate supply of these vitamins is therefore necessary. Thiamine, riboflavin, nicotinic acid, pyridoxine, cyanocobalamin, pantothenic acid, biotin and folic acid will be considered separately.

Thiamine (vitamin B_1) plays an essential part in the normal functioning of nervous tissue and forms part of the enzyme required for the utilization of carbohydrate. The greater the consumption of carbohydrate the more thiamine is needed. Unfortunately most of the thiamine available in wheat is lost during the baking process used to produce white bread. It is therefore a legal requirement in Britain that all flour except wholemeal should be fortified with thiamine and since bread forms a major staple in the British diet adequate supplies of the vitamin should be available in daily bread supplies. Cornflakes also have thiamine added and other major sources are potatoes and milk. Yeast extract and Marmite are rich in this vitamin. Moist heat during baking can destroy 20–30% of the thiamine present in flour. Cakes made with baking powder may lose all their thiamine content through interaction with this.

Riboflavin (vitamin B_2) has a similar function to thiamine, although there is little relationship between the individual's energy requirements and the amount of riboflavin required. About one-third of the average intake of riboflavin in Britain is derived from milk. It should be noted that riboflavin is destroyed by ultraviolet light and milk left exposed to direct sunlight for $3\frac{1}{2}$ hours will lose its riboflavin content. Rich sources of riboflavin are yeast extract, liver, kidney, meat extract (Bovril, Oxo), fortified cornflakes and eggs. Deficiency of riboflavin is associated with sores at the corner of the mouth and redness of the tongue and eyes. There may be a check on growth and lesions on the lips.

Nicotinic acid (vitamin B_3) has similar functions to vitamin B_1. The amino acid tryptophan can be converted to nicotinic acid in the body, hence a diet which contains foods rich in this substance, e.g. eggs and milk, can compensate for the lack of nicotinic acid intake. Nicotinic acid is not available to man in the form in which it is found in cereals, therefore amounts have to be added to flour synthetically. Approximately 25% of the total intake of this vitamin is provided in the British diet by bread and flour products. The major sources are meat extract, Marmite, liver, kidney, chicken, beef, pork, canned salmon, herring, cod, wholemeal bread. Peas and beans are a useful vegetable source, and fortified breakfast cereals provide some of this vitamin in a convenient food.

Pyridoxine (vitamin B_6) is involved in the metabolism of amino acids and requirements are thus related to protein content of the diet. This vitamin is also required for the formation of haemoglobin. Liver, bran, wheatgerm and wholemeal flour, fish and eggs are all good sources of pyridoxine. Deficiency diseases associated with this vitamin are rare. Infants fed on milk powders deficient in pyridoxine were found to suffer from convulsions but responded rapidly to doses of the vitamin. The precise function of vitamin B_6 has not yet been fully established.

Cyanocobalamin (vitamin B_{12}) contains the trace element cobalt (hence its name) and is essential for the formation of red blood cells. It is found mainly in liver, fish, milk, eggs, cheese, beef, lamb and pork. As it does not occur in vegetable foods, vegans (vegetarians who live on a strict diet without meat, fish, eggs, and milk) may suffer from a deficiency. A substance known as the 'intrinsic factor' which is found in the stomach and is essential for the absorption of vitamin B_{12} may be lacking in people who suffer from pernicious anaemia, which is the deficiency disease associated with lack of cyanocobalamin. Pernicious anaemia used to be fatal but is now treated with injections of vitamin B_{12}.

Pantothenic acid, like other B group vitamins, forms part of the enzymes used in metabolism. It is found in liver, kidney, yeast, egg yolk, cereals and leguminous vegetables (i.e. peas, beans). Pantothenic acid is so widely distributed in foods that there is no danger of deficiency.

Biotin also acts like a co-enzyme and is found mainly in offal and egg yolk. Smaller amounts are obtainable from milk, dairy products, cereals, fish and bananas. Distribution is wide and there is no likelihood of deficiency.

Folic acid is required for production of

normal red blood cells as in cyanocobalamin. It is found particularly in offal (liver, kidney), spinach, broccoli tops and fish. Other sources are peas, beans, cabbage, lettuce, wholemeal bread, bananas, oranges, beef and eggs. Folic acid is destroyed in cooking, so care should be taken to ensure adequate sources of this vitamin in the diet. Elderly people and pregnant women who have an inadequate diet over a period of time may suffer from a type of anaemia which is associated with folic acid deficiency. It is called megaloblastic anaemia and refers to the process by which red blood cells mature, which is interrupted if insufficient folic acid is consumed.

Nutritional anaemia is caused by lack of iron in the diet. Signs and symptoms are paleness of mucous membranes, conjunctiva and skin, fatigue, breathlessness on exertion, fainting, lethargy, frequent colds and lack of appetite.

By the age of 6 months, the store of iron in the baby's liver is running low and neither human nor modified dried milk feeds contain enough for his needs. Weaning foods rich in iron, such as egg yolk, are suitable for babies, but many mothers persist in providing cereals as the first weaning food. Health visitors accept this, but suggest that mother should use only fortified cereals which contain iron and vitamins. A minority of children are allergic to eggs, so other foods rich in iron can be used for later stages of weaning – red meat, liver and kidneys can be sieved, minced or grated. Sieved green vegetables and oatmeal in porridge can also be given. Where eggs are acceptable, they can be given in various forms to babies and young children – lightly boiled or scrambled for breakfast, poached eggs with baked beans for lunch or a snack, or eggs with cheese for supper (not all on the same day!). Liver with bacon is often popular with young children and liver is rich in iron. A cup of cocoa makes a nutritious drink as cocoa contains iron and milk is as good source of protein, calcium, phosphorus, carbohydrate and fats.

Vitamin C is essential for the absorption of iron and can be readily obtained in rosehip or blackcurrant juice, oranges, lemons and grapefruits. Children are often given drinks rich in vitamin C as accompaniment to meals, or for in-between-meals drinks.

A well balanced diet with adequate amounts of protein, fats, carbohydrates, vitamins and minerals, opportunity for a controlled amount of exercise in fresh air, adequate sleep and rest, suitable clothing, footwear, and a loving secure environment are also essential for treatment of anaemia.

Vitamin C. Vitamin C (ascorbic acid) is necessary for the maintenance of healthy connective tissue, the proper formation of teeth, bones and blood vessels, growth processes and absorption of iron. It is also involved in the clotting of blood and promotes healing of wounds. Ascorbic acid is found mainly in fruit and vegetables. As it is water soluble and destroyed by heat, prolonged cooking of vegetables and drying processes can remove the vitamin C content altogether. Dried peas, beans and dried fruit do not contain any ascorbic acid.

The richest sources of vitamin C are blackcurrants, rosehip syrup, strawberries, oranges, lemons and grapefruit (citrus fruits), and pineapple. Cabbage, cauliflower, brussels sprouts and spinach all contain large amounts of vitamin C in the raw state, but after cooking these are considerably reduced. To avoid loss of this vitamin in cooking, vegetables should preferably be steamed with the minimum quantity of water. Vegetables and fruit should not be crushed or finely chopped before cooking and a sharp knife is preferable for cutting as a blunt knife causes loss of vitamin C.

Placing vegetables in boiling water and cooking for as short a period as possible also helps to retain vitamin C content. Bicarbonate of soda should never be added to fruit or vegetables in cooking as the alkaline conditions created destroy the ascorbic acid. When cooked, foods should not be kept hot for longer than a few minutes, as 25% of ascorbic acid in cooked food is lost if the food is kept hot for 15 minutes. Food in restaurants and canteens which is cooked from a central kitchen and kept hot for long periods before serving will obviously have little ascorbic acid content left.

Watercress, which is eaten raw, is an excellent source of vitamin C. Fresh peas and new potatoes contain this vitamin and since large quantities of potatoes are eaten in Britain they constitute an important source of this vitamin. Raw cabbage is a much better source of ascorbic acid than lettuce. It is also cheaper and when served with grated carrot can make an acceptable salad. Tomatoes are often included in salads and they too are a useful source of vitamin C. Raw bananas, apples, pears and plums are moderately good sources but storage and cooking affect their vitamin content. Blackcurrant jam and plum tarts would not be regarded as useful sources of vitamin C.

Cows' milk has less ascorbic acid than human milk and some is destroyed during pasteurization. Exposure to sunlight, which as we have already noted destroys the riboflavin content, also reduces the ascorbic acid content. It is important that babies on milk diets should be provided with other sources of this vitamin, such as concentrated orange juice, rose hip or blackcurrant juice. Canned and bottled orange juice can retain their ascorbic acid content as long as the container is kept closed. Once opened, the vitamin content can be reduced by 50% within a week. Supplementary doses of vitamin C are also given in iron-deficiency anaemia, because of its function in aiding the absorption of iron.

Scurvy is the deficiency disease associated with lack of vitamin C in the diet. This disease is characterized by weakness, swelling and bleeding of the gums, bleeding under the skin and slow healing wounds. Scurvy in infants is associated with tenderness and pain in the lower limbs and changes in bone structure. Scurvy is not common in this country but occasionally mild deficiencies may occur in infants who are given cows' milk preparations without supplements, in elderly people living on poor diets, and in 'health food' addicts who eat mainly whole cereals which contain no vitamin C.

Vitamin D. Vitamin D is essential for the absorption of calcium and phosphorus which are needed for the formation of bones and teeth. It is fat soluble and found only in animal food products. Fatty fish such as halibut and cod are the most important natural sources of this vitamin and as it is stored in the liver, liver oils used to be the form in which babies and children were given vitamin D supplement. Nowadays vitamin supplements are usually given in one preparation which includes vitamins A, D and C. Herrings, kippers, salmon and sardines also contain good supplies of vitamin D. Margarine has vitamin D added artificially and contains more than butter. Egg yolk contributes only a small quantity of vitamin D to the diet. Milk in summer contains more vitamin D than in winter, but there is insufficient in milk and it is not regarded as a good source.

Vitamin D is also obtained from the action of sunlight on a substance called ergosterol in the skin and most people obtain all they need from this source. However, children, pregnant and lactating mothers, elderly people on inadequate diets and others who live in areas where sunlight is masked by pollution, or where custom decrees clothing as protection from sunlight, e.g. in Asian communities, all require adequate intake of vitamin D in the diet.

Lack of vitamin D causes *rickets* in children and osteomalacia in adults hence its name 'the anti-rachitic vitamin'. Without vitamin D, calcium cannot be absorbed properly in the body and thus bones and teeth do not develop. Rickets was a very common disease in this country at the beginning of this century and although rare nowadays outbreaks can still occur due to overcrowding in industrial areas, deprivation of sunlight and inadequate diets. Children under 2 years of age are at risk as the first 2 years of life are the most rapid period of growth and the bones therefore require more vitamin D.

The signs and symptoms of rickets are irritability, restlessness, painful bones and joints, diarrhoea, colic and chest infections. Slow dentition and dental decay may also be characteristic signs. The bones are not formed correctly, often they are soft and when weight is put upon them, e.g. as in legs when the child begins to walk, they become misshapen. Bowlegs may develop and the bony pelvis may be flattened (with serious implications for future childbearing in girls). The ribs may have bumps at the end known as 'the rickety rosary' and the child may become 'pigeon chested'. Where the child is crawling, pressure on the arms and hands causes widening of the wrist bones. Delayed closure of the anterior fontanelle may occur in a young baby affected by rickets. The anterior fontanelle is usually closed by 12 months nowadays. Growth is generally stunted as a result of rickets. A well balanced diet with adequate amounts of calcium, phosphorus, vitamins A, D, and C, plus fresh air, sunlight, adequate rest, sleep and exercise should prevent the occurrence of rickets. Excessive carbohydrates can hinder the absorption of essential minerals and vitamins and should be avoided. The pregnant and breast-feeding mother should have a sensible diet with vitamin supplements to provide a good foundation for the baby's growth and development.

Osteomalacia is the adult deficiency disease due to lack of vitamin D. In this condition, calcium is actually lost from the bones which become soft as a result. It is found most commonly in women who have lived on a poor diet and have had frequent pregnancies. The development of the fetus requires increased calcium and the woman's own body supplies become depleted to allow for this. A good diet with plenty of milk and dairy products to supply calcium and eggs to provide vitamin D is necessary to compensate for this and to prevent osteomalacia.

Overdosage of vitamin D is rare but it can occur where control is not exercised over supplements given to children. Too much vitamin D causes more calcium to be absorbed than can be excreted. The excess is then deposited in the kidneys where it can cause damage.

Vitamin E. This fat-soluble vitamin is found in vegetable oils, cereal products and eggs. It is an antioxidant, but its function is not yet fully known.

Vitamin K. This is also fat soluble and is required for the clotting of blood. It can only be absorbed in the presence of bile salts. It is found in spinach, cabbage, cauliflower, peas and cereals. Lack of vitamin K can occur in newly born, breast-fed babies and causes haemorrhagic jaundice of the newborn which occurs in about one in 400 babies.

Vitamin supplements. These are usually given to children under 5 years of age. Breast and cow's milk both contain sufficient vitamin A and B but insufficient vitamin D. Powdered milks are fortified with vitamin D and baby cereals now have vitamin D added. A danger of over dosage was possible when babies were given supplements to fortified milk and cereal and consequently artificial milk powders for babies had the vitamin D content reduced. Concentrated drops of vitamins A and D are often given instead of fish liver oils, and babies started on supplies from a few days after birth. At first the amount is minute as the baby sucks on a teaspoon from which the oil has been poured back into the bottle. Gradually it is increased to one teaspoonful each day. Oil should not be put in the bottle if the baby is bottle fed since it may not mix with the milk and stick to the sides of the bottle. Double doses should not be given to compensate for a missed dose.

Vitamin C supplement is necessary for babies fed on cows' milk as it does not contain enough for their requirements, and boiling and other preparatory processes destroy the vitamin C content. Orange juice is usually given as vitamin C supplement but rose hip syrup and blackcurrant juice are also popular. Concentrated fruit juices are diluted with boiled water which has been cooled before mixing to prevent loss of vitamin C due to heat. As vitamin C is rapidly destroyed by exposure to air, all preparations of fresh fruit juice should be given to the baby after mixing, not stored after preparation. Fresh orange juice can be used but it may need to be strained first. Orange squash does not contain vitamin C and should not be used for babies, but canned and frozen orange juice is a satisfactory source. Although rose hip syrup contains more vitamin C than orange juice, it is very sweet and should not be given in undiluted form on a dummy as this can cause tooth decay. It is better to give rose hip and blackcurrant juice as drinks and they should never be used as comforters with a miniature feeder to soothe a child at bedtime.

Water

This is essential for life as the body cannot survive without it for more than a few days. It provides the medium in which all body cells function and about two-thirds of the body is water. Water is required for the formation of blood, for transport of nutrients throughout the body and for protein, fats and carbohydrate metabolism. The end-products of glucose metabolism are carbon dioxide and water but the total amount produced from oxidation of foodstuffs is inadequate for bodily needs and therefore major supplies are obtained from water, beverages and solid food with a high water content.

Service of Food

Food which is attractively presented stimulates the appetite, and the flow of saliva and gastric juice subsequently aids digestion. Good health with adequate fresh air, exercise, rest and sleep are essential prerequisites for a healthy appetite. When children feel slightly unwell, a colourful meal well cooked with varied tastes and textures, presented in small portions, can often encourage them to eat instead of refuse. The routine of regular meal times and a happy family atmosphere for their service can often make children feel emotionally secure and aids their social development. If young children are allowed to eat at the same time as the rest of the family, they can gain through the interaction in language development and learn acceptable behaviour and 'good manners' naturally.

Food Requirements

Food requirements vary according to age, sex, size, occupation and climate. Tables of recommended intakes which are produced by DHSS (or Scottish Home and Health Department, SHHD) are not the same as requirements, which are usually less than the amounts given to meet

Table 4.1   Recommended daily intake of energy

Age range	Body weight in kilograms	Energy requirements kcals	Energy requirements kJ
Boys and Girls			
0–1 year	7.3	800	3 300
1–2 years	11.4	1 200	5 000
2–3 years	13.5	1 400	5 900
3–5 years	16.5	1 600	6 700
5–7 years	20.5	1 800	7 500
7–9 years	25.1	2 100	8 800
Boys			
9–12 years	31.9	2 500	10 500
12–15 years	45.5	2 800	11 700
15–18 years	61.0	3 000	12 600
Girls			
9–12 years	33.0	2 300	9 600
12–15 years	48.6	2 300	9 600
15–18 years	56.1	2 300	9 600
Men			
18–35 years			
Sedentary	65.0	2 700	11 300
Moderately active	65.0	3 000	12 600
Very active	65.0	3 600	15 100
65–75 years			
Sedentary	65.0	2 600	10 900
Moderately active	65.0	2 900	12 100
Very active	65.0	3 600	15 100
65–75 years			
Sedentary life	63.0	2 350	9 800
75 and over	63.0	2 100	8 800
Women			
18–55 years			
Most occupations	55.0	2 200	9 200
Very active	55.0	2 500	10 500
55–75 years			
Sedentary life	53.0	2 050	8 600
75 and over	53.0	1 900	8 000
Pregnancy 3–9 months		2 400	10 000
Lactation		2 700	11 300

'the nutritional needs of practically all healthy persons in a population'. The recommendations refer to food that is actually eaten and as all the nutrients can be stored in the body for at least a few days, it is not essential to consume the recommended intake everyday.

Developmental changes affecting nutritional requirements

In infancy and childhood rapid growth must be met by large supplies of proteins, calcium and iron for all tissues, bones and blood cell formation. Vitamin supplements of A and D are required to ensure that deficiency does not occur and affect growth processes. Children growing up in poor industrial areas may lack the opportunity to gain vitamin D through sunlight. The diet may have an excessive carbohydrate and fat content, which is easier and cheaper to supply than protein foods, and there may be little or no fresh fruit and fresh vegetables available to supply vitamin C which also plays a part in growth and is essential for the absorption of iron. Vitamin C supplement will therefore be necessary.

Adolescence. The final growth spurt may lead to demands for more energy foods, mainly carbohydrate and the diet must be controlled to ensure adequate supplies of protein, fats, minerals and vitamins are available. Excess carbohydrate hinders the absorption of mineral salts and vitamins, exacerbates the common teenage condition of acne and may cause obesity with possible adverse emotional effects.

Adulthood. The need for adequate supplies of iron in the diet has already been explained. It has particular significance for women as their haemoglobin levels (13 mg/100 ml of blood) are lower than men (15 mg/100 ml of blood) due to monthly blood loss in menstruation. In pregnancy the fetus will take the iron and calcium it requires for development from the mother's stores even if this depletes her supply for her own needs. A well balanced diet rich in these should be taken by the pregnant woman and sometimes iron and folic acid supplements may be given to compensate for the baby's demands. Proteins should be taken in larger quantities than carbohydrates and fats as they cannot be stored. During lactation (breast feeding) the mother's store of nutrients is again depleted as the baby obtains his nutritional supplies from her, and the diet should compensate for this.

Old age. The appetite is usually lessened as people grow older and their daily intake is reduced. It is however important for elderly people who are living at home in retirement to obtain an adequate diet with first and second class protein and iron, as many can suffer from nutritional anaemia due to a disinclination to cook or prepare foods, and a tendency to miss meals or merely pick at foods.

Customs

Customs and religious taboos can have considerable effects on diet. Asian communities tend to have rice (polished) as a staple item, which may cause deficiency of vitamin B. They regularly eat chappatis, made from high-extraction wheat-flour rich in phytate, which apart from preventing absorption of iron has also been blamed as the cause of the high incidence of rickets in Asian children in the late 1970s. A number of rickets prevention programmes have been successful in encouraging Asian mothers to give their children vitamin supplements which are available free at Health Board clinics. The ingestion of pork is taboo for religious Jews and Muslims, as is beef for Hindus. Some Jews will not accept food unless it is 'Kosher', and similarly, some Muslims will refuse to eat all types of meat unless it has been ritually slaughtered using the 'Halal' method. Otherwise mutton is usually a common choice for these families, as it is cheaper than lamb, but as it is more difficult for children to digest they could suffer from anaemia due to lack of red meat in their diet.

Vegetarian and Chinese foods have a high fibre content which avoids constipation but results in low weight gain, which occasionally leads to lightweight people of small stature. Vegetarian diets may sometimes lead to deficiency diseases as they lack first class protein in meat, fish and eggs, but combining different pulses and grains can overcome this problem. In vegan diets eggs, cheese and milk are excluded, which means that the diet is low in cholesterol but without the binding agents, so the stools tend to be liquid. This means that the necessary absorption of essential nutrients does not always take place.

and curry is a welcome addition to school menus. In Afro-Asian cultures, milk, orange juice, lemonade and blackcurrant juice are considered to aggravate coughs and colds, and parents may write to the teachers forbidding them to give these to their children. Appreciation of diverse customs is required of all who look after children in muticultural societies.

A Guide to Infant Feeding

This guideline should help mothers to provide an adequate and nourishing diet, as well as a happy feeding experience for their infants.

Stage One

The baby's diet for the first stage (Table 4.2) consists of either breast milk or milk mixture, with the introduction of vitamins A, C and D at about 4 weeks of age (breast fed only).

Table 4.2   Example of feeding routine

6 a.m.	Breast or bottle feed
10 a.m.	Breast or bottle feed, plus vitamins A, C and D
2 p.m.	Breast or bottle feed
6 p.m.	Breast or bottle feed
10 p.m.	Breast or bottle feed
Unsweetened boiled water at any time.	

Second Stage – When to Start Weaning

When baby is about 3–4 months old, mixed feeding may start with the introduction of one or two small teaspoonfuls of iron-fortified cereal at one feed per day (Table 4.3). Cereals are usually readily accepted by infants, though, occasionally, the new taste causes initial refusal. If this should happen with cereal, or any of the foods subsequently offered, they should be discontinued for a week or two and tried again. Of course, no foods should be forced, and the spitting out of food when first offered is very common. Cereals should not be put into the bottle as the milk will taste different and the baby may refuse his feed.

The baby's diet must always include the basic nutrients – proteins, fat, carbohydrates, minerals and vitamins. To begin with, these nutrients are provided by milk feeds, but as weaning progresses the baby learns to enjoy the basic ingredients of a balanced diet in more 'grown-up' forms and flavours.

Table 4.3 Example of feeding pattern

6 a.m.	Breast or bottle feed
*10 a.m.	Breast or bottle feed, plus one teaspoonful cereal or fruit as advised
2 p.m.	Breast or bottle feed
*6 p.m.	Breast or bottle feed, vitamin supplement given once daily
10 p.m.	Breast or bottle feed

*Interchangeable if the baby is more hungry at 6 p.m. than at 10 a.m.

Table 4.4 Example of feeds at 4–6 months of age

6 a.m.	Breast or bottle feed
10 a.m.	Cereal or fruit, plus vitamin A, C and D drops followed by breast or bottle feed
2 p.m.	Select from: soup or creamed vegetable, egg yolk, fish, minced liver, finely grated cheese, fruit, minced chicken, minced kidney, mixed green vegetables
	Breast or bottle feed may now be substituted with water or fruit juice when a larger solid feed has been taken
6 p.m.	Breast or bottle feed, plus fruit if hungry
10 p.m.	Breast or bottle feed may well be discontinued before 6 months of age

At this early stage of weaning, all foods should be offered to the baby in mashed or puréed form (by rubbing through a sieve), and should not include fried or spiced foods, sugar or salt. All meals must be closely supervised. A baby must never be left while feeding.

If your baby is becoming too fat, you may be advised by your doctor or health visitor not to give cereal as a 'starter' but to offer fruit or vegetables instead.

As you can see from Table 4.3, milk should continue to be baby's main food and new tastes are introduced in small quantities in order to educate the baby's palate as well as to give him extra nourishment.

When solids are introduced at two feeds in the day you may find the baby enjoys them best when they are given at the 10 a.m. and 6 p.m. feeds.

Never leave the baby while he is feeding from a bottle.

At 4–6 Months

During this time, solids may be very gradually introduced at other feeds until, at 6 months of age, your infant is having three small meals a day (Table 4.4). The quantities used at each meal may vary according to the individual needs of the baby. As the amount of solid food taken increases, there will be a reduction in the amount of milk consumed, but this should never be less than 1 pint per day. One milk feed may be discontinued, e.g. at 2 p.m., when water or fruit juice may be offered instead from a cup.

A wide range of foods may be offered at this stage (excluding fats, fried foods and highly seasoned foods). As was suggested earlier, in this first stage, food should be puréed, then towards the age of 6 months the baby may accept slightly thicker foods, and perhaps a hard toasted crust may be enjoyed. Soft-boiled egg yolk, which is a good source of iron, should be introduced sparingly and gradually from about the age of 4 months.

At about 9–10 Months of Age (or sometimes earlier)

Now the baby will enjoy using his fingers to feed himself. This will be fun for the mother and the baby if mother can accept the baby's needs to learn and enjoy self-feeding. This is a messy, but very necessary, process! A pelican bib is useful to catch food items.

About 1 Year of Age

Now the baby can join in in family meals, but should not be expected to manipulate the spoon correctly until he is nearer 18 months of age, nor should he be expected to have a sophisticated standard of table manners. Child-sized cutlery and a dish with straight sides will help him to eat more easily.

At the age of 1 year it is recommended that milk drinks be changed from dried or modified milk to cows' milk (preferably pasteurized).

There is less need to mince food, soft casseroles of meat and fish can be given.

At 11–12 months, drinks of milk or water from a cup should be encouraged.

To encourage a good feeding pattern, eating between meals should be discouraged. This particularly applies to biscuits, sweets, and sweet drinks. Apart from fattening qualities of these foods, they encourage dental decay. Normal foods can be given at normal times.

Some fruit or vegetable should be offered if a child is hungry, e.g. a piece of peeled apple, as this helps to keep their teeth clean and sharp. As with all foods babies should not be left alone with this in case they choke. Give large pieces

Table 4.5   Example of feeding at 6–12 months of age

6 a.m.	Drink of fruit juice or water
Breakfast	Select from the following: egg, fruit, cereal, bacon, fish, finger of bread or toast, plus bottle or breast feed
Mid-morning Lunch (select from)	Drink and A, C and D vitamin drops
	Vegetable, meat, fish, soup, egg, cheese, fruit, milk pudding, water or juice to drink from a cup
Tea (select from)	Egg, cheese, finger of toast with Marmite, cheese spread, honey; hard crust to chew; fruit, e.g. mashed banana; milk to drink

they cannot choke on, and ensure that there are no pips or stones in the fruit.

At the toddler stage, mother sometimes has to deal patiently with food refusal. If this persists, her doctor or health visitor will be glad to help.

Vitamin Supplements

These are given to breast-fed babies, as human milk has very little vitamin C, A and D. (Modified milk feeds usually have added vitamins and minerals.) Vitamin C is readily obtained in fresh orange juice, but nowadays drops containing vitamins A, D and C are usually given to both breast-fed and bottle-fed babies. The drops daily can be given on a spoon from the first month, increasing slowly to the full dose of seven drops daily for babies on breast milk. If fed on fortified milk, two drops daily should be given at 1 month, increasing to four drops at 4 months. The full dose of seven drops should only be given when bottle feeding stops.

Feeding Problems

The baby who is constantly screaming could have a feeding problem, but other possible reasons, such as gastroenteritis, otitis media, intussusception or nappy rash should be excluded first by reference to the GP or Health Visitor.

1   *Underfeeding.* Possible causes include:
Physiological (e.g. cleft palate)
Poor feeding technique (breast feeding posture, bottle feeding difficulty)
Oral thrush
Sore nipples
Engorgement
Poor feeder (e.g. sleepy baby)
Poor sucker (e.g. premature baby)
Not enough feeds per 24 hours
Not enough milk per feed

2   *Overfeeding.* Possible causes include:
Wrongly made up feeds
Too many feeds per 24 hours
Too much at each feed
Greedy baby
Milk given as 'drink'
Cereal added to bottles

3   *'Colic'.* Possible causes include:
Constipation
Air swallowing

4   *Teething.* This could be a cause, but this normal part of physical development should not be blamed exclusively for all the baby's discomforts and ills.

5   *Failure to thrive.* This could be a feeding problem, and possible causes include:
Underfeeding (see above)
Pathological/anatomical: jaundice, congenital defect, infections
Sociological factors: marriage problems, unwanted baby, lack of stimulation, lack of continuity in care (mother in hospital, broken home)

6   *Maternal anxieties*:
Guilt: bottle versus breast, previous cot death, career or job (using au pair, nanny or childminder)
Insecurity/inexperience: age, lack of support (from professionals or family), domestic problems
Failure to thrive (see above).

7   *Vomiting/possetting* (causes due to infection excluded by GP). Possible causes include:
Overfeeding (see above)
Over-rich formula (making feeds up incorrectly)
Milk intolerance: milk protein intolerance, carbohydrate intolerance
Air swallowing
Poor hygiene

8   *Diarrhoea.* Possible causes include:
Maternal diet in breast feeding
Badly balanced artificial feeds
Overfeeding (see above)
Poor hygiene
Teething

9   *Colour of stools* may be due to:
Chemical reaction from formula milk
Introduction of solids

Changes from one milk to another
Overfeeding (see above)
Underfeeding (see above).

Overweight and underweight

The importance of good nutrition is now better understood by more people, due to the influence of television, popular newspapers and journals. Many people are still obese, and vast fortunes are spent on 'the slimming business'. Anorexia nervosa, in which the goal becomes slimming at the expense of good health, is also frequently seen. These are obviously two conditions which are peculiar to societies where more than basic food supplies are available and where people use eating (or not eating) for psychological reasons rather than physical necessity.

Obesity is a disease of malnutrition, in that the body has an excessive intake far more than its energy output requires and this is converted into fat. A person is regarded as obese if they are 10% above the standard weight for their height and frame. Hereditary factors may play a part in obesity, but environmental factors are more important. Family eating habits influence the amount of food children consume and many babies are overfed in infancy. It is not yet proved that fat babies tend to become fat adults due to deposition of extra fat cells, but they may undergo psychological and emotional trauma in childhood and adolescence because of obesity. Physically, there is a greater risk of metabolic, respiratory and cardiovascular disorders in obesity and a tendency to 'accident-proneness'. Fat babies are often acceptable as adults find them attractive and there is still the mistaken attitude that a fat baby is a healthy baby, but fat children often suffer from taunts of other children and may be less popular as they will find participation in vigorous activity more difficult than other children.

Weaning babies on to cereal can often lead to obesity, and respiratory difficulties are sometimes another unfortunate consequence suffered by babies and young children whose first and major solid food is carbohydrate. Contrary to popular opinion fat people are not always jolly – many become depressed as propaganda for slimness increases in intensity. Paradoxically they find solace for their unhappiness in further eating and so the obesity pattern continues.

Weaning

The commonest reason for starting solid foods as given by mothers is the baby's apparent hunger. Bottle-fed babies are usually weaned before breast-fed babies (on average 2 months to 14 weeks). This may be because the breast-fed baby sucks harder when he is hungry and stimulates the production of more milk. Vomiting, low weight gain, the desire to make the baby sleep through the night, feeding difficulties and advice from friends and relations are also given as reasons.

Adequate milk during the day should make a baby sleep well, but there are many reasons why he might not sleep well and feeding him with solids will not provide the solution. Extra milk should be sufficient for the first few weeks. If weaning takes place before 4 months the danger of food allergies with eggs, fish and gluten are greater, but some babies are also allergic to cows' milk. The baby may have difficulty in feeding from a spoon and suffer from deficiencies if weaning is delayed for longer than 4 months. From the age of 6 months the baby needs foods for biting to encourage teething and the opportunity to develop the skills of feeding himself from a spoon and drinking from a cup.

Early weaning may be advised for pre-term, low-weight babies who will require iron supplements from 2 or 3 weeks of age. Unfortunately, solid foods tend to contain more sodium and protein than immature kidneys can cope with and dehydration may occur after an illness with possible effects of convulsions, brain damage and death. It is wrong to interpret all the baby's cries as caused by hunger; they could be due to thirst, discomfort, being too hot or cold or simply a cry for attention! Many mothers still answer a cry with more food or artificial milk and increase the load on the baby's digestive system. Salt and sugar should *never* be added to infant food as these can upset the fluid and salt balance.

The object of introducing solid foods apart from provision of iron is to introduce a variety of tastes and textures to the baby. Starch foods like cereals do not provide this, and their exclusive use can prove harmful as they are fattening and obese babies are more prone to illnesses. New tastes should be introduced gradually a little at a time on a coloured, plastic spoon, as this gives novelty which the baby enjoys. One taste at a time after his milk feed may be appropriate. It is important that the mother does not show anxiety at refusal.

At *3 or 4 months of age* the baby's taste buds have not fully developed and he is learning to acquire likes and dislikes. He also learns that there is a great adult interest in his reaction to new foods and always a response when he spits food out! Egg yolk is easily introduced as a first source of iron. Strained liver and vegetables can be bought and are a useful convenience, but many tinned foods contain cereal. Many mothers nowadays have a liquidizer–blender which enables them to utilize food prepared for the rest of the family. Mashed potatoes and gravy, shredded steak and liver, chicken, fish in milk sauce, sieved stewed fruit and green vegetables are all easily prepared and provide the baby with essential nutrients. If the baby has an infection, or is suffering from the effects of hot weather, it is better to delay the introduction of new foods. The baby's stools should be observed and if the child has *loose stools* or appears constipated the new food should be left out for a few days then introduced again with a small taste. Some babies still like to have their milk feed at bedtime during the weaning process and this should be given. It is better to introduce the first solids at the second feed of the day, as the baby will be impatient for his first feed. Water is needed as well when the baby is having much solid food.

Most of the food given to babies at 4 or 5 months will be smooth and free from lumps as their digestive system is unable to cope with these until they are 8 months old. At 4 months the baby does not have any teeth but usually bites on anything that reaches his mouth. He is able to chew at 6 months and can be given a crust, piece of apple or rusk at this stage. While he is able to hold it by himself at this age he should not be left alone while feeding in case he chokes on a large piece. With supervision, the baby will enjoy feeding himself and although he will make a mess at first, his self-confidence and interest in food is increased. If the mother has a teaspoon as well as the baby, she can give the baby food while he plays with his own spoon. Babies can usually drink from a cup at 6 months of age, although they only take 2 fluid ounces at mealtimes at first. It is useful to keep the breast or bottle as a milk supply for 12 months, as the baby has difficulty drinking from a cup in times of illness when his nose is blocked.

The child will be able to progress to an adult range of food by the age of 10–12 months but he will need a pint of milk every day for the first 2 years of life. Vitamin supplements should continue until the age of five.

Planning Menus for Children

Babies and young children have higher energy needs than older children as they are growing rapidly. Energy intakes are measured in kilocalories ('calories') or kilojoules. (1 kcal = 4.19 kj).

As protein is required for growth and vitamins are needed as essential factors in this and other processes, carbohydrates and fats are needed to provide energy, warmth and fat-soluble vitamins, minerals and water to maintain body fluid balance, a balanced diet is required containing

Table 4.6 Example of a midday meal which can be prepared by the children in the nursery

Savoury stuffed baked potatoes with salad
Instant Whip dessert with fresh fruit
Fresh orange juice

Savoury stuffed baked potatoes. Each child in the group cleans a medium sized potato and wraps it in cooking foil. The adult places wrapped potatoes in the oven for 1 hour. On removal children are shown how to scoop out centre of potato, mix it with 2 oz of grated cheese and raw tomato pulp. Children can use a grater and knives under supervision. The potato cases are then filled with the mixture and a slice of tomato placed on top. A salad is made from raw grated or sliced carrots, raw shredded cabbage, celery sticks and watercress. This gives an attractive, colourful and nutritious first course.

Cheese. Protein, calcium, phosphorus, vitamins A and D. Promotes growth and repair of tissues including bones and teeth.

Potato. Mainly starch, little protein, calcium and vitamin C. Provides energy and supports growth.

Tomato. Vitamins A and C, calcium. Helps growth and development, aids resistance to infection.

Carrots, cabbage, celery, watercress. Vitamins A, C, calcium. Celery in particular contains useful fibre for roughage.

Dessert. Instant Whip made with milk (this is often the only way some children will take milk) is easily mixed by a child. Fresh fruit as available may include apples and pears, sliced or cubed with skins (these provide roughage), raspberries and oranges. Milk provides protein, fat, carbohydrate, calcium, phosphorus, vitamins A and D, and is valuable for growth and repair of all tissues and resistance to infection. Fresh fruit provides vitamins A and C with calcium.

Fresh fruit juice. Either orange or blackcurrant can be made with a juice extractor and contains vitamin C for growth.

Table 4.7   Suitable foods for inclusion in nursery menus

Food	Amount 1 oz = 28 g 100 g = 3.5 oz	Content
Breakfast		
Cornflakes	104 kcal/oz 365 kcal/100 g	Mainly carbohydrate, small amount of protein, usually fortified with vitamin B
Oatmeal	113 kcal/oz 395 kcal/100 g	Less carbohydrate than cornflakes, more protein and fat, calcium, iron, vitamin B
Bread	72 kcal/oz 253 kcal/100 g	Carbohydrate, calcium with added traces of vitamin B and iron
Margarine	208 kcal/oz 728 kcal/100 g	Fat (vegetable, unsaturated) little calcium, vitamins A and D added
Butter	207 kcal/oz 724 kcal/100 g	Same fat content as margarine but animal saturated type. More calcium and vitamin A than margarine, less vitamin D
Milk	19 kcal/oz 66 kcal/100 g	Good source of calcium and vitamin A. No iron, traces of vitamins, contains proteins, fat, carbohydrate
Cocoa	126 kcal/oz 441 kcal/100 g	Mainly carbohydrate, contains calcium, iron, fat, protein, vitamin A, traces of vitamin B
Egg	45 kcal/oz 158 kcal/100 g	Protein, fat, calcium, vitamin A, traces of vitamins B and D and iron
Bacon	136 kcal/oz 476 kcal/100 g	Mainly fat, some calcium and protein, traces of vitamin B
Lunch		
Liver	244 kcal/oz 854 kcal/100 g	Protein, fat, carbohydrate, calcium, iron, vitamins A, B, C, little vitamin D. May need mincing or straining
Corned Beef	61 kcal/oz 216 kcal/100 g	Protein, fat, calcium, iron, vitamin B
Chicken	42 kcal/oz 148 kcal/100 g	Protein, little fat, calcium, vitamin B, trace of iron. Easily digested
Roast lamb	83 kcal/oz 291 kcal/100 g	Protein, fat, calcium, iron, vitamin B
Beef	63 kcal/oz 223 kcal/100 g	Stewing steak, highest in protein content. Contains less fat than liver or lamb, calcium, iron, traces of vitamin B
Pork sausage	104 kcal/oz 367 kcal/100 g	Mainly fat, some protein and carbohydrate, calcium, little iron, vitamin B
Cod, haddock, white fish	21 kcal/oz 76 kcal/100 g	Protein, little fat, calcium, vitamin B
Herrings	66 kcal/oz 234 kcal/100 g	More fat than protein, rich in vitamins A and D, some calcium, vitamin B
Brussel sprouts	7.4 kcal/oz 26 kcal/100 g	Little protein, carbohydrate, calcium, vitamins A and C
Cabbage (raw)	6 kcal/oz 22 kcal/100 g	Rich in calcium, vitamins A and C, some protein and carbohydrate. Boiling reduces all nutritional content
Carrots	6.5 kcal/oz 23 kcal/100 g	Carbohydrate, calcium, vitamin A, little vitamin C
Cauliflower	4 kcal/oz 13 kcal/100 g	Mainly water. Rich in vitamin C, some calcium, little vitamin A
Celery	2.2 kcal/oz 8 kcal/100 g	Mainly water, rich in calcium, some vitamin C
Lentils	84 kcal/oz 295 kcal/100 g	Mainly carbohydrate but good amount of protein, calcium, iron, vitamins A and B
Lettuce	2.2 kcal/oz 8 kcal/100 g	Mainly water, calcium, rich in vitamins A and C
Onions	6.5 kcal/oz 23 kcal/100 g	Some carbohydrate, calcium, iron, vitamin C
Peas (fresh or frozen, boiled)	14 kcal/oz 49 kcal/100 g	Carbohydrate, protein, calcium, vitamins A and C
Green peppers	4 kcal/oz 14 kcal/100 g	Mainly water, rich in vitamins A and C
Potatoes	21 kcal/oz 76 kcal/100 g	Carbohydrate, protein (reduced if boiled, increased if fried or roasted). Some calcium, vitamin C
Sweet corn	22 kcal/oz 79 kcal/100 g	Carbohydrate, some protein, calcium, vitamins A and C

Table 4.7   *Continued*

Food	Amount 1 oz = 28 g 100 g = 3.5 oz	Content
Tomatoes (fresh)	3.4 kcal/oz 12 kcal/100 g	Mainly water, some carbohydrate, calcium, rich in vitamin A
Watercress	4 kcal/oz 14 kcal/100 g	Rich in calcium, vitamins A and C
Turnips	5 kcal/oz 18 kcal/100 g	Calcium, vitamin C
Beans (runner)	6.5 kcal/oz 23 kcal/100 g	Some protein, carbohydrate (haricot beans contain more protein than any other kind), calcium, vitamins A and C
Bread and butter pudding	44 kcal/oz 154 kcal/100 g	Carbohydrate, fat, protein, calcium, vitamin A
Tea/supper		
Cheese	117 kcal/oz 412 kcal/100 g	Rich in protein and fat. High calcium and vitamin A content
Black pudding	87 kcal/oz 305 kcal/100 g	Mainly fat, carbohydrate and protein. Rich in iron and calcium
Baked beans	18 kcal/oz 63 kcal/100 g	Carbohydrate, protein, calcium, vitamin A, little vitamin C, iron
Fish fingers	50 kcal/oz 178 kcal/100 g	Carbohydrate, protein, fat, calcium
Spaghetti	104 kcal/oz 364 kcal/100 g	Mainly carbohydrate, some protein, little fat. Calcium, little iron and vitamin B
Steak and kidney pie	86 kcal/oz 304 kcal/100 g	Fat, carbohydrate, protein, calcium, vitamin A, iron
Apple pie	80 kcal/oz 281 kcal/100 g	Mainly carbohydrate, fat, little protein. Calcium, little vitamin A and C
Trifle	46 kcal/oz 162 kcal/100 g	Carbohydrate, some fat and protein, calcium, vitamin A
Ice-cream	54 kcal/oz 192 kcal/100 g	Carbohydrate, fat, protein. Rich in calcium.
Fruit cake	105 kcal/oz 368 kcal/100 g	Mainly carbohydrate, fat and little protein. Calcium, vitamin A, iron
Rice pudding	40 kcal/oz 142 kcal/100 g	Carbohydrate, fat, protein, calcium, vitamin A
Custard	26 kcal/oz 92 kcal/100 g	Carbohydrate, fat, protein, calcium, vitamin A, some iron
Apples	13 kcal/oz 46 kcal/100 g	Carbohydrate, little calcium, vitamins A and C
Apricots (dried)	52 kcal/oz 182 kcal/100 g	Carbohydrate, protein, calcium, iron, rich in vitamin A Canned apricots contain hardly any protein, less calcium, vitamin A, very little iron
Bananas	21 kcal/oz 76 kcal/100 g	Carbohydrate, little protein, calcium, some vitamin A and C
Figs (dried)	60 kcal/oz 213 kcal/100 g	Carbohydrate, protein, rich in calcium, some iron and vitamin A
Oranges	10 kcal/oz 35 kcal/100 g	Carbohydrate, calcium, rich in vitamin C
Peaches (canned)	25 kcal/oz 88 kcal/100 g	Carbohydrate, little calcium, vitamin A, little C
Pears (fresh)	11.7 kcal/oz 41 kcal/100 g	Carbohydrate, some calcium, little vitamins A and C
Prunes (dried)	46 kcal/oz 161 kcal/100 g	Carbohydrate, little protein, some calcium, little iron, quite rich in vitamin A
Rhubarb	1.7 kcal/oz 6 kcal/100 g	Mainly water, rich in calcium, some vitamin A and C
Pineapple (canned)	21 kcal/oz 76 kcal/100 g	Carbohydrate, some calcium, little iron, vitamins A and C
Raspberries	7 kcal/oz 25 kcal/100 g	Rich in calcium. Contains vitamins A and C
Plums	9 kcal/oz 32 kcal/100 g	Vitamin A, carbohydrate, calcium, little vitamin C
Strawberries	7.4 kcal/oz 26 kcal/100 g	Rich in vitamin C

these in the ratio proteins one-fifth, fats one-fifth, and carbohydrates three-fifths.

Milk will figure in the diet of young children because it is a valuable source of many nutrients. However, whole milk is high in fat and can therefore contribute to overweight. Milk should be regarded as a 'food' rather than as a drink. It is not thirst quenching and thirsty children should therefore be offered water or diluted fruit juice first.

Raw fruit and vegetables give useful fibre and also help the teeth to develop and the gums to harden. Sweet, sticky foods should be avoided in the diet of young children. Energy-giving foods can be supplied in bread and vegetables which also contain other useful nutrients. Cakes, jam and biscuits contain little except starch and sugar and can cause dental decay and obesity when taken in excess. Often children come to prefer a piece of cheese if this is offered instead of sweets as a snack between meals. Chocolate is more nutritious and less harmful than boiled sweets but children should be encouraged to clean their teeth after any meal and particularly one which offers sweets.

When planning menus for children in the nursery, it is beneficial to include foods which allow them to help prepare the meal whenever possible. Many foods can be cooked with little difficulty in the cookery corner with a small table-top cooker, or in the nursery kitchen. Some foods can be grown in the nursery garden and indoors. Potatoes, carrots, cabbage and celery can be grown out of doors and provide a useful education about how plants grow and the part played by the sun, water and soil. Watercress, a popular and nutritious sandwich filler and accompaniment to salads can be grown in individual trays on blotting paper and provide a simple explanation of seeds and plant growth.

The production and preparation of food helps the shy children to engage in a social activity, increases self-confidence, develops awareness of size, shape, texture and effects of baking and cooking, helps language development and colour recognition, and stimulates appetite in children who normally eat little. Children must be supervised at all times during preparation of food.

Management of Mealtimes

If food is to be easily digested it is important that there is stimulation of saliva and gastric juices. The sight, smell and at times the memory of food leads to the stimulation of the appetite, literally with 'mouth-watering' effects. Food must be adequately cooked, attractively served and appear palatable for full enjoyment. Small portions and choice of colourful vegetables, e.g. carrots and green cabbage or peas, make food more pleasing for children, particularly when they are off-colour and lack appetite. The food does not need to be mashed up; this often discourages children who prefer to imitate adults at the table.

Mealtimes can be a valuable occasion to further the child's social development if they are shared with nursery staff or parents and children. The child learns acceptable table manners and is encouraged by the example of the adults to eat his food slowly and with little mess. At first younger children of 2 to 3 years of age will need large bibs to protect their clothing as they may find eating unaided difficult. Bibs which are made of plastic or washable material with a pocket at the base are most useful.

Children of this age will find a fork and spoon useful and can progress to using knives and forks as their manual dexterity improves. Mastering the skills of feeding can help development of hand–eye coordination. Coloured table cloths and plates provide an attractive presentation of food and help visual perception. Senses of taste, touch and smell are also enhanced when the meal is attractively served.

Mealtimes in the home or nursery can be the main social events of the day when adults and children join together and enjoy an exchange of experiences. Social skills in listening to others and courtesy towards others can be practised at this time, which is unlike any play situation. Self-confidence is increased as the child learns to feed himself and possible frustration at his comparative helplessness in an adult situation is removed.

Regularity of mealtimes contributes to good eating habits, gives a sense of security and discourages the need for snacks between meals. As these are usually sweet, fattening and contribute to dental decay they are best avoided. Variety in daily and weekly menus is also desirable as it has been shown that less food is eaten when one type only is served. Mealtimes should not be allowed to become a battle of wills between adult and child. Children will show variations in appetite, tastes, likes and dislikes and refusal to eat should not be seen as defiance. Desire to please adults and conflict at mealtimes can make children sick. Conversely, when children realize how anxious the parent or nursery nurse becomes at their refusal of food, they may use this as an attention seeking device. The adult must control the situation and not view it as an emotional battleground. A 2- or 3-year-old child can gain emotional satisfaction through an understanding attitude at mealtimes as he is allowed to enjoy the same foods as adults (where appropriate and adaptable to the child's needs), and satisfy his desire to be treated as 'a big boy'.

Language development and vocabulary extension can take place in a relaxed atmosphere at mealtimes and it becomes another learning situation. Some adults try little quiz games at table which older children enjoy but this can give an inappropriate formality to the occasion for young children. There is much that can be achieved through an informal discussion about the food. Questions as to its origin (from farm, factory or dairy, not just shop!) can extend the children's knowledge and satisfy their natural curiosity. Concept formation can happen almost incidentally as various sizes and shapes of fruits and vegetables are considered and differences between the two explained. Stories about shopping trips can follow or precede mealtime and the children could be taken from the nursery for a visit to the local greengrocers and other kinds of shop or possibly an open-air market to develop the theme further.

Mealtimes in the nursery should be the highlight of the day's routine and although careful planning is necessary, it is not a good idea to anticipate them too soon beforehand. In some nurseries tables are set for hours before the meal is served and while this is done to prevent undue disruption in other activities, the nursery nurse should ask herself whether this is a natural activity which would be done at home.

Special Diets

Gluten-free for Children with Coeliac Disease (see p. 170)

The following items are allowed:

All kinds of:
  meat, including poultry, bacon, ham, and offal.
  fish and shellfish
  cheese
  milk, plain yogurt

  fats
  fruit and fruit juices
  vegetables
Gluten-free flour and pure wheatstarch
Rice
Potato flour, soya flour, maize, corn, sago, tapioca and arrowroot
Gluten-free bread, pastry, cakes, biscuits, puddings
Cornflour
Breakfast cereals made from corn or rice, e.g. Rice Krispies and cornflakes
Raising agents – bicarbonate of soda, cream of tartar, tartaric acid, yeast
Homemade soups, sauces and gravy thickened with cornflour, rice or wheat starch
Bovril, Marmite, salt, pepper, herbs, spices, sugar, honey, jam, marmalade, plain boiled sweets and lollies, jelly, gelatine
Tea, coffee, fruit squash
Flavourings

Gluten-free flour, bread, biscuits, cakes and pasta can all be obtained on doctors' prescription.

Forbidden foods which contain gluten:

All meats cooked with flour or breadcrumbs, corned beef, corned mutton, tinned meats, sausages, meat pastes
Fish prepared in batter or breadcrumbs, fish pastes
Cheese spreads, synthetic cream, packet shredded suet, fruit yogurt, fruit pies, baked beans, potato crisps, vegetable dishes with flour
Wheat, rye, barley, oats, semolina, pasta, wheatmeal flour, oatmeal, flour, flour products
Custard powder, ordinary bread, pastry, cakes, biscuits, puddings, pancakes, cake and pastry mixes, crispbreads, 'slimming' biscuits
Breakfast cereals made from wheat or oats, rye; Weetabix, Puffed Wheat, Bemax, Farex, baby cereals
Ordinary baking flour, homemade soups, sauces, gravies, tinned and packet soups, Oxo cubes, Bisto, bottled sauces, packet stuffing mixes, mustard, curry powder, pastes, malted milk drinks, drinking chocolate, barley-flavoured drinks, ice-cream, wafers and cones
All sweets and chocolate, unless gluten-free

Nowadays, there *are* gluten-free foods available from health food shops and chemists.

Milk-free diet for children with milk allergy (Galactosaemia)

Allowed:

Milk substitute for infants – Velactin or Prosobee

Fats – Outline margarine, lard, suet, salad oil, cooking oil

Meats – all fresh, plain frozen, plain tinned in brine

Fish – fresh fish, tinned fish in oil or brine

Eggs, nuts, plain unprocessed cereals, rice, semolina, sago, tapioca made without milk, macaroni, spaghetti, other pasta

Bread and bread rolls free from milk and milk products

Biscuits, cakes, pastry – only if no milk involved in baking

Baby foods – baby rice, rusks

Sugars, sweets, conserves, jam, marmalade, syrup, plain milk-free chocolate

Fruits, desserts, puddings, ices, jelly, ice lollies, water ice

All vegetables

Soups, if free from milk products

Drinks – tea, coffee, drinking chocolate/cocoa made without milk, squashes, fruit juices, lemonade, Nesquick, Oxo, Bovril, Marmite

Sauces, dressings, stuffings, stocks, checked for any milk content

Forbidden:

Milk in all forms, milk products, meat and fish dishes with milk in pastry or dressings

Cereals, unless known to be milk free

Bread, unless known to be milk free (home-made bread is cheap, very easy to make, milk free and very nutritious)

Fudge, toffee, milk chocolate, lemon curd

All puddings made with milk

Tinned vegetables in milk-based dressing, potato mixes

Soups containing milk

All milk-based drinks

Goats' milk is sometimes used as a substitute for cows' milk, but should be boiled for infants and either boiled or pasteurized for other children. It must never be given full strength, but diluted 400 ml goats' milk to 100 ml water and 20 g sugar. Some babies and children cannot tolerate goats' milk, and soya-based milks may be useful here.

Vitamins A, D, C and folic acid supplements must be given.

Food Hygiene

Care in handling and storage of food is essential to prevent the spread of food-borne diseases and to preserve the food in a fresh state ready for eating when required. Food spoilage can be caused by chemical reactions such as oxidation which changes the appearance of meat, causes an unpleasant smell and brings about rancidity in fats. Contamination with dirt or chemicals, infestation by insect pests, moulds, yeasts and bacteria also render food inedible and must be prevented.

Antioxidants such as vitamin E can be added to foods to prevent rancidity. Moulds require oxygen for development and are usually found on the surface of foods such as meat, cheese, and jams. Sterilization under pressure (more than 100°C) or heating food to 70–80°C will destroy spores. If all food is covered and kept in the refrigerator, it will reduce the incidence of spoilage by moulds, but the only truly effective way is to use perishable foods within 2 days unless they are kept in a freezer. Yeasts can spoil fruits but they are killed by heating to 100°C. Bacteria can multiply very rapidly at body temperature 37°C, most are destroyed at 100°C, but other types which form spores, e.g. typhoid bacillus, are resistant to extremes of heat, cold and drying. Some need oxygen, others, including *Clostridium welchii*, which causes botulism, a fatal type of food poisoning, are anaerobic, and multiply in cooked meats, canned fish, raw meat, milk and raw egg products. *Salmonella*, the bacterium which causes food poisoning, typhoid and paratyphoid can also be carried in the same foods. Infected water can contaminate food and diseases such as typhoid are spread in this way.

Bacterial contamination can also occur through food handlers neglecting to wash their hands after using the toilet or changing a baby's nappies. An uncovered septic cut on the hand and food which has been contaminated by flies can also be vehicles for the spread of infection. Bacillary dysentery still occurs frequently among babies and children and is often spread by hand from faeces to food. Bottle-fed babies in hospitals are at risk from food-borne infection.

Strict cleanliness in the handling and preparation of food with the exclusion of disease carriers who are able to infect food, without showing any symptoms themselves, is essential. All food must be kept covered and as salmonella organisms can survive cold storage, frozen chickens must be thawed properly before cooking and cooked at 100°C for at least an hour to prevent the spread of food poisoning.

Preservatives

Chemicals are often added to food for preservation purposes. The addition of salt, sugar and vinegar has been carried out for many centuries. Salt is added to meat and fish before smoking, and curing meat is now carried out for the taste rather than as a preservative measure. Sugar is used to preserve fruit and added to milk in condensed milk, which remains fresh and free from microorganisms for weeks after opening. Sulphur dioxide, sodium or potassium nitrates or nitrites and sorbic acid are some permitted preservatives. There are many others which are added to foods such as spices, glycerol and lecithin which are not legally regarded as preservatives.

Anxiety is often expressed at the number and level of additives in food. Sodium and potassium nitrates are used as preservatives for bacon, ham and pickled meat. Sodium nitrate is added before the bacon is cured and it is reduced to nitrite by bacteria. Nitrites are toxic as they can have an adverse effect on haemoglobin. Nitrates can be harmful to babies under 6 weeks old as their stomachs do not have sufficient hydrochloric acid to prevent production of nitrate-reducing bacteria which convert nitrates to nitrites. Some varieties of strained food have been discontinued as they were found to contain sodium nitrate.

Milk

This contains *lacto bacilli* which are the bacteria responsible for souring and production of butter. Where milk production is not controlled hygienically, it may also contain pathogenic organisms from the cow, milking machine, container or handler. Now that cows are immunized against tuberculosis and there are herds which are attested as tuberculin-free, the spread of bovine tuberculosis through milk is rare. Other diseases such as scarlet fever and brucellosis which used to be spread through milk are also rare due to heat treatment of milk.

Pasteurization

Pasteurization of milk involves heating it to 72°C for not less than 15 seconds after which it is rapidly cooled. This destroys most harmful organisms while retaining the flavour. Some of the vitamin content is lost during storage if it is stored in direct light.

Sterilized milk

This has been homogenized by heating the milk to 65°C and forcing it through a small opening under high pressure. This breaks up the oil droplets and forms an emulsion. After homogenization the milk is filtered into narrow-necked bottles and heated to boiling temperature 100°C where it is maintained for an hour, although higher temperature for a shorter time is more common. Sterilization destroys the vitamin content of the milk and gives it a peculiar taste, but it can be kept for a long time unopened and is safe to use.

Evaporated milk

This is pasteurized milk which has had 32% water removed and is then homogenized and sterilized in sealed cans.

Roller-dried milk

This is used for feeding babies and is produced when whole milk is dried by passing a film of it between heated rollers and the resulting powder is then scraped off.

Spray-dried milk

This is completely soluble in water and can be stored for long periods in sealed containers. The milk is first concentrated under vacuum at a low temperature and it is then dried by spraying it in the form of minute droplets into a hot air current. It is nutritionally similar to pasteurized milk.

5

Infection and Childhood Ailments

Infection

Infection is the successful invasion of the body by disease-producing organisms in sufficient numbers and of sufficient virulence to defeat the body's defences.

It is important to realize that infection and disease are not the same. Disease literally means the absence of ease, a state or morbidity of mind or body. It is expressed objectively by *signs* and subjectively by *symptoms* in the sufferer and the pattern of the disease is determined by the nature of the condition.

Bacteria

Microorganisms, so called because they can only be seen with the aid of a microscope, do not all cause disease. Bacteria, which form the largest group of known organisms, can be *pathogenic* (disease producing), but many are *saprophytic* (non-disease-producing) and of benefit to the body. Saprophytic organisms include:

1 the lactic acid bacillus, which causes milk to sour and enables butter, yoghurt and cheese to be produced;
2 organisms in the bowel which break down cellulose, the fibrous starch in certain foodstuffs;
3 organisms in the bowel which synthesize vitamins, e.g. vitamin K, which helps in the production of blood clots;
4 organisms in the soil which break down nitrogen into a form usable by plants;
5 organisms which break down sewage in the purification process.

Commensals are bacteria which live in and on the body and which are normally saprophytic. They may become pathogenic in a different habitat, e.g. *Escherichia coli* found in the intestines, which can spread disease (if ingested) in water and food.

Bacteria are unicellular organisms, consist of a nucleus surrounded by protoplasm, and multiply by simple fission – splitting into two. Ideal growing conditions include a warm, even temperature less than 100 °F, moisture, a neutral medium (i.e. neither acid nor alkaline), adequate food and darkness. When these conditions prevail, one bacterium becomes two in 20 minutes and will multiply to 17 million overnight.

Adverse conditions are:

Cold or excess heat
Dryness
An acid or alkaline medium
No food
Light (especially sunlight)

Certain bacteria thrive in oxygen (aerobes) while others such as tetanus and anthrax organisms, die in the presence of oxygen (anaerobes). Some, known as facultative organisms, can live in the presence of oxygen.

Bacteria which are able to form spores or cases round themselves can live for long periods without food or moisture and resist boiling and freezing. They are also capable of reproduction after sporulation which is really a method of preservation. Hence spore-forming bacteria such as tetanus and anthrax can live for years in the soil and are difficult to destroy.

When examined under the microscope, bacteria appear in different shapes. Pathogenic bacteria which are round or berry-shaped are known as *cocci*. They may appear singly, in chains, pairs or clusters and the names given to causative organisms of certain diseases reflects their shapes.

1 *Streptococcus*. The cocci appear as a chain. This organism produces sore throats, tonsilitis, scarlet fever and erysipelas.
2 *Staphylococcus*. The cocci appear as a cluster or bunch. This organism produces boils, styes and chronic (long-term) infections.

3 *Diplococcus*. The cocci appear in pairs. Diseases caused by this type include pneumonia, meningitis and gonorrhoea.

4 *Bacilli*. Rod-shaped organisms including the tubercle bacillus (*Mycobacterium tuberculosis*) which causes tuberculosis, typhoid bacillus (*Salmonella typhi*) which causes typhoid fever. Tetanus and anthrax bacilli (*Clostridium tetani* and *bacillus anthracis*) are spore-forming.

5 *Spirilla*. Wavy organisms such as are seen in relapsing fever.

6 *Vibrios*. Comma-shaped organisms, e.g. *Vibrio cholerae*.

7 *Spirochaetes*. Corkscrew-shaped, e.g. *treponema pallidum* (*Spirochaeta pallida*), the causal organism of syphilis.

Toxins are produced by bacteria. They are poisonous to living tissues. *Exotoxins* pass out from the organisms to circulate in the blood stream causing damage to tissues, e.g. diphtheria, tetanus. *Endotoxins* are released on the death of the organisms and act locally, e.g. tubercle bacillus.

Viruses

These are ultra-microscopic organisms – they can only be seen through an electron microscope, will only grow in live cells and tissue cultures and are much more difficult to identify than bacteria. Viruses are also very resistant to drugs – many antibiotics such as penicillin have no effect on them. Various types of viruses cause diseases such as smallpox, measles, mumps, influenza, poliomyelitis and encephalitis.

Spread of Infection

The spread of infection begins with the source. This may be a clinical case where the infection has been diagnosed, a 'missed' or unrecognized case, a carrier or an animal. *A carrier* is one who has either had the disease and is convalescent or who carries the causative organism with no adverse effects to himself (the 'healthy carrier'). Carriers have been found to cause outbreaks of typhoid where the cause has been obscure. That animals can spread infection is not often recognized by those with babies and young children. Household pets such as dogs and cats can transmit streptococcal infections, worms and fleas, yet they are often allowed to sit near the table when the children are feeding and even

patted and fondled by hands which then convey food to the mouths. Parrots can spread psittacosis, a fatal disease.

Secretions such as saliva, mucus and sputum, *excretions* such as urine and faeces, and *discharges*, pus from wounds, boils, ears etc., often provide sources of infection.

Infection can be spread directly or indirectly. *Direct spread* involves actual contact, e.g. a child touching another's face or hands with infected fingers or kissing. *Indirect spread* involves handling of infected objects (sometimes called 'Fomites' such as crockery, books, dressings, thermometers, dust, potties. Food, milk and water supplies, if infected, can spread typhoid, cholera, salmonella-type food poisoning and poliomyelitis. Botulism, although rare, is still contracted mainly from tinned meat and fish foods where the packing process has been inadequate. The toxins produced by bacillus *Clostridium botulinum* often prove fatal to the victims.

Vectors such as flies, rats, fleas and mosquitoes also spread disease indirectly. Flies can spread diseases such as influenza, dysentery, gastroenteritis and poliomyelitis through their custom of feeding on dung heaps and then alighting onto food. In order to make the food soluble, they vomit their stomach contents onto it before ingestion. Infective organisms are thus left on the food. Rats are known to spread bacterial food poisoning, Weil's disease, rat flea-borne typhus, flea-borne relapsing fever and plague. *Airborne* or *droplet* infection refers to those respiratory infections which can be caused by minute droplets from nose and mouth of infected persons drying out and floating in the air.

Routes of Entry

Pathogenic microorganisms can get into the body by:

1 *inhalation* through the nose and mouth, e.g. droplet infections,
2 *ingestion* through taking in food, e.g. salmonella food poisoning,
3 *inoculation* through the skin, e.g. tetanus (by a graze or cut),
4 *implantation* through infected instruments, dressings.

Whether the organisms which enter the body actually produce disease depends on the virulence (strength) of the organisms, their concentration (many or few), resistance of the new host, and the site of entry. General bodily state (influenced by environment, work, rest, sleep, nutrition, hygiene and recreation), the external and internal defences of the body determine the body's resistance to infection.

The External Defences

These defences of the body include the skin which has a protective function, and tears which bathe the eyes and contain lysozyme, an antiseptic substance. The mucous membrane linings of mouth, respiratory and alimentary tracts produce mucus and provide a barrier against entry of infective organisms, as do the cilia which are microscopic hairs lining the nose. Gastric juice secreted by the glands lining the stomach contains hydrochloric acid which acts as an antiseptic, as does bile which is secreted by the gall bladder.

Internal Body Defences

Lymphoid tissue which is found in the tonsils, adenoids, neck, thymus, spleen, axillae, groins and intestines acts as a static defence in that the lymphocytes, which are cells produced in lymphoid tissue, fight against pathogens.

Lymph glands (or nodes) are regarded as anti-infective filters. In tonsilitis the lymph glands in the neck are swollen as a result of their increased activity. Phagocytes are white blood cells circulating in the bloodstream which are able to infest pathogenic organisms. When the skin is broken and pathogens invade body tissues large numbers of phagocytes are found in the area. This causes the swelling and redness (due to dilatation of the capillaries) associated with inflammation. Pus, which may result from an infected wound, contains dead bacteria and dead phagocytes.

The number of white blood cells present in the blood (usually 10 000 per cubic millimetre of blood in children) is often an indicator of the body's reaction to infection. In an acute infection, e.g. appendicitis, the number of white blood cells may be trebled or quadrupled. Lymphocytes respond more slowly and are usually associated with chronic infections such as tuberculosis. They also form antibodies and respond to many viruses, e.g. that of glandular fever, while other white cells do not.

Antibodies and antitoxins provide a circulatory defence against infection. An antibody is a protein formed in the spleen or lymph gland when the tissues are invaded with a foreign protein or antigen. Antibodies inactivate antigens and combine with the proteins of bacteria to act as a defence against disease. Antibodies are peculiar to certain diseases, e.g. antibodies against measles are ineffective against chickenpox. While it takes about 2 weeks for antibodies to be primed against new antigens, they can be quickly renewed in case of future attacks. Hence an attack of measles gives lasting immunity to the disease. Unfortunately antibodies can also be formed against non-pathogenic alien proteins which may be introduced into the body, and produce an allergic reaction.

Antitoxins are formed against the toxins released into the blood stream by certain bacteria such as tetanus and diphtheria. These toxins damage nerve cells, and diphtheria toxins also affect the heart. The toxins are antigens and antitoxins respond to them as antibodies. Serum containing antitoxins of diphtheria or tetanus is used in the treatment of these diseases.

Prevention of Infection and Disease Spread

Young babies are particularly susceptible to infection as their immune defence mechanisms are still immature. Children too are vulnerable to foreign bacteria and viruses – especially when they first join a nursery group. Thus, parents and adults working with babies and children should ensure that their own health is good in case they act as a source of, or spread, infection.

General rules of hygiene help to promote resistance to infection. Cleanliness (care of skin, hair, teeth, routine, regular bathing, adequate stimulation, fresh air, good ventilation, sunlight, rest, sleep, good nutrition, suitable clothing and footwear, clean water supply and good sanitation, love and security . . . all enhance the state of health.

Hygienic practices are necessary in prevention of infection and disease. Washing and drying of hands before handling food and after using the toilet or changing baby's nappy should be mandatory as gastroenteritis spreads rapidly in groups of young children and often starts through carelessness in this habit of basic hygiene. E. coli, often the causative organism, is a commensal and normally inhabits the bowel.

When transmitted to a new host through dirty handling of food it can cause enteric infections, sometimes with fatal results for young babies.

Hands should be thoroughly washed with soap and nails scrubbed as infection often lurks under the nails. Drying hands is also important. Roller towels have now been replaced with warm air dryers which are far more sanitary than wet, infected towels. Paper towels, which can be disposed of in an incinerator, are also frequently used.

Particular care should be exercised by those who have to prepare feeds for babies after sluicing soiled nappies. Before washing, the nappies should be placed in a disinfectant solution, such as Napisan. After rinsing, they should then be washed as a separate machine load from children's clothing, and at home mothers might don a clean overall before preparing a feed.

When an infectious disease is diagnosed, the child is sent home from school or nursery and the school medical officer notified as necessary. The isolation period is the amount of time deemed necessary by the physician for someone with an infectious disease to be kept away from all other potential sufferers for their protection and his own. It is less often used since the advent of antibiotics. In a case of gastroenteritis the isolation period extends until the child is recovered and three negative swabs of fecal matter have been obtained. A child with measles, on the other hand, may be excluded for only 10 days after the appearance of the rash and then readmitted to the nursery if he appears well. While ill, the child should be nursed in bed (on his own, if possible) and should have his own crockery and cutlery which should be kept and washed separately from the crockery of other family members. If the child is admitted to hospital, he may be barrier nursed in an open ward (as in amoebic dysentry), barrier nursed in a side room or cubicle (as in infective hepatitis), or barrier nursed in an isolation ward.

Barrier nursing

This involves the following:

1 Wearing of gowns (or overall garments) is necessary for all bed-making and attending to the patient, but not for serving meals. Gowns should be kept in the sickroom or cubicle and only used for one patient to prevent cross-infection.

2 Masks (which are usually made of disposable material nowadays) should be worn if the doctor so instructs. They can protect the patient from droplet infection.

3 Feeding equipment should be washed in a special bowl or sink and kept for one patient only. Terminal disinfection (at the end of the illness) should be in an autoclave–steam under pressure which increases the temperature to 121°C – or boiling for 10 minutes.

4 Bed linen and pyjamas should be put in a special laundry bag for steam disinfection before being added to the general wash.

5 Mattresses should be enclosed in a plastic cover and swabbed with Savlon 1 in 30 after the infection has gone. The mattress can then be aired before further use.

6 Blankets should preferably be cellular cotton as these are lighter and overheating of a feverish patient can cause fluid loss and dehydration. Terminal disinfection is easier too in that these blankets can be boiled or steam disinfected.

Care of the sick child

Good ventilation. This is essential in an isolation room as fresh air reduces the number of airborne bacteria and thus reduces the risk of other infections. An extractor fan leading to the exterior is ideal. A fresh atmosphere gives the patient a feeling of wellbeing which aids recovery.

Good nutrition. Although the child's appetite may be poor, small, light, nutritious meals should be offered. Soups, party-size sandwiches, eggs, yoghurt, jellies, fruit, all usually go down well. Yoghurt in particular may be acceptable when other foods – even milk – are not; it is high in both protein and calcium.

Fluid intake. This is important to a feverish patient and the doctor may ask the mother or nursery nurse to keep a record of fluid intake and output, to ensure that excess fluid loss does not take place. Often children are reluctant to take drinks when they are ill and if so a small glass or cup of iced water or fruit juice may be acceptable taken in sips at a time.

Skin care. This is important for the sick child's comfort and a daily bed bath is particularly pleasant when he is feverish, while the opportunity for observation of further rashes and skin conditions is useful.

Mouth care. When the patient has a high temperature and breathes through the mouth, mouth care is essential. The tongue may be furred and should be swabbed with a solution of bicarbonate of soda. Rinsing with a mild mouthwash is refreshing. A little vaseline can be applied to dry, cracked lips.

Light. Some patients, particularly with measles, may complain about the light and the bed should preferably be placed so that the light does not shine directly on to him. However, blacked out rooms can be frightening to a child and should be avoided.

Excreta. Any excreta may need to be kept for observation. In cases of gastroenteritis or dysentery, disinfectant (Izal 1 in 20) is added to the potty or bedpan which is then covered and left for 2 hours before emptying into lavatory or sluice. The potty can then be washed and soaked in Milton 1 in 80.

The most important aspect of isolation procedures is thorough hand-washing to prevent spread of infection.

Immunization

Immunization procedures have helped to reduce the incidence of childhood diseases and almost completely eliminated those such as smallpox, diphtheria and poliomyelitis.

Reasons for immunization of children under 5 years include the following:

1 Some infectious diseases are extremely dangerous and can be fatal in babies under 1 year old, e.g. whooping cough.
2 Complications of infectious diseases may cause handicaps or disability, e.g. measles can affect eyesight and hearing, poliomyelitis can cause permanent paralysis.
3 Illness resulting from infectious diseases may affect the child's intellectual development directly – e.g. brain damage from convulsions (a complication of whooping cough) – or through interruption in schooling.
4 Reduction in number of susceptible people and elimination of diseases.

Immunity is the power of resisting infection due to the elaboration of antibodies. Generic immunity or natural immunity is due to the quality of body tissue, e.g. man is immune to dog distemper. Immunity can be described as active or passive.

Active Immunity

This refers to the antibodies and antitoxins formed in the body in response to bacteria or their toxins.

Natural active immunity is acquired through:

1 an attack of the disease – e.g. measles, rubella and chickenpox – in which antibodies formed against it provide rear lifelong immunity;
2 sub-clinical infection, in which an invasion of body tissues is of sufficient virulence to alert the body defences but not severe enough to cause an acute attack. Repeated minute doses of an infection also produce the same effect.

Artificial active immunity means inoculation with:

1 living organisms, e.g. vaccination against smallpox,
2 living weakened (attenuated) organisms, e.g. BCG for tuberculosis,
3 dead organisms, e.g. whooping cough vaccine,
4 modified toxins – toxoid, e.g. APT against diphtheria.

Artificial methods should be used well in advance of exposure. In active immunity the body takes 5–10 days to produce antibodies and antitoxins but they remain for long periods.

Passive Immunity

This may be acquired naturally or artificially.

Natural passive immunity is that possessed by babies in the first few months of life. Antibodies are produced in the mother and passed from mother to child via the placenta before birth and in the mother's milk after birth.

Artificial passive immunity means that serum containing antibodies and antitoxins produced by a human or animal are injected into those who require protection. The protection is conferred immediately but only lasts for a short time. It may be given just before an anticipated infection to very susceptible subjects such as weak infants and invalids, or it can be given

Table 5.1   Active immunization for a child

Age	Immunization
3 months	Combined diphtheria, whooping cough and tetanus plus oral poliomyelitis (1)
5 months	Combined diphtheria, whooping cough and tetanus plus oral poliomyelitis (2)
11 months	Combined diphtheria, whooping cough and tetanus plus oral poliomyelitis (3)
12–18 months	Measles
5 years	Booster: diphtheria, tetanus, poliomyelitis (oral or inactivated)
11–13 years	(Girls only) rubella
10–13 years	BCG (to protect against tuberculosis; for tuberculin-negative children)
15 years	Booster: tetanus, poliomyelitis (oral or inactivated)

during an illness to combat the causative organisms and its toxins.

Immunization schedules may differ slightly in various regions but the general sequence is shown in Table 5.1.

While childhood diseases such as measles and diphtheria are no longer fatal because of immunization, it is but one aspect of preventive medicine which has helped to eliminate many infectious diseases in this century. Improved nutrition, housing and sanitation have all contributed to the health and longevity enjoyed by most people in the UK today.

Unfortunately, a considerable amount of adverse publicity has affected the decision of parents to have their children immunized against whooping cough. The Joint Committee on Whooping Cough Vaccination (1977) stated that the benefits of pertussis vaccine continue to outweigh its risks. Whooping cough is particularly dangerous in babies under 1 year old, and as the mortality rate has not changed for the past 20 years the recommendation has been made that first dose of triple vaccine (for diphtheria, tetanus and pertussis – DTP) should be given at 3 months with completion of three doses by 8–10 months. Sadly media focus on vaccine-damaged children tends to give a one-sided view of immunization and many parents have neglected to protect their children from other diseases such as diphtheria, tetanus and poliomyelitis. Despite the low risk of infection from diphtheria and tetanus nowadays, cases still occur and tetanus, often caused as a result of slight injuries, still causes deaths. Poliomyelitis also occurs, although fortunately only in sporadic cases (i.e. occurring here and there occasionally) but the danger of permanent paralysis is greater than the risk of immunization against the disease.

Tuberculosis, which was once regarded as a major scourge and claimed the lives of thousands of children and young adults, is now controlled thanks to mass immunization with BCG (Bacillus Calmette-Guèrin) and effective chemotherapy with drugs like streptomycin and isoniazid. However, babies born to immigrant mothers and contacts of tuberculosis cases who have negative results to tuberculin tests (which shows they have no immunity) still require BCG vaccination.

Vaccination against rubella (once called German measles) has been mainly directed at teenage girls in this country, while in the USA immunization of all infants has reduced the prevalence of the disease there. As the rubella virus can cause blindness and malformations of the fetus if contracted by the mother during the first 3 months of pregnancy, all women of child-bearing age should be immunized against it. Those particularly at risk are doctors, nurses and nursery nurses in hospitals and obstetric departments, teachers and those whose serum tests show that they have no antibodies specific to rubella. When women are vaccinated, they are advised to avoid pregnancy for 3 months afterwards.

The success of immunization against small-pox can only be repeated with the childhood diseases mentioned above if adequate measures are taken by parents. Unfortunately, there is still no effective vaccine against the strains of influenza which cause outbreaks and fatalities on occasion and the same is true of the ubiquitous common cold. Here prevention must be mainly maintenance of good health, body defences and emphasis on precautions against disease spread.

Terms Associated with Infectious Diseases

Epidemic. An outbreak of disease occurring in a region or community at a certain time, which spreads rapidly within the area.

Endemic. A disease which is always present in a specific region or peculiar to specific peoples.

Sporadic. Outbreaks which occur from time to time, only occasionally and unrelated to others.

Table 5.2   Common infectious diseases of childhood

Disease	Cause	Method of spread	Signs and symptoms	Complications	Treatment
Common cold (Coryza) Incubation period: 1–3 days	virus	airborne, but can also be spread by hands through infected person touching eyes, mouth and nose, and hence carrying pathogens in secretions	sneezing, sore throat, stuffy nose, running nose; headache, partial deafness; slight rise in temperature (pyrexia), child irritable, not interested in play	sinusitis, laryngitis, tracheitis bronchitis	no specific cure; symptoms treated; comfort and hot drinks; junior aspirin if prescribed by doctor; vaseline applied to nostrils to prevent soreness due to discharge
Measles Incubation period: 1–2 weeks	virus	airborne	running nose, watery eyes, fever, cough; Koplik's spots – red with white centres – may be seen inside the mouth in 1 or 2 days then disappear; 3rd day fever subsides; 4th day temperature rises again maybe as high as 104°F as rash appears; blotchy red rash spreads down over the body from the face; child fretful, irritable, hot, with cough and painful eyes	otitis media (middle ear infection), pneumonia, corneal ulceration (rare), encephalitis (rare)	requires special attention, chemotherapy may be prescribed to prevent complications; relief of symptoms; bedroom/ sickroom shaded if photophobia present; attention to diet as vomiting may occur; plenty of fluids; convalescence in fresh air and sunshine
Chickenpox (Varicella) Incubation period: 2 weeks	virus	airborne (and by discharge from skin lesions)	mild onset – off colour, slight pyrexia; rash appears first on trunk, then face, then limbs; lesions are little vesicles (blisters) surrounded by a ring of inflammation; blisters can erupt easily; vesicles become filled with pus (pustules) then dry up to form	scarring and secondary infection only if there is scratching of spots	calamine lotion is soothing for irritation; relief of other symptoms; particular care of skin to prevent chafing and complications; child's nails should be cut short to prevent secondary infection through scratching, gloves applied

Table 5.2   *Continued*

Disease	Cause	Method of spread	Signs and symptoms	Complications	Treatment
			scabs; rash appears in crops so three stages vesicles, pustules and scabs may all be seen at one time; child will feel ill, with severe headache and find spots irritating		if itching is severe; if lesions are profuse penicillin may be prescribed to prevent secondary infection
Mumps (epidemic parotitis) Incubation period: 2–3 weeks	virus	airborne	general malaise, pain and swelling of parotid glands (in front of and under the ear) on one or both sides of the face; rise in temperature, sore throat, headache may develop before glands swell; flow of saliva may increase or diminish – affects feeding; jaws painful – patient may refuse feed or find difficulty in chewing	meningitis (rare), orchitis (inflammation of testes, usually only in adolescent boys) rarely causes sterility	no specific cure; care of mouth – cleanliness and moistness; plenty of fluids, through a straw (which has a good effect on the child who may be feeling miserable and will enjoy departure from normal methods of drinking)
Whooping Cough (pertussis) Incubation period: 1–2 weeks	bacillus	airborne	affects mainly children under five; cough usually first symptom often accompanied by clear, watery, nasal discharge coughing becomes more frequent then paroxysmal and temperature rises; whoop follow a number of short, sharp, expiratory coughs; the cough reflex closes the glottis and the	otitis media, bronchopneumonia, convulsions in babies under 1 year old – may lead to brain damage	requires extra special attention, coughing may continue for several weeks; the child may be reluctant to have feed because of vomiting; paroxysms are less frequent after 2–3 weeks and temperature is usually normal in about 2 months Child must be kept warm, moist inhalations can be given and

Table 5.2 *Continued*

Disease	Cause	Method of spread	Signs and symptoms	Complications	Treatment
			child cannot take a breath until the outburst is over: thus he appears to be suffocating – may turn blue, red or purple, eyes seem enlarged and protruding; drawing in air against the resistance of the glottis causes whoop Production of thick mucus and vomiting usually follows the cough; paroxysms of coughing may leave the child exhausted; babies do not usually acquire whooping cough		linctus may be prescribed for the cough; antibiotics maybe prescribed to prevent complications in the chest Support and comfort should be given during paroxysms which are frightening; a feed may be given after an attack to give time for absorption before the next coughing fit
Rubella (German measles) Incubation period: 2–3 weeks	virus	airborne	mild symptoms – headache, stiff neck, running nose, rash of pink spots behind the ears and forehead may be swollen glands at back of neck; child may feel unwell	only if contracted by women in first 3 months of pregnancy – baby may be born with deafness, heart abnormalities and general malformations	treat symptoms
Dysentery (means inflammation of colon and rectum; can be caused by amoebae or bacilli, but bacillary type most common in UK) Incubation period: 1–7 days (usually 3–4 days)	bacillus	excreted in stools so spread through poor sanitation, poor sewage disposal and by lack of hand-washing spread in food	diarrhoea often with blood and mucus; fever, headache, muscular pain; diagnosis made by taking specimen of stools, or from a rectal swab	shock and prostration dehydration through loss of fluid and salts; can be fatal, particularly in young children and babies	isolation and barrier nursing; excreta disposed of only after disinfecting with Izal 1 in 20 for 2 hours; fluid or low-residue diet, i.e. foods which are easily digested such as fruit purees,

Table 5.2 *Continued*

Disease	Cause	Method of spread	Signs and symptoms	Complications	Treatment
					jellies, thickened soups, eggs, minced meat and fish, ice-cream Drugs as prescribed by the doctor Three negative swabs required before patient is pronounced cured Strict hygiene in food handling
Gastroenteritis (infantile)	*Escherichia coli*, *Salmonella* or dysentery bacillus, viral infection or secondary to other infection, e.g. otitis media	rare in breast-fed babies	looser bowel action sometimes with blood or mucus or coloured green or bright orange; occasional vomiting and rejection of feeds despite obvious thirst and hunger. Reduced urinary output, weight loss, dehydration; restlessness and general malaise	dehydration often rapid and severe with metabolic and electrolyte disturbances; these, if uncorrected, can lead to convulsions, renal failure and death	requires special attention

Incubation period. The interval between infection onset and the first symptoms and signs (see Table 5.2 for variations in length of incubation period).

Isolation period. The length of time deemed necessary by the doctor for infected or carrier child to remain separated in isolation ward or at home, away from the rest of the family to prevent spread of infection.

Contact. This can refer to the person who contracts a disease through association with an infected person or to the method of spread (direct and indirect contact). Contacts used to be kept away from nursery or school but this rarely happens nowadays, although immunization is recommended if relevant.

Quarantine period. This refers to the amount of time contacts are advised to remain at home to prevent spread of infection. In practice nowadays, advice varies widely as in chickenpox, for example, patients are highly infective early in the disease even when without symptoms. Quarantine is therefore of little value in preventing spread of this infection. Quarantine period is usually 2 days longer than incubation period.

Carriers. See above.

Fomites. These are inanimate articles such as towels, toys, books which can carry infection in diseases such as gastroenteritis and respiratory infections (since they are touched by hands which may carry infected secretions from eyes, nose and mouth of children). They should be disinfected weekly and steam-sterilized when an outbreak of gastroenteritis occurs.

Anti. As in 'antibodies', means someone or something which acts against another.

a. Without; as in aseptic, without infection.

dys. Pain or difficulty, as in dysentery – a condition in which there is pain in the intestine.

cyte. A cell, as in lymphocytes, produced in lymphoid tissue.

enter. The intestine, as in gastroenteritis – inflammation of the stomach and intestine.

-itis. Inflammation of, e.g. gastroenteritis, hepatitis (inflammation of the liver).

path. Disease, as in pathogenic – disease causing.

encephal. The brain, literally 'in the head', as in encephalitis.

aden. A gland, e.g. adenoids.

-rrhoea. Discharge or flow. Diarrhoea means a running through.

phobia. Fear or dislike, e.g. photophobia dislike of light, sometimes seen in children with measles.

micro. Small, e.g. a microscope is for seeing items usually invisible to the naked eye.

Childhood Ailments

Eye Infections

Discharging eyes

This may be due to an infection, a blocked tear duct or debris left in the eyes during birth. The eyes usually appear to be sticky due to the discharge. Where this occurs in the first 2 or 3 days after birth in hospital, a swab is taken to discover if any pathogenic organisms are present, but as it is usually caused by the remnants of amniotic fluid, it does not require an antibiotic and can be cleaned by bathing the eyes in a solution of salt and water. When the eyes are cleaned, a swab of cotton wool should be used for each eye. To avoid the risk of spreading infection from one eye to the other, the swab should be applied from the inside corner to the outside of the eye and by swabbing the least affected eye first and using each swab once only. The adult's hands should be carefully washed before and after swabbing the eyes and used swabs and unused solution discarded safely.

A discharging eye can be due to infection with the *Staphylococcus aureus* organisms. This organism causes boils and styes. Any infection can spread rapidly in a nursery so scrupulous cleanliness must be observed by staff and children at all times. After swabbing the eyes with saline solution, an ointment (or drops) which will be prescribed by the doctor can be applied. Tear ducts are vessels which carry tears from the eyes to the nose and blockage of them can cause continual watering of the eye. This usually clears up spontaneously by the age of 6 months.

Conjunctivitis ('red eye' or 'pink eye').

This means an inflammation of the conjunctiva, which is the colourless covering of the eye. The eyes have a sticky discharge when the child wakes in the morning and although the eye looks very painful, there is usually no pain or photophobia (literally, fear of light, where the child turns his eyes to shield them from the light). *Staphylococcus aureus* can cause conjunctivitis but a number of other bacteria and viruses may be responsible.

Drops may be prescribed by the doctor and should be inserted in the following way. The child is reassured and then sits on a chair beside a table on which is a tray with a container for cotton wool swabs, saline solution, drops and receptacle for waste. A small towel or cape can be placed over the child's shoulders to protect clothing. After thoroughly washing hands, the adult gently swabs each eye with a swab soaked in saline solution, remembering to swab from the inner part outwards. The child's head is then inclined slightly backwards and the upper eyelid raised gently while the drops are inserted in the inner part of the eye under which a swab can be held. This is repeated for the second eye, after which the used swabs are placed in a receptacle for safe disposal. To prevent risk of infection spread, the hands must be thoroughly washed after this procedure. The child must also be encouraged not to rub his eyes.

Upper Respiratory Tract Infections

These are common in infancy and childhood owing to the narrowness of the air passages in the lungs and the body's immature defence mechanism.

Acute upper respiratory tract infections, e.g. bronchitis, are indicated by alteration in breathing pattern (shallower and more irregular); flushed cheeks, dry skin and thirst – the result of fever and dehydration; irritability and restlessness because of the difficulty in breathing; and sometimes pain and exhaustion due to the coughing.

Treatment is by bed rest, with ample fluids, nourishing and appetizing meals, humidified air to increase sputum productiveness, support with pillows (or no pillows and the bottom of the bed raised for postural drainage) and antibiotics to attack the infection.

Respiratory infection frequently precedes or follows other infectious illnesses such as measles or whooping cough. Recurrent infections are seen in children who have a chronic underlying disease, e.g. congenital heart defect, and in those who are malnourished and living in overcrowded or damp conditions.

Enlarged tonsils and adenoids

These are seen in respiratory infections. Acute tonsillitis is usually caused by a streptococcal organism. Often earache and swollen neck glands accompany enlarged tonsils and the temperature is raised. Tonsils and adenoids are composed of lymphoid tissue which acts as a defence against infection hence their swelling when bacteria invade the upper respiratory tract. The child with a sore throat may have difficulty in swallowing and feel ill. If an abscess develops, as in quinsy, he may even find swallowing saliva painful. Swollen tonsils can be seen by asking the child to open his mouth wide and by gently holding the tongue flat with a spatula or the handle of a spoon. They appear as red lumps on either side of the uvula, a pointed piece of tissue which hangs from the roof of the mouth at the back. Swollen adenoids cause the child to breathe through the mouth as they are situated on the posterior part of the nasopharynx and when inflamed, block the nasal passages.

Snoring and frequent head colds also characterize adenoiditis, and more serious complications such as sinusitis and otitis media can develop.

Antibiotics are usually effective in curing infections of the tonsils and adenoids. In tonsillitis, the child is best kept isolated with his own cutlery and crockery. Analgesics as prescribed by the doctor should be given. Gargles may be useful for older children.

Strict attention to oral hygiene is essential. A mouthwash may be useful and there are a variety of these although a simple solution of water and sodium bicarbonate helps to clean the mouth. In the case of quinsy, a receptacle should be provided for the child to spit into. Usually throat swabs are taken to determine the cause of tonsillitis and a negative swab is required before the child is declared better. Sometimes chronic tonsillitis follows an acute attack. Here the tonsils become a focal point for infection and sore throats occur whenever the child becomes unwell.

Nowadays surgical removal of tonsils and adenoids is not performed until medical treatment has been carried out or complications develop and the child fails to thrive. The most effective preventive measure is to follow the rules of health: balanced diet, adequate rest, sleep, exercise, fresh air and sunlight, suitable clothing and footwear.

Asthma

Asthma is a condition in which there is an obstruction of the airway due to spasm of the bronchial muscle and increased secretion of mucus in the bronchi. Asthma attacks can be brought on by various agents, can occur at any age, and sometimes appear shortly after birth. In more than half the cases, there is a family history of allergies, such as hay fever, eczema, or urticaria. The incidence of asthma seems to increase after the age of 3 years, while some childhood asthmas disappear at puberty.

Causes of asthma include:

1 allergy, e.g. pollen, animals, feather pillows, certain foods,
2 infection,
3 physical factors, e.g. cold, humidity, sudden changes in temperature or barometric pressure,
4 irritants, e.g. dust, chemicals, air pollutants,

5 psychological and emotional factors,
6 exercise.

The signs and symptoms of asthma are gradual onset with snuffles, sneezing and watery nasal discharge. Attacks may occur at night when the child wakes suddenly with wheezing, anxiety, uncontrollable cough, sweating and fear.

Complications include severe lung disease and, in infants under 2 years, serious respiratory failure.

Treatment lies in removing the triggering factor; building up the child's resistance to allergens and infection; drug therapy which will include bronchodilators to help the child breathe more easily, and expectorants to help him cough up excess mucus.

Convulsions (fits)

Convulsions are an extremely serious sign and usually occur as a result of sudden high temperature or diseases such as pneumonia and meningitis. Febrile convulsions are most frequent between the ages of one and three and they rarely occur after the age of 5 years. A child who has suffered brain damage at birth may suffer from convulsions and in some cases convulsions can be the forerunner of epilepsy which is diagnosed after an encephalogram (EEG), a test used in hospital for recording brain waves. Irregular brain waves are seen in children and adults who suffer from epilepsy. The tendency to febrile convulsions runs in families and usually disappears as the child becomes older.

During a convulsion there may be twitching of the muscles of face and limbs as a result of irritation of the nerves which supply the muscles. The eyes stare or roll up and the face looks bluish. Respiration stops and the child becomes unconscious, still twitching uncontrollably. Breathing usually begins in a few seconds with grunting noises and the child becomes conscious again. The teeth are clenched but the child rarely bites his tongue and it is unwise to try to prise the jaw open. *Do not try to put anything between the teeth or gums.*

Medical attention should be sought immediately, but in the interim, treatment should aim at reducing the high temperature which causes a febrile convulsion. This can be done by sponging with *lukewarm* water. Cold water takes the blood away from the skin, which delays cooling.

Sponging should only be continued until the child's temperature falls to 38.8°C, given for half an hour only each time, and no more frequently than every 2 hours. The child should be placed on his right side, on the floor if this is quicker than providing a bed, with his face turned towards the floor to allow any vomit to drain out. A good supply of fresh air should be ensured and clothing undone to promote cooling. The child should be moved away from danger in case he falls or hurts himself in his twitching movements. Following the fit, the child will usually fall asleep.

Where convulsions are repeated they may be diagnosed as epilepsy which is controlled by drugs so that most activities of childhood can still be safely undertaken. A history of convulsions precludes vaccination for measles and whooping cough as these vaccines could exacerbate the condition and cause permanent brain damage.

Skin and Scalp Conditions

Sweat rash

This occurs in parts of the body, where the sweat glands are most numerous: face, neck, chest, shoulders, particularly where there are creases between folds of skin. Often babies are overheated due to fear of chills and their crying in discomfort may be wrongly interpreted. Regular bathing and cleansing with mild soap and water and thorough drying of the skin are important particularly where skin surfaces meet. Clothing should be absorbent and allow for free circulation of air. Wool vests should be avoided as cotton is coolest next to the skin. Babies should always be dressed for the climate, not the season, and it is unnecessary to have them fully clothed with mitts and bootees in warm weather.

Scratch mitts may be used to prevent the baby from scratching the skin, but they should not be used for too long or too frequently as they may deprive him of tactile stimulation.

The cot sheets should be cotton rather than flannelette – woolly blankets should not be next to the baby's skin – and the light, cellular type is preferable. Talcum powder should only be applied in moderation after the skin has been thoroughly dried following the bath.

Sore buttocks (nappy rash)

These can be caused by (1) neglect of proper

washing, rinsing and drying of buttocks, (2) leaving baby in wet and soiled nappies inside the waterproof pants, (3) reaction to detergent washing powders, (4) seborrhoeic dermatitis (scurf). The buttocks should always be carefully washed in a mild soap, rinsed and gently but thoroughly dried. Nappies should be changed regularly, soaked in Napisan, washed in soap flakes rather than detergent, and thoroughly rinsed. The baby should be left to exercise without a nappy on as exposure to air is helpful. Zinc and castor oil cream can be applied to the buttocks after bathing but talcum must never be applied on top of this as the cream acts as a barrier between the skin and the wet nappy. In seborrhoeic dermatitis, scurf from the scalp can spread to the buttocks. Treatment for the condition (see scurf) will remove the nappy rash. *Ammonia dermatitis* produces the most severe type of nappy rash. It produces a strong smell and can spread over the groins and lower abdomen. Breast-fed babies are less susceptible to this condition as the causative organisms thrive in the alkaline conditions produced by cows' milk feeds, and breast milk produces acid stools which are inhospitable to them. After nappies have been sterilized, washed and rinsed they can be given a final rinsing in acetic acid (vinegar) as this prevents the bacteria, which are present in the stool and which react with the urine, from producing ammonia.

Urticaria (nettle-rash)

This can occur in any part of the body and is an allergic reaction. It is seen as a rash of raised white or red spots, which may bleed, and is very itchy. Calamine lotion has a soothing effect and helps to reduce the irritation. Urticaria is not infectious and can be caused by hypersensitivity to certain foods, for example eggs, strawberries, shellfish. Reaction to drugs, e.g. penicillin, colouring matter in orange juice and Haliborange, and allergy to materials like wool may cause urticaria. Rarely sensitivity to bites from dog or cat fleas and mites from budgerigars cause a type of urticaria where the red blotches have blisters. Use of insect repellants and anti-flea powders may be helpful. Antihistamine preparations are prescribed by the doctor to prevent reoccurrence of urticaria. A change in diet and wearing of non-allergenic materials may be necessary. Calamine lotion or cream can be applied for a soothing effect.

Impetigo

This is caused by an infection from staphylococci and streptococci. It may develop as a complication of another condition such as eczema, scabies or uticaria. Impetigo starts as red spots which develop into blisters and then form large brownish-yellow crusts which should not be removed as this may impede recovery. It is seen on the face, scalp and hands. As it is spread very quickly by contagion, extra care must be taken to ensure maximum cleanliness. The child must have his own bed linen, towels and face flannels. Antibiotic cream may be applied and antiseptic baths (Savlon) can be used. Oral antibiotics may be required as the infection spreads so rapidly.

Seborrhoeic dermatitis

Sometimes called scurf or 'cradle cap', this is caused by the sebaceous glands on the scalp producing too much sebum or grease. It sometimes spreads to the skin, when it is seen as red scaly patches or as cracks in the skin above the ears, and on face, neck, axillae and eyebrows, or as brown scaly patches which may cover the whole scalp. Some mothers are afraid to wash over the anterior fontanelle, but it is quite safe to do so as this is covered by a tough membrane; washing with a solution of sodium bicarbonate 1 in 20 may remove scurf soon after it appears. Gently covering the scalp with olive oil and leaving it overnight helps to soften the crust. The family doctor or health visitor will be able to offer advice and help. Sometimes a lotion is prescribed which can be rubbed in at night and used to wash the scalp in the morning. It is important to ensure that the whole head is washed with medicated shampoo and rinsed thoroughly in clean water every day.

Tinea (ringworm)

This is a fungus known as a dermatophyte because it invades skin, hair and nail. The fungus spreads down the hair follicles on the scalp and penetrates the soft keratin which causes the hairs to break and gives rise to bald, scaly patches, which are ring-shaped, hence the term 'ringworm' (used less frequently now). A special lamp is used to detect fungal growth on the scalp. *Athlete's foot* is a common type of tinea. This causes intense irritation between the toes or painful blisters on the sole of the foot in hot weather. The space between the toes appears soggy and cracked and the feet have an unpleasant odour. Dry scaling on the soles and sides of the feet can spread to the nails causing discolouration and thickening. Finger nails can also be affected by this type of tinea known as *Tinea rubrum*. As all tinea is highly contagious, an infected child should be kept away from the nursery and all his toys used by himself alone. Any brushes, combs and towels should be destroyed as they will carry spores which cannot be removed. Athlete's foot is easily transmitted in communal baths and wet bathroom floors.

Griseofulvin may sometimes be given to clear up tinea, or Whitfield's ointment may be prescribed. After bathing, the space between the toes should be properly dried and a powder lightly applied. Special powders effective against tinea may be prescribed for use and some are available as over the counter preparations, e.g. Tinaderm.

Head lice (Pediculus capitis)

These are 1–4 mm long and appear greyish white. They can be seen in the hair or behind the ears. The mature louse lays eggs known as nits which are affixed to the hair by a cement-like substance which prevents them from flaking off like dandruff. Sixty or more eggs are laid in a month and as these hatch in a week and the lice are fully grown in 10–21 days, it is important to initiate eradication quickly. Lice suck blood and their bites cause intense irritation which may cause sleeplessness and reduced resistance to infection in the infested child. As lice were found to become resistant to some DDT preparations these are no longer used in treatment. Malathion used as Prioderm shampoo or lotion destroys head lice and nits and exerts a residual effect sometimes for several weeks afterwards. Lice have no resistance to Malathion.

Regular inspection of heads by nursery staff or health visitor should detect infestations before they spread. Children must have their own combs and brushes. During an infestation, dressing up clothes and hats should be removed from the nursery after careful inspection and disinfection. Observations usually leads to detection as infested children will scratch their heads frequently. When infestation occurs the child's parents should be informed and advice given as to treatment. The health visitor may do this but the child's teacher should also be informed as it affects activities. Small group activities where children work with heads close together should be avoided as lice can move from one head to another in this way. When the adult is beside the child to help, it is wise to keep the head above that of the child. Where coats and hats are hung together in the hallway, they must always be kept sufficiently apart.

Scabies

This is caused by the itch mite (*Sarcoptes scabiei*) which is ½ mm long. They spread by close, personal contact with infected people or more rarely by clothing, and an infestation can affect all the members of a family or a large number of children and staff in a nursery. The female mite burrows under the skin at the rate of 3 mm a day and lays her eggs after which she dies. When the larvae emerge after a few days they soon become adult and cause intense itching. Scratching with dirty nails leads to secondary infection and impetigo can develop. The burrows can be seen as dark lines about one and a half centimetres long and they are usually found on the wrists, at the ankles and elbows, between the fingers and in the armpits. A widespread rash also occurs, not necessarily in the same place as the burrows.

Treatment is usually aimed at the whole family. A hot bath is given and the whole body thoroughly washed and an emulsion of 25% solution benzyl benzoate is applied all over the body from neck to toes. When this has dried the patient can dress in clean clothing. A bath is taken after 48 hours and usually only one treatment is necessary. The infested person is advised to apply the emulsion to his hands everytime he washes them. To prevent reinfestation the clothes of the infected person are disinfected. Spread in a nursery can be prevented by early detection of the condition and referral to a doctor.

Threadworms (Oxyuris vermicularis)

These are very small and appear as white threads in the infected child's stool. They live in the bowel and the mature female crawls to the anus to lay her eggs at night. This causes intense itching and when the child scratches the eggs are picked up under the finger nails. When the fingers are put in the mouth the child swallows them and reinfestation occurs. Other children can be affected by contact with the infected child or by eating infected food. Threadworms cause sleeplessness, bedwetting at night (enuresis) and occasionally convulsions.

Treatment for threadworms involves prevention of reinfestation. The child's nails should be cut as short as possible and hands washed frequently under supervision. Pripsen is usually prescribed by the doctor. This is in the form of a raspberry flavoured drink which is usually taken by all the family (in the evening for adults and in the morning for children). A secondary precautionary dose given 14 days later is 95% effective and prevents cross-infestations in the family. To prevent scratching, the child should wear cotton mits or gloves and close-fitting pants at night. The anal area should be thoroughly washed (in the bath) and an ointment prescribed by the doctor should be applied around the anus. Strict adherence to rules of hygiene and cleanliness must be observed, particularly in preparation of food. The infected child should be told that the worms are more like threads as he may feel dirty and horrified to think that he has worms in his bottom. Reassurance is very important to prevent long-term effects.

Fleas (Pulex irritans)

These are another blood-sucking parasite. They can be up to 2½ mm long and the female lays large eggs singly, usually in bedding or dust. Fleas are wingless but they can jump and in this way are easily transmitted from one host to another. Flea bites appear as red lumps with a puncture spot on top and are very itchy. A search through bedding or clothing often locates a single flea but in serious infestations fumigation may be necessary, although fleas are now seen only rarely. Fleas from cats and dogs have also been known to bite humans and we have already noted that some children develop urticaria after contact with household pets. All animals should be disinfested and in a healthy state before young children are allowed to play with them.

Gastrointestinal Disorders

The signs and symptoms of gastrointestinal disorders in babies and children may be any or all of the following, to a greater or lesser degree: vomiting, pain, alteration in bowel habit, diarrhoea, constipation, offensive stool odour, change in stool colour (e.g. black, red, green, bright orange), abdominal distension, reduced or concentrated urinary output, weight loss, dehydration (dry wrinkled skin), restlessness and general malaise. All these symptoms should be taken seriously, documented, and promptly reported as the child may deteriorate rapidly.

Upper gastrointestinal tract

Vomiting. There are many causes of vomiting, but it should never be taken lightly as mineral and electrolyte losses may be severe. Vomiting following a head injury should be reported to a doctor without delay. It is important to note the timing, mechanism (e.g. effortless regurgitation or projectile) and content of the vomiting, and if the vomitus appears to contain more than merely partially digested food (e.g. blood) it should be reported and kept for medical inspection. It should also be noted whether the vomiting is merely an isolated episode or persistent.

Vomiting is distressing to the child who therefore needs to be supported by holding and being kept comfortable. Once the vomiting episode is over a mouthwash may be offered to remove traces of vomitus and the unpleasant residual taste. Fluids should be offered frequently in small quantities, as follows: 1 level teaspoonful of sugar in 120–180 ml water per kg of body weight per 24 hours for babies and young children.

Vomiting can be seen in infectious diseases such as whooping cough when it often occurs after an attack of coughing, but it can also be seen in the early stages of diseases such as pneumonia, otitis media and meningitis in which cases it will be accompanied by raised temperature, pulse, diarrhoea, loss of appetite and acute abdominal pain. Whenever these signs and symptoms accompany vomiting medical aid should be sought as these are serious conditions. Dehydration is possible in feverish illnesses and in gastroenteritis since fluid is lost in both vomiting and diarrhoea. Loss of sodium, phosphorus, potassium and other salts are also possible, with adverse effects on the sick child.

Feeding problems. Over- and under-feeding, food or milk allergy and lactose intolerance often present with vomiting as the main symptom.

Overfeeding is usually the result of an overzealous parent or nursery nurse and is easily corrected. Vomiting usually occurs immediately after the food. Overfeeding is rarely a problem in breast-fed babies.

Underfeeding means that the child, because she is hungry, takes the food very quickly, gulping down a lot of air at the same time. This causes abdominal distension and forces the stomach contents back up.

Allergy to proteins in cows' milk may make some children very ill and there may be skin rashes and diarrhoea. Advice from the GP or health visitor should be sought and soya milk (not goats' milk) substituted.

Lactose intolerance results from a deficiency of the enzyme lactase which splits the milk sugar lactose into glucose and galactose for proper absorption. Substitution of lactose-free milk or soya milk usually brings about a dramatic improvement.

Congenital pyloric stenosis. This is the thickening of the pyloric sphincter which causes a narrowing of the opening from the stomach to the duodenum. Signs of pyloric stenosis are obstruction, irritation of the stomach lining, projectile vomiting and weight loss. These usually first appear within 2–6 weeks after birth. Some cases resolve spontaneously at about 4 months but early severe cases require surgical correction.

In the intervening period between diagnosis and operation, the baby will require intravenous fluids to correct dehydration and electrolyte imbalance, and also gastric lavage to remove stale milk products from the stomach.

Hiatus hernia. This is caused by a congenital defect in the muscles of the diaphragm so that part of the stomach is pulled (herniates) through the opening into the thoracic cavity. Sphincter control is also affected, causing constant reflux of food and stomach secretions into the oesophagus (gullet).

The baby vomits food, mucus and sometimes even blood soon after feeds, and as a result loses weight. Treatment is by keeping the baby upright at *all* times (so that the stomach is below the diaphragm), giving feeds slowly (with the baby upright) and hernia repair by surgery.

Lower gastrointestinal tract

Abdominal pain. The causes of abdominal pain are varied: it can be a sign of acute appendicitis, a consequence of illness, or a reaction to stress. If cuddling or comforting the child does not resolve matters and there is fever, diarrhoea and/or vomiting, medical attention should be sought. If the baby or child turns white or grey, or lies curled up or bent double, he or she should be taken directly to hospital.

Acute appendicitis. This is most common between 5 and 12 years. The onset may be gradual, with restlessness, loss of appetite, nausea and occasional vomiting and constipation, or sudden, with fever, rapid pulse, furred tongue and a tender abdomen. The child is usually very irritable. A white blood cell count will usually be high, showing that infection is present. Treatment is by immediate surgery as perforation is more common and more serious in children than in adults and can lead to peritonitis.

Intestinal obstruction. This may be due to a congenital abnormality, e.g. duodenal atresia, or acquired, e.g. volvulus, intussusception, strangulated (inguinal) hernia, pressure from tumour, or a swallowed foreign body. The signs are vomiting, pain, total constipation and abdominal distension. Treatment is by surgery and is very urgent both to correct the obstruction and to resolve fluid and electrolyte imbalances.

Duodenal atresia. This is a narrowing or absence of the lumen of the duodenum causing obstruction with symptoms beginning some 4 hours after birth. Vomitus is usually bile-stained.

Volvulus. This is where a loop of bowel gets twisted around itself causing obstruction. Treatment is by urgent surgery to avoid prolonged ischaemia to the bowel and gangrene.

Intussusception. This is one of the most urgent emergencies of childhood, though fortunately quite rare. It refers to the telescoping of one portion of the bowel into another and frequently occurs shortly after weaning, when possibly, the change in diet sets up an inflammatory reaction in the ileocaecal region, where the small bowel enters the large bowel. Typically the child is aged between 3 months and 2 years, and suddenly has an acute attack of colic, causing him to draw up his legs. The pain is so intense that the child or baby turns white or grey. The pain may, however, go off in a few minutes and all will appear well, but it recurs some 20 minutes later. The child may pass 'red currant jelly' stool.

Diarrhoea. The term refers to frequent bowel motions, loose and fluid. The causes of diarrhoea include:

> Excess carbohydrate in feed
> Excess fat in feed
> Physiological diarrhoea (e.g. breast feeding)
> Epidemic diarrhoea
> Amoebic dysentery
> Allergic diarrhoea
> Staphylococcal enterocolitis
> Appendicitis
> Coeliac disease
> Ulcerative colitis
> Shigella (bacillary dysentery)
> Pathogenic *E. coli*
> Medication
> Febrile illness
> Gastroenteritis
> Emotional upset
> Salmonella (food poisoning)

Diarrhoea can often be prevented by basic hygiene, e.g. hand-washing before preparing food, or stricter anti-infective measures, e.g. sterilizing bottles, barrier nursing. Diarrhoea associated with feeding is frequently the result of incorrect preparation of the milk formula making the feed too concentrated and rich. Many other kinds of dietary problems can also cause diarrhoea.

Diarrhoea due to an infective organism is very rare among breast-fed babies.

Fluid loss – dehydration – is the most serious consequence of diarrhoea as it can have a detrimental effect on all the organ systems of the body. Mineral and electrolyte disturbances, if not corrected, can precipitate metabolic disturbance.

The GP should be informed, as rehydrating the baby is a priority. In mild dehydration, rehydration may safely be carried out at home and the child given half-strength feeds topped up with pre-boiled water, and plain boiled water on its own, between feeds until the diarrhoea has stopped. In more severe cases, the child will be referred to hospital for intravenous fluid and electrolyte correction.

Signs of marked dehydration include: sunken eyes, depressed fontanelles in babies of less than 12 months, laxity of skin (especially over the tummy), irritability or drowsiness, dry mouth and poor urine output.

Gastroenteritis. Gastroenteritis in children should not be confused with gastroenteritis in adults or ordinary diarrhoea. The causes are different and potential outcome far more serious in the younger age group.

Gastroenteritis can occur in children of all ages but is more common in premature babies and in babies who are not breast fed.

The causative organism is usually bacterial, e.g. *E. coli* or *Salmonella*, or dysentery; rarely, it may be viral. Gastroenteritis may also occur secondary to a primary infection elsewhere in the body, e.g. otitis media. The usual presenting symptoms are looser, more frequent stools, and sometimes offensive odour with traces of fresh blood or mucus present. However, the stools may also be green or bright orange and the child may pass free fluid. The frequent, loose motions contribute to significant fluid loss and although the child may obviously be hungry and thirsty feeds are often vomited back. The urine may become darker and more concentrated, which is a serious sign.

A baby does not need to lose much fluid before serious dehydration and electrolyte losses become life-threatening. The GP should be notified immediately the diarrhoea doesn't appear to resolve, or is greenish, or very smelly or very watery. Admission to hospital may be arranged for intravenous feeding and fluid and electrolyte correction. As gastroenteritis is very infectious, barrier nursing precautions will be undertaken.

Chronic diarrhoea, or that which persists after acute gastroenteritis, may be due to lactose intolerance (see Vomiting), cows' milk allergy (see Vomiting) or other food allergies, coeliac disease, cystic fibrosis, ulcerative colitis or immune deficiency states.

Where chronic diarrhoea is associated with failure to thrive, the problem may be malabsorption in the intestine. Weight loss can be dramatic in these cases, and if there is no response to the removal of possible allergenic foods in the diet the child is usually referred to hospital. The child with ulcerative colitis has similar symptoms to dysentery – blood and mucus in the diarrhoea, cramping pain in the lower abdomen. Fortunately this is still an uncommon condition.

Toddlers' diarrhoea. From the end of the first year to the age of 2–3 years, the commonest form of chronic diarrhoea is toddlers' diarrhoea, but this is not associated with the 'failure to thrive' syndrome. The GP will want to know the dietary pattern of the child and the family, as the cause is thought to be some exaggerated reflex between the stomach and the bowel, maintained by large meals, frequent snacks and cold drinks. The child appears happy, has no recent illness, a good appetite, and shows normal weight gain. Apart from the frequent smelly nappies that the parents have to cope with, there are no real problems associated with this type of diarrhoea, and adjustment of the size and type of meals may be all that is required.

Constipation. This is characterized by the hardness of the stools and the infrequency of defecation. It is not serious if a child only has a bowel action every 2 days, but if he frequently passes small, hard stools with great difficulty, he is constipated. Headache and furred tongue often accompanies constipation; the child may be irritable and complain of abdominal pain. The causes of constipation are an unbalanced diet which lacks bulky fibre (or roughage) necessary for peristalsis, lack of sufficient fluid, bowel obstruction, faulty management and training in habit formation, emotional reasons, lack of exercise, or regular laxatives which weaken the bowel muscles. Painful motions from constipation further complicate the condition.

Unfortunately a great deal of attention was traditionally focused on bowel activity. Breast-fed babies do not suffer from constipation but with underfeeding this may occur in bottle-fed babies. It is better to offer fruit and vegetables rather than large quantities of cereal when mixed feeding begins. Laxatives must never be given and expressions of anxiety by parents should be avoided. Rarely constipation may be due to intestinal obstruction but this will be referred to hospitals. An anal fissure may occur as a result of straining with hard stool and milk of magnesia may be prescribed to soften the faeces and make the passage less painful.

Chronic constipation sometimes causes soiling due to the seepage of fluid behind the hard stool which blocks the rectum.

Rarely, hypothyroidism may be the cause of chronic constipation in childhood.

Infestations

Gastrointestinal upsets with diarrhoea due to infestations are not common in the UK, but threadworms and roundworms, with a protozoan called *Giardia lamblia*, can be causative. Most children show no signs or symptoms in infestation of roundworms. In heavy infestation, the child becomes ill and fails to thrive, the abdomen is distended, and there may be colicky abdominal pain. The ova or worms can be found in the stools, and a drug such as piperazine may be prescribed.

Threadworms

These are about 5–10 mm long and affect mainly children aged 5–9 years. Very heavy infestation can result in diarrhoea and abdominal colic. Diagnosis may be made by seeing the short white threads in the faeces, or by strapping a piece of sellotape to the anus and surrounding skin at night, which traps the ova and occasionally an adult female worm, and these can then be seen under the microscope. Treatment is with piperazine as Pripsen, and the whole family may have to be involved in this.

Disorders of Metabolism and Absorption

Cystic fibrosis

This is the commonest (yet only seen in 5 percent of live births) of the congenital metabolic disorders and is the result of a recessive gene. There is generalized exocrine gland dysfunction with excessive sweating. The sweat contains high levels of sodium chloride and there is an abnormal viscosity of mucous secretion throughout the body. This results in chronic lung infections, and pancreative insufficiency which in turn gives rise to malabsorption with fatty stools, stunted growth and abdominal distension. Intestinal obstruction is seen in the neonate and this – i.e. meconium ileus – may even be present at birth.

Management is by pancreatic enzyme preparations, vitamin supplements, a low-fat, low-sodium diet, daily chest suction, physiotherapy, and humidification of air. Contact with the Cystic Fibrosis Society and genetic counselling is recommended. (See Chapter 1 on Genetic Defects.)

Phenylketonuria (P.K.U.)

This is due to a recessive gene (incidence 0.1 per 1000 live births) and arises when the enzyme necessary to convert phenylalanine, a protein substance, to tyrosine is absent. Phenylalanine accumulates in the blood and causes severe mental handicap. A rare condition, it can now be detected by a test performed 6–7 days after birth. The Guthrie test estimates the level of phenylalanine in the baby's blood and can be followed by using Phenistix for a quick estimation at frequent intervals. Milk preparations are available with low phenylalanine content but as they are unpleasant to taste and smell the child is weaned early on to foods which do not contain phenylalanine and has to persist on this special diet in childhood.

Galactosaemia

This is a condition in which the baby lacks the enzyme required to convert galactose, a milk sugar, into the simplest form of glucose for absorption. The condition is usually recognized early nowadays as babies are routinely tested for metabolic disorders by midwives or health visitors in the first weeks after birth. Low-lactose milk can then be given to babies suffering from this condition. Later, when mixed feeding is introduced the child must not be given foods which contain milk (this includes most cakes and puddings). A number of preparations are now available which do not contain milk in any form and are palatable and attractive.

Babies who are allergic to caseinogen or lactalbumin, the proteins in milk, are given milk preparations made from soya bean, and where there is a danger of obesity low-fat milk can be used.

Coeliac disease

Coeliac disease is a permanent, inherited inability to tolerate dietary wheat and rye gluten. Gluten is the protein part of flour, and in susceptible children can cause damage to the lining of the small intestine. Diagnosis of the condition usually takes place between 6 and 24 months. In the baby of 3–9 months, the illness may be acute, with severe diarrhoea and vomiting, and failure to thrive due to malabsorption of food. At 9–18 months of age, signs and symptoms give the 'typical' coeliac appearance: weight loss after a period of normal growth in the early months of life, abnormal and frequent stools, abdominal distension, anorexia, muscle wasting, mild clubbing of the fingers, vomiting (often in the

evening) and mood changes. In later childhood, the results of malabsorption are seen in anaemia, low levels of protein, calcium and vitamin K with sugar intolerance. When diagnosis of the condition is made, the child is given a gluten-free diet (see Special Diets p. 148).

Diabetes mellitus

This is rare but as one-fifth of all diabetic people in Great Britain are children, we have to be aware of the signs and symptoms of the condition.

It is due to insufficient secretion of insulin, the hormone produced by the pancreas. As the level of glucose in the blood is affected by insulin (which allows glucose to be stored as glycogen in the liver and muscle cells) the mechanism of supply to the tissues breaks down and glucose is excreted in the urine, while blood glucose levels are higher than normal. A sudden intense thirst accompanies excessive urine output – the child may begin to wet the bed. Some children may have abdominal pain and even vomiting, while others may become drowsy and eventually lose consciousness. Simple blood and urine tests are used by the GP to determine diabetes.

Treatment involves insulin taken by injection and mothers are taught to give injections and perform simple urine tests with Clinitest strips and tablets which give an orange colour if too much sugar is present. Children are often able to carry out their own treatment after they have been shown the correct way. This is important psychologically as they are not made to feel dependent because of their condition.

Illness and Hospitalization

When to Call the Doctor

The sudden nature of children's illness tends to cause panic in parents. Their child can be happily playing in the morning and yet have a high temperature associated with an infection by the end of the afternoon. Sometimes the child complains of 'tummy ache' but, as children under three are unable to verbalize sore throats or earache, the 'tummy ache' could refer to any of these. The entry to nursery or primary school frequently brings childhood infections and nursery/school staff become familiar with the various signs and symptoms which they are able to point out if the parents have missed them. Of course a 'tummy ache' may be a child's way of showing dislike of separation from parents. Sally Ann went through a period of unhappiness at playgroup around the time of her baby sister's arrival. Every day she came home saying 'I sick' but a cuddle and extra attention soon put that right! Parents worry about sending for the doctor – will he be annoyed if it turns out to be only trivial? However, ear, nose and throat conditions are particularly rife in young children and throat infections can lead to otitis media (middle ear infection) as the throat is connected to the middle ear by the Eustachian tube. Sometimes the child will rub his ear to indicate that it is painful. The child of five to seven will be able to indicate verbally the location of pain and the doctor should be informed, since otitis media can cause deafness if it occurs frequently, due to the accumulation of mucus which prevents the ossicles (tiny bones which vibrate as sound waves pass from outer to inner ear) from vibrating properly. This condition of 'glue ear' is very common and it is wise to have the child's hearing checked after ear infections. Very rarely, otitis media could lead to meningitis, so it is essential to consult a doctor.

Diarrhoea and vomiting are always alarming, particularly in a young baby. The loss of fluid from the body can cause dehydration which requires urgent replacement of lost fluid and antibiotics for the causative infection.

'Croup' is another condition in young babies which necessitates a doctor's visit. Here, the respiratory tract is swollen and narrowed, which causes grave difficulties in breathing. A steaming kettle in the baby's room will help until the doctor arrives.

The Sick Child

Signs of illness

Signs of illness in a child include raised temperature, increased pulse and respiration rate, loss of appetite, sweating, flushed or pale complexion, listlessness, lack of interest in play, abnormal posture, photophobia (fear of light), sleeplessness, unusual crying bouts, irritability and fretfulness, vomiting and change in frequency, colour and consistency of stools. A raised temperature alone is not necessarily a sign of illness. Children can become very hot at times without abnormality whereas babies with a temperature which is lower than normal may be ill. A depressed anterior fontanelle in babies under 18 months is a sign of dehydration. Abnormal posture is seen in pain and discomfort; a baby with 'colic' – abdominal pains – usually draws his knees up to his chest and lies in this position. Photophobia is indicated when the child turns his head away from the light or buries his head under the bedclothes when in bed. Loud crying and rubbing the affected ear occurs in earache. Strong continuous crying is heard when the baby is hungry, a feeble moan in pain and exhaustion, and a sharp piercing cry in brain injury. Vomiting and diarrhoea may indicate a serious infection such as dysentery and should be notified to the doctor immediately. Careful observation by the mother or nursery nurse of any departure from normal appearance and behaviour often leads to early diagnosis and quicker recovery in childhood illnesses.

Care of the child in bed

The sickroom. In the house this is usually the child's bedroom. In the nursery, a small room is usually furnished and maintained for use until the child has seen a doctor, or until he recovers from a mild bout of sickness. The sickroom should be as cheerful as possible, painted in a restful colour (pale green has been found to have a peaceful effect on sick people), well ventilated and furnished in a homely rather than a clinical fashion. A sink is useful for the patient and the nurse or visiting doctor but, in most families, bowls of hot water will be brought from the bathroom. Clean towels for bath and handwashing should always be available. The bed should be high enough from the floor to facilitate cleaning below it and should not have bars at top or bottom in case a small child pokes his head through these. Bedclothes should be light but warm and carefully tucked in. Pillows should not be too bulky.

The child who is sick at home may be happier on a couch or camp bed in the living room if the mother is able to cope with this arrangement. Safety precautions must be stringently observed – breakable articles should not be within reach, fires should be well guarded and fluffy cushions should not be used as pillows. This saves the mother frequent trips upstairs and the expense of extra heating but is not a practical idea if the child has an infectious illness or is irritable and upset by noise.

Nursing. A sick child will often want to sleep most of the time, and as this gives the antibodies in his blood an opportunity to fight against the infection good conditions which predispose to sleep should be encouraged. The curtains can be closed to prevent the distraction of bright light; this is particularly important in an infection like measles where photophobia may be present. If the child has bouts of vomiting a receptacle should be kept at his bedside, emptied and washed after rinsing in Savlon.

The doctor may wish to see vomited matter in case of abnormality, so a covered specimen should be kept if the mother or nursery nurse is uncertain of the child's condition. Soiled linen and blankets should be changed to prevent discomfort. It is not necessary to put extra blankets on the bed. Frequently the child is overheated rather than cold and if he has a feverish illness it is better not to clothe him with extra layers as he may require cooling to lower the temperature. When a child's temperature rises above 39.4°C (103°F) tepid sponging may be advised by the doctor as it lessens the chance of febrile convulsions which occur as a result of fever.

Usually removal of extra blankets or a junior aspirin reduces the temperature but if the child is too ill and uncomfortable the cooling effect of sponging is pleasant. The mother or nursery nurse should take the child's temperature every 10 minutes throughout the treatment and stop when it falls below 38.5°C). Instructions for this procedure are usually given by the doctor but it can be carried out quite simply. The child is undressed and placed on a waterproof sheet covered by a towel or blanket. Tepid (cool) water is preferable to cold as cold water causes contraction of blood vessels in the skin and cooling requires dilatation of blood vessels. Cloths soaked in tepid water can be wrapped loosely round the child's neck and thighs after sponging all over the body. Sponging usually takes place every 2 hours and for 30 minutes only at one time.

Temperature, pulse and respiration. These are usually observed and recorded together as they are indicators of illness. It is important to realize that babies and children normally have faster pulse and respiration rates than adults.

Normal body temperature is 37°C (98.4°F) and this is usually indicated by a dot or arrow on the thermometer. Pyrexia means that the temperature is raised and when severe this can mean over 40.6°C. Hypothermia is a state of reduced temperature and usually means a temperature below 36.4°C.

The usual site for taking the temperature in a baby under a year old is the rectum and, for children over that age, the axilla (armpit) or groin. This is to avoid the possibility of a broken thermometer and the subsequent alarm if it is placed in the mouth and the child bites it. Older children are able to hold the thermometer in the mouth without great difficulty.

When taking the temperature of a baby, the mother can lay the naked baby across her lap on his tummy. The thermometer should be shaken down before use so that it does not register above 35°C (92°F). Some doctors use a special thermometer for babies which registers a temperature of 29.4°C (85°F) as their fluctuations in body heat can be greater than the normal range. The bulb end of the thermometer which contains the mercury is lubricated with a little petroleum jelly and gently inserted into the baby's rectum while he is held firmly with the other hand to prevent sudden movements and a broken thermometer. After holding the thermometer in place for 1 minute, the mother removes it, reads the temperature, wraps the baby in his shawl and then records the temperature. The rectal temperature is 1°C higher than the temperature taken in the axilla or groin. Before returning the thermometer to its case it should be washed in cold water (hot water may break it) and placed in a disinfectant solution, e.g. Savlon (1 in 20).

Where the axilla or groin is used to take the temperature the child should lie on his side in a comfortable position. The thermometer should be dry and not register above 35°C when put into position. It is useful to have a small tray to hand with a towel, cotton wool swab in a dish, the thermometer ready for use and receptacle with disinfectant for the thermometer after use. As the sick child may be fretful it is wise to reassure him and the adult can tell him the exercise is 'to see if he is hot'. After wiping the skin with cotton wool or towel, the bulb end of the thermometer is placed in the axilla or groin and held there for 3 minutes. It is important to ensure that there is no clothing between the skin and the thermometer as this will give an incorrect reading. When the thermometer is removed the child is covered up and the temperature is recorded. The thermometer is then disinfected, dried and returned to its case.

Pulse and respiration vary with age, physical and emotional activity. At birth, the rates are rapid and decrease as the child grows older. As excitement at temperature taking may increase the pulse rate, it is best to record it while the child is asleep. The anterior fontanelle is the usual site for a baby, and the temporal artery (which passes over the temporal bone in front of the ear) or the radial artery at the wrist (outer side parallel with the thumb) for older children.

Nutrition. The sick child may not want any food while he feels feverish and of course food should never be forced upon the child at any time. A supply of drinks (preferably fresh orange or blackcurrant juice as these contain vitamin C) can be kept available at the bedside. It is best to have the bottle or jug of juice on a bedside table, covered to prevent droplet infection or dust, and a plastic mug (washed and replaced everyday) on a tray. To prevent stained carpets and bedclothes a piece of plastic sheeting can be placed on the floor beside the bed and a towel or bib put around the child to enable him to drink without wetting his pyjamas. Milk is a very nutritious drink and if the child dislikes milk a spoonful of milkshake syrup can be added to make it more palatable for him. The addition of sugar to drinks provides a sick child with a ready supply of energy – ordinary table sugar (sucrose) is just as effective as expensive glucose preparations. Some children like meaty drinks and Bovril, Marmite and Oxo are easy to digest if the child wants a savoury rather than a sweet drink. Fruit purees, thickened soups, ice-cream and jellies are usually also acceptable.

Most sick children do not find ordinary food attractive but they may be willing to have small pieces of buttered bread or fingers of toast after a couple of days. A lightly boiled egg is easily digested and is also suitable. Egg custard is a nutritious sweet and some children will take milk puddings without difficulty. If the child has whooping cough or some condition which causes frequent vomiting he may become dehydrated, so copious fluids will be required, and also bland foods which do not cause regurgitation. 'Thickening' fluids (such as cornflour or arrowroot made with milk) can be given in small amounts after each bout of coughing. As with all meal times the adult must not show anxiety at the child's refusal of food. Children may lose weight when they are ill but they soon regain weight on return to health.

Administration of medicines. This is not usually difficult as most children's medicines are flavoured to make them more palatable and easy to swallow. If capsules or tablets are prescribed they can be crushed and given in fruit juice. A kindly, firm approach is required if the child refuses medicine and the adult must be prepared to explain why it is necessary, and to persuade the child. If a reluctant child is forced to take medicine he may spit it out or make himself sick. A baby should be held in the adult's arms while sips of medicine are placed at the back of the tongue with a spoon. If the baby refuses to take any medicine despite all the adult's efforts this must be reported to the doctor as it will affect the child's recovery.

Where medicines are distributed to different children in a nursery the nursery nurse must always check the name on the bottle and the dosage before administration. Serious accidents can occur if the child is given the wrong medicine or the wrong dosage. A teaspoon is a doubtful measure unless it is known to contain 5 millilitres and it is customary to use a small graduated medicine container which can be glass or plastic. The container should be held at eye level while the medicine is poured into it from the bottle (held with the label upwards) to ensure accurate measurement of the dose. It should not be necessary to bribe the child with promise of a reward and the practice of giving sweets after medicine can have unfortunate effects on teeth and behaviour. After administration the bottle should be wiped, the top replaced and then returned to the medicine cupboard. In the home or in the nursery the medicine cupboard should be at a height which is inaccessible to the children and kept locked. This is particularly important when adult medicines are stored there since many coloured pills resemble sweets and there could be serious consequences if children were to swallow some of them. Medicines should be given as frequently as prescribed, e.g. three times a day could be given after breakfast, lunch and supper, unless it states 'before food'. If medicines and tablets are left when the person has recovered from the illness, they should be discarded as some can be harmful if taken after long storage. Medicines should never be transferred from one container to another as this makes identificaton difficult if a child takes an overdose. Most bottles now have 'child resistant' caps and these should always be replaced properly to be effective.

Some mothers dislike taking their child to the doctor unless he is in severe pain. They resort to medicines bought from the local chemist and while these may be useful in mild illness, it is safer to inform the family doctor when the child refuses foods, has diarrhoea, vomiting or headache or other signs of illness. Aspirin is frequently given to children and the 'junior' type is of a suitable strength for them, but aspirin should never be given to children under a year old and dosage should never last long. Often a walk in the fresh air or rest is sufficient treatment for a minor illness.

Convalescence. If the sick child is confined to his bedroom he will need some activity when he sits up and begins to feel better. He could be brought downstairs for the afternoons and allowed to watch children's TV programmes. It is not necessary to buy new and expensive toys to amuse a convalescent child; he will enjoy a favourite jigsaw puzzle if a tray is provided for him to lay it out. Painting and crayoning can be carried out without damage to bedclothes if a plastic sheet is placed over the bed. It is useful to have a 'surprise box' for when children are ill. Into this can go odd scraps of material left over from dressmaking, threads, wools, odd buttons, Christmas cards, small toys thrown aside and one or two cuddly dolls or teddy bears. An 'Action Man' or paper doll dressing kits are enjoyed by children over 5 years who have the manual dexterity for this exercise which can lead to imaginative play.

Pictures can be cut from used cards or coloured magazines and stuck into a scrap book. Small cardboard boxes become spaceships, forts and fire stations in the hands of children. The convalescent child who is still inclined to be clinging and requires fussing and petting may be happy just holding a comfort toy such as a doll or teddy bear. Some children become attached to a small blanket or shawl during illness and use it as a comforter for some time after their recovery. A number of books are now available with stories about sick children and the child will appreciate the full undivided attention of the adult while a story is read to him at different times of the day instead of just at bedtime. Where the child is very young or disinclined to

activity, a series of mobiles made from foil milk tops, animal shapes or even model cars and aeroplanes can be suspended by wires or nylon thread over the bed. A device used in hospitals now enables the child to reach for toys which are attached to a metal frame fixed to the bed within easy distance.

If the child is suffering from an infectious disease he will not be allowed to have visitors in the early stages. Many parents are not keen to have their children exposed to colds and other infections and keep children away from the sick child. The family doctor will decide when the child is fit to return to school and length of absence will be determined by the local regulations relating to infectious diseases.

Hospitalization

Hospitalization is often a frightening prospect for children and their parents as they fear the effects of separation, unfamiliar surroundings, strange nurses and doctors, and possibly painful procedures on the child. Nowadays most hospitals allow easy access to parents for visiting and many accommodate parents for the duration of the child's stay, to prevent a sense of abandonment and long-term emotional disturbance. Not all children will suffer adverse effects of hospitalization – some older children enjoy the novelty and as teachers are usually provided in children's wards for long-term illnesses or orthopaedic conditions they do not have to worry about falling behind their schoolmates in school work.

Ideally, children should have the opportunity to visit a hospital before they become ill. This is difficult as some hospitals refuse visitors under the age of 12 but even a visit to the Out-Patients' clinic with another member of the family can help to overcome the fear of the unknown. When a date is given for hospitalization the parents should take the child for a preliminary visit to meet the ward sister. This enables them to inform the nurses of the child's eating and sleeping patterns and his words for the toilet. Children under five often find hospitalization most difficult as they cannot communicate and make their wants known. Nursing staff know this and are usually eager to discover from the parents all they can to help the child feel more at home and recover quickly.

Preparation of the child for entry to hospital

Studies show preparation for hospitalization can be carried out effectively through play and story telling. Children love playing at doctors and nurses and although they do not need to have expensive uniform kits bought for them it is useful to accustom them to the idea of white coats and nurses' aprons, as these can be frightening because of unfamiliarity. A toy stethoscope can also be used to remove fear of examinations, and masks and thermometers shown and explained to the child. Television provides a useful medium for removing fear of hospitals through programmes about nurses which, though fictitious, present an accurate picture of hospital life. As children with no previous experience of separation from their mothers are said to be most distressed at hospitalization it is a good idea for the parents to leave the child with a relative or familiar babysitter on a few occasions, to accustom them to brief separations. Only children, youngest children, those from extended families, insecure, aggressive, inhibited, over-dependent children and those with anxious mothers are known to be most at risk from adverse effects. Children may also believe that their hospitalization is a punishment for being particularly naughty. Continous preparation is preferable as children may be too young or admitted in an emergency and cannot therefore be adequately prepared prior to admission.

Care of the child in hospital

This can be shared by the nurses and parents where the latter are allowed to sleep in. If a bath is required on admission the parent can help with this and settle the child to sleep which otherwise might be difficult in a strange setting. Nurses should explain procedures and techniques to parents to reassure them and in order that they can then explain simply to the child. A variety of puppets and dolls with either real equipment or models can be used for children to play out medical procedures. The child is more likely to eat normally when his parents are at hand and he does not suffer from role conflict between the nurse and his mother as he observes them working together. Since fear of parental rejection is the main feature of hospitalization, the child feels more secure through maintenance of family contact. The parents feel happier when

they can continue in their role as parents and need not fear a takeover by their substitutes. Their anxiety is removed as treatments are explained to them and any guilt feelings they may have if the child's admission followed an accident are reduced.

If an operation is performed, the parents can help to prepare the child with explanation of the need for urine samples and abstinence from food or drink beforehand. They can also reassure the child that he will fall asleep when given an injection before the operation, and that the operation will not commence until he is fully asleep. The child will also need reassurance that he will wake up again after the operation and if the parents are sitting at his bedside when he recovers from the anaesthetic he will feel more comfortable and secure.

As soon as the child begins to feel better he will be encouraged to participate in play activities on the ward. Many hospitals employ play specialists who may be trained nursery teachers or nursery nurses. In some areas playgroup workers set up play facilities in children's wards with the cooperation of the nursing staff. Nurses who are trained to look after sick children usually have a good understanding of the child's need to learn and develop through play and are able to supervise play facilities. Parents can help the nurses or play specialist by indicating the level at which their child enjoys plays and encouraging him to participate. They can often help with other children whose parents are not with them.

Some paediatric units have specially furnished playrooms with toys and play materials to suit a wide range of children. They may be staffed by play therapists who have undergone a training course which enables them to understand children who have special needs. Even children who behave normally at home may resort to aggressive outbursts in hospital and the play therapist knows how to cope and tries to increase the child's sense of security and remove the fears which are the reason for his aggression.

The National Association for the Welfare of Children in Hospital produces a number of useful leaflets and books for parents and children (address in Appendix). There is also a National Association of Hospital Play staff (address in Appendix).

When parents are not able to be with their child throughout his stay in hospital they should visit as frequently as possible to maintain family contact, prevent the child from feeling rejected, reassure themselves and speed the child's recovery. Often an anxious parent can transmit fears to the child and frequent communication with the nursing staff can allay anxiety to the ultimate benefit of the child. A surprise box or a favourite toy can be brought in by the parents to maintain links with home, and his brothers, sisters and friends in nursery or school can be encouraged to send cards. It is very exciting for the child's name to be used by the ward sister as she brings him a card or letter and he feels more confident and secure in his importance. All human beings need to feel loved and small events like this can enable the sick child to enjoy this basic satisfaction.

Effects of hospitalization

Children require a continuous loving relationship for healthy development so any interruption of this presents a risk to their emotional wellbeing. If the length of stay is under 1 week it is unlikely to have adverse effects but, after this, social and psychological factors may lead to even longer stays. Most children, particularly if they are under five years of age, are likely to show some behaviour disturbance when they return home, but this may be because of the contrast between home and hospital environments and daily routines. A number of children show bowel and bladder disturbances and a few may have nightmares and interrupted sleep patterns. Few children suffer from persistent disturbance and most recover within 6 months.

One study of adolescent children admitted to hospital for more than 1 week under the age of five revealed an increased risk of behaviour disturbance and poor reading attainment, and a greater likelihood of delinquency and instability in job patterns. Studies of children aged from one to 14 years found the effects of hospitalization decreased with increasing age and the crucial time is known to be between 6 months and 3–4 years.

Parents should recognize that the child needs to adjust and not be too alarmed at uncharacteristic aggression or over-dependence. Understanding and reassurance will help the child to feel secure in his family relationships again, although this may take a few weeks and, like any other aspect of development, it must proceed at the child's own pace.

Convalescent care after a stay in hospital

When a child returns home he will require a period of transitional care as he gradually adjusts to the routine of family life from the clinical routine of the hospital ward. He may have become accustomed to early morning waking and be disgruntled or anxious when his family are still asleep at 6 a.m. and no-one brings him a drink. A glass of orange juice or milk can be left beside his bed at night-time for this purpose and some toys or games put out on the bedside table, so that he can play quietly until his parents come in to see him. He may have little appetite but a high-protein diet may be prescribed by the GP, together with foods rich in iron and vitamins, to promote recovery, prevent further infection and replace haemoglobin, which is often depleted after a major illness or operation. Fresh juices of citrus fruits (orange, lemon, grapefruit, lime) are pleasant to drink and contain vitamin C, essential for post-operative tissue repair. At first milk puddings only may be accepted and eventually fruit can be added – banana slices, dried apricots, until he takes chicken or turkey and perhaps a little fish cooked in a pleasant sauce. Obviously the presentation of food is important where lack of appetite persists – small amounts, colourfully arranged on the child's 'own' plate will be more readily accepted. Apart from spreading infection, allotting china and utensils for the child's exclusive use makes him feel 'special' and eases him from a situation where he had constant attention to one where he has to share parental attention with others. Familiarity of his room and possessions help to accustom him to the normal routine of the home but he will need reassurance, and possibly want a nightlight if he exhibits regressional behaviour.

The mother should be aided by the father and siblings in sitting, playing or reading stories with the child to encourage the security of 'belonging'. It is a good idea to allow the child to talk about hospital and still play with 'medical' equipment as he relives his experiences as this allows him to vent any frustration or problems he has repressed. Friends from school or nursery should be encouraged to visit as his recovery progresses. As soon as possible he should be allowed to join in family meals and join in light exercise with his brothers and sisters outside if possible. Outings to places of interest, such as the seaside, enable the child to benefit from fresh air and sunlight, when present, but all activities must be gradually introduced as over-stimulation and too much, even of good things, can be harmful and impede recovery.

Day hospitals

The idea of treating children as out-patients was pioneered at the beginning of the century by a paediatric surgeon, James Nicoll, at the Royal Hospital for Sick Children in Glasgow, who operated on 9000 children with congenital abnormalities in this way. Despite the advantages to children of this idea it is only in the past 15 years that paediatricians have organized day hospitals for children. As explained previously, 'glue ear' is a very common condition in young children and a day hospital now operates in Cambridge to deal with this and other ear, nose and throat conditions. To prevent deafness through 'glue ear', small tubes called grommets are placed through the ear drum. They equalize the pressure across the ear drum so that fluid can drain away through the tube and hearing returns completely. If the condition is untreated, prolonged deafness can result so a purpose-built hospital unit for day cases is an essential preventative measure. Parents are given clear instructions as to preparation of the child. The GP is contacted by the hospital who informs the staff if the home conditions are not conducive to good recovery. Both parents usually accompany the child and remain while he is examined, having completed a questionnaire as to the child's history of illness. Then parents don masks and gowns and go into the operating theatre with their child, holding his hand until he falls asleep under the anaesthetic. After the operation the child is taken to the recovery area and, where his condition permits, is placed in his mother's arms, to wake up to a familiar face and voice. Obviously, this is of great benefit to the child who avoids the often drastic effects of hospitalization. Studies show that children who are informed and prepared, and those who are accompanied by their mothers, suffer less emotional disturbance and make a better adjustment to the hospital environment.

6

Children with Special Needs

Children with special needs are children who have learning difficulties of some kind – whether because they are partially sighted, of limited intelligence or autistic – and those with physical disablities of various types.

Research suggests that one in six children will need special educational provision at any one time, and that one in five will require it at some point in their school career. It is important that the emphasis of special education is placed on the child's *needs* and not his disabilities, and that parents should be regarded as partners with professionals in helping their children.

Educational home visitors are trained nursery teachers who visit homes to help mothers stimulate their children. They are invaluable in areas where nursery facilities are lacking.

Parents should be given information, advice and practical help with their children, including a variety of short-term relief placements. There is no doubt that many children in long-stay residential hospitals would not need to be there if community and local authority services were adequate.

Mental Handicap
(now termed as 'Learning Difficulties')

This must not be confused with mental illness. Psychiatric disorders may be seen in some mentally handicapped children, but they do not cause mental handicap. Mental handicap has many causative factors, some of them unknown. Chromosomal defects, as seen in Down's syndrome (where there are 47 instead of the normal 46 chromosomes in the genetic make-up), and the effects of disease such as meningitis which may cause brain damage, are known causes of mental handicap, but there are over 300 types of unknown cause. Early detection and identification is important 'so that treatment, if available, for a specific condition can be started as early as possible; so that complications can be

prevented; in order to help and support a family in their care of the handicapped child; for genetic counselling with regard to the possible involvement of subsequent offspring; to alert the health, social and educational services that extra help will be required for a particular family' (Dr M. Griffiths, 1973).

Certain conditions such as Down's syndrome can be recognized at birth or soon after because of characteristics seen in the baby. Others, such as severe cerebral palsy and spina bifida, are regarded as conditions in which mental handicap may be present, but this is not always so. Not all mentally handicapped children have the condition at birth. Some become so as a result of physical trauma (disease or accidents).

Cultural, familial and environmental factors can also cause mental handicap or make it more obvious. Parents of low intelligence and no academic interest often have an adverse effect on the IQ levels of their children. Poor housing conditions, physical illnesses and malnutrition can all affect intellectual development. It has been established that a large number of 'mildly' mentally handicapped people belong to a sub-cultural group who suffer from adverse environmental factors. Lack of stimulation can depress IQ levels even further and nursery group provision with opportunities for further essential learning activities and play related to the child's needs has been found to have a positive effect, but only when parents carried on the stimulation at home. The Educational Home Visitor can help parents of mentally handicapped children by devising programmes which are an extension of the nursery activities, to help the child.

Malnutrition has been said to be responsible for retarded intellectual development mainly because of its effect on the brain. The human brain has two 'critical time' periods at 1–8 weeks of gestation and from mid-pregnancy to the age of about 3 years; 25% of the adult complement of brain cells are present at birth and 90–95% by

1 year of age. The cerebellum is relatively underdeveloped at birth, but has a shorter more rapid period of cell multiplication in the postnatal period. Lack of adequate nutrition at this stage is more likely to be injurious, resulting in poor fine motor performance. Breast feeding has been found to reduce the risk of brain injury from malnutrition.

Developmental tests can be made on babies under 1 year of life, and these may lead to diagnosis of mental handicap in a child who has not reached the 'milestone' of grasping for objects, but who has escaped detection at birth. Often parents suspect abnormalities when their child does not sit up, walk or vocalize at the usual age, but this may mean that the child is a year old before the condition is diagnosed and specialized help can be offered. The monitoring of developmental progress by primary health care teams could help to prevent missed diagnosis and promote early identification. Referral to a district handicap team could provide the 'appropriate and appropriately timed help' so desperately required by the handicapped child and his parents.

Mental handicap is not a specific term. Terms such as 'Severely' or 'Mildly' mentally handicapped are no longer used. Children previously described thus are now said to have 'special needs'. Within the group of children so described there is a wide range of abilities and disabilities. Those in the IQ range 70–100 were termed 'mildly mentally handicapped' (Educationally Subnormal ESN(M)) and often function well in the 'normal' population. Others have IQs in the 50–70 range and were described as 'moderately mentally handicapped', while those with IQs below 50 were said to be 'severely mentally handicapped' (ESN(S)). Some mentally handicapped people have other handicaps of a physical or sensory nature; many have speech defects, some suffer from epilepsy, and some may be described as 'multiply handicapped'.

However, labels and IQs do not really tell professional carers or parents much that will enable them to aid the development of the mentally handicapped child. Social skills are more relevant and measurements of Social Competence such as the Gunzburg Assessment Charts or the American Association of Mental Deficiency tests can be made by teachers and others after instruction. These tests give a profile of the child, what he can and cannot do in many aspects of development. One finds examples of

people in the IQ range below 50 who can live independently while others of higher IQs cannot. Much depends on the quality of compensatory care and the time of detection. Children brought up in long-stay institutions have been described as vulnerable to various forms of deprivation which may eventually create additional handicaps for them.

Behaviour problems are sometimes an accompaniment to mental handicap. Studies show that children in some special schools have increased depression, inhibition, tension and aggression towards adults. There are three times as many of these children (once termed as maladjusted) than in ordinary schools. Children placed in the maladjusted group were more likely to have unstable family backgrounds, poor health and physical defects. Disturbed children often have parents who showed hostility to school themselves.

Down's Syndrome

This was first described by John Langdon Down in 1866 and is the commonest syndrome associated with mental handicap. Down used the word 'mongolism' to explain the physical characteristics of the child, which he found similar to the features of the Mongolian people.

Unfortunately this incorrect term (many Down's syndrome children do not have the same facial appearance) still persists today. The cause of Down's syndrome was not discovered until 1959 when leJeune, Gautier and Turpin showed that the cells of children with this condition contained 47 instead of 46 chromosomes, the additional one being attached to the 21st chromosome. Later discoveries showed that translocation of the chromosome to another group could be responsible. In trisomy 21, the defect is likely to occur during conception; in translocation the condition may be present in the mother and there is a 1 in 10 chance that a subsequent child could be affected.

A third type of Down's syndrome is Mosaicism, in which some cells are genetically Down's syndrome, while others are normal. The age of the mother and, to a lesser extent, the father has been found to be a major factor. Mothers at 20 years are said to have a one in 2300 chance of conceiving a Down's syndrome child; at 45 the likelihood is one in 54. Australian research has shown a link between infective hepatitis and

Down's syndrome, but it is thought unlikely that this is connected with maternal age. Between 65 and 80% of Down's syndrome conceptions are lost as spontaneous abortions. Half of all Down's syndrome children fail to reach their fifth birthday, but an increasing number now survive to old age. Respiratory infections are the commonest cause of death. The condition occurs in all national and racial groups, and has an incidence of one in 700.

Physical characteristics involve a number of factors, but not all of these appear in every child. Fingers are short and broad, with the little finger often incurved and a single or 'simian' curve across the palm. The neck and feet are usually shortened, the face is usually relatively flat, the tongue and lips often fissured, the ears small and angular with a small lobe or no lobe at all. The eyes tend to slant upwards and outwards and to have epicanthic folds (vertical folds of skin at the inner corner of the eye), hence the description 'mongolism'. Additional handicaps are often seen with these.

Eyesight is often abnormal, squints and myopia are common and cataracts may exist. Hearing is sometimes impaired and there is a tendency to upper respiratory infections and bowel abnormalities. Circulation may be poor, leading to marbling of the skin. Many congenital abnormalities such as leukaemia, dislocated hips and cardiac malfunction are also more common than in the 'normal' population.

All Down's syndrome children have learning difficulties to some extent, although many can be taught to read and write. Measured intelligence tends to decrease with increasing age (from average of 70 at 6 months to 30–40 at 6–9 years). Girls tend to score higher than boys who are often more severely handicapped. Motor and mental scores were found to improve with regular home visits and support from professional staff. In tests of specific abilities, these children perform better on tests of visual shapes than other severely retarded children, and are good at understanding pictures and expression by gestures. They do less well at tasks which involve tactile recognition, and show increased language delay as the years go by. All studies of parents of Down's children show their need to be told of their child's handicap as early and as honestly as possible, and stress that the earlier parents receive support and advice, the earlier this can help their children.

The only method of prevention of Down's syndrome is antenatal screening by means of amniocentesis, and subsequent termination of pregnancy. Parents' groups offer support and help to parents of these children – the Down's Babies Children's Association has published leaflets for them, and local MENCAP groups offer support for parents. These groups appreciate the role of professionals in providing advice for parents and in helping them to develop positive and optimistic attitudes towards their children and their development potential.

In the nursery environment, professionals have to understand the effects of the handicap on the child, and reinforce and extend the stimulation provided by enlightened parents. Play should help the child to develop independence as there is always a danger of over-protection from parents and others. It is of little practical value to talk of 'mental ages' – one still hears it said of a mentally handicapped adult: 'He has the mind of a 2-year-old', which is inaccurate. Worse is the description of severely handicapped children as 'cabbages'. Why this particular vegetable is chosen to depict a human child who, however grossly handicapped, possesses human qualities, remains a mystery and an insult to all parents of these children, since it implies that they have produced an inhuman object.

Mentally handicapped children need love as all children do, and part of this must be respect for their dignity as human beings, and care which involves presentation of tasks within their capacity, and those which will 'stretch' their potential, however limited. Nothing succeeds like success, and while progress is often minimal, one tiny achievement is a major step forward for the child and a major reward for his mentor.

Cretinism

This is a very rare condition nowadays. It is caused by hypothyroidism (under-secretion of the thyroid gland), which affects all aspects of growth. Maternal hormones supply a baby's needs for the first 3 months after birth. Then if the baby's thyroid gland is underactive, stunting of physical and mental growth is seen. If left untreated, the child becomes a mentally retarded dwarf with coarse facial features. Early detection of the condition and administration of thyroxine reverses the symptoms but mental retardation persists in some cases.

Epilepsy

This is a reaction rather than a disease. It is called *symptomatic* when a cause is found and *ideopathic* when the cause is unknown. Most epileptic people do not have mental handicap, but it is sometimes seen in mentally handicapped children as a result of convulsions in infancy. Fits or convulsions may occur as a result of injury, infection, electric shock, various drugs and asphyxia.

The episode of disorganized and excessive activity in some part of the brain causes disturbance of sensation, movement or consciousness according to which area of the brain is involved. There may be preliminary symptoms or aura which can be uncontrolled movements in some part of the body, or a sensation. During the attack the patient falls unconscious, his muscles stiffen and then twitch violently, and the bladder may empty. The attack lasts a couple of minutes and some patients then go to sleep. Epilepsy is usually controlled by drugs, so attacks should not normally occur in the nursery or school. If they do, the adult must treat the child without panic.

Various Skull Deformities

These can be associated with mental handicap. The normal circumference of the skull at birth is 33–35 cm and when it is considerably smaller than this, the brain is under-developed and the child is described as microcephalic and will be severely handicapped. He will require intensive care as there may be lack of control over the bowel and bladder, and other facilities may never develop.

Hydrocephalus

Literally 'water on the brain', this is caused by pressure building up in the ventricles of the brain by impairment of the circulation of cerebro-spinal fluid. This gives the appearance of a large head, and it can occur without spina bifida. It is sometimes associated with mental handicap and is treated by surgery and the insertion of a Spitz-Holter valve which drains the cerebrospinal fluid into the bloodstream.

Children with Physical Disabilities

The opportunities offered to these children will determine whether their disabilities become handicap.

Spina bifida

This is a congenital abnormality (incidence 2.4 per 1000 births) in which the arches of one or more of the vertebrae have not fused together so that the spine is 'bifid' or split into two. This occurs during the first 10 weeks of pregnancy. The spinal cord or its membranes may protrude through this gap. 15–20% of children with spina bifida cystica suffer from meningocele, but the majority are more severely handicapped with myelomeningocele. The severity of the handicap varies with the site, extent and type of spinal defect, but can include paralysis, deformities of the lower limbs, skin insensitivity, bowel and urinary incontinence and kidney infections.

Hydrocephalus is present in 80% of children with myelomeningocele. Children with both spina bifida and hydrocephalus are usually mentally handicapped, while those with spina bifida and no hydrocephalus are usually of normal intelligence. The verbal abilities of these children may make parents and others believe them to be more intelligent than they are, but many lack comprehension of written and spoken language and visual–motor performance is poor. It is as yet unknown whether these disabilities are due to neurological abnormalities or to deprivation of normal experiences due to the restrictive handicapping condition.

The cause of spina bifida is still unknown, but many complex factors are thought to be responsible. It seems to run in families and brothers and sisters of affected children are likely to have the condition. There is also a link between spina bifida and maternal deficiency of essential nutrients – notably folic acid – in very early pregnancy. Diagnosis is made by amniocentesis when a sample of amniotic fluid is taken from the uterus and tested for alphafetoprotein (AFP) content. High levels of AFP indicate spina bifida.

Cerebral palsy

Often called spastic paralysis, this is the main cause and largest category of physical handicap in childhood. Regions of the brain which control movement and muscle tension are affected by

Figure 6.1   Children with special needs at play.

this conditon. Muscles may be very stiff (literally spastic) or very floppy. There may be malformation of the brain, athetosis and ataxia, which cause difficulties in eating and walking. *Ataxia* is characterized by jerky and uncontrolled movements which are due to poor muscle control and children with this may be unable to judge distances, may fall or trip easily, and may need a great deal of help in adjusting to the environment. *Athetosis* is found in many cerebral palsied children and involves constant wriggling and writhing movements.

In his first year of life the child is usually floppy and lacking in normal movements. Then the physical manifestations of writhing, twisting and grimacing are seen. Many children with athetoid cerebral palsy are of normal or high intelligence. Fifty per cent of all these children will have movement difficulties in whichever muscles are affected, e.g. walking, feeding, speaking. Hands may appear to be in a strange position, with bent wrists, which makes manipulation difficult. Where leg muscles are affected the child may walk forwards on his toes, with knees bent and the legs crossing in a weaving or scissor gait. Many spastic children have:

1 diplegia (in which the four extremities are affected, but legs more than arms),
2 quadriplegia (where all four extremities are affected),
3 hemiplegia (one side of the body is affected and disability may first present as clumsiness), and many are non-ambulant.

Brittle bones (Osteogenesis Imperfecta)

This is an inherited condition. About 7 in every 1000 births are affected. There is a tendency to fractures in children. As the child gets older, characteristic deformities caused by fractures and softness of the skull appear. The child may appear dwarfed with shortened limbs and humped back. Most of these children are of normal intelligence.

Paraplegia

This is usually caused by spinal injury. If the spinal cord is injured below the neck, movement and feeding may be affected. Tetraplegia is more serious since the damage to the spinal cord is higher up at neck level and all four limbs (and possibly lungs) will be affected. Problems of bowel and bladder control occur as a result of spinal injury.

Muscular dystrophy

This is a muscle-wasting disease. The commonest type is Duchenne's, which occurs only in boys and is transmitted through the mother, who, unaffected herself, carries the X chromosome responsible. After a case has been diagnosed, the mother, female siblings and any female offspring are examined to see if they are carriers. The diagnosis of the condition is usually made between 3 and 5 years when the parents may report abnormalities in neuro-muscular function which has led to description of the child as 'lazy', 'clumsy' or 'flat footed'. Boys with this condition have difficulty in walking at first, later the arms are affected and the child is usually in a wheelchair at 11 or 12 years. There is no cure for this conditon and a third of boys affected are known to suffer mental retardation.

Haemophilia

This is a rare 'Sex-linked' condition transmitted through X and Y sex chromosomes, but commonly affecting the male offspring. Clotting factors present in the normal blood are missing in haemophilia. Injections are now given at Haemophilia Centres or at home to supply the missing factor, Factor 8. Scratching or cutting a finger is not the trigger for uncontrolled bleeding and death. Serious damage can be done to joints and muscles by slow and insidious bleeding internally, which can follow knocks and bangs. Knees, elbows and ankle joints are commonly affected. Some severely affected children will have to spend periods in wheelchairs while their limbs recover or to avoid injury.

Haemophilia and AIDS

Unfortunately, some Factor 8 blood used in the UK prior to the compulsory testing of donated blood from 1985 onwards, was imported from the USA where it had been donated by carriers of the Human Immunodeficiency Virus (HIV). Some haemophilia sufferers infected with HIV have subsequently developed AIDS (Acquired Immune Deficiency Syndrome). As the name suggests, this syndrome impairs the immune system, and sufferers are therefore unable to combat opportunistic diseases, such as atypical pneumonias, etc.

HIV can also be spread by the sharing of needles between drug addicts; through sexual intercourse; and from HIV positive mothers to their unborn children.

Nursery nurses working in maternity or children's wards may care for babies or children who are HIV positive. Due to the routes by which the disease is often acquired and fears about contagion, haemophiliac children who have been infected through contaminated blood supplies are often subjected to hysterical and unnecessary reactions from other parents and children. Nursery staff must ensure that no child is ostracized because of imagined fears of contagion, and since the virus can only be spread through the direct exchange of bodily fluids, there is no need for isolation. When caring for children suffering from dysentery (where blood may be present in the faeces), or any similar condition, and during first aid with *all* children, it is advisable to wear disposable gloves which are now stocked by most schools.

Blindness and Partial Sight

These are rare; about one per 10 000 births for blindness and about three per 10 000 for partial sight, but this is often accompanied by additional handicaps. Universal early screening of all children for visual handicap is essential, as parents will need advice about helping the child's development and schooling. As emotional handicap in these children is likely, psychiatric help may be needed, and the children will have regular links with the Child Guidance Centre and a consultant psychiatrist where necessary. Educational counselling for the family needs to be carried out by a specialist teacher or educational psychologist.

There is no reason why all visually handicapped children, except some with multiple handicaps or very poor home conditions, should not live at home as long as parents have specialist help. Ordinary nursery school provision is satisfactory for the partially sighted and, in some cases, for the blind. A peripatetic teacher of the blind could support staff and supervise the progress of a visually handicapped small child wherever placed. Nursery education is of even more importance for these children than for sighted children, but flexibility of hours and ages is essential.

Deafness and Hearing Disability

This is sometimes caused as a result of maternal rubella or drug-taking during pregnancy. Perceptive deafness results from changes in the cochlea itself or in the nerve pathways from the ear to the brain. Some spastic children suffer from this form of deafness. All babies should be tested for hearing soon after birth, but many go undetected until the mother reports that the baby does not vocalize in response to the adult or that they are not speaking at the usual age. Once diagnosed, children over three can be fitted with a plastic hearing aid which fits into the ear. Nursery school provision promotes language development and a peripatetic teacher of the deaf can support staff and supervise progress.

The Child with Special Needs in the Nursery

Knowledge of the needs of handicapped children is essential for adults who are attempting to satisfy them in the nursery or playgroup. Many handicapped children will have suffered emotionally through either overprotection or the effects of parental anxiety and depression. Social opportunities will have been limited and the child is probably not used to mixing with other children. Intellectually, learning opportunities will have been restricted, unless the parent has known how to give effective stimulation. Physically, he may have had little chance or space for exercise, which could result in a tendency to sluggishness and obesity.

Independence and self-confidence can be promoted by teaching the child to dress, feed and wash himself, play freely and attend to his own personal hygiene. Intellectual development will benefit as he learns new skills and develops whatever senses he has through play. Socially he will enjoy playing with other children and physically benefit from exercise and extended freedom of movement.

Dress

The physically handicapped child requires clothes which are adapted to his handicap and can be easily taken off and put on, especially for toilet purposes. Learning to undress should come before dressing, and the child should learn to cope with one garment at a time so that he gains emotional satisfaction through each stage. The child's clothes should be laid out in order of putting on, within easy reach, and suitably arranged for easy dressing.

Practice must be consistent, top clothes a size larger are easier to get on and off. The physical and emotional needs of the child should be considered in choice of fabrics. Strength and durability, washing, freedom of movement, light, ventilation and temperature control are all important physical factors. Colour of clothes and attractive appearance are important to give emotional satisfaction. Front fastenings are easier to cope with than at the side or back. A tape attached to the back of the boots or shoes will help the child to pull them on. Ties permanently knotted and fastened with elastic can be bought or made. Tight neck openings in sweaters should be avoided. Stretchy polo necks and V-neck styles are suitable. A double-sided neck opening with loops for buttons is easier to fasten on a hyperactive child. Large armholes, open sleeves and sleeveless garments make dressing easier, and the last two are better for children with short arms. Velcro tabs can be used instead of buttons. A large ring on a zip helps the child to grip it.

Skirts and trousers should have elastic waistbands which can be slipped off easily if the toilet is needed in a hurry. Suction aids help spastic and limb-deficient children to pull up their own pants, and sock aids also help towards independence. Protection against physical injury is required for some spastic children and helmets are designed to prevent head knocks on floor or furniture. Catsuits are suitable for children whose mobility is restricted to rolling and crawling, but if incontinence is present or the child is in nappies care must be taken to change frequently to prevent discomfort and skin disorders.

Specially Adapted Cutlery

Wide-handled spoons and forks, and plates with a high edge and non-slip base help self-feeding. Plastic flexible straws are useful for children who cannot hold a cup. Non-slip mats hold plates and cups. A strong polythene bib prevents messy clothes, as it catches spilled food.

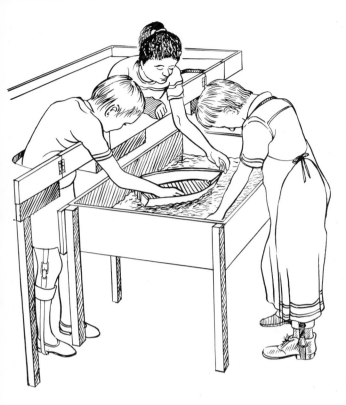

Figure 6.2 Adaptation of equipment for use by physically compromised children.

Figure 6.3 Sturdy materials may be required.

Wedges made of strong foam rubber and wooden trolleys on which the child can lie and push himself along with his arms allow the child to explore his environment.

Play Materials

These must be very strong and sturdy and constructed to enable the spastic child to use them. PVC balls and musical instruments are useful for wheelchair children. Large inflatable squashy bags to bounce on are great fun and give a sense of freedom. Tables with a space cut out to fit the child in a wheelchair enable fine motor activities such as jigsaws to take place. The younger child can have a variety of small toys on a pulley at the end of his cot or table operated by himself. He can pull toys towards himself and, when he is finished, they move back to their former position.

Blind and partially sighted children will need play materials they can feel. Magnifiers, talking and large-print books, tape recorders and Braille equipment are all utilized. Deaf and partially hearing children will need visual interpretation of the spoken word – pictures and signs. Speech therapists will devise programmes for children with aphasia (no speech) or dysphasia (lack of speech or speech difficulty) which can be followed up by nursery staff.

Children without arms or legs may be given prostheses – artificial limbs and hands – and encouraged to use their feet for grasping and mouthsticks or headsticks for painting and drawing. If the physically handicapped are in ordinary nurseries, ease of mobility must be provided by uncluttered space and access to toilets and doorways.

Children with learning difficulties tend to be at an earlier stage of development than other children of their age. In the nursery, education through play must be considerably extended to promote language development and social skills. Hospital provision is unsuitable for these children unless they have other problems which require nursing care. These children do not have the curiosity through which other children learn, so play activities for them must have wide variety, and should be presented in simple stages so that they can gain one skill at a time. This breaking down of skills is called 'task analysis' and can be done with the needs and abilities of each child in mind.

Final Goal

Children painting with a brush on paper attached to an easel:

Stage 1 Finger painting on a large white plastic cloth completely covering table or floor. This is particularly enjoyable for those children at the anal stage who like the feel of messy paint, and enjoy smearing it on paper.

Stage 2 Instead of using fingers for painting introduce 1-inch dowels with 2-inch sponges of different shapes attached to the end. One primary colour of paint is provided in a margarine tub.

Stage 3 Replace the dowels with the large paint brushes normally used.

Stage 4 Introduce paper, still working on the table.

Stage 5 Introduce paper and paint at an easel.

The adult working with mentally handicapped children must be aware of normal stages in child development. A good programme will have a balance between active and quiet play (see Play and Exercise). The quiet period should provide materials which will improve hand–eye coordination, and encourage increased attention span, and colour and shape differentiation. Attention span is often limited in these children, particularly if they are hyperactive. Development of the senses can be helped through 'feelie' materials, music of various kinds, and a variety of items for smell and taste.

As with 'normal' chidren the handicapped child is eventually able to choose an activity in which he can play purposefully. With the support of an understanding adult, aware of the child's capabilities and able to give guidance, he too will experience success. Success at one stage may make him want to stay there. The adult's task is to show him he can be successful at the next stage as well, however small, but it is important to know when to withdraw support and when to reintroduce it. Thus the foundations of learning are laid, for all children, including those once deemed 'ineducable'.

Autism

The term 'autism' can cause confusion as it refers not only to a state of withdrawal but also to a condition characterized by a failure to develop relationships. There are various degrees of autism, and it is often but not always accompanied by mental handicap. Certain groups of symptoms are said to be peculiar to autistic children: profound and general failure to develop social relationships, language retardation, short attention span, stereotyped repetitive movements of the hands and fingers, self-injury and delayed bowel control.

Long-term follow-up has shown that the intelligence levels, which may range from severely mentally handicapped to normal or superior in autistic children, do not usually improve their level, even if the condition appears to improve. Autism affects boys more than girls, and although signs of organic neurological (brain) abnormality are not often present, epilepsy may begin later in childhood. The outcome of autism has been related to (1) intelligence, (2) attainment of useful speech by 5 years of age, (3) use of educational opportunities, and (4) severity of autistic behaviour. Parental emotional warmth, consistency and adequacy of communication were not related to the outcome but this is now highly debatable. Autism is due largely to sensory brain factors, and as autistic children grow older, most remain dependent which can cause problems for their families.

Dr Lorna Wing stated in her book on autism that all the problems seen in autistic children can occur in normal children. In normal children, however, these phases are mild and temporary. Normal children have wide repertoires of behaviour in their play and social relationships, which contrast sharply with the limited range of abnormal behaviour that characterizes autism.

Assessment and Diagnosis

Parents' suspicions about their child's development after 18 months to 2 years, based on behaviour problems such as restlessness, overactivity, tantrums, destructiveness, self-injury and sleep disturbances, usually lead to the child's referral for assessment. This is usually carried out at a nursery or opportunity group linked to an assessment centre or paediatric unit, by a paediatrician, a child psychiatrist, a psychologist and a speech therapist.

Provision for Autistic Children

The 1981 Education Act gave local authorities the power to assess a child under 2 years of age with the consent of their parents, and are required to do so at the request of the parents.

Some mildly autistic children with normal or near-normal intelligence are able to cope in ordinary schools, with the support of the Child Guidance team or a child psychiatrist. Those children with reasonable intellectual potential who show very marked obsessional symptoms may need special education from an early age. A constructive programme of training which is appropriate to the child's level of development is devised, to involve the parents as co-therapists in modifying the behaviour of the child, if he is living at home. The National Society for Autistic Children in England and the Scottish Society for Autistic Children run a number of special day and residential schools. The aims of treatment are to foster skills in self-help, socialization, language, cognitive and motor development, and to eliminate abnormal behaviour which tends to interfere with learning and impair social functioning. Activity charts are used to record successes and failures each day in certain tasks. A child may be given the task of learning to button up his shirt. At first he will be given large buttons with large button holes, then smaller sizes as he progresses in manual dexterity. Each step is carefully noted and rewarded with praise and perhaps a star on his chart.

Dyslexia

The word 'dyslexia' literally means difficulty in reading and writing. It is unrelated to intelligence or educational opportunities, and seems to appear more in social classes, 1, 2 and 3, though this may be because parental expectations in groups 4 and 5 are lower, and poor educational provisions combined with an unstimulating environment may mask personal deficiencies.

There may be disorders of sensory input, so that the child does not receive the 'right message' when he looks at a page of a reading book. Defects in motor performance sometimes occur with clumsiness, poor writing, disorders of fine movement and lack of balance. The child's lack of ability in sport may hamper his social development when he tries to participate in peer group relationships. His difficulties in sequential learning, including days of the week, months, seasons, time-telling by clock, compass directions, telling left from right and word recognition, may be accompanied by remarkable creativity in painting and building with

Lego or bricks. Some dyslexic chidren may be hyperactive in the nursery and insomniac at night. Teachers may complain that they lack concentration, and they can develop low expectations of the child so that he falls further behind in school and may become naughty and troublesome.

The inability to read and write may not become evident until the child reaches Primary 2 or 3, and when he is first introduced to formal reading. Teachers will usually ask for a referral to the Child Guidance team of Educational Psychologists, who will be able to diagnose the problem, and a paediatric physiotherapist may discover minor neurological abnormalities such as immature reflexes. Remedial teaching, backed up by the child's parents, provides exercises to improve physical dexterity and balance, together with a positive outlook towards areas of sport. Computer-based education now provides an enjoyable way of learning, and can be used alongside writing exercises to relieve the tedium often felt in these.

The major part of treatment is to build up the child's frequently weakened self-esteem, encourage the development of those skills in which he excels, while tackling energetically those in which he is weak.

Toys and Activities for Children with Special Needs

The play experiences needed by children with special needs are mainly the same as those for other children, but in slow motion and with different emphasis. It is not 'special' toys that are needed, so much as the *right* amount of the *right* toy at the *right* time, presented in the *right* way.

Early Awareness and Exploration

As with all children, those with physical or mental handicap will require an environment with adequate stimulus, provided by parents or care givers in the form of mobiles of different shapes and colours, to be changed frequently, and opportunities for self-exploration. The baby may need help to reach out with his arms and hands towards a hanging mobile or toy tied with elastic to the end of his cot, since some Down's syndrome babies show little response. When the baby is in the bath, or on a play rug, he can be encouraged to move his body and play with his arms, legs, fingers and toes, as he discovers the capacities of his body, and achieves some mastery over it. Where the child has no movement in his arms or legs, he can be encouraged to exercise the parts of his body which can be utilized. Deaf babies can still be stimulated with adult direction in movement, and brightly coloured mobiles are effective. Blind babies can often be stimulated by parental massage, which is an excellent form of communication of love, since touch is one of the primitive senses, and with hearing, it should be exploited. Mobiles which tinkle with little bells, or move in the currents of air like wind chimes, made from plastic shapes, together with talking and singing, enable those to whom sight is denied the opportunity to develop their other senses. Mothers who carry their babies around in a sling contribute to the baby's exploration also. Toys that easily squeak with *slight pressure*, and rattles, contribute to the baby's need to feel mastery over his environment. Lack of interest is of course a common response, and patience with tenacity are required to ensure that progress, however little, is made.

Pre-walking: Adult Supervision Required

Equipment for crawling includes open-ended barrels, tunnels (not a good idea for blind and deaf children, as they may feel 'cut off' from the others) and sit-and-shuffle toys, such as a Glideabout car or a sturdy wooden animal with wheels, which will move with little effort. Rocking toys, such as seesaws, hammocks, swings and rocking horses of a suitable size for the children, all provide stimulation and fun, provided they are safe and an adult is close by. Hand-propelled vehicles such as the Chailey Chariot, Land Boat, or porters' trolleys with long swivel handles are excellent for group play with non-ambulant children, who can be given 'lifts' by the ambulant children. Wigwams offer an opportunity for children with a variety of disabilities, since the Indian Chief spends a lot of his time sitting, planning manoeuvres with his war counsel, or watching tribal dances round the camp fire!

All safety factors must be observed, including deep sides on slides, safety rails on rocking horses and seesaws, no sharp edges or corners, and no splinters or protruding nails. Non-toxic paint and safety mats on the floor or ground

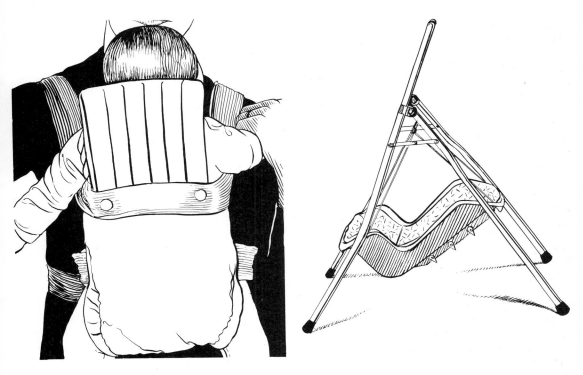

Figure 6.4   (a) Baby carrier, (b) baby rocker.

must also be provided. Baby bouncers are not suitable for use with handicapped children.

Walking Toys

Baby walkers with adjustable handles, pedal cars, extra-large tricycles (for strengthening muscles of lazy walkers), push and pull toys, wagons and wheelbarrows provide exercise for feet and legs. A small trampoline with a safety bar is useful for partially sighted and blind children as it gives them whole body movement in security through their hold on the bar. Children with spina bifida who have no leg movement can also bounce up and down on the trampoline and enjoy the lovely feeling this gives.

Tactile (Touch) Experiences

These are particularly necessary for those who have leg impairment, since much exploration of the environment can only occur with these children through arms, hands, fingers and various tactile experiences. Provision of water, for whole or part immersion, even a paddling pool,

can be most valuable for all aspects of development. Dabbling hands and feet in warm water is very soothing for the child who is struggling daily to overcome the inhibiting effect of his handicap. The discovery of items which will float or sink can be made in the bath or in the water play area of the playroom, and the child in a wheelchair can add to his intellectual development if he is given a tray broad enough to carry a basin of water, and a variety of items to test. Hand–eye coordination can also be promoted as he pours from one beaker to another. Dabbling hands in dry sand, salt, talcum powder and bath foam provide different experiences for comparison. Further textures can be explored in the use of clay and dough, and for those children who have little or no finger dexterity the primary organ of discovery – the mouth – can be used, with objects like plastic rings of various shapes and sizes, large beads (too big to swallow, stick in ears or nose) and wooden play shapes. A squeeze box which rewards the child's efforts with a musical sound as the correct amount of pressure is applied, a Jack-in-the-box which jumps out when the lid of his box is lifted and football rattlers which require some pressure before they can be swung around and produce a sound help to sharpen the tactile sense. Large lightweight plastic balls suspended from the ceiling can give the non-ambulant child a sense of mastery as he learns to push them, which will cause them to move away from him. Rolling about in large beanbags or on rolls of polythene foam also help the child to gain some idea of his whole body mass. Paint which can be applied with fingers or feet to the class mural is a delightful activity, since messiness is allowed, and some children who have no movement in their hands go on to paint with their feet, holding the paintbrush between the toes, or, where feet are also inoperative, painting with the mouth as the anchor for the paintbrush. Crayons can also be utilized in this way, and various devices are obtainable to enable an adapted typewriter or computer to be controlled by sensors held in the mouth or, in some cases, attached to the forehead.

Toys to Stimulate Smell

Great fun can be enjoyed apart from learning experiences, when the adult sets up a testing station, like the laboratories seen in perfume factories on television. Small containers can be filled with coffee beans, moth balls, dried lavender, rose petals, lemon juice and vinegar, and an assortment of empty perfume bottles can be used for guessing games if the children are forbidden to look inside the container. Removing tops left on the perfume bottles brings another aspect into the play, as children are usually not allowed to do this, and it is always more delightful to do something regarded as strictly forbidden!

Other Toys

Where children suffer from cerebral palsy, toys and equipment should be lightweight and easy to grasp or clutch. 'Comfort' toys such as cuddly teddies or stuffed animals made by the staff are just as necessary for handicapped children, particularly if their life is arranged around mechanical aids. Children who have an impairment of the heart muscles may often be breathless and unable to undertake any energetic

activity, unless under the direction of a physiotherapist, and will also require light toys to cuddle as they listen to stories or music.

Constructional equipment such as blocks, small Lego pieces and parts that screw together help coordination. Jigsaw pieces should be large enough for the child to grasp them in a palmar grasp, as his fingers may not be capable of fine movements. Simple ball games, skittles using foam wedges, posting boxes and balls on elastic help hand–eye coordination, which is usually difficult for spastic children. Opportunities should be made to adapt toys and equipment to give each child the opportunity to excel at something, however minor, as this is important for the child's self-image.

Children who have defective vision can still learn about shapes and sizes with large bead sets, pegboards, jigsaws with various pieces, boats, trains, cars, and, as a pre-reading activity, blocks with raised shapes and letters. Much emphasis is placed on learning through hearing and touch with blind children, so tape recorders and record players will be extensively used, as will musical activities.

Deaf and partially hearing children will have activities to emphasize visual abilities and to develop speech. The former will include threading beads of different sizes, tool sets, building sets and picture puzzles, and the latter telephones (which can pre-empt future daily practice by provision of a mirror, or television screen, if available, at each end of the line, so that the children can see themselves and their friends as they speak to each other) and card and board games like snakes and ladders, Monopoly and Bingo.

Many nursery nurses opt to work with handicapped children, and soon realize that each is a child first, and the handicap is secondary. Assessment of the child's abilities, rather than disabilities, will determine his learning programme, and the approach should be to accentuate the positive, i.e. exploit the other senses when one is lacking or deficient. When the children have learning difficulties, carers have to appreciate that progress usually occurs only in small steps, in some instances almost imperceptibly, but the joy one experiences when they see that tiny step forward compensates for the long period of expectancy.

7

Play

Defining Play

When we ask 'What is play?' the answers will be many and different: 'Play is the way children learn', 'Play is a serious business', 'Play has a purpose', 'Play is a spontaneous activity'.

Play is also described as 'activity with no goal other than the enjoyment derived from it', and certainly children should be able to play for the sake of playing, but play is also a powerful medium for learning. Through play children learn many skills, gain concepts and understanding, and draw relationships between concepts. This is illustrated in block play. Here, children are concerned with sizes, shapes and relationships as they build with blocks. They measure, match, classify, face problems of construction, share materials with others and communicate their ideas and feelings. Play is a valuable part of cognitive (intellectual), physical, social and emotional development. Many of the things children collect on Nature walks, such as leaves, twigs, berries, shells and rocks, are valuable tools for pre-number and prereading activities. The child who sorts and classifies the objects himself to his own criteria learns more than when he is handed a box of beads and told to sort out the colours. The physical properties of each require the use of senses which greatly contribute to intellectual development. Involvement in play allows a child to explore his thoughts and feelings about himself as a person and a learner. In play the child finds different ways of dealing with social situations too. He discovers more about the world he is in and the roles people play in the world. Part of his successful interaction with others involves a balance between dependent and independent behaviours. Within established limits he is able to use materials creatively, interact with others and simultaneously learn to control his behaviour. The achievement of self-control in interaction with other, and in dealing with both success and frustration is an important part of social and emotional development.

As a child makes discoveries through play his personal involvement adds depth to the experience. He learns more when he sets his own challenges; he identifies his problems and begins to see the link between cause and effect. Each child has his own way of learning and should be allowed to proceed at his own pace. Play also promotes the development of speech as the child verbalizes his problem: 'How can I move all those bricks to build my fort? A wheelbarrow is best!'. As he plays with others his vocabulary is increased and facility with appropriate language developed.

Functions of Play

1 Play provides suitable opportunities to enable the developing body to be continually and purposefully active.
2 Play enables the developing mind to be alert, curious and thus improved.
3 Play enables the developing personality to be eager to establish rewarding relationships with other people and to acquire social competence.

Play is therefore as necessary for a child as food, warmth and protective care, and contributes to the four aspects of growth – physical, intellectual, emotional and social. Play is an activity in which a child is able to define and select his own goals, which means increasing control over materials and situations in his every day life, and this gives confidence. There are four essential provisions of play: playthings, a range of rich experiences, some novelty, an environment with interesting material and equipment relevant to the ages and stages of the children, and an atmosphere in which each child is allowed to proceed at his own pace.

Role of the Adult in Play

Observations of individual children at play help nursery staff to appreciate the optimum quantity, duration and timing of adult intervention. The role of the adult does not always require intervention and too much organization and direction in play can produce passive and uninterested children. Studies of adult–child interaction in a number of pre-school situations show that where children are left to their own devices and expected to learn continually from their own efforts they fare less well than where the adult worked together with them, sometimes on a one-to-one basis. Researchers also came up with the fact that the adult's part in play makes it richer and longer lasting. Even in this adult–child interaction, however, researchers found that there was little to do with shared activities, nothing on play, and nothing by way of logical reasoning or causal thinking. The language used was mainly that of management and description, with an element of conversation about events and happenings outside the immediate environment. At present much nursery practice is mainly 'non-directive' by the adult or 'child-directed', which usually means that the role of the adult is just to provide a stimulating environment with interesting materials and equipment to which the child will respond as he wishes. There is a danger here that the importance of the adult role is overlooked and production of too many materials can be confusing and disconcerting to children. Materials should be made available in such a way that the child's curiosity leads him to explore, discover various properties of the play equipment, and ask questions about them. The adult helps to clarify concepts and correct misconceptions. Provision for individual differences in both learning style and rate is made as the adult helps the children towards problem solving in a way related to their developmental stage. It is often difficult to determine the difference between a positive form of intervention and interference. If comments are made too often children become dependent and stop play when the adult moves on to another group, but they also lose interest if the play is not theirs independent of the teacher.

Questions asked should be open ended (i.e. not allow 'yes', 'no' or any one syllable as answer) e.g. What are you going to do with this? (stating the problem), How will you manage to put all those bricks into the wheelbarrow? (testing understanding), Why did you have two wheelbarrows yesterday? (recall), What do you think will happen if you pile them all in the

small wheelbarrow? (predictive), Why did we need two wheelbarrows again? (recap process), Which way is easier for the work people [remembering non-sexist descriptions] to move all those bricks? (evaluation), What would have happened if we had only one wheelbarrow? (imaginative). Any comments made by the adult should extend the child's learning (What a long sausage that is), encourage thinking (Can you cut it up in little pieces so that we can all have some for tea?); and clarify concept (Yes, we'll all have little sausages, the butcher cut up his long sausage into short pieces for us).

Apart from provision of interesting materials suitable to the ages, stages, interests and needs of the children, the adult also sets necessary limits. Equipment must be used in a safe way and children cannot be allowed to hurt each other. Where possible, however, the limits should be set by the materials rather than the teacher, e.g. a climbing frame which does not reach shelves to tempt some adventurers to jump on to them only to fall to the floor.

Even in imaginative play there is scope for adult involvement. It might simply be the invitation to 'a tea party' in the house corner or provision of a model for 'the hairdresser'. It has been found that adults helping in imaginative play led not only to increments in originality and creativity for disadvantaged children, but also to some increases in verbal skills and language.

When the workplace is a nursery school or children's centre the nursery nurse has to participate as a team member in the organization and supervision of play. Needs and interests of individual children have to be considered with those of the group. The ages and stages of the children will be involved as the 3-year-olds are still enjoying discovery of various properties of materials, while the fours and rising fives have progressed to more complex problem solving, improvisations of equipment and broader vocabulary. Their self-confidence has increased but they are still not ready for primary school and the present emphasis on placing rising fives into primary classrooms is not conducive to healthy development. The child needs 'room to grow' in all aspects of development. A variety of experiences, involving personal relationships, intellectual stimulation, creative and imaginative play, with opportunities for language development through hearing and listening, physical development of large and small muscles, and hand–eye coordination should be offered. Sometimes there will be noisy active play, sometimes quiet periods in the book corner or with jigsaws. Repetition of routine activities provides a sense of security in young children but the timetable must be flexible so that the children are able to finish a new project or enjoy outings. Astute observation of the child's development stage enables the adult to approach the child at the right level, utilizing his experiences with various materials. The adult can encourage the children to discuss their work and know when to step in or hold back. Constant awareness of safety factors – broken toys, leaking water tray – and time factors, so that children are not upset when they have to terminate an activity in time for lunch or break time, are both part of the adult's responsibility.

Play in Development

Play is not merely a means of relaxation to children – it is their main medium for learning and has implications for all aspects of development. Enlightened parents and care givers should therefore never be heard to say 'we'll finish this first and then you can play' when the task in hand resembles 'serious educational activities', such as reading, or domestic work such as washing up, both of which are regarded by the child as play activities.

Physical Development

Physically the child benefits from play as it helps him to acquire body control. Coordination develops through movement and exercise. Random movements become purposeful as he grasps a moving object. Later he progresses from crawling to walking and running, from standing on one foot to hopping; and eventually to more complicated games requiring physical skills with large and small muscular movements.

Intellectual Development

Intellectually the child is able to develop new skills and abilities with words and objects, experiment with the properties of creative media and play equipment and solve his own problems in his own way.

Exploratory play begins at the breast with the most primitive senses of touch and taste, then proceeds through random movements to voluntary control of hands, arms and legs which enables the child to grasp, hold and examine small objects. Through these movements the baby comes to acquire control over his body and attempts to control his environment as he progresses from crawling to walking and running. He discovers textures of food and other materials first by putting them all into his mouth, later by feeling and close examination. Different shapes and sizes come to recognition as he tries to grasp the coloured mobiles strung over his cot. Experimentation begins as he pulls the cord which will set the tiny chime-bar into action and introduce another dimension, sound, into his achievements.

Play with sounds develops with his own babbling which is obviously a pleasurable activity apart from its later significance as a means of communication. Concepts of colour, form, size and properties are developed as he explores different materials in block play, form-board, sand, water and clay. Discovery of the properties of different play materials leads him to classify and categorize items to his own criteria. Eagerly he questions in his enthusiasm to learn. A discovery, such as the necessity to add water to sand before one can build with it, is greeted with the alacrity of Archimedes, and is no less important to the child. Emotional aspects are closely interwoven in his pride at achievement and appropriate appreciation should be expressed by the adult. Building a tower of three cubes is a major feat and should at least be rewarded by an acknowledgement.

Emotional Development

Play provides an outlet for feelings and the child can use playthings on which to vent his anger – smacking teddy or kicking the ball is preferable to smashing valuable ornaments, and obviously more acceptable. Later he learns to use his anger constructively by hammering nails into wood or pounding clay.

Play involves not only the negative feelings of fear, aggression, anxiety, hate, guilt and frustration, but also pleasure, happiness, exuberance, love and affection. Sometimes, children's feelings toward their parents are ambivalent – 'I don't love you any more' or 'I hate you' can often be heard as the child enters a power struggle which revolves around a simple matter, like a second ice lollipop. Sometimes he will turn towards a quiet, peaceful activity with a favourite jigsaw, stacking toy, water or sand play. This ability to utilize objects for his own needs will, in future, enable him to cope with difficulties in real life.

From Baby to Child through Play

1–6 Months

Too much is as harmful as too little at this stage. Over-stimulation distresses babies, so selection of items is important.

Mobiles. Mobiles can be carefully suspended (on string) either above or across the cot or pram. Homemade mobiles using clean foil milk caps, yoghurt containers, cutout shapes from cards and calendars or cereal boxes are just as effective as expensive shop models. Glaring items should be avoided, as they cause discomfort. At first the baby will simply look at the moving objects; later he is able to see more clearly, fixate briefly, and at 6 months hand–eye coordination is developing as he reaches out in the right place to catch these objects and bring them closer to him. Apart from exercising the muscles of his arms, wrists and eyes, he is also mastering skills towards independence in his own environment (see Intellectual Aspects).

Pram beads. These are often part of the accessories that go with a pram. They must be too large for the baby to put in his mouth, as during this period everything is taken to the mouth for exploration. They fulfil the same function as a mobile in that the baby will make random movements towards it at 3 months, and try to grasp them at 6 months. They have an added thrill in that the beads can be moved across horizontally (by the adult at first), and the baby's eyes will follow this movement briefly initially and for longer periods after the age of 4 months.

Rattles. These provide opportunities for visual and small muscle movements. Even at 1 month the baby notices a toy shaken about 15 cm away from his eyes and follows it briefly. At 3 months he will hold the rattle for a few minutes if it is placed in his hand, but he does not necessarily look at it. At 6 months he has learnt that shaking a rattle produces a pleasant sound, and an opportunity for mastery over an aspect of his

environment is also gained. Now he will shake the rattle vigorously and look at it closely while he delights in the sound.

Teething ring. This is usually made of hard plastic and may be used as part of a mobile until the baby is about 4 months old, when he will put it to his mouth, as he does everything at this stage. As his teeth erupt, the baby may find it comforting to bite on the hard ring. Care should be taken to ensure that a teething ring is not used by more than one baby and that it is washed thoroughly, if it drops to the ground, before the baby sucks it again.

Floating bath toys. These need not be expensive manufactured models. Plastic lids, beakers and tin foil containers allow scope for floating, sinking, filling and pouring. Often plastic ducks are given as presents to babies and these are fun, but they do not represent a real duck to the baby at this stage. However, any bath toys help to make the bathtime enjoyable, a time when parents or care givers can relax with the baby. They are also a pleasant learning experience as he becomes more active and starts to reach for objects that float past him!

Activity aids. Baby bouncers are designed for babies of 3 months upwards. They help to develop muscles used in walking and give the babies enjoyment in the gentle bouncing exercise. The British Standards Institution inspects numerous items in household and nursery use, has very rigid safety standards, and insists that activity aids are not regarded as toys or playthings. Their mark of approval – the kitemark – is only seen on some makes, and it is best when buying these items to look for this, to ensure maximum safety. When a baby is put into a baby bouncer, he should *never* be left unsupervised, nor allowed to play too long in the bouncer. Bouncers are often hooked to a beam or attached to the top of the door surround (architrave) and suspended in the open doorway.

Safety factors include the following:

1 The door surround must have a horizontal ledge at least 13mm (½ inch) wide on either side of the door. The two ledges must be at the same level and at the back of each ledge there must be a vertical surface or wall of at least 13 mm height against which the clamp can operate.

2 The height of the bouncer should be adjusted by hooking the chain section of the rubber extender into the clamp hook at a link which will ensure that the baby's toes just touch the floor.
3 The door surrounds must be strong enough to support the bouncer.
4 The door must be anchored back with a door stopper.
5 The rubber extender strap should be examined regularly and taken back for replacement if signs of wear or cracks appear in the rubber.

A bouncer on a four-legged portable stand which can be carried from room to room is now available, but this is more expensive.

Baby walkers. The BSI insists that the spread of the four legs of the baby walker must be sufficient to prevent it tipping over if the child bumps into an obstacle. Another specification before the 'kitemark' is given to baby walker models, is that the diameter of the castor wheels should not be less than 50 mm, and the fabric used for the harness and the saddle (seat) must be fireproof. Models that store flat should lock safely without any danger of collapse when in use. The baby walker seat should be adjustable to varying heights for different stages of a baby's growth. His feet should just touch the ground when he is in the saddle. This activity aid can be used until the baby is walking without help, hence it must be made of sturdy materials, and it is worth spending more initially if the expense is justified in lengthy use. Some baby walkers have a row of coloured play balls in front which the child can reach for, grasp and move along as his arm and wrist muscles develop.

Once a child is mobile in a baby walker he may bump into hazards such as trailing flexes, loose rugs, portable fires, coffee tables, large toys, play equipment or glass-fronted cupboards. The adult must therefore ensure that the room is cleared of hazards and that the child is *never* left unsupervised. Safety gates should be placed in position to prevent the child falling downstairs.

Swinging chairs. Some modern tubular highchairs are made to allow the moulded seat to be detached and suspended to form a low swinging chair. These are designed to give the baby a gentle swinging motion and can be used for babies from 3 to 6 months of age. Small children should never be allowed to push the swing.

Adaptable highchairs are economical as their use solely as a separate eating place for babies is limited and they are too expensive for many mothers to afford just for one purpose.

6–12 Months

Nesting cubes and beakers. These are usually made of strong coloured plastic. Cubes can be made in wood, but, if painted, the paint used should be non-toxic, as the baby takes everything to his mouth until 12 months of age. At 6 months the baby uses his whole hand in palmar grasp to pick up cubes which he can focus on at 6–12 inches distance. Often he uses two hands to scoop them up, but occasionally one hand only is used. Later he passes them from one hand to the other and is able to put them inside larger cubes when this is demonstrated to him. At 9 months he delights in finding a cube hidden under a beaker, this being another form of 'peek-a-boo'. At 12 months he is adept at putting cubes in a box or beaker, and his small muscle movements are now precise enough to enable him to do this with ease.

Soft doll. This can be made by the adult. Eyes on wires and small buttons should be avoided. Often a simple shape in a cuddly material, with a face embroidered on (provided the dye cannot be sucked out by the baby), is most acceptable. At 9–12 months, this may be used in the experiments of dropping toys from the pram or cot and watching them fall. Later, he will possibly use it as a comforter. If taken to bed, it must not be of a fluffy material and large dolls should be avoided.

Saucepans and lids. These provide an inexpensive way for the baby to develop control as he picks them up, rattles and bangs them together, and puts smaller pans into larger ones. When space permits, mothers can simply sit the baby on the floor beside the cupboard and allow him free play. If she is cooking, obviously this could prove a hindrance and possible danger to the child. Baking and washing do not pose the same hazards, particularly if the baby is in a playpen away from the cooker and he can play happily near his mother.

Wooden spoon and drum. A wooden spoon can provide much fun as the baby loves to bang it, rattle it in a saucepan, or use it as a drumstick. The drum need not be an expensive model. A cake tin can be covered with a piece of rubber (inner tubes of tyres can be used), which is held in place by string tied tightly round the tin. Container tins used upside down also provide drums, though the level of noise must be considered, as too much noise irritates adults and children.

Cotton reels and large beads. These are useful for threading onto string and can be easily picked up with the whole hand at six months. The pincer grasp at 12 months enables the baby to hold the thick string or cord onto which the reels can be threaded with the help of an adult at first. Fun and a sense of mastery are enjoyed as the baby pushes them along. The beads must be large to prevent swallowing, should be free from paint, harmful dyes and varnish.

Songs, rhymes and simple games. Using hands can be very enjoyable as the baby is able to clap his hands by the age of 12 months. Songs like 'Clap hands for Daddy', 'Pat a cake', 'Round and round the garden' provoke delighted attempts at imitation. 'This little piggy' has a pleasant jingle and increases the baby's interest in his fingers which are now of increasing use to him. Rhythm is one of the most primitive attributes of man, and babies respond well to all forms – the voice is as effective as a musical instrument. Occasionally the baby will hear music from the radio or records as he 'listens with Mother' and pleasurable reactions to this will be observed, provided it is not a cacophany of sound!

12–18 Months

Boxes, tins, cartons provide lots of fun as the child now tries to fit them into each other, fills them with sand or water, empties the contents, sits in the larger boxes, pushes and pulls them along with his teddy inside.

Cotton reels, apart from threading on to string, may now be arranged in rows or in towers of three.

Pans, lids, wooden spoons will still be used to produce sounds but the child may briefly imitate Mother (or Father) stirring soup in the pan. Several cuddly toys and animals – the child can become very attached to his teddy bear or doll at this stage, and may be seen walking around with it, or kissing it in imitation of the adult.

A wooden train of a simple design, with two or three pieces fitting together easily, helps manual dexterity as the child is able to lift pieces up and place them together if shown how.

Hammer pegs help hand–eye coordination and development of small muscles, and provide an outlet for frustration as they are banged into the board. Pieces of material of different types and colours in a box can provide fun as the child puts in his hand and brings out a different piece each time. Velvet, fur, suede, wool, cotton, satin, silk, sandpaper, crêpe paper, cottonwool, duck's down all give new sensations and develop the sense of touch.

Models of house furniture and staircase provide scope for imaginative play as the child helps to put pieces away in the correct part of the doll's house and walks with his fingers up the stairway. Walking, singing and talking games should be used to encourage activity at this stage, as the child loves the sound of words and rhymes and attempts to join in.

2–3 Years

Active equipment for developing large muscles, balance and coordination include push and pull toys (e.g. carts or trucks which can carry bricks), animals on wheels, large riding toys such as a rocking horse or horse on wheels, on which the child pushes himself along, climbing frame with small spaces between the bars steps for running up and down and a slide with steps at the back. 'New' children often forget their anxiety if they are given a chance to use this when they first visit the nursery. It provides the simple thrill which persists throughout childhood and is seen in adolescence and adulthood, when people still slide on large slides at fun fairs.

Large and small balls: at 2 years, the child can throw the small ball, at 2½ years, he can kick a large ball without over balancing. A trampoline with handle can provide fun, but supervision is required. Walking planks with a mirror for the child to see himself helps balance, as does a tricycle, but space is needed for this if accidents are to be avoided.

Housekeeping toys enable the child to copy parents and take part in household tasks such as sweeping up with a dustpan and brush, washing pots and pans in a child-sized sink, 'cooking' meals on the stove unit in the House corner, having a tea party with dolls and a teaset, answering the telephone, ironing dolls' clothes

Figure 7.1   An old mattress can provide fun and activity indoors.

with an iron and board and putting the dolls to bed.

Dress-up clothes are also useful for make-believe play. Floor toys include blocks or boxes, wooden bricks, toy trains and cars (preferably those in which the child can sit and 'drive', and smaller ones for 'traffic jams'). At 2–2½ years, the child will play alone with these, but at three he may play with others.

Scissors and paper for cutting can be safely used if the scissors have smooth tips; these help small muscle control.

An abacus with large balls in primary colours aids recognition of red, blue and yellow.

Wooden puzzle – a simple puzzle with two or three main pieces promotes manual dexterity and recognition of shapes and parts, which is a pre-number activity.

A posting box with square, triangle and circle cutouts helps the child to gain confidence through recognition as shape and correct 'posting'.

Formboards for lacing, buttoning and zipping practice increases skills in dressing and undressing.

A selection of jars, bottles and tins with screwtops enables the child to exercise his new skill in unscrewing them.

Auditory materials include bells, chimes, sealed containers with rice, peas or lentils in for shaking and drums.

Painting materials: large brushes, easels and poster paints. At this age the child is most interested in covering the paper with paint.

Books with few words and large coloured pictures are enjoyed now.

Nails, board and hammer provide a harmless outlet for aggression.

3–4 Years

All the above equipment can be used, but puzzles can have more pieces (4–6), building materials will be used more constructively as a 'house' or 'garage' is made, and a wider range of dressing up clothes appeals to his imagination and desire for make-believe play. Dolls figure in this and, to encourage abilities in dressing, they should have detachable clothes which button, zip or lace up. A wooden board with lock and key and latch helps mastery of another skill, and could prevent his being locked in a room by accident. Coloured matchboxes with coloured counters in primary colours for matching, large and small beads to sort and buttons of different kinds further acquisition of skills required for later literacy and numeracy. Drawing should be done with a thick crayon or pencil as the fine muscle control is not yet fully developed. A long thick brush is still used for painting.

Lego sets are popular at this stage, but should be simple interlocking pieces at first.

Picture Lotto games provide a pre-reading activity as they help the child to realize the sequence of events in a story and rearrange them accordingly.

Books with large pictures are still enjoyed as they help understanding of the story text, which can be supplemented by the adult if it is too brief.

Finger puppets can be used by the adult and the children to illustrate or invent a story.

4–5 Years

As above, with the following additions.

More painting, drawing, modelling materials, construction and building sets can be included.

More tools (screwdrivers, screws, plane and drill) can be used as greater manual dexterity is gained.

Nurse and doctor kits, as well as plenty of dressing up clothes for hospital play, often dispel fears of children about to be hospitalized.

Ropes and ladders to climb, plus a climbable tree in the garden if possible.

Garden tools (a trowel and fork) help each child to grow vegetable and flowers in his own little plot.

Scales for weighing should be real household scales and weighing activities can precede number play.

Jigsaws can be more complicated now.

Play shops allow the children to take turns to be shopkeeper and customer.

Realistic jars, tins and boxes should be used for meaningful role-play.

Glove puppets can be used to make up stories and in drama with children recording the parts on a tape cassette recorder.

Clean junk with glue, string, paper fasteners, paint and rubber bands is useful for collage and model making.

Books can now be of the type used for learning to read. Some of these will be of the phonic type with pictures of objects which begin with certain sounds. Most are intended for 'look and say' reading, where familiarity with the whole word, which is repeated frequently throughout the script, enables the child to read meaningfully.

5–6 Years

Large equipment for activity includes slides, swings, rope ladders, a trampoline, a child-sized bus, bikes, scooters, the swimming pool (with children's area and adult supervision), balls and bats.

Musical instruments – some made by the children – include drums, triangles, castanets, shakers, recorders, guitar and piano.

Drawing and painting materials still include thicker pencils and brushes, progressing to finer implements.

Complex floor games include railways with a number of parts and Lego building sets.

Jigsaws with 6–12 pieces, and matching and sorting materials still provide fun.

6–8 Years

Large equipment as above. Dramatic play materials – cardboard television set, earphones for 'newscaster' of the day.

Musical instruments plus record player, tape recorder.

Filmstrip and slide projector, clocks, radios and telephones allow discovery and manipulation of more complicated mechanisms.

Calculators for counting and spelling (simple types) provide enjoyment in formal arithmetic and mastery of new skills.

Computers – a BBC basic for games at first, followed by communication through graphics and symbols, problem solving, basic spelling and number skills, and story telling are intended as useful *aids* to learning, not to take over the whole household or classroom!

Types of Play

Imaginative Play

This helps children to gain pleasure, learn self-expression, explore and solve problems, and enables them to pass through egocentrism to objectivity (see above). Pretence and symbolic play are early forms of representation, and fantasy play helps children cope with emotions and problems in childhood.

Fantasy play is said to last from 18 months to 7 or 8 years although much well formed pretend play does not appear until after 3 years. Some maintain that make-believe play diminishes at 6–7 years when reality and fantasy are distinguished by the child's reasoning ability and experience.

In imaginative play the child rehearses his interests, skills and obligations, and makes experiments in social living without having to pay the penalty for mistakes. Imaginative and recreational play are often interwoven with practical activities and this 'pretend play' is seen in vastly different cultures.

Symbolic play enables the child to relive his past experiences and makes for the satisfaction of the ego rather than for its subordination to reality. In older children, the symbols are replaced by rules in social play. Role play refers to any activity in which the child assumes a distinct identity different from his own – a special case of the more general category of pretend or make-believe play. In the first, the child announces 'I'm the doctor, you're the nurse and Kirsty's the sick one', while the second type is seen when another child says 'I'm driving my ambulance to the hospital' while sitting on a wooden truck.

Toys are not necessary for imaginative play – children will gather or request the necessary symbols and play with great inventiveness, as the wedding dress becomes Wonder Woman's cape and the handbag becomes a sack of coal. The 'Indian' daubed with paints and sporting magnificent head gear made from a feather duster can quickly change sides to become a 'cowboy' simply by announcing it!

The excitement of the nursery picnic, riding on the bus, eating an exciting meal of items not usually enjoyed at home – baked potatoes, chicken drumsticks, fresh fruit and vegetable salads – will be relived many times. There is no danger of food poisoning, however, since children appreciate that their dough or clay cakes are not edible! Sometimes parents worry about the amount of violence and 'war games' they see in play but these are often excellent for catharsis of hidden fears and anxieties as to size and inadequacy of themselves in relation to adults. Some children can express aggression in art form – perhaps lurid colours, scrubbed in vigorously, to represent various frightening animals while he makes the appropriate sounds. The destruction of the painting either by tearing up or colouring over it with black paint gives relief from the tension which often accompanies the aggression. This therapeutic nature of imaginative play is not a necessary characteristic of rough and tumble play in that many battles won and lost may simply be a pleasurable activity. Differences in terms used indicate this – rough and tumble is 'composed of run, hop, jump, fall, wrestle, laugh, chase, flee, make a laugh'.

Imaginative play aids the physical development through hand–eye coordination involved in dressing up and pretend play. 'Crossing the deep river' on a plank suspended over two blocks is a dangerous feat, but aids balance.

Intellectually various concepts of size and number can be gained. A sense of time and duration and sequential order (relevant to pre-reading and pre-number) may be emerging, as role playing entails remembering past and present and planning for the future.

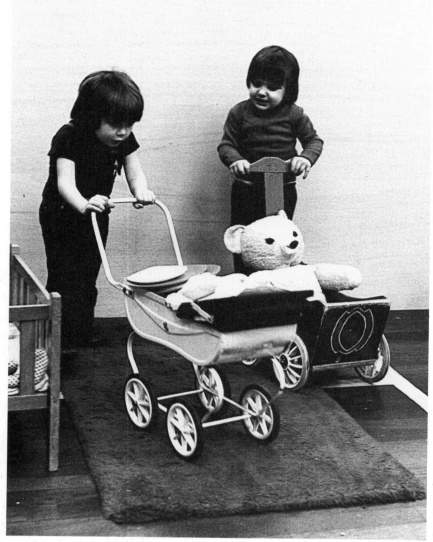

Figure 7.2   Role-playing parts give children the opportunity to create an imaginative world dominated by themselves.

Social development

When imaginative play is in groups, social development is aided as children exchange ideas, take turns and learn how to be social beings. The origins of most of the aspects of play can be detected in the earliest contacts of the child with his parents or care givers. A 2 year old child's 'social expertise' is based on experience with cooperative adults, and he has to learn how to cope with his peers who may irritate through their tendencies to snatch toys, poke and scream in much the same way as himself. Three-year-old children take part in active social play but less often than older children, and the preceding watching and observation may be a form of exploration or timidity due to the new experience of nursery or playgroup. Once a child reaches a level of cognitive maturity that permits him to operate with roles and plans for pretend games, he becomes less dependent in the pretence of the real properties of objects. Socially, certain props or settings that suggest or permit group activities in which functional roles can be differentiated, such as shops (sales assistants, manager and customers) or buses and trains (driver and passengers) can encourage group play among three or more children.

Socially, the child develops an awareness of himself in relation to others and discovers the joy of shared activity and mutual respect.

Progression of Play

Play is not only a part of development but it follows a sequence linked to the stages of development. The enlightened parent or care giver recognizes the importance of providing the right kind of play equipment and toys suited to the child's needs and interests at each stage. Any organization of play, including choice of toys and equipment must take into account *stages*, *ages* (which are not always the same as the stage, but may produce difficulties if a 5 year-old boy plays with babyish toys because he is not at the 5 year-old stage), *interests* and *needs* of the children for whom it is designed. One can only become aware of these through knowledge and observation of each child involved. Each child is an individual and, while developmental schedules are useful as a guide, they only indicate the average and not even the normal, because it is normal for each individual to progress at his own rate through the pattern of development.

Constructive Play

This is the forerunner of creativity as the child experiences satisfaction in the end-product. He begins simply with building mountains in the sand pit, making clay or dough pies and playing with blocks, beads, wood, paint, scissors, paste and crayons or chalks. The actual end-product is less important than the production at first, and usually the child is 4 years old before he is interested in actually producing something,

Figure 7.3 Spectator or parallel play?

although at three he will often utilize his block constructions as houses or boats in dramatic play. Modelling with clay or dough, finger painting and collage pictures are the next development in constructive play, although up until the age of 5 or 6 years the child has no preconceived plan or pattern. After 6 years of age he is able to use materials for specific purposes in an appropriate way.

Recognition of effort is important at all stages and every day because all activities require some degree of effort and without encouragement children soon lose interest and the motivation to try again. Sometimes it may be helpful to suggest how a task can be completed or to offer a few alternative suggestions when a child is frustrated and unable to finish an importtant job. This timely intervention may help the child who in later life opts out whenever difficulties arise and dissipates his energy in anger and evasive behaviour.

Research has shown that the longest, richest and most elaborated sequences of play were produced by materials and activities which made it possible for the child to construct something. These were constructions whose progress could

be appreciated by the child without the aid of an adult. Surprisingly, the most popular activities of water, sand, clay and finger painting were not at the top of the list of these activities. So we will look at constructive play through the media of blocks, woodwork, building sets and in our provisions and timely interventions help the children to become 'engineers of play'.

Block Play

The amount of space given to a block building area will depend on the size of the room and the importance placed on the activity by the teacher, but obviously children need space for their constructions. The block area should be out of the way of traffic in the nursery so that children do not interfere with the building, and other activities are not prevented because of it. A carpet needs to be flat for a firm building base and, of course, a carpet lowers the noise level. The block storage cupboard should be low enough to enable the children to take the blocks out and put them away easily, and with sufficient shelves and sections to store blocks of similar shapes together. Cupboards must be sturdy to avoid

Figure 7.4   Other children's activities can sometimes appear more interesting.

any danger of their collapse. Storage in shelves is better than in a box, as the children experience classification and whole-part relationships as they arrange them to put away. Large unit blocks allow children to discover equivalences and other mathematical relationships as they handle them, enable the construction of sturdy structures and offer the best possibilities for imaginative play. Blocks are constructed of non-splitting hardwood and although expensive are durable. Large hollow blocks allow children to build houses, garages and airports which are incorporated into dramatic play.

Accessories to enhance play include trucks of various sizes, floor trains, cars, animals, people, railway and road signs, aeroplanes and helicopters. Where accessories are not available other materials can be adapted. If accessories are available all of the time they may detract from the improvisation which is an essential part of imaginative play, when the block can become a car or a person.

Benefits of block play

Physical. The child uses gross motor skills as he bends, lifts, stretches and crawls. As he handles and places each block, he develops fine muscle control and hand–eye coordination. Control of fingers and hand is seen in the palmar grasp for large blocks, pincer grasp for the smallest. Balancing on his 'bridge' as he 'crosses the river' promotes foot control, and as he handles the blocks for the pleasure it gives he becomes aware of their properties through manipulation. As he reaches for blocks and stands on tiptoe to place them high, he enjoys a great deal of physical exercise.

Intellectual. Concepts of size, shape, position, heavy, light, tall, small, large, little and big are gained as the children play with blocks, taking out and putting away as the adult helps until they are familiar with the right method. Where there are pictures of blocks on the shelves, to correspond to their position, children experience the relation of a three-dimensional object to a two-dimensional form, and if the labels include the appropriate block names, children learn to identify a block with a symbol. In block play, children gain concepts which are basic to a number of subjects in the curriculum of primary and secondary schools – mathematics, language, science and social studies. Certain blocks stack more easily because of similar shape and, as the child learns to stack in series, he practises one-to-one correspondence in keeping the stacks equal. This one-to-one correspondence is basic to the study of mathematics. Blocks are the parts which make up the whole structure of a tower and the concept of the whole and its relationship to its parts is important for the child's understanding of the basic mathematical processes of addition, subtraction, multiplication and division. If the tower is too high the child subtracts one or two blocks. When he decides to make a dual carriageway out of a single road, he is practising division. In using two half units to construct a whole, he is becoming familiar with fractional components in a concrete way. Problem solving is another benefit from block play. The child observes 'the crane is too high to go under the bridge', identifies the problem and tests two solutions – make the crane smaller or the bridge higher. Working through similar problems increases the child's knowledge of his environment. Eventually experience enables him to move away from trial and error to more scientific approaches. He realizes that small blocks will not support large ones. He can experiment – how many blocks can be added before his construction will collapse?

His vocabulary is increased during block play, perhaps by the teacher providing labels and pictures of various edifices discussed previously. Words like 'skyscraper', 'multistorey', 'factory', 'warehouse' are used with ease and memory recall heightened as the children remember visits to the town when they saw the real things.

Emotional. As the child builds something to his own specifications, he feels enormous pride as a creator, possibly of something higher than himself. The sense of mastery adds to his self-confidence as he repeats his success over and over. Blocks are not fragile or expendable so he can take risks and make mistakes without fear. They can also be safely knocked down when he feels aggressive or frustrated, without the guilt which may accompany destruction of some other medium. The child's ability to balance objects becomes more precise as he finds ways to make the structure more solid and, in the process, he develops a positive self-concept.

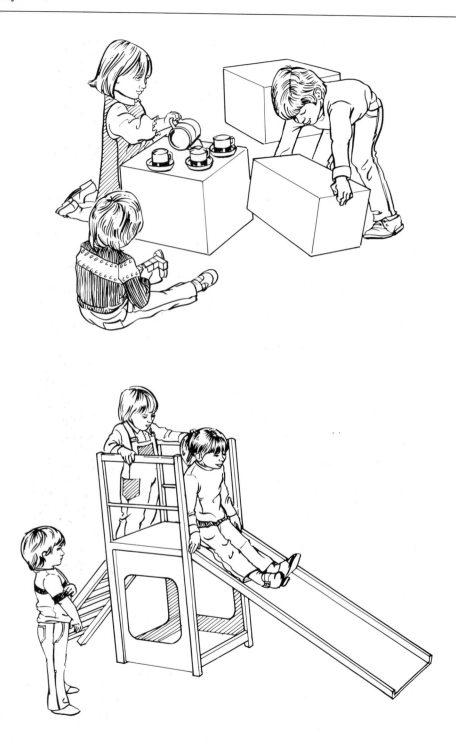

Figure 7.5 The progression of play:
(a) cooperation, (b) taking turns on the
slide.

Figure 7.6   Construction materials allow opportunities for solitary, parallel and cooperative play.

Social. Block play allows children to play cooperatively in groups, sharing ideas, respecting each other's opinions and contributions. They can share vocabulary and their experiences at home, at school and in their communities. Sharing block play experiences with other children provides a means for discovery of self in relation to others.

Different stages of play can be seen in block building. Some children may play alone (solitary), others play alongside each other (parallel), while some plan and work together on a building (cooperative play). Yet others may work and talk together about their common activity without dividing their labour to accomplish a common goal, as in associative play. A child may play alone one day and join in with others the next. Their different interactions depend upon their state of readiness, their experiences in and out of school and their own feelings about themselves.

Role of the adult in block play

The adult's support is essential to purposeful play with blocks. Even their presence is often enough without intervention, but it may be necessary to direct a child toward a project or bring about involvement – 'Can Yvette help you build the palace?' and 'Where will you put the door?'. The adult can also help by naming blocks and by timely progress to more prolonged play with 'new' supplies. They will take turns to use a hammer, 'lend' and 'borrow' nails, share space and ideas with other children.

Building Sets

Sets should be displayed on low toy cupboards, easily available to the children. A variety of equipment is needed, as each different set provides its own stimulation and develops different skills. Older children (5–8) should not have sets with small pieces. Some sets interlock, some fit in grooves and others have dowelling that fits into holes.

Suggestions. Lego builder, model builder, peg blocks, plastic bricks, town-building set, block-craft, large dominoes, balancing builder set.

Play shapes can be used with a wide age range of children 1½–5 years. They are made in soft, washable vinyl in bright colours and interesting shapes which interlock easily to form all sorts of objects and animals.

Sticklebricks are ideal for very young children (1–2 years) and possibly for slow learning children who have retarded development. The large pieces interlock very easily, giving quick satisfying results. Older children (2–7 years) can build quite complex and imaginative structures as well as wheeled vehicles.

Stacking and nesting beakers and dolls are good for young babies as an introduction to construction play in that they involve placing brightly coloured beakers inside each other or stacking large plastic rings on to a base. These can be used with babies from 6 to 18 months.

Pop-up Rocket, a suitable toy for a space-age baby, involves stacking rocket pieces on top of each other and pressing button for lift off. The reward is to see the pieces fly up! These are suitable for 2- to 3-year-old children.

A *vehicle construction set* with bases, wheels, seats, ladders and people are useful for 2- to 4-year-olds to build their own vehicles.

Lego plastic building bricks are very useful and provide for a wide age range. The Basic Set is suitable for 3- to 9-year-olds; Fabuland which has animal characters and a story as well as a set of bricks is suitable for 3- to 5-year-olds; Legoland includes sets for cars, a town, castle and space travel, and is suitable for children over 4 years; and the Technic Set builds into detailed working models with pistons, gears and steering mechanisms and is for children of 8–9 years.

Bolt 'N' Build, Wreck 'N' Repair, while the name has to be deplored as it encourages spelling difficulties, can be pulled to pieces after construction and the bits used again – an excellent release for tension! It can also be motorized so that it really moves and is for 7- to 10-year-olds.

A wide variety of toys for every age group and most play purposes can be identified in the *Good Toy Guide* published by Play Matters/The National Toy Libraries Association.

Value of play with construction sets

Physical. The child develops large and small muscles, pincer grasp, hand–eye coordination and manual dexterity.

Intellectual. Recognition of shapes and sizes, textures, colours, smells, concepts of small, large, long, short, fitting pieces to make patterns or three-dimensional objects – all can be achieved at various stages in baby and child development. Increased vocabulary occurs through naming buildings, vehicles, animals and people. Imaginative and dramatic play develop as the hero rescues people from the top of a tower, or King Kong demolishes the skyscraper. Association of ideas develops as the child links DIY efforts of parents at home to building labourers on new building sites and re-creates his experiences from observation of these events.

Emotional. Pleasure and enjoyment in his own creations. Sense of mastery gives self-confidence, pride in achievement. Release of tension.

Social. Construction crews work together planning, sharing ideas and parts, taking turns to be the foreman or architect. Girls can be the engineers as well as boys to prevent sex-stereotyping.

Role of the adult in Construction Set play

The adult must not be tempted to show the child how to use the various items. In play, as in cooking, too many hands spoil it for the child. He should be allowed to examine and experiment with parts before he seeks help. Careful observation will ensure that no child becomes frustrated with some set which is too complicated and walks off in disgust to something else. Questioning as part of timely intervention helps the child to express his difficulty which is of great value emotionally, as verbal discussion of frustrations often prevents physical manifestations. The adult may be invited to join in imaginative and dramatic play and add to the children's vocabulary and understanding of concepts – high, higher, highest, space capsule, satellite, fitting in, on, up, down, below and above.

Woodwork

Siting

The woodwork work bench should be placed in an accessible area out of the line of traffic in the nursery and, if possible, where the noise will not interfere with other activities. Tools can be kept on a pegboard on the wall or in a cupboard. Outlines of the tools on the places where they fit helps the children to match the tool to the configuration on the board in a one-to-one correspondence. With this method the children can learn to put them away without assistance. A sturdy box beside the work bench can store wood scraps for independent selection by the children. A working area of 2½ ft × 4 ft allows two children to work at the same time.

Equipment

Good work benches can be improvised by using a heavy table with the legs sawn off to an appropriate height. A height of 24 inches is satisfactory and a platform 3–4 inches high can be used to raise smaller children to this height.

All tools used by the children should be regular adult tools of good quality and appropriate weight and size, not toy versions. Hammers should be small, well balanced and of sufficient weight to provide plenty of force when swung lightly. (It takes more, not less, strength to work with a lightweight hammer.) Nails may be of several sizes, very sharp and with good-sized heads. Half to 1¼ inch nails are good. Saws can be handled by most 4-year-olds if they are not too large and are kept very sharp. Fretsaws may prove generally more useful, especially when used with fairly thin wood. The blades should be medium weight as fine blades tend to break too easily and very coarse ones are somewhat harder to use. Clamps are almost a necessity for nursery children who find it hard to hold a piece of wood with one hand while sawing it or hammering it with the other. Wood scraps in a variety of shapes, spools and other round shapes are useful. Wood shapes used for hammering and sawing might include larger pieces than those used for glueing. Large planks, bunker boxes, orange crates, small barrels and large industrial spools may be used for wood construction with hammers and saws. Sandpaper wrapped and tacked round a small wood block permits uniform pressure on wood and is easy for children to handle. A plane is unnecessary for 3- to 5-year-old children as their hands are not developed enough to grasp it securely. Screwdrivers are not necessary either and can be dangerous if they slip. Hardwoods and plywoods are too difficult for children to work with as hardwood is resistant to nailing and plywood splinters.

Value of woodwork

Physical. Woodwork provides many opportunities for manipulative experiences. The child uses every part of his body – large and small muscles are involved as he hammers the nail held between finger and thumb into wood. Balance is involved as he positions his body to hammer more directly and his efforts to hit the nail with the hammer aids hand–eye coordination. He uses bodily force as he conquers the resistance of the wood. Release of energy is seen as he pounds on the wood.

Intellectual. The child discovers the properties of different woods – sees the grain, smells the aroma, touches the smooth, sanded surface, noting differences in texture. He learns about sizes, shapes and weights of different woods. As he saws, he practises basic mathematics – division as he cuts up a board into small pieces, addition as he puts them together with nails. The nails are sorted and classified into long, longer, longest, thin, thick and placed in appropriate containers. He notices how the nails are arranged in the wood as if in a pattern and proceeds to make more complex arrangements. Two pieces of wood are joined, then twisted about to give the desired shape as in a boat. Processes of selection, testing, elaborating and evaluating are all involved.

Emotional. The child experiences great relief as he is able to bang joyfully, making a noise, without guilt or fear of reprimand and welcomes a great outlet for pent-up feelings of frustration and anger. Mastery of the tools leads to self-confidence and development of positive self-concept. His imagination soars as his masterpiece becomes an aeroplane, a ship, a bird, a house. He appreciates the aesthetic qualities of wood – the beauty of grain patterns, the pleasant feel of smoothness. Pleasure is further enhanced with an end-product he can show off, but this is less important than the experiences gained.

Social. The children can work together in a cooperative way or in solitary or parallel play.

Creative Play

Creativity involves discovery, invention, experiencing, imagination, experimentation, doing something different in problem solving, establishing new links between what already exists, e.g. a blanket, table and chair become a series of caves for exploring. If creativity is to be fostered in the nursery, the attitude of staff must allow for children to deviate from the norm – one piece of original work is worth much more than 20 pieces cut from the same adult-made template. Apart from the obvious creative activities such as painting, collage, dough and clay play, junk play often results in the production of a space shuttle from a few cardboard boxes. Music and movement give scope for free expression and no interpretation is considered wrong. Dramatic play, whether with dressing-up clothes or not, also provides for individual responses. Swimming provides a vehicle for active imaginations – it is safer to fly like Superman when you are in reality jumping off the diving board into the water.

Instead of conventional playgrounds many schools and communities have now utilized the space as Adventure Playgrounds. This idea came from Denmark where they can be seen beside every high-rise block of flats, providing scope for free expression. Tree trunks are transformed into pilot's seats, table tops for tea parties and, with a large cardboard box, become hideaways. Strong tree branches become fixed points for Tarzan swings, tyre swings, tents made from blankets and tablecloths.

In order to foster creativity time must be allowed for children to end their play, so flexible timetables are necessary. Rigidity about cleanliness can dampen creativity. The children should not be under pressure; new ideas must be allowed even if they irritate the adult, and risk-taking must also be allowed. There should be a balance between stimulus, excitement and delimitation. The stimulating environment should include problems demanding solutions, e.g. 'How can I make a spy hole in that tree?' But these should not be posed or solved by the adult. Encouragement, space and helping children towards outlets for creativity should be the adult's role. As creativity stands against well established rules and customs it must be recognized that a democratic society caters for deviants, otherwise there would never be a flourishing of great talents.

Value of creative play

Physical. Large and small muscles are developed as the child carries blocks and boxes to his 'fort' in the large outdoor sandpit, holds his long thick brush in painting or stubby crayons for colouring. Progression to finer implements requires fine movement of hands and fingers. Use of a variety of raw materials in creative play as in finger paint leads to exploration and movements of arms and shoulders as he enjoys creation of different shapes. Touch becomes more sensitive as he realizes that different levels of pressure produce different patterns.

Intellectual. The child learns about the properties of creative materials through sensory experience – the smell of clay and dough, the difference in texture and flowing abilities of wet and dry sand, the thrill of mixing colours and creating new ones. As he 'draws' shapes he becomes aware that symbols (square for house, round for moon) can be used to represent real objects. In production of pictures and objects the child comes to appreciate beauty. Putting out materials and clearing away after the session help sequential thought, essential to later reading skills.

Emotional. Children gain enormous satisfaction and enjoyment from creative expression. As each effort is appreciated by the adult, his individuality is stimulated and encouraged. The availability of a wide range of materials enables him to enjoy the independence of choice. Dancing around like a Spaniard or Greek seen on television to guitar music, pounding dough, sloshing paint on to paper or tramping around in wet paint for a 'foot' mural gives pleasure and relief from tension and worries.

Social. The child learns to share space and materials and take turns with paste jars, joins in the clearing away of materials which is an essential part of the activity. It helps to develop a sense of responsibility in the children.

Role of the adult in creative play

The adult must provide adequate space, time and materials for creative play. The placing of materials has to be careful to avoid traffic from other children not involved in the activity. Materials must be large enough (small pieces of paper are useless for painting) and chosen carefully to avoid frustration such as dark-coloured sugar paper which makes a poor background for red, purple, brown and blue paint. Experiences like visits, outings and classroom displays provide the rich background essential to creative expression. As children touch and smell and look, the adult helps them to verbalize the experience and thus gain more understanding of what they have done. However, non-verbal communication is often more effective than asking a question or making a comment – just adult presence encourages children to be more adventurous with the material. Intervention as to content or techniques can stunt and stultify the exploration essential to satisfaction with the medium. There is no need to comment on the artistic value of a painting or model: the adult must be non-judgemental and appreciate that it is the process – the doing – which is important, not the product. Hence, children's artwork should not be held up or displayed as good or better – each one is valued as self-expression. Demonstrations as to

use of materials are unhelpful and inhibiting as are patterns cut from one template for use with a whole class, or showing children a picture someone else has produced and inviting them to imitate it.

The adult must also be expansive during times of creative activity and not become over-concerned at the 'mess' made by the children in their enthusiasm. There must be an opportunity for the child who wants to spatter and drip paint from a height on to his paper, but when this is intended to ruin another child's masterpiece it must be disallowed. Overall the adult's role in creative activities involves an attitude which encourages curiosity, exploration, initiative, improvisation and provision of materials suited to the ages, stages, interests and needs of the children involved.

Benefits of painting and arts activities

Physical. The child uses many parts of the body and gains motor control. Painting on the floor, a table or an easel involves different positions for arms and shoulders, and changes in whole body posture. In finger painting he uses his fingers, fingernails, knuckles, hands and arms to test what he can do with these parts of his body as he gives variety to his designs. With experience, children experiment with different parts of their hands in order to refine shapes they create. It takes a different movement to paint a tree top from those used to depict grass. Foot painting involves muscles of ankle, foot and toes. Painting of 'sculptures' and models made from junk materials involve fine muscle control. Management of the brush involves control as he decides to let it drip or make drips part of the painting.

Intellectual. The child has to make decisions as to where he will put the first stroke or position the first shape on the paper. Many children talk as they paint and begin to use words to describe the properties of paint – wet, thick, thin, lumpy – as well as naming colours and symbols. As he moves a brush, pencil or crayon across a page, he is practising hand–eye coordination. When he looks at the shapes he has created on paper he sees figure against background. He becomes aware of comparative shapes and eventually begins to classify them as circles, squares and triangles. Hand–eye coordination, figure–ground and the creation of shapes are all part of pre-reading experience.

Figure 7.7   Adults can learn much from listening to children's conversations with each other.

Emotional. Great enjoyment is experienced in the process of using different types of paints, crayons and other artistic media. The sheer joy of being able to make a mess without incurring an adult's reprimand makes for freedom of expression. Exploration is possible with mixing colours, and if they are not all introduced at once discovery of 'new' colours is exciting. Painting is a means of self-expression in that the child can express feelings through paint that he cannot talk about. His feelings emerge as he paints and he becomes aware of those he did not know he had. Strong feelings can be safely expressed on paper. He is free to set his own standards and work at his own pace. The routines of putting on an apron, placing one brush in each cup, washing brushes, removing pictures from the easel and hanging up to dry encourage independence.

Figure 7.8   Painting can be a quiet and all-absorbing activity.

Social. Children can work together in twos and threes or larger groups to produce a class mural. They learn to be considerate of each other, respecting individual space requirements, sharing communal aspects as they help to lay out materials and place them safely away.

Painting

Painting with tempera paints using thick, long-handled brushes is an absorbing and relaxing activity. Children are equally happy painting at the double standing easel, wall easel, on tables or on the floor. Paper for painting should be at least 18 × 24 inches and bright colours should be available. Tempera paints can be obtained in powder or liquid forms. They can be kept mixed and ready in airtight jars. For children's use the paint can be poured into smaller jars which are covered when not in use. If the paint becomes too thick a little water added will thin it, but care should be taken that paint is not too thin. Brushes should be kept clean by washing daily in warm water. If painting is done on the floor, the paper should be placed on top of oilcloth, plastic sheets or newspaper to protect the floor. Finger, hand and foot paintings are novel sensory experiences and if done by a group of children on a large piece of paper make an entertaining mural. Painting of carpentry, wood or clay models is also enjoyable and calls for finer control.

At first painting is enjoyed more for the doing than the end-product. The sloshing of paint on paper is purely manipulative and enjoyed for the sheer delight of handling·the materials. Gradually skills will develop in creative activities; the ability to control the brush, crayon or dough and to reproduce forms. There is real pride in a child's discovery that he can make a form or shape, and he will repeat it over and over for his own satisfaction. These forms will gradually change with his increasing skills and when a child begins to arrange materials in a way satisfying to him this is the beginning of design.

Recognizable pictures or forms come only after considerable experimentation and the first attempts are very primitive. Often the first real picture that a child makes is one of himself – it emerges as a head with eyes and perhaps a mouth and nose. To the head are added arms and legs. The making of the body comes later, as does more detail. Most of the child's picture-making is of activities and events which are important to him, usually with himself as the focal point of interest, 'me with mummy and daddy shopping'; often these show a little mummy and daddy and a big 'me'.

All these stages in a child's art growth are important as he explores at his own rate of progress. The adult's role is important too, as he/she shares the child's enjoyment and accepts efforts as worthwhile, thus giving him the confidence and interest to keep on experimenting. All young children are interested in drawing right from the scribbling stage of the beginner through the more controlled steps on to picture-making and design, so crayons and paper should always be available for the children to use.

Pencils are not recommended for pre-school children as they are too slim and children tend to hold them in a stiff cramped position which makes drawing a poor activity. When the children have developed freedom of movement and considerable skill in the use of crayons, usually at 5 or 6 years of age, pencils can be provided but they should be thicker types. *Crayons* should be large, hexagonal shapes as the small muscles are not yet developed in pre-school children and freer movement is possible with large

ones. Colours should be clear and bright and crayons can be washed with soap and warm water if they become grubby. The use of different kinds of paper adds to the interest in crayoning. Newsprint, wallpaper (smooth, rough, embossed), cardboard and wrapping paper can all be used.

Candle painting. Rub the candle vigorously over piece of paper making pattern and wash over with non-thickened paint.

Potato painting. Mix a thick paint. Cut potatoes into shapes. Put a little of each colour into small containers (marge) and dip potato into mixture and stamp on paper.

Painting on wet paper. Wet paper and paint over while paper is wet. Use four tablespoons of powder colour to ⅔ tablespoon water.

Finger paint recipes

1 2 cups (yogurt) taken from ready-mixed Polycell
6 heaped teaspoons of powder paint
Put Polycell on to a Formica-topped table or an enamel tray and add powder paint – keep adding as the mixture thins out on the table, interchanging colours and perhaps taking prints as green and yellow turn to blue, etc. Fine sand can be added to give a different texture.
2 ½ cup starch
½ cup of powder paint
Mix the starch well with ½ cup of cold water, then add 1 cup of boiling water and the paint. To preserve add 1 tablespoon of sodium benzolate.
3 2 large cups of Daz or any washing powder
¾ cup hot water
2 rounded tablespoons powder paint.
4 1 cup of cornflour
½ teaspoon powder paint
Mix with 1 cup *cold* water, add 3 cups hot water, boil for 1 minute, cool and add the powder paint and 1 drop oil of cloves to preserve mixture.
5 ½ cup soapflakes
½ cup cold water starch (without borax)
¾ cup cold water
Beat all together until the mixture is the consistency of whipped potatoes. Colouring can be added if desired (see recipe 1).
6 1 large saucepan
1 cup cornflour or maize starch (available at Boots)

a drop of cold water
2 pints boiling water
1 cup white soap flakes
colouring

Dissolve the cornflour or maize starch with a little cold water in the saucepan, add 2 pints boiling water and bring back to the boil. Remove from heat, add soap flakes. It will be runny, but it gets firmer as it cools.

Some hints

Colours. Vary colours to give a new look.

Prints. Prints of finger painting can be made by pressing paper over the patch that has been fingerpainted. Colouring can be added to the glue, or it can be mixed without colour: let children work a blob of paste with their fingers first and then let them scatter one or more colours on to their paste on the table and make their own colours as they smear. This allows them to see colours actually at work instead of the ready prepared colour. You can get food colouring in bottles with dropper taps, or provide powder paints in dredgers to make it less wasteful.

Miscellaneous

How to use up old bits of wax crayons:

1 *Stubjuice.* Melt odd bits of wax crayons in an old tin and let children paint with them. Adult supervision is needed to watch that children won't burn themselves on warm tin! Not all makes of wax crayons will melt. Suitable activity for small group only.
2 Let children shave off bits from wax crayons (use blunt knife or a potato peeler for this) onto a clean piece of paper. Spread the chippings over the paper, lay a piece of paper on top and iron all over with a warm iron. Let the children peel off the top paper.

Coloured sand: Dye silver sand with food colouring, and dry it in the oven. This can be used for collages (children paint with glue and sprinkle sand over it . . . excess sand can be shaken back into tray). Children also enjoy using it in the sand box.

Finger puppets (knitted)

All puppets are knitted on size 12 needles.

Large size. Cast on 15 sts in DK wool. Knit 1 row in K1 P1 rib to prevent the base curling, then 14 rows stocking stitch for the body, and 10 rows stocking stitch for the head. Do not cast off.

Medium size. Cast on 14 sts in 4-play. Work 24 rows in garter stitch for the body and 8 rows stocking stitch for the head. Do not cast off.

Finishing off.
1 Thread the end of the wool into a long needle and pass this through the stitches, slipping them off the knitting needle at the same time. Pull up tightly and secure with a few stitches.
2 Sew up seams (centre back). Turn right side out.
3 Stuff head part very firmly with a little knob of kapok or cotton wool, shaping and rounding it well.
4 Run a gathering thread round neck, pull up tightly and fasten off securely by stitching backwards and forwards through the neck.

Junk play*

Junk is extremely satisfactory for creative work and has a sequence for the child to work through as in painting–dough–clay–water–sand.
    At first the child may cover a cardboard box or paper or card completely with the glue or paste as if he were painting, and not stick anything on at all. Then he may stick two or three things on top of each other – no adult intervention is required here as his explorations will eventually lead him to use the cartons and materials in other ways, and finally 'make' something!

Storage

There are various ways of presenting junk; remember, however it is presented, children can very easily become confused and if they are faced with a great heap of old cartons, boxes and bottles, they can lose interest very quickly and the table or corner could become just JUNK.
    Homemade storage can very easily be adapted

*(Adapted from Mrs Bertha Hayworth, Tutor to General and Advanced Playgroup Courses, Stevenson College.)

to playgroup use and for easy storage. Various ways are:

1 a selection of various size shoe boxes stuck into a bread board or cardboard container to give different size storage trays,
2 tomato boxes (cardboard) stuck together or separate and partitioned off inside with 'walls' of cardboard,
3 round transparent hard plastic containers (obtainable from certain Component Factories), which come packed in a long box,
4 old portable filing cabinets – partition the drawers off into sections,
5 old cotton reel drawers partitioned off into sections,
6 vegetable racks,
7 large cardboard boxes with plastic sweet jars on their ends (stored inside the box) to enable the children to get their hands into the necks,
8 pieces of material with pockets sewn on and hung on a wall or behind a chair,
9 a camp kitchen – three tiers with a solid *wall* on the top layer.

The adult could have sharp-ended scissors on hand, also a Stanley knife, to be used only with her supervision. If the child knows these other materials are there for his use he will soon begin to ask for them himself instead of the adult suggesting she has them if he needs them. There is an endless list of materials which can be used – in fact, anything one would normally throw out can be recycled on the Junk Table. Listed in Table 7.1 are some bits and pieces children, Mother, Grannie or friend could be asked to collect and save and bring along to the playgroup. A basket or cardboard box could be placed in a prominent part of the room with a notice or chart above it suggesting to the Mums what they could collect. The box can be cleared out by the playgroup staff frequently so that it never looks over-full or cluttered.
Other useful things include:

Table 7.1　Items to collect for the junk table

Aluminium foil	Elastic	Plastic bottles
Buttons	Fur	Paper
Beads	Feathers	Pipe cleaners
Bottle tops	Fringes	Pebbles
Braid	Fablon	Plastic and polystyrene trays
Birdseed	Felt	Ribbon
Books	Foam rubber	Rice
Brushes	Fir cones	Raffia
Cotton reels	Foil dishes	Sand
Cartons	Glitter	String
Cards (birthday, Christmas, holiday)	Grasses (dried)	Sawdust (can be coloured with food
Cereal packs (cut to give a good solid	Ice lolly sticks	colouring or powder paint)
base)	Insulating tape	Sweet papers
Coat hangers	Jewellery	Silver paper
Candles	Kitchen roll centres	Sheep's wool
Cotton wool	Lolly sticks	Shells
Cardboard	Leather	Sequins
Cellophane (off sweets, etc.)	Lace	Straw
Chalk	Leaves	Squeezy bottles
Corrugated paper	Lino (scrap)	Seeds
Cheese boxes	Magazines (for cutting out)	Shoe boxes
Cocktail sticks	Match boxes	Trimmings, e.g. lace, braid, ric-rac
Coloured paper	Material (scrap)	Tiles (ceiling)
Corks	Melon seeds	Threads
Christmas paper	Margarine containers	Toilet roll centres
Crayons	Meat trays	Tissue boxes
Doilies	Milk bottle tops	Tape
Drawing pins	Netting	Velcro
Dried:	Net bags	Wool (used and new)
egg shells	Newspapers	Wood
tea leaves	Nut shells	Wallpaper (rolls and old books)
coffee granules	Polystyrene	Wood shavings
melon seeds	Paper plates and cups	Yoghurt cartons
sand	Pine cones	
Egg cartons	Ping pong balls	

Old tea trolley – two tier

Shelving

Scissors, plus storage – a bought box, a four sided frame with 'hole' to fit scissors into, a pegboard frame with some holes made bigger, an egg box with a hole cut in each section, a brick with air holes in it

Glue storage – again glue pots can be bought

Paint palettes – certain individual ice-cream cartons fit directly into the holes and when they get too gooey can be thrown away.

Glue spreaders can be bought

Paint brushes can also be used but sometimes it is difficult to wash PVA glue out of them.

Glues are:

Flour and water paste

Wallpaper paste (without fungicide)

School glue (white PVA which washes out of clothes)

PVA (doesn't wash out as it has a plastic base)

Bostic (good sticker but watch the children's clothes)

Evostick (to be used with an adult and has 'fumes' so be careful if using it)

Cow gum

Gloy

Fixol (instant adhesion – even sticks plastic egg boxes)

Have on hand:

Sellotape
paper clips
stapling machine
rubber bands

Good (round–ended) cutting scissors are an essential at the table.

Failing all above, a container (sturdy) tall enough for scissors to sit upright but not covering the handles.

Whatever type of storage is available or supplied, remember that children are much smaller than adults, and therefore ensure that boxes are low and shallow enough for a child to see into them.

There are various types of glue one can introduce to this activity. Some stick paper and collage work and won't stick boxes, others have instant adhesion and others have to be held for a short while before they stick. One theory is that a child should be allowed to discover himself what glue sticks what, but there is another argument against this: a child can become terribly upset, angry or frustrated with his model when wall-paper paste won't stick two egg boxes together. This is where very careful thought in the setting up of the Junk Table should be taken. The adult should be in the near vicinity of the table and if she observes this frustration building up be on hand to suggest to the child that perhaps X glue would be quicker or would he perhaps like the Sellotape or a paper clip? How often has a nursery nurse been heard to say 'I set up the Junk Table in the morning and never go near it again'. She thinks she is doing the 'right thing' by not 'showing' the child what to do – but she is going to the other extreme and perhaps doing a lot of harm to certain children by not being on hand to suggest alternatives if necessary.

Tissue paper is an added luxury. Tissue paper circles and squares are available in several different sizes and colours. Shiny coloured paper to be cut and doilies could all be introduced.

Rice, lentils, macaroni, pasta (various shapes), peas (dried), split peas, etc; have all been used at the Junk Table but even if the playgroup can afford these items it is a very debatable point, with the present world food shortage, whether we should be using food as a play material.

Try having different days at the Junk Table or different type boxes, e.g:

1 *A colour day* – have all the material a certain colour, e.g. red silver paper, tissue paper, wrapping paper, ribbon, buttons, wood, saw-dust, etc. Some of the children may notice and you could talk about it, notice that one colour was darker than the other although they were both red, etc. Flour and water paste or wallpaper paste could be used.

2 *A flat scrap day* – have everything that is flat, e.g. paper, material, seeds, shells, twigs, etc; to be stuck on to flat paper or card with flour and water paste, wallpaper paste, or PVA for shells, etc.

3 *A big box day* – big cartons. Have good sticky glue and household paint brushes and paints near at hand. Be sure that the children, tables and floors are well protected before the activity begins.

4 *An interest table* could be set up near the Junk Table with Junky pieces as the setting, e.g. a Spring day with cottonwool lambs and tissue paper flowers, etc.

5 *Small cartons* – have a large selection of various small cartons available with a good sticky glue; also paints near at hand. (Should

one use small medicine boxes, pill packets, cigarette packets, etc; on this table?)

6 Another idea is to have a 'feely' book for the children. If at all possible let the children make it. Some of the 'feely' things could be:

a Materials: velvet, satin, cotton, tweeds, candlewick, tartan, nylon (plain and brushed), corduroy, etc.

b Furs: smooth, furry, astrakan, leather, suede, sheepskin, etc.

c Woods: sawdust, shavings, balsa, hardwood, sandpaper (rough and smooth).

d Papers: silver, tissue, brown, cellophane, greaseproof, newsprint, corrugated, etc.

e Buttons: all shapes, sizes and colours.

f Wools: thick, thin, hairy, smooth, straight, curly, etc.

Role of the adult in junk play

The adult has to ensure careful storage and siting of Junk materials. Too many items in a messy situation will deflect even the keenest children. If junk materials are stored to prevent lack of free passage but arranged on open shelves so that children can see what they want and collect it on their own if they wish, there will be less confusion. Safety factors are also the adult's concern. Children under three should not be allowed to play with tiny beads and buttons in case they swallow them or put them in their ears or nose. Attention must be given to the children's ages, stages, interests and needs when planning for junk play. Sharp scissors and knives may be required for production of some desired project but these should be kept by the adult and their use restricted to him/her until the children are able to use them under supervision. Paste, glues and paints must be free from toxic substances. Children will have greater freedom if their clothes are covered with disposable plastic aprons, since some glues cause problems when stuck on to clothes. As with any large activity, preparation and clearing away should be seen as part of the exercise. Novelty is a great stimulus so one new item each week is effective.

Benefits of junk play

Physical. Preparation for the activity gives the child some idea of comparative weights and heights. He becomes aware that he can make things which stand taller than they do. Large and small muscles are developed as they stick on delicate pieces of lace and small beads. They learn to use both hands and feet to steady their 'house' while they put 'curtains' in the 'windows'. Scissors develop hand–eye coordination and manipulative skills.

Intellectual. Numerous sensory experiences are part of junk play – what will and won't break or tear, glue with paste, or glue only with strong gum. Making flour and water paste leads to talk about dough and baking and how does it stick?

Figure 7.9   Manipulative play.

Language is greatly increased – the sounds of paper crunched up, crinkly, shushing, tin foil compared to crêpe paper. Wood is hard and needs a saw to split it into smaller pieces. Cardboard looks hard like wood but can be split with a knife. The properties of materials add to knowledge – the soft pile of velvet, the warmth of lambs' wool, the smoothness of fur. Junk play is an activity that can be extended by the child's own interest and initiative.

One day a wallpaper book was left on the floor when the Supervisor went to the Junk Table; she found the children 'papering the walls'. This activity was carried out on three separate days by the same children. The children were just doing and being allowed to do what Daddy was doing at home.

Another group had had a story about a nest and the next day the supervisor introduced straw and feathers to the Junk Table. There were quite a few 'nests' taken home at the end of that session.

Junk is an activity which can be taken into the home. One mother commented 'I'm like a magpie with junk. I throw nothing out – it's great when it's raining – I put everything on the kitchen table and the children sit for hours'. How much better this is for a child, an opportunity to use his imagination, than an expensive toy with only one purpose to its use!

Recently a 'mobile' was admired in an ex-playgroup Mum's house. She said the girls had made it one wet day – it was a concertina-type apple box packing which they (the girls) had opened up by sticking bottle tops and coloured card and paper into the holes. They had put string through the top and stuck a few streamers of paper over it, and it looked very colourful and attractive.

Concepts related to size, shape, colours and textures are all promoted in junk play.

Emotional. The pleasure of using a feely book for the first time, experimenting with various sizes of boxes, glues and paints, makes junk play very rewarding. The sense of mastery and pride in achievement often fades, however, when parents arrive to take their children home. Some mothers can't be *bothered* to take a model home, or they are just going to the shops, or it's too wet, or they have too much to carry. The supervisor or member of staff should be ready to step in and suggest that little John had spent quite a lot of time 'making' his model for . . .

wouldn't it be nice to keep it for a day or two at least? Sometimes a child makes his model for the nursery nurse; in that case, thank him, show his Mum what he has done and keep it in the playgroup.

A child's creativity can so easily be destroyed. An adult has a group of children round her making, for example, rockets – it's nice to take home to show Daddy but what has the child really done? He has pleased the adult but is it really his own work? When he starts school and is left to his own devices, what does he produce – a soggy mess and Mum says 'What's wrong, John – you did far better at playgroup?' This will probably (not always) have some effect on the child. He may even stop making things, knowing he can't please his Mum with what he makes and takes home.

Through careful, individual observation, the adult can discover the child's current interest and help even the timid child on the road to achievement, raised self-confidence and improved self-concept.

Some children lack confidence in themselves and would rather sit back than do something. If the adult knows a child is interested in, for example, cars she could perhaps have pictures of cars near the table and materials to hand which would perhaps suggest wheels, a car body, etc., in the hope that the child may be stimulated to do something himself. A play leader had amongst her junk some odd gloves; they were put out one day, and one little girl spent a long time making a scarecrow and, of course, using the gloves for hands.

Water play, sand play and modelling with dough and clay are all relaxing and absorbing creative activities. One or more of these activities should be in the play room every day.

Water Play

This can be indoor or outdoor but is a basic play material. *Planning* is essential for all play but particularly for water and messy play. A large plastic water tray set in a portable frame allows access by a small group of children. A set of equipment for the various kinds of water play is useful and saves time if dried and stored together after use. Plastic aprons, sleeves rolled up, plastic sheet or newpapers on the floor for protection, are essential. A sponge and mop should be available and paper towels for drying hands.

Figure 7.10   Water play.

Plenty of space and materials should be made available for each child.

The kit for *floating* should include a plastic dishpan, tub or tray, boats and fish made of plastic or wood, corks, empty plastic pill bottles, balls, plastic toys. Small boats of various kinds, docks and bridges, a lighthouse made from a juice can and placed on a rock, provide dramatic and social play. Purely manipulative water accessories may be provided one day, boats and docks another.

The kit for *pouring* can include a plastic dishpan large enough to prevent splashing, small plastic jugs, small cans with holes punched in bottom and sides, rubber tubing attached to a funnel and plastic lemons.

Equipment for 'bathing a baby' should include a plastic bowl, sponges, small cake of soap on a dish and a towel to dry. Washing dishes can begin with a few plastic dishes, plastic bowl, washing-up liquid, tea towel, small dish rack on a tray. Other 'real' work activities include washing easels, washing tables after clay or finger painting, scrubbing shelves, scouring basins, washing toys, and cleaning paint jars and brushes. A basin of water, sponges, scrubbing brushes and soap, with a mop close by for splashes, should be provided and a longer period of time allowed than an adult would take. Outdoors, washing steps with soapy water and mop and hanging dolls' clothes out on a line at child height provide real work activities.

Blowing bubbles is great fun but also leads to 'scientific' questions about how they are formed and why plain water does not produce shiny, 'coloured' bubbles. These items should be assembled on a tray: a jar of thick yellow soap solution (made by pouring boiling water over pieces of soap, outside the play room away from children) containing one cube of sugar and a few drops of glycerine, sturdy plastic pipes, straws or plastic tubes (straws may be slit ½ inch at the bottom and spread), a half-pint plastic cheese container for each child, a jug of water to dilute the solution in cheese container, a jar of water with Savlon added to sterilize the mouthpiece of the pipe as each child finishes, old newspapers for the table and paper towels to dry hands.

Benefits of water play

Physical. Muscular coordination is developed through the use of various accessories for pouring, filling and squeezing. Large and small muscle movements are made as they dip hands in the water, watch them drip, make wave movements, then wash and dry hands. Testing difference between sensation when fingers, then toes are dipped in. For an outside activity in warm weather, immerse the whole body, in swimsuits, shorts or in 'the buff' if parents and children don't object. Floating requires balance in the horizontal plane and is something most children can do if they are not panicked by others. Others can use rubber rings or 'wings' but the joy of splashing about in the garden pond – whether man-made or not – is something shared by babies and grandparents alike! Why does wetness make you feel cold? Can you shake your hands dry? Can you walk on water? Sit on water? How does a boat stay up when you put it in the water? Why won't it float when it's full of pebbles? Since the first experience of water is usually in the bath, the large outdoor pool – natural or plastic – enables almost full immersion and allows practice in 'swimming' movements. Paddling in little pools and puddles, sloshing through muddy fields – a whole variety of movements, sensations, manipulations, in fact a complete body experience – is possible in water play.

Pouring from a funnel into a container involves hand–eye coordination and control which will be useful when the child is asked to pour juice at break time.

Intellectual. Water helps *learning skills* through experiments with the properties of water: displacement, buoyancy, cause and effect of wet and dry, dripping and pouring, what floats, what sinks.

Concept formation can be developed during water play. Questioning strategies aimed at development of concepts, vocabulary and reasoning ability should be planned before water play to ensure that it is a learning experience, as well as one of enjoyment. Closed questions which call for only 'yes' or 'no' in reply should be avoided. Some typical questions which might suit the situation are given here but only as a guideline. It is hoped that nursery nurses will indicate their own creativity in formation of other questions!

Descriptive questions include: What does the water look like when you pour it from high up above the water tray? What does the water feel like? What colour is it?

Reasoning questions include: What happens when we fill two buckets with water and pour them away in the sink? If you fill one big jug, will you have enough to fill the two smaller ones? Which of these toys will float? Which will sink? Why do they float? Why does it sink? What happens when you pour the water out? Why does it not sink now? Why do we use warm water to wash? Cold water to drink? (Some of these questions are predictive, when the child is asked to predict what will happen in different situations.)

Memory questions include: Tell me about your bath time at home – how is the water different from this? What happens when your Mother puts the foam in your bath? What sort of games do you play in your bath? Where else do you have water at home? What kind of water does Mummy or Daddy use when they wash the dishes? Why do they add liquid soap? What happens when all the dishes have been washed? Why don't we like to eat food from wet dishes? Who has been to the seaside? What did you see there? What did you do there? What do we call the water there? How is the sea water different from the nursery water? Your bath water? The washing up water?

Imaginative questions include: What would happen if you tried to walk on the water like a water-boatman? (Children could observe its movements in the aquarium.) Why can't people walk on water? What would have to happen to the water before you could walk on it? Does water freeze when it's very warm? If you were an ice dance skater how could you dance on the ice – would you not fall on the slippy parts? What would happen if you poured very hot water on the ice? How are ice lollies made? How does your ice lolly taste like oranges? Why is the ice useful to us? What would happen if we didn't have fridges and freezers? What does food look like when it's bad? What does it smell like? How could we make ice-cream? (Making ice lollies can be a fun exercise as a follow-up if there is a fridge in the nursery.)

New concepts of sinking, floating and other properties of water are developed with the adult who asks and answers questions as they arise. Forms of water as ice, snow, hailstones, all require explanation and exploration and add more to the vocabulary.

Simple experiments like the 'magic' which occurs when a spoon is placed in a jar of water or a laundry pin is placed very carefully on the surface of a glass filled to the brim with water lead to later scientific curiosity and discovery.

When the aquarium houses some water-skaters in Spring, they can be seen skimming along on the surface water of the aquarium.

Other experiments to encourage enquiry and stimulate thought include:

1 Find out where the water in the tap comes from.
2 Trace the pipes at school and at home.
3 Arrange a visit to a reservoir if possible.
4 Visit a large pond – which animals and plants live in water? Remember those in the aquarium!
5 Boil a kettle (safely). What happens to the water? Note steam on the windows (or a pair of glasses). Is that the same water we boiled?
6 Test absorbency of skin, straws, paper, foil and different materials.
7 What does 'waterproof' mean?
8 Examine our macs and wellingtons. (Where do these names 'Mackintosh' and 'Wellington' come from?)
9 Wash dishes in the house corner. Test various materials for drying – which is best? Why?
10 Drop a large coin into a trough of water – what happens?
11 Think of all the things we could *not* do if we had no water.
12 What are the names of the places in hot countries where there is very little water?
13 Look at our cactus plants. Giant cactus plants grow in deserts. How do they manage to keep a supply of water?
14 What happens to your skin if you keep your hands in water for a long time?
15 Set up three bowls of water – one hot, one cold, one warm and soapy. After painting and glueing sessions ask three groups to wash in prepared bowls. Which makes hands cleaner?

Emotional. Running one's fingers or hands through water is a pleasant experience for most people. In cold weather, warm water for washing and bathing makes one feel more comfortable and safe. There are so many activities in water play – even those who are physically handicapped can perform well in the baths or swimming pool, often to the envy of their friends! If the child enjoys a particular experiment with water he can repeat it as often as he wishes. There is no sense of failure with

water. Water satisfies all the senses: it makes a lovely sound, whether splashing or tinkling in a water tray waterfall; it looks delightful as it pours from a great height or rests in a few drops on the leaves of a plant; and nothing tastes as good as fresh clear water to the person who is desperately thirsty. While fresh, it is odourless; this is simply an invitation for children to add juices to see if they can smell it!

Water is particularly enjoyed by the timid child who has not found his place in the group, by the child who is over-active and needs to relax by himself, by the aggressive child when situations become difficult, and by all children for pure sensory pleasure with plenty of time to explore.

Dramatic play with water can involve bathing a baby or washing dishes. The 4-year-old may want to help with washing up at home, and opportunity should be made for him to do this, even if it just involves rinsing cups and plates at first. With adult supervision the child learns the delights of helping in the house and being treated as a grown-up able to do the tasks, which is often a bigger boost to his self-confidence than any other play situation. Fantasy and make believe are enjoyed during dramatic play with boats and accessories.

Water play has a relaxing and liberating effect which often carries over into children's use of other material. Its versatility encourages spontaneous and imaginative play. It also provides sensory satisfaction often denied because of lack of time during washing routine.

All these activities can be applied to different age groups, from the exploratory novel nature of water play in the nursery through the primary one child with his desire to experiment, test and recall previous experience, to the junior 7- or 8-year-old fired with the enthusiasm of inventors like Archimedes and James Watt.

Comparisons between rain water and tap water can be made, then tap water and soda water. Sodastream water mixers are great for illustration of how the bubbles of gas get into the water. Further experiments with water can be found in Chapter 8, under The Child's Discovery of Life and Science.

Language development can be promoted through 'word boats'. These are large outlines of boats (made by the adult first perhaps, later by children) which can be filled with words like 'float' 'sink' 'wet'. Rhymes about water like

Insey, Winsey Spider and *Dr Foster* (the unfortunate medic who ruined his best coat in a Gloucester rain shower!) can be recited with glee and mimed as appropriate to the age of the children. Musical chairs can become musical puddles, all the inhabitants of the sea can be mimicked – whale, shark, crab, octupus (long pieces of string or wire can be wrapped round the child to provide the extra arms). The Owl and the Pussycat can become alive again as they 'sail' in their green boat across the 'sea' of the classroom floor, if swimming baths are not available. The Pobble who had no Toes can be directed in his boat to the Land Where the Bong Tree Grows. Pictures of icebergs and Eskimos can lead to transformation of the classroom into the Northern Territories of Canada. Discussion can centre round wet weather clothes and wellies, warm water and cold weather outfits, modelled by children using dressing up materials.

Social. Water play can be enjoyed as solitary, parallel or group activities. Certain accessories prove to be eagerly wanted and children learn to share these and take turns with sieves, tubes and jugs. Solving problems of flotation and displacement (a body immersed in water takes up a certain volume which can be measured, and demonstrated with a doll in a bath; this was the theory of Archimedes, the Greek scientist) often involves two or three children who easily come to recognize their dependency on each other for satisfaction of curiosity. As shown above, a number of communal activities develop from the water play.

Role of the adult in water play

When a bath of water or a wading pool are used inside or outside the play room, there must be constant careful supervision by the adults – young children can drown in a few inches of water. Reckless splashing of water or pouring on to the mats or floor covering should obviously not be allowed but too many restrictions spoil the carefree enjoyment. Too many accessories at once should be avoided, with some withheld to introduce some novelty day by day. The adult can also add to play and extend it through questions which require the child to test and evaluate new techniques, report on past experiences and possibly predict what will happen if he follows a certain suggestion. Questions should preferably be prepared to obtain maximum benefit for the child.

Sand Play

This offers an opportunity for manipulative activity through pouring, sieving and making models with damp sand. Discovery is also made about the properties of sand compared to water, salt, sugar and the difference between wet and dry sand. A sand table of strong plastic in a portable frame allows group activity. Two sand tables, one with wet the other with dry sand, provide greater opportunity. Accessories are similar to water play but include larger pots, sieves, toy cranes with lifters, baking tins, trucks, cars, trains and shovels. Animal and people figures lend scope for dramatic play about life in the desert. Palm trees can be made of paper and dates introduced to show children the fruits. 'Cakes' of damp sand need a board as a base for when they are turned out. A dustpan and brush hanging by the sand table encourages the children to clean up any spills.

When planning sand play the adult should think of questions to ask which will promote language development, learning skills and sensory awareness. Questions should be worded in such a way that they require more than 'yes' or 'no' in reply. For example: What does the (dry) sand feel like? Why is it like water? How is it unlike water? What happens when we add water to sand? Why is it easier to make models with damp sand? How many times do you have to fill the little tin with sand and empty it into the big tin before the big tin is full? What is the difference between empty and full? Why does sand go through the sieve but stay in the big spoon? What does the crane do to help lift a heavy load of sand? Which of these tins is the lightest? Why is it lighter than the full tin? How is sand different from salt and sugar? Why is sand not used for building houses? Why are bricks better? Is the sand warm or cold? Is this sand the same as the sand at the seashore? How is it different? Which plants grow in sandy areas? Why don't plants grow in sand on its own? What is the weather like in desert countries? How do palm trees grow there? Why do people dress in white clothes in hot countries? Which animals like to live in the sand? What does the sand smell like, taste like, look like, feel like?

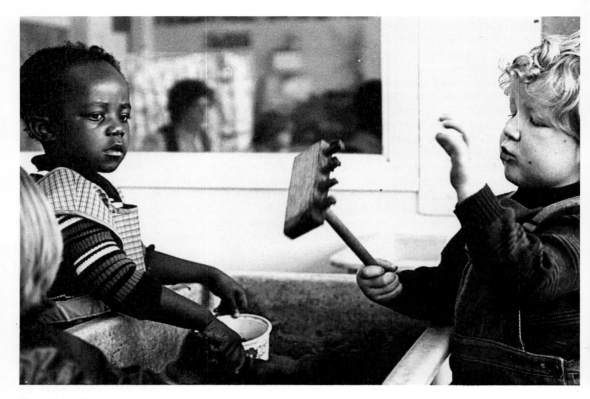

Figure 7.11   Sand play.

Responses to questions indicate the child's level of experience and understanding of concepts of size, texture, temperature, weight, colour and different living conditions. Sand may be transported from the beach (but care should be taken to ensure that it does not have too many stones in it), or from a dealer. The latter will provide silver sand which is more expensive. Ordinary builder's sand is satisfactory if it is washed thoroughly.

Benefits of sand play

Physical. The size of the sand area determines how much of the child's body can be involved. If there is just a sand tray, the child will run it through his fingers. Where wet and dry sand trays are available, he will model with lumps of wet sand. If the sand area is large enough he can bury his feet, legs and torso up to his neck. This is very exciting but not a good idea with under-sevens who may feel afraid. The 7- to 8-year-old, filled with his vivid imagination and lively sense of adventure, will probably challenge his friends to this particular 'torture'. Supervision of large sandpits is of course a very important part of the adult's role and sometimes under-fives will throw sand over other children in aggression, which could cause accidents.

Intellectual. Questions as indicated above help to clarify and form concepts and increase understanding. Sand has weight and volume, wet sand is heavier than dry sand, and it can be measured in various amounts. Various shapes and moulds can be made with wet sand, tunnels, roads and bridges can be made by the budding engineer. As he constructs, he may talk to himself or to other children. His vocabulary increases as he assumes various roles as builder, baker or sculptor. The medium of sand lends itself to limitless uses of imagination. When a tunnel collapses he can try to build it up, or come up with another idea and try that.

Emotional. Sand play is non-competitive so the child can set his own challenges without fear of failure or other children's observation of his failure. This promotes a positive self-image. Children can become completely absorbed in sand play, hence it is a useful activity for recovery after a temper tantrum or other aggressive behaviour when the child requires peace as his anger and fear are dissipated. There is also scope for individuality and a sense of mastery as he creates his models. This improves self-confidence which enables him to enjoy dramatic play when ideas from books, movies and television films can be translated into action. He becomes a sheikh with a teatowel tied round his head and a small stool with two cushion 'humps' surrounded by sand becomes his camel as he rides towards the oasis (water tray) on his dromedary. Girls dress up to resemble the beautiful Arabian women seen in adverts for Turkish Delight, and perhaps some groups will want to be camels with appropriate humps on their backs, if there is a large sand area outdoors. Some may even try carrying small bowls of water on their heads as they have seen on television.

Social. Sand is a medium which allows older and younger children, those with little experience and those with lots, to play and learn together. Highly developed cooperative play is possible with sand as the children construct highways, cities, temples (like the mosques now seen in many British towns) and castles. Consideration for others is developed as they prepare and clear away, and all through the process, when care is taken to ensure they don't spoil the play of others.

Role of the adult in sand play

Siting and arrangement of sand is important to ensure that there are no obstacles to freedom of play. Sand can be utilized indoors and out but in each case should be out of the line of traffic. If outdoors, a partially shaded area is best. The sand area at ground level should have a specially prepared base about 12 inches deep with 2–3 inches of gravel covering the bottom so that there will be drainage. This should allow for about 9–10 inches of sand. A ledge bordering the area will confine the sand. An enclosed area near the sand is best for storage of sand toys.

As stated before, careful supervision is required to prevent accidents, and rules of play must prohibit sand throwing. Tools are to be used as such, not as weapons. If all the children want to play in the sand area at once they should be persuaded to have a shift system since too many bodies and too much clutter spoil the play for everyone. Sometimes the children can be introduced to sand in the natural setting of the seashore before developing play in the sandpit.

If children are sitting, standing or lying in the sand, they will need space on the covered floor to shake out sand from their shoes, socks and clothes. In this way, there is less danger of slipping and the sand is recycled. A good rhyme for this activity is given on p. 256.

Dough Play

Dough and clay are such pliable materials that they provide a really relaxing activity, besides providing an outlet for frustration and aggression as they are pounded and bashed into shapes. Children should be given a large quantity of dough, at least as large as a grapefruit, and rolling pins, cutters, tart dishes and small pans. It should be noted that younger children are more interested in the handling than in production of a cake or model. This comes later. Dough can be made in bulk each week and divided into lots for colouring. It can be wrapped in clingfilm and kept in a fridge to keep it fresh from day to day. Pink and red colours plus a lovely marbling effect can be provided with cochineal. Green and blue colouring can also be used. A little powder paint can be added to the dough for different colours. Black is a popular colour, not because it is funereal or a sign of disturbance in the child who chooses it, but possibly because it looks like liquorice or like something from outer space. It is interesting to provide a choice of colours, and observe which are chosen, and whether their choice is enlightened or not. Again, planned questions make this a more meaningful activity and dough is more pliable than clay, so rolling out is easier and words like round, flat, long, short, sticky, stretchy, elastic, will be part of the play.

Arrangements for dough play

A table with a washable surface should be used at a height of about 18–20 inches, sturdy enough to withstand the banging and thumping that children give to large lumps of dough. The floor should be protected with heavy-duty plastic sheeting. The dough area should not be in an area of through traffic and should, if possible, be near hand washing facilities. It may be near the house corner, where it will be used for cakes and pies for tea parties. To allow for freedom from worries about damage to clothes, plastic disposable aprons can be worn.

A simple recipe for dough is:

2 cups flour
1 cup salt
2 tablespoons of olive oil
water

The salt helps to keep it fresh, the oil makes it more pliable, and if self-raising flour is used a different consistency from plain flour is obtained. If no colourings are available many children are content to use dough in its natural state. Any colourings must be non-toxic as the children will want to taste it.

Role of the adult in dough play

Provision of facilities as above and the presence of an adult is often sufficient to promote rich and elaborate dough play. The adult can listen to the children as they play and extend their vocabulary of 'doing' words as well as adjectives given above. Children should never be expected to be spectators while adults demonstrate – there must always be an environment free from interference for good creative play. If children ask for help the adult can discuss what they want to make, what it looks like and encourage them to make it for themselves. At first dough play need not involve accessories – these can come later.

There must be some limitations in dough play to ensure fair play for everyone. Children must *not* be allowed to throw dough about the playroom, hit each other with rolling pins or any other tool, mix the dough with sand or refuse to share materials and space. Observation of each child's developmental stage and personal needs enables the adult to know when to suggest new ideas to take the play further.

Benefits of dough play

Physical. Large and small muscles are developed through pounding, squeezing, slapping, pinching, rolling, poking, prodding, stretching, stroking, thumbing – and look at all these lovely action words! The children utilize all their senses with dough – handling, smelling, tasting, noting changes in colour and texture, feeling it against their skin.

Intellectual. Dough is made in every culture. The fact that children can see the process of making dough from the beginning and engage in its preparation is very valuable to their experience. Its resilience and pliability enables many different shapes to be made and helps the child to understand how a natural material behaves. Long snake-like forms can be made into symbols as children experiment with letters, figures, roads and houses. Sometimes they create symbols with cutters. Dough provides great opportunities for creativity and imagination.

After initial exploration children may produce a recognizable end-product, e.g. man or animal, but this stage is not usually reached until the child is four or rising five, when he will have had plenty of opportunity to become familiar with the properties of dough. As in all creative activities, however, it is the 'doing' that is most important. Apart from an increase in the vocabulary of action words, the concepts of comparison as in 'longer', 'shorter', 'shortest' and of prepositions, 'in', 'under', 'on', 'up', 'down', form part of his conversations with other children or the adult.

Emotional. Dough play is very enjoyable and can be comforting for the shy child or one who is new to the nursery if placed near the entrance. The child can use the dough table as a vantage point as he plays with the dough and looks around at the other children. When he feels a little more confident he may venture in further. Some children have carried a piece of dough around in their pockets as a comforter during their 'settling in' period. Timidity and inhibition can be seen in the way dough is handled by certain children – they will roll and pat it rather than pound and pinch. The consistency of dough will allow children to express both negative and positive feelings. Dough play can provide very satisfying experiences, as tension is released and anxieties soothed. The aggressive child can exert great energy as he thumps, tears and kneads the dough. Older children express dramatic fantasies as they use red and purple dough to make frightening monsters which can be destroyed if they evoke too much fear in the younger children. Brown and green dough may be used as a setting for a magnificent battle with tanks and soldiers.

Social. Playing with dough is particularly conducive to social interaction. As the children play they recount experiences, interests or anxieties, share tools, admire another's work or boast about their own.

Clay Play

Clay is tougher than dough and may need to be wet and prepared beforehand, otherwise frustration will result as endless pummelling produces no effect. Clay should be kept in a container covered with a damp cloth to prevent drying out. Accessories are not necessary for clay play, as the children use it for pounding, banging, squeezing and moulding and endeavour to overcome the resistance it offers, which makes it more satisfactory for slapping than dough.

Arrangement

Clay can be used indoors or outdoors. A large washable table top is best and the floor should be covered with plastic sheeting. Plastic aprons are necessary to prevent clothes becoming messy. Ideally, washbasins should be near so that the children can clean up easily, which may be part of the fun if plenty of sponges, bowls of water, dustpan and brush are available. If the clay becomes hard, the children can bang it into small pieces with a hammer, then water should be poured over it. After a few days it should be soft enough for use. If too wet it should be kneaded (like bread dough) in a circular fashion. All the soft lumps can be gathered together and thrown down on the table with great force (this part will be eagerly sought after!). Kneading on an absorbent surface such as wood, concrete or paper towels removes the excess moisture and makes the clay more pliable. If the clay is used with 5- to 7-year-olds who wish to bake it, kneading must be thorough to remove air bubbles which cause explosions when the clay is heated.

Clay can be obtained from local craft or pottery workshops or school suppliers. Tools are not necessary until the children have had the opportunity to explore the medium fully. A satisfying experience can be obtained simply by investigating its properties. After some experience tools may be provided from time to time. Cutters, wooden sticks, rolling pins, spatulas can all be used to give variations.

Role of the adult in clay play

As with all creative media the adult should not demonstrate how to play with clay or, worse, make an object for children to copy. This inhibits the child's creativity and may cause frustration and anxiety as he is unable to produce something of similar standard. The adult's presence at the clay table is often sufficient incentive and indicates to the children that the material is valued. Vocabulary is extended as the adult names 'doing' words and clarifies concepts.

Questions here should include: What is the difference between dough and clay? Why do you prefer dough (or clay)? Why does clay feel colder than dough? How is dough made? Why does dough feel warmer when you have played with it? Which kind of plants would grow in clay? What happens when we add water to dough, clay? What happens when we put dough and clay in the oven to bake? Why can't we eat clay? Safety is an essential part of the adult's role – wet clay can be very slippy and could cause accidents if it were not sited in a sensible place away from through traffic.

Benefits of clay play

Physical. There is direct contact between child and material as he creates shapes, and physical satisfaction in coordination of large and small muscles in limbs and trunk. Fingers, hands, wrists, arms and shoulders tense and stretch as they manipulate a large piece of clay. The struggle brought about by the resistance of the clay requires control which gives a feeling of strength and helps development of self-control. These unusual properties of clay cannot be found in many other substances. Sometimes children will sit at the clay table as they pummel and pound; sometimes they will stand to exert greater pressure with shoulders and arms.

Intellectual. Clay is a valuable medium through which a child can clarify concepts and shapes, such as flat, round or spherical. Shapes can be changed by adding or removing a piece, and textures by impressions made with hand or tools. Clay is a three-dimensional medium with which objects can be made to be held up and admired. Figure–ground relationships are created with the use of cutters to produce a variety of shapes. As noted before, this understanding of figure-ground relationships is part of pre-reading activities.

Emotional. Clay play can be very enjoyable, satisfying and therapeutic. Children who are feeling angry or frustrated at their own inadequacies use it as a safe outlet. Aggressive moods and jealousy of a new baby or younger sibling can be dissipated as he punches, pokes, twists and squeezes the lumpy inanimate object which represents the hated or envied child.

As clay is a messy substance and bears some resemblance to faeces it may help the child to resolve any conflicts or guilt he has about messiness. These feelings may relate to the 'anal stage' (see Development) or to some problem associated with toilet training. If children are able to overcome this feeling of revulsion it may enable them to deal sensibly with other revolting experiences in later life.

Social. When the child slaps and pounds the clay he becomes aware of his own body rhythm. Later he notices the rhythm of other children and, after considerable experience, he comes to incorporate these rhythms into his own. Preparation and cleaning activities can be shared to prove the old adage that many hands mean light work, but it is salutary also to remember that too many cooks spoil the broth – or good play!

Physical Play

Provision of a happy, secure, safe environment for indoor and outdoor play

In order for play to be enjoyed and for the child to gain intellectual stimulation and develop self-confidence from it, the environment of the home or nursery must be stable, with adults who can unselfishly forget their own problems and tensions. Stability and security can be provided through a daily routine which, while flexible, has enough familiarity in it to make it acceptable. Obviously adults have fears and worries and frustrations which have to be resolved but they should not allow these to affect their relationships with other adults as children are

sensitive to tension and may react through disturbed behaviour or by aggression.

Play activities can be devised to cope with potential behaviour problems and the provision of outdoor play or space indoors is particularly important. Curiosity is often the key which unlocks whole new worlds for children, but curiosity, like a flower, will wither away and die if it is not nourished and kept alive by a stimulating environment, by adults who appreciate that the small world of the nursery, while usually larger than that of the home, cannot provide all the intellectual stimulation required by children today. In an age where young children are exposed to television from an early age (one mother recently complained on a viewers' panel programme that there were not enough programmes for babies!) more effort is required to extend their 'sophisticated' knowledge further.

The value of space

Indoors. Babies and young children are given the opportunity to enjoy their own room and play area. The baby will sleep more easily (and prove less of a strain to his mother and the rest of the family) if he can rest in the peace of his cot, uninterrupted by his brothers and sisters trooping into their beds in the same room. Where cots are placed beside each other in nurseries, there should be at least 3 feet of space between them to reduce the risk of infection spread. Adequate space also avoids the necessity for the baby's pram in the sitting room with family activities (including television) carried on all around him. The risk of infection spread and exposure to head lice infestations is also reduced.

Children with space to move (including crawling and toddling) without bumping into furniture will develop independence more quickly. Space to play indoors (perhaps in a playpen in kitchen or living room where mother can keep a watchful eye on him) gives both child and mother a sense of freedom. It also decreases anxiety and worry about accidents which can happen when the child or children have to be under the mother's feet all day. Children can also enjoy play with water, sand, clay and dough on the floor when space is provided, and there will be room for various large toys and play equipment to be stored. On rainy days young children enjoy having two or three friends in to

Table 7.2 Physical activities children can enjoy indoors

Activity	Apparatus
Crawling	Benches, tunnels, on boards elevated on boxes, through hoops and tyres
Lifting	Moving trestles, boards, boxes, suitcases
Pedalling	Tricycles, cars
Swinging and stretching	On climber, suspended ladder, rings or trapeze, parallel bars made with pipes
Rocking	Rocky boat, rocking horse
Pulling	Wagons (with loads), each other on ropes, set along a rope securely attached at one end
Climbing	Indoor climber (could be made in section for storage or with folding parts – a climber could be made to fold against the wall when not in use), boards and ladders as accessories, hanging rope ladder, trestles, boards, ladder, boxes, kegs
Sliding	Portable slide or board attached to climber, platform, play-gate, table or from upturned adult chair
Pushing	With legs: wagons, circular board with castors. With arms: wheelbarrows and carriages, boxes and hollow blocks, brooms, each other in cardboard cartons
Pounding	Hammers and nails, dough, clay
Balancing	On bench, on board and trestles, plywood board elevated from ground – can be made so that height from floor can be increased
Jumping and tumbling	Over elastic rope, on tumbling mat, from jumping boards, boxes, bench, over blocks
Building	(Combine lifting, pushing, pulling and balancing with creative and dramatic play) – boards, boxes, kegs – blocks (hollow floor blocks) – all sizes, accessories, trucks and cars, steering wheel on block, traffic signs, petrol pumps, lengths of rope and hose; dressups – workmen's hats, bus driver, fireman, policeman
Running	To jump over rope, with reins
Throwing	Beanbags, balls
Sand play	Sand table – this could have a cover so it might serve as a table for paint, finger paint, etc. dishes, scoops, spoons, jugs, sieves, articulated toy trucks, cars, water (to observe differences between wet and dry sand)
Water play	Tubs, galvanized metal or plastic water table, accessories for pouring, squeezing, measuring, sprinkling, washing

play with them and this relieves the mother from continual one to one play, while she prepares meals and does washing.

Indoor play. Active indoor play which involves exercise of large or small muscles, hand–eye coordination, balance, muscle tone, poise and balance can be arranged with the efforts of an imaginative teacher/nursery nurse or mother, and some equipment. This can easily be produced with the help of the woodworking class, fathers and/or eager do-it-yourself child care givers. A number of timber firms are willing to give odd pieces of wood for children's use and in some areas old school desks can be obtained for conversion into play equipment. Learning about space and gaining confidence in movement skills are activities which have life-long benefits for children of both sexes. Pre-school children have a need for strenuous activity and it is important to satisfy this need. The playground/garden is the ideal situation for vigorous play, but some days it is impossible to play outdoors. Plans should therefore provide an indoor active play period for these days. For the nursery/home that cannot provide a playground, an active period indoors should be part of the daily programme. A large room where portable equipment to encourage active play can be set up is ideal, but the regular playroom can be used by moving tables and chairs and leaving space for the children to play actively. Windows should be open and the temperature lowered during this period.

At the end of the active play period the children can help in carrying equipment to the storage area. A reading circle in the book corner can occupy the children who are not busy tidying and setting up the room for the regular period. Or one area could be tidied away and replaced with tables for creative materials, play with small toys or set out as a Wendy house or cookery corner. This would mean no break in play but a gradual change to quieter activities.

Outdoors. Safe play areas away from busy roads, near to home and preferably with grass surfaces give children a sense of freedom as they can run about without restriction. The resultant feeling of well being helps their emotional development. Children can use space to gallop, walk and run as a means of getting rid of aggression and frustration. Exposure to fresh air and sunlight promotes physical development, as the sun's rays acting on ergosterol in the skin produce vitamin D, which helps the formation of good bones and teeth. Unfortunately pollution in some industrial areas excludes the sun and this, combined with poor diet, can lead to cases of rickets in children. Running about improves breathing and circulation, while outdoor exercise promotes resistance to infection.

Use of large apparatus such as climbing frames, rope ladders and trampolines helps development, muscular control, poise, balance and self-confidence. If there is a tree in the play space, it will not only provide a challenge for the older children to climb, but even younger children can enjoy the thrill of swinging from a (thick) branch or a tyre which has been discarded from the family car or local garage and suspended on a rope by an adult. Swings, see-saws and slides provide great sources of fun – even a young baby can enjoy his own safety swing with moulded seat and safety belt.

It is important to recognize safety factors in outdoor play and adventure equipment. Care in selection and maintenance plus continual supervision by the mother or other adults can ensure an accident-free environment. Trampolines often enable 3- to 6-year-old children to experience the thrill often felt by jumping up and down on mattresses, but trampolines should have a safety jumping handle, heavy-duty mat and sturdy rustproof legs. Slides should have non-slip platforms and flat head steps, and hammocks (which are not suitable for children under 4 years of age) should be of strong cord and not slung too high from the ground. If a corner is available (or can be created with mounds of earth and stones) great scope for imagination and adventure is provided as children hide in 'caves', or play 'Red Indians and Cowboys'. It is also a good idea if space is available to have a restful corner where children can sit and play quietly or enjoy a story read to them. A two-storey climbing cabin with a roofed in den which can become a lighthouse, hidey hole or lookout also provides ample opportunity for imagination and adventure play.

Space gives freedom to use bikes without danger to other children. Balancing on brick walls or large blocks encourages self-confidence, independence and a sense of discovery, thus promoting intellectual development. Water play can involve paddling if a pool is available (some can be used as sand pits). A low level of water and constant supervision is necessary but it widens the child's experience of water, which may previously have been restricted to pouring and measuring in the water container indoors. Creation of a nursery garden by planting seeds and watching them grow gives a sense of achievement – each child can dig his own patch if there is sufficient space. (See Science/Discovery)

Use of the sand pit outdoors gives more freedom and more opportunity for self-expression than in the confined space of the playroom. Group and team play outdoors (which may be impossible indoors) improves children's social development. An old car or bus with engine removed and repainted by the children themselves (perhaps with help from the local secondary school pupils) also provides group activity and enables the child to enjoy fantasy and role play as he becomes Mummy/Daddy driving the family car or a bus driver/conductor. A double decker bus also allows him the opportunity to run up and downstairs as often as he likes without adult interference expending energy in a harmless way. 'Pretence' trains with two or three other children can also move around imaginary tracks (without the danger of bumping into others and causing frustration and quarrelling) when there is adequate space.

Outdoor play. While the same benefits described above can be enjoyed outdoors there is the bonus of additional space. Large equipment and playing in fresh air and sunlight which adds to the feeling of wellbeing, alertness and ability to gain maximum benefit from exercise.

Apart from all the apparatus described in Table 7.2 (and in the section on Space), large hollow wooden blocks can be made for outdoor play. These are $11 \times 11 \times 5\frac{1}{2}$ inches ($27 \times 27 \times 13$ cm) or $11 \times 22 \times 5\frac{1}{2}$ inches ($27 \times 55 \times 13$ cm) and should be painted as a protection against the weather. Despite their size, they can be handled by the children without strain. They encourage the development of large muscles and focus a great deal on the motor activity of the children. Some planks, sanded and painted $\frac{1}{2} \times 8 \times 36$ inches increase the children's enjoyment and extend the range of exercise. They can build bridges, provide roofs for their garages and make their own walking boards with them. Twelve to 15 of each size of hollow block is recommemded for a well equipped area.

Substitute blocks can be made from butter boxes, banana boxes or any strong cardboard box. These can be taped, glued and painted by the children giving them an opportunity to develop their creative talents. They are not as durable as the hollow blocks but can provide lots of fun and opportunities for exercise. If three or six barrels can be obtained these can make useful and interesting playground equipment. Placed on a wooden base, planks, wooden ladders or solid boards such as a used door can be added on either side of the construction. The three-barrel construction has been proved to be safe as the barrels will not roll away, a wooden door and ladder at either side allows good strenuous play. Adventurous children climb the ladder, stand on top of the barrel and slide down the door. When it snows this is very popular as the children can imagine they are on a ski-ride. A six barrel construction should be tested first to find out if the middle barrel will stay in place when the weight of the child is on the top barrel – if not then it can be welded or bolted. A 'jungle gym' can be made from 16 wooden uprights (5½ × 5½ inches), 6ft 2 inches above ground, 1 ft underground, set 18 inches apart and 1¼ inches round hardwood rings spaced 16 inches apart. This provides scope for a number of children to climb, crawl, and swing but obviously it is better to place it on grass rather than a concrete surface. An outdoor climbing platform can also be made by supporting a wooden ladder horizontally on rungs made of old pipes attached to sturdy posts.

Climbing is always a source of enjoyment and discovery apart from exercising large muscles. A climbing tree can be made by cutting a live tree, leaving only the strongest branches. Remove the ends, leaving a clean rounded edge. Take off the bark and give two coats of preservative. Set in a hole 3 × 3 × 3 ft filled with concrete. A pile of logs, shortened to the desired length, sanded and fastened together with spikes then covered with two coats of preservative and arranged in a triangular shape provide another interesting item. Play logs can also be cut in various lengths of 4–8 ft (at least 1 ft in diameter). The wood should be green from a freshly cut tree. Remove the bark and cover the logs with two coats of preservative. Dig a trench 3 ft deep and long enough to hold all the logs in the group. Place the logs so that the short ones are steps to the higher logs. Fill in with earth and flatten down firmly. If any of the logs have split fill with concrete, and put concrete between logs at the base to hold together in the group. Logs can also be used as the body of a horse mounted on four 'legs' made of criss-crossed short posts joined lengthwise by a long plank. The horse's head can be made from another piece of log and a realistic mane from rope ends. Reins and a tail add the final touches. Another log can be placed horizontally supported at the higher end by shorter logs sunk into the ground and an old car wheel mounted on a wooden spoke to provide a realistic car.

Apart from hanging tyres on ropes attached to tree branches, tyres can also be used as 'flat' seated swings when connected with strong rope or chains to an overhead horizontal pole. A large tyre can provide a seat for two as the children sit on the sides and put their legs through the opening in the middle. Tyres also make fun seats for ordinary swings. The seats can be removed from swings, and two tyres hung on the chains. A plank is then placed on the tyres (each end through a tyre). At each end of the plank a small piece of wood is fastened vertically to give some variety to the swing. It also means the children swing together and learn to cooperate with one another, which encourages social development.

Books and Storytelling

The Bullock Report, *A Language for Life*, 1974, stated that it is 'a priority need to introduce children to books in their pre-school years and to help parents recognize the value of sharing the experience of them with their children. The printed page, the physical comfort and security of sitting on an adult's lap, the reassuring voice and the fascination of the story all combine in the child's mind to identify books as something which hold great pleasure'. Apart from physical aspects and enjoyment through books children also benefit emotionally, intellectually and socially, and perhaps most of all in language development, which has implications for all aspects of development. 'By fostering a delight in books you are helping a child on the way to literacy – the ability to read and on to literature – the heights of language and communication' (Brenda Thompson).

Physical Benefits

At 15–18 months of age babies like to look at pictures in books and pat them fondly. At 2 years of age they can recognize familiar objects in pictures and at 2½ years point out minute details. Physical characteristics of books are obviously important from a sensory and economic point of view. It is hardly worthwhile introducing books to young children which can be easily torn; they will merely misinterpret the function. Hardboard or cloth books with good clear illustrations should be used for babies. Cloth books are more hygienic, as they can be washed in disinfectant to prevent infection spread. Books for children of 2 years onwards should have smooth, but not glaringly shining pages so that they can enjoy the feel of them, without experiencing discomfort.

At first the pages will be turned over two or three at a time, later singly as fine movement is mastered. Colours of illustrations are also important – these should be in clear primary colours at first, without fuzzy, blurred outlines. The clarity of illustrations is important as the children love to recognize familiar objects and point out minute details. Pictures must be complete – cars must have four wheels and a body, animals a head, body, four legs and a tail. Some illustrations depict only the front part of the object, e.g. the head and front legs of an animal, the bonnet of a car, and this is confusing and even distressing to some young children.

Emotional Benefits

Books can facilitate a close emotional relationship between adults and children. Sitting close to the adult or cuddled up on a knee the child feels secure. Fears and anxieties about his size, insignificance, place in the family or naughty behaviour can all be resolved as he reads about characters who have similar experiences and the happy ending reassures the child and dispels his worries. Repetition of favourite stories is also reassuring.

Intellectual Benefits

Apart from learning that print can give pleasure in the form of stories, children learn new words and experiences. Through stories they can share experiences which might not otherwise be possible, including make-believe situations. They can accumulate knowledge of people and of their attitudes and behaviour and learn about the world around them. Curiosity is stimulated as the children ask questions and have their knowledge broadened by the answers. Observation of the way the adult holds the book the right way up and turns the pages from right to left while reading from left to right and the way in which words are put together to form sentences,

helps the child to understand how reading is done, and promotes language development.

Social Benefits

The child benefits from belonging to the small intimate circle which surrounds the adult as a story is read. He learns to discuss and share his likes and dislikes of various stories and through books comes to appreciate how other people feel and to share feelings with story characters. He is enabled to feel sympathy and compassion. Conversation with the adult is possible, although this will only bring forth an adequate response from the child, when the adult knows him and can relate the story to his personal experiences. Visits to the zoo, park, farm or seaside should be preceded and followed by stories related to the happenings which occur on these occasions and conversation with the adult who has shared these experiences with the child will obviously be able to help the child derive most from them. In many nurseries and playgroups, parents are often encouraged to be involved in activities like reading to the children but as with 'professional' care givers, their success in enabling social and language development will be limited unless they are able to link up the child's experiences to the conversation which results from reading books.

It is also important that reading activities should be used to encourage children to use speech – often conversations in the book corner are dominated by the adult with one or two-word responses from children. A child only learns to read after he has learnt to talk, to listen and to understand what he hears.

Setting up a Book Corner

The book corner should be attractive and inviting if children are going to want to be there of their own volition. A warm, well lit, quiet position away from noisy activities is essential. A carpet, rug and cushions make it comfortable and a few small comfortable chairs for those who want to sit rather than lie on the floor. The books can be displayed on two baker's boards hinged together, a clothes rack backed with hardboard, a folding wooden bookcase, a large canvas book holder (with pockets of different sizes and small enough to allow the book title to be seen) attached to a wooden frame. A cloth

Figure 7.12   Sitting in the book corner, but concentration isn't always easy.

rack can also be put over chairs or an easel. If no book holders are available, books can be displayed by resting them on a chair seat with an elastic band holding the books upright. A wooden display rack can be used to screen off the book corner from the rest of the playroom. Alternatively, a clothes horse covered with clean, brightly coloured material makes a good screen and the books can be placed on low shelves inside the area.

The most important factor to remember is that the books should be easily accessible for the child. Young children are easily distracted and find it difficult to concentrate if there is constant noise and activity around them. Silence and solitude are necessary at times and these needs should be catered for since they are as important as the needs of the aggressive and boisterous child. It may be difficult to arrange a quiet corner but books are a play activity and are as important for all-round development as table toys, painting or sand and water play.

An adult should be near and available to the book corner not only to read stories, but to see that the children handle the books properly and replace them in the bookrack. Children should be shown how to look after books. 'A 3-year-old is sensible enough not to mangle books and can be quickly and gently taught to appreciate them' (Brenda Thompson). Of course appreciation of books does not come to the 3-year-old without adequate preparation. Books for the book corner should be in good condition as old,

tattered and dog-eared books are not attractive.

Good binding is an important factor when buying books: paperbacks will need replacement more quickly than hardbacks. While it would be undesirable to have books in a pristine condition indicating that they have never been read, they should be clean and attractive. Tears can be mended with Sellotape and new books can be covered in transparent cling foil. The children can help to prepare and repair their own books as this enables them to feel more responsible for them. Children who have little beauty in their everyday lives will love the feel of the paper and the sight of the coloured pictures. They often rely more on the impression gained from picture and from their own experiences than from the story and will often return to a picture they like and from this alone they will derive a lot of pleasure. 'Because children are travellers setting out on voyages of discovery, picture books can offer them one of the earliest, most enchanting ways of extending their experience of the world. Poring over their books, they can behold the delight of new places and of new people, of strange birds and beasts of lands very different from their own. Magic casements are opened for them looking out on the vastness of the earth with its perpetual promise of new surprises' (Joan Cass).

Books, like other play materials are meant to be used and not just kept in the cupboard or on display. While the 'old familiars' are always requested, the selection should be changed from time to time as different topics of interest emerge, e.g. changes in season, events such as gardening, trips to places of interest. The Science and Discovery corner could be near to the book corner and books on plants and animals laid out at appropriate times. Pictures, carefully mounted, can be stuck onto a display board in the book corner to stimulate conversation and aid language development. Those from Sunday colour supplements or from 'Child Education' are particularly suitable as they are clear, colourful and convey the subject matter well.

Choosing Books

Books are not merely a collection of pictures and stories: 'a good book is the lifeblood of the master spirit'. They can impart knowledge, provide enjoyment, help understanding of self and others, and promote security and self-confidence. Hence the variety of books chosen for the nursery and infant groups should include story books, information books, rhyme and poetry books.

Story books

These should include stories about everyday experiences, special occasions (new babies, starting school, going on holiday), naughty children and new experiences (going to hospital, the dentist). Animal stories which arouse compassion and cause amusement and have characters with which the children can identify are also important. A simple style with good illustrations is essential, and books should be suited to the ages and stages of the children's development. Picture books are sufficient at first, then pictures with a few words; longer stories can be appreciated at four to five, and more complex words. One should not be afraid to introduce new long words, however, children are able to pronounce intricate names of foreign cars which they hear their fathers talking about and often remember the difficult words, perhaps because it requires effort to articulate them!

The Dick Bruna books are suitable for 2- to 3-year-old children. There is only one clear illustration on each double-page spread so that the 'readers' are not confused and the illustrations tell the stories to the child without words so that he can venture his own story line. These books also open out flat for easy display to the child.

Some Ladybird books are also good but, apart from the simplest, they tend to have too many words, although the stories can be adapted from the original by the adult to suit the children's needs. The illustrations in these books are good and, as the books are cheap and small enough for little hands to grasp, they are popular.

Books with pop-up centrepieces are not suitable for group use as they tend to get torn and thus lose their interest. Usually the language and illustrations in these books are poor and beyond the level of the children. The novelty of the pop-up picture is not enough to compensate for these deficiencies. Scratch and smell books have the same drawbacks and often the smell is not realistic. Books with gimmicks such as these may be enjoyed at home with one or two children but are not good for group use. Fantasy and fairy stories are not suitable for 3- to 4-year-old children as they are often unable to distinguish between reality and make believe until they are 6 or 7 years old and cannot appreciate that good usually triumphs over bad. A child can 'quickly pass from a world of confidence to a world of fear and uncertainty' (D. Mackay and J. Sims) if witches and giants are introduced without explanation. Of course the all-persuasive influence of television must not be ignored and it may be that some children will happily listen to gory details of ogres devouring human beings, but again the adult has to be aware of individual stages and needs before choosing books and stories. As children identify with the people or animals in the stories they hear, it is a mistake to tell them stories where parents desert or show cruelty towards their children. Many traditional fairy stories are like this in the original form, e.g. Babes in the Wood, Hansel and Gretel, and are best left until the child is older.

At the pre-school stage, children need to know that their parents love them and will not desert them and even where this has happened through divorce and separation of parents, children should not be reminded of it in an environment that is intended to be compensatory. The warm security of home in stories about loving, happy families remind children of the significance of home and may help a deprived child to share by proxy some of the joys he is missing at home. Ordinary simple tasks such as cooking, cleaning, washing, driving a car, plane or ship, occupations of nurse, policeman, bus driver, fireman which are all part of the grown-up world come within the child's world through stories and he can imagine himself as the strong hero or heroine who puts everything right.

Information books

These are essential for young children, whose curiosity is insatiable. Part of knowledge is knowing where to look for facts and it is good for adult and child to discover answers together as it helps the child realize that adults are not omniscient but they know that books hold the key to discovery of the unknown. The Things I Like series by Peggy Blakely include the following titles: *My Home and Yours*; *Big and Little*; *Colours*; *Fast and Slow*; *Rough and Smooth*. McDonald Starter's Series cover topics like trains, bread, snow, kitchens. Questions about nature and the seasons arise at all times of the year and Ladybird series is useful here: *What to Look for in Spring, Summer, Autumn, Winter*; *Birds*; *Wild Flowers*; *Indoor Plants*; *The Weather*. Ron McTrusty has also written some useful nature books: *Dandelion Tear*; *Apple and Butterfly*; *Egg and Chicken*; *Tadpole and Frog*. *The Hungry Caterpillar*, apart from being an amusing fascinating story which lends itself to painting and collage follow-up activities, also reveals how the caterpillar changes into a butterfly. In these days of technological development, children are used to tape recorders, filmstrip projectors and computer games but their apparent sophistication is not knowledge. They may ask how television works and a large picture encyclopaedia with explanations which are simple but scientifically correct will be a useful asset for adults and children in the nursery or home.

Rhymes and poetry

Sadly, many children in primary schools today have no store of nursery rhymes in their foundations of speech and language. They have missed out on an important learning possibility and since traditional favourites are usually first learned at mother's knee, their own children may be deprived in the same way when they grow up and reproduce. Nursery rhymes belong to a stage of intensive learning in childhood, when children are learning about the world through language. Rhymes help children to learn names of numbers and days of the week in a pleasurable way and even if the concepts come later, they are already familiar with labelling.

Rhymes also reflect a range of moods which children themselves experience every day. The love of stories often begins with the repetition of favourite familiar rhymes. Stories told in rhymes have great appeal for children and they love to complete the next line of a familiar verse. *Old Mother Hubbard and her Dog*, illustrated by Paul Galdone, is a favourite and the amusing and ridiculous events which characterize most nursery rhymes are always enjoyed by the children. Poetry was defined by Coleridge as 'the best words in the best order' and children show their appreciation of this form of written language by their frequent demand to hear them, and constant repetition. At 6 or 7 years of age, children like to write their own poems and while these may not always rhyme it provides them with a medium for expressing themselves in language.

Storytelling

This was a custom long before books were written, and like any art it needs preparation and practice to be effective. There are a number of ways to tell a story but perhaps the traditional way of the adult sitting with one or two small children on her lap and a few others on cushions, close enough to see her expressions as she recounts a familiar favourite, using the same words she has used on the past dozen occasions, is best. Of course this means that the adult has to memorize a few stories and some find this difficult. Illustrations can be used when telling a story and some stories can be made up around illustrations. Other ways of storytelling are given below.

Reading from a book. This seems to be the most popular method but it is essential that the adult has read the book beforehand to ensure continuity. There is the difficulty of holding the book so that the child can see it which means the adult has to read upside down; not an impossible task when the story is familiar.

From a picture. The picture may be of a shopping trip but even the younger children will have some contribution to make to a familiar topic.

Flannelgraph. Large outlines and shapes of fruits, animals, houses, trees, flowers and people can be cut out in felt or lint and a piece of sandpaper stuck on the back for adhesion. Here, the children can join in the story adding to and removing pieces as the story unfolds.

Puppets. Any sock can become a talking animal when it has ears and eyes sewn on. Finger puppets are easy to make with scraps of material or they can be knitted, and each child could represent a character in turn. The children can make their own puppets from paper bags, dish mops, clothes pegs and wooden spoons. The fascination shown by generations of children for Punch and Judy shows can be brought into storytelling as puppets are used to represent naughty, aggressive and frightening characters.

Models. Models of farm animals, soldiers and a doll's house with furniture are all useful as illustrations.

Record or tape recorder. Records should be listened to by the adult beforehand in order that omissions can be rectified and illustrations prepared. A picture book of illustrations can be made for the children to look at while listening to the record. A recording is often better as songs and sounds can be added. The children can take part and love to hear their voices on tape. It is also a good exercise for the adult to hear their own voices so that improvement can be made in quality and tone.

Movement, Dance, Rhythm, Music and Drama

Children can create their own movements, music, dance and drama. Each event is a creative expression. There is no memory work, nothing can be repeated in an exact form as it will change or be forgotten. Running throughout a semi-dark room can be a start. Good-quality musical instruments, some homemade, brightly coloured cloth 'socks' big enough for a child or two children to get inside, flash lights, a single light in a partially dark room, electronic or space music from a record or tape, streamers of cloth, silk, etc., can all be used. Action words, chosen by the children, are put in one hat and emotion words in another. Each group of children gets one word from each hat. After preparation, each presents its 'drama'. The other groups try to guess the two words. The presentation makes use of special lighting effects, sounds, musical instruments and creative movement.

Music

All kinds of sounds are music to different people – how often does the child hear his parents say 'That's music to my ears!' when the car is heard revving after a period of non-starting? Even before birth, the baby hears the heartbeat and peristaltic sounds inside his mother's abdomen. This pleasant rhythm remains as a soothing memory, and has been found so effective in calming crying babies that the makers of the Lullababy rocker (see Chapter 1) have now produced a tape of 'womb sounds' for use with fractious babies. Sounds heard from outside the mother's body such as loud rock music also impinge on the baby in the uterus, and babies have been found to respond to these as well. After birth, the mother may hum or sing a gentle melody to help the baby to sleep, which, combined with a comforting, secure position in her arms, is very effective.

Benefits of music

Physical. Music should give expression to individual interpretations, rather than have themes imposed by the adult. So-called classical music often gives a good medium for free movement, and of course coordination is achieved as children weave, jump for joy, crouch, crawl, step lightly or heavily, waving arms in front or extended as wings, stretch, wiggle, curl up as they interpret the various moods of the music. At other times, they may be able to translate their experiences of visits to a farm or zoo into actions they consider appropriate for a Carnival of Animals, using Saint-Saens' exciting music. They can become as tall as a giraffe, dumpy as an elephant, graceful as a swan. Opportunities should be provided for the children to develop their own rhythms. Rather than give specific instructions, the adult should encourage the children to move their bodies in their own way: 'Use your own space – don't touch anybody.' This helps space and body awareness and expression of original ideas. Children love to interpret animal movements which they have seen on a trip to the zoo, or on television. The action of a huge crane, an aeroplane or a truck may provide ideas for movement. The use of contrasting movements heightens awareness of the abilities: Walk tall like a giraffe – higher, higher! Now be a sleepy kitten – curl up in your basket. Now you're a big clumsy elephant. Can you walk like a ballet dancer on your tiptoes? Can you leap like a frog? Wiggle like a long worm?

With sufficient stimulation children will develop their own ideas, increasing skills in self-reliance, awareness, imagination, coordination and aesthetic appreciation.

Intellectual. Hearing and listening are not the same thing, since nowadays many children are exposed to sounds, mainly loud and often cacophonous, from the incessant, ubiquitous transistor radio or television. They soon become used to this background sound, and often are not really aware of it. Listening then is a sensory development, essential to academic and social success, which can be developed by the provision of different sounds from various instruments, including those the child can produce for himself. Simple listening games help to 'sharpen' the ears of small children to music. A baby can distinguish his mother's voice from others at 3–6 months and recognizes familiar noises in his daily routine. The mother builds on this early recognition and nursery staff can do the same. A bell is rung, hands are clapped. 'Listen – does that sound the same?' The floor is tapped, then heavily knocked, different drums are played, hands are cupped for a hollow sound. 'Is that the same sound?' Children respond to this 'game' happily and offer contrasting noises they have discovered themselves. They also enjoy 'listening to silence' at different times.

In response to the whispered question 'What can you hear?' they reply 'a tap dripping in the kitchen', 'rain falling on the window', 'children playing', 'birds singing'. The different nature of calls in the robin and the crow should be noted as children can appreciate specifics. Qualifying sounds with a descriptive adjective heightens feeling for language, e.g. a tinkling sound, a booming noise, scratching, buzzing, tapping, singing. Children soon develop their own vivid way of describing sounds. Four- and 5-year-olds like to recall the first sound they hear in the morning (Rise and shine, Breakfast's ready) or the last sound at night (car door slamming, light going out).

Children can detect very simple rhythmic patterns: Clap, clap. Listen! Is that the same as this? Clap, clap, clap. Can you do it? Let's clap names – Jonathan. Clapping the three syllables slowly, repeating it until it becomes a chant, with the first syllable heavily stressed so that the

pattern is well defined yet part of a rhythmic momentum. After this another pattern 'Sally' as two syllables. Then the adult claps one and asks which one is this: Clap, clap, clap. When a child makes up his own rhythm, the adult takes it up by singing la la la, clapping, playing it on another instrument – anything to support and heighten his awareness of his own sound design. Verbal comment ('Good rhythm, Jamie') also reinforces this awareness.

Emotional. Music provides an effective release for emotions, from sheer joy and pleasure to frustration, anger and fantasy. There is no competition involved in music – children have only to please themselves – hence it is also a release from tension. Making a noise with musical instruments may be thought of as the best way to express negative feelings, but quiet, soothing music 'to soothe the savage breast' is often more effective.

Children are primitive beings who express their music on simple instruments that can be shaken or banged. Drums of different sizes, gongs, shakers, dulcet chime bars, and assortment of bells, castanets, brass or copper tubing cut in different lengths and taped on to rubber-tipped dowelling, tambourines and cymbals are all required.

Easy accessibility is as important as variety. A child can communicate his own feelings through instruments that are as familiar to him as paint, paper and his favourite climbing tree. Uncritical approval fortifies his self-reliance. Suitable instruments can be set out in the playground, gym and in a cleared corner of the playroom where he is free to dance 'as his music makes him'. A guitar left on a table or a piano always open are not a novelty, and musical children gravitate towards them to play them with genuine listening, experimentation and care. When a musician comes to play instruments, their contribution is doubled if they let the children feel and try them.

Social. Sometimes children will share a musical chant as they discuss their play. 'See me painting' chants one child, and another replies 'I can see you' in a different key. Eventually others may join in and the sensible adult knows when to allow these spontaneous suggestions to develop into rhythm and music-making sessions. After children have had many opportunities to create their own rhythms and body movements, simple dances may be introduced, in which all have a part, whatever their physical prowess.

A music corner

This can be set up with homemade and factory made instruments. It should be accessible, but not in an area where the noise will disrupt others who are reading. Noise levels can produce irritation in staff and students (or harassed parents at home) and the level should be carefully monitored. Care should be taken to ensure that the sound produced by a musical instrument is musical and not just a noise. The instruments should be attractive to look at and represent a variety of musical qualities. They should be simple to use and safe. Homemade shakers with metal bottle tops attached to sticks with nails protruding can be very dangerous. Shakers are best kept to washing-up liquid containers with rice, peas and beans inside for different sounds, and fastened securely.

Music workshops

Drums. These can be of different sizes, and homemade ones made from large tins covered with a piece of rubber (from the inner tube of a tyre) are often effective. Coconut shells, paint tins and waste-paper baskets can be used. Leather is useful for covering the drum base as different kinds produce different sounds. Some types need to be wet before they are stretched and put on the drum. A linen dish towel can be used as a drumhead. The dry linen is stretched tight, fastened with tacks and given a coat of shellac. The linen drumhead remains tight and gives a good sound. Drumsticks can be made from dowelling pieces about 20 cm long. If a number of rubber bands are wrapped round the end, this makes a different sounding head. A softer sound can be produced if a dish mop is covered with velvet, corduroy or felt and tied very firmly.

Castanets.
Materials:

2 half walnut shells or plastic bottle tops
wax polish
Sellotape
strip of plastic or tape approx. ½ inch wide
   and 6 inches long
Bostik

Stick a small piece of Sellotape to each shell where tape or plastic is to be attached, this is to keep the wax from this area. Using a soft cloth and wax polish, polish the shells well. Remove Sellotape. Cut tape or plastic into two 3-inch lengths and stick them into a loop, then stick them into position on the shells. Leave to dry. Play castanets by looping one shell on thumb and one on first finger and then clicking them together.

Wooden xylophone. Pleasant-sounding wooden xylophones with a chromatically correct range of tones can be purchased and give experience in pitch.

Triangle. The triangle is a metal instrument which produces a long sound.

Cymbals. These should be played with a soft hammer, not by hitting two together. They are useful for special effects.

Tambourines and jingle bells. These are also useful for children to experiment with and produce a variety of tone and pitch.

Children should be made aware that instruments are valuable and have been constructed to produce beautiful sounds. Individual experimentation enables them to have experiences with tone, pitch, duration of sound and rhythm. One or two children may be allowed to accompany a song or dance. Too many accompanists can result in unpleasant din, so structured musical play should give opportunity for individual playing in production of harmonious sounds.

An instrument such as a xylophone or tuned chimes can be a quiet pleasant accompaniment for a rest period. The children enjoy hearing the adult play a simple, familiar melody and it introduces them to the beauty and musical possibilities of the instrument. Rhythmic movements can be accompanied by an appropriate instrument. A drum can accompany a movement such as a heavy walking step. An instrument with a long sound quality such as a triangle, finger cymbals or gong might represent a wider movement such as swinging. Only by experimenting will the children become aware of the possibilities of each instrument and adults must feel able to experiment also if they are to help children learn the joys of being creative in music.

Singing

Physically, singing involves use of the vocal cords, and it is interesting to note that children who stammer are able to sing without difficulty.

Intellectually, the children learn new sounds and the meanings of words like low, high, loud and soft as they are applied to singing. Their vocabulary is increased as they repeat the traditional nursery rhyme songs, their constant repetition acting as a reinforcement.

Emotionally, children may be able to express feelings in songs which cannot be stated verbally, and of course singing is an enjoyable activity. The repetition of familiar words and tunes is comforting and makes the child feel more secure.

Socially, the children enjoy singing together, and often the anonymity of singing in a group makes it preferable to individual activities.

Singing is always a popular activity, particularly if the songs are familiar with galloping rhythms and accompanying actions. Familiar tunes are often used to make up songs about everyday events: 'Joanie has a new house', 'Playing in the garden today.' Children like to sway to music, swing their arms or jump up and down. If a peaceful break is required a restful tune can be selected and hummed or sung quietly.

Record Players and Tape Recorders

Some teachers and nursery nurses will bring a guitar to the nursery, which is used as a stimulus for music activities. Many schools have record players and a collection of records which covers a wide range of differing tastes and includes music from a variety of countries and cultures. Music should not be played while other activities are taking place, as this makes it difficult for the children to attend to the music, and may distract them from another activity. Fostering good listening habits is unlikely in this situation. Playing records and tapes can also inhibit natural creative movement and singing. The activity becomes an exercise in matching his rhythm to the music. When the adult plays records for dance, children have to fit in to the framework of the music, whereas it is more meaningful for the children to create their own rhythms. Hence, use of these aids should not replace the natural music-making activities of the children, but they may be used to add another dimension at later stages.

Fingerplays

These provide rhythm and activity on a small scale, but perhaps their greatest attribute is the enjoyment children get from repetition of the words and actions. Love of language and security develops from these fingerplays which are often learnt sitting on mother's lap and become part of the firm foundation children build new skills onto. Some examples are:

Wiggle

I wiggle my fingers	Now no more wiggles
I wiggle my toes	Are left in me
I wiggle my shoulders	So I will be still
I wiggle my nose	As still as can be.

The Spaceship

1 We must climb into our Spaceship
   For the latest way to fly
   To travel through the Universe
   Away up in the sky.

2 But first we'll put on space suits
   From our helmets to our feet
   Then get on board the spaceship
   And settle in the seat.

3 There's a man who gives the signals
   And you will hear him say
   'Now we have checked the instruments
   And everything is okay'.

4 Stand by now for the countdown
   And again you'll hear him say
   '3–2–1 and zero
   Blast off and we're away.

   Chorus   A Zoom m m m
                 A Zoom m m m
                 A Zoom

5 Soaring high up among the stars
   Now the earth is many miles below
   Soaring to reach the moon or Mars,
   On and on and on we'll go.

Knock at the door	(Hit forehead with fist)
Peep in	(Raise eyelid slightly)
Lift up the latch	(Touch tip of nose)
Walk in	(Put finger in mouth)

Five little firemen sit very still	(hold up 5 fingers)
Until they see a fire on top of the hill.	
No. 1 rings the bell ding-dong	(bend down thumb)

No. 2 pulls his big boots on	(bend down index finger)
No. 3 jumps on the fire engine red	(bend down middle finger)
No. 4 puts a fire hat on his head	(bend down ring finger)
No. 5 drives the red fire truck to the fire	(bend down little finger)
As the big yellow flames go higher and higher	(spread arms)
Whooooooooooo . . . Whooooooooooo . . . hear the fire truck say,	(imitate siren)
As all of the cars get out of the way.	
Shhhhh goes the water from the fire hose spout	(rub palms together)
And quicker than a wink the fire is out!	(clap hands)
An owl sat alone on the branch of a tree	(fold hands)
And he was as quiet as quiet could be	(whisper)
It was night and his eyes were round like this	(make circles around eye with fingers)
He looked all around, not a thing did he miss.	(turn head from side to side)
Some birdies crept up on the branch of a tree.	(make fingers creep up opposite arm)
And they were as quiet as quiet could be	(whisper)
Said the wise old owl,	'To-whoooooo, to-whooooooo'
Up jumped the birdies and away they flew.	(hands move behind back)
The owl sat alone on the branch of a tree	(fold hands)
And he was as quiet as quiet could be	(whisper)

Dramatic Play

Stories can be acted out in rhyme or otherwise by the children. Many nursery rhymes lend themselves to active interpretation, e.g. *Humpty Dumpty*, and stories can be adapted: *The Gingerbread Man, The Three Little Pigs*. As far as possible each child should have a part to play, or take turns. Speech, vocabulary and comprehension are all promoted through dramatic play and the children identify with the story characters more readily. They even change their voices to suit when playing the role of the little pig and the wolf, if they have been introduced to the story by an adult with an expressive voice. Self-confidence and emotional satisfaction is achieved by acting out real life emotions as an imaginary character. They are sufficiently removed from the emotion to feel safe and as the stories have happy endings, fears and anxieties can be seen to be resolved without danger to the child.

When telling a story, it is important that the children should be able to see the adult's face as expressions should add to the context of the story. The adult should also be able to see the children, they should be close enough for eye contact so that their responses can be noted as the various emotions of excitement, surprise, joy and sadness are traced in the story. Obviously a small group is better than a larger one, as a close intimate atmosphere is conducive to the occasion. The adult should sit at the same level as the children in a relaxed manner. Interruptions must be dealt with naturally and if a child gets up to wander away he can be brought into the story 'And what do you think he said then, Philip?' Of course there will be occasions when a child will prefer to look at a book on his own rather than listen to the adult and there should be provision for this. On no account should a child be reprimanded for not showing interest – it may be that storytelling does not satisfy his needs and interests that day.

Repetition of favourite stories makes children feel secure – they love the predictability of events and reactions. The adult has to ensure that the same format and words are used each time to avoid annoyance and interruptions as the children rush in to correct the 'new' version and the listeners often provide the punch line when it comes, so they feel cheated if it does not arrive at the expected time.

As with other aspects of development certain major factors have to be considered if children are to benefit. With books and stories these factors are: Stages, Ages, Interests and Needs of the children. This SAIN approach should ensure that each child gains individual satisfaction from this traditional activity.

Dramatic play begins spontaneously with the familiar. At first children may offer coffee to the teacher or imitate mother or father in the kitchen. They love to cook or wash dishes or walls. Sometimes playing families comes next or possibly role playing a fireman or policeman. There are times, however, when it is appropriate for the adult to stimulate dramatic play. Children who are young or new to group experience may need prompting. Sometimes children from underprivileged neighbourhoods seem unable to release themselves into dramatic play. Here the stimulation of new themes and the provision of continuity in play is appropriate.

Ordinary cooking could be changed through carefully directed conversation into a family breakfast with fried eggs and someone rushing off to the shops. In this case the adult draws on real experience. The idea is to start with an experience already chosen by the children, to expand the play and then to withdraw inconspicuously. Dramatic play should not be confined to the home. Ambulance and hospital services, nurses and doctors may be involved in taking a 'sick person' to hospital. Flexible furniture, boards and archways may attach in different ways to accommodate quickly inspired and easily lost themes. Some empty floor space with large blocks and rideable vehicles which can become ambulances, fire-trucks, buses, etc., should be available. If musical instruments are available, the children will quickly build and change, creating stores and dams, ambulances and spaceships, exciting rhythms and chants.

Role of the adult

The adult's role in play is to help the child grow and learn. Extension of interest and activity, cultivation of the individual viewing of the forces and objects of the world are some of the goals set by the adult. The right question at the right time can spark the children's search and stimulate them to make their own discoveries. In addition to specific questions the teacher could ask 'Is there a different way of doing this perhaps?' or 'What do you think about this?' The confidence that children can learn on their own is the essence of this role; it would be inappropriate to say whether any particular response is right or wrong.

Dramatic play should be:

1 broadly comprehensive for a variety of experiences in role play;
2 flexible with materials for any theme;
3 child-centred – the children do the learning, thinking, experimenting, acting, while the adults

Figure 7.13   Play can also be a medium for learning.

set the stage, observe, consolidate and stimulate so as to extend the experience of the children;

4 integrated – a theme in dramatic play may derive from, or be extended to include, arts and crafts and will include indoor and outdoor play;

5 a mirror of the child's experience of the world – this needs to be based on real experiences of field trips, shopping trips and visitors to the nursery.

Benefits of dramatic play

Physical. Movement in dramatic play is often determined by the imagination of the child and his interpretation of the role he is taking, which may be real or fantasy. Vigorous exertions may relate to the keep fit sessions of his parents or breakfast time television. Sometimes he will gallop about on his horse (which need not be represented by a stick to be real to him), as his favourite cowboy does; sometimes he will jump off chairs or boxes as he becomes Superman. (Sadly, his enthusiasm must be curbed if he attempts to jump off walls or tables in case he believes that, like his hero, no harm can come to him.) When outside, he may become Tarzan, Robin Hood or a Sioux warrior as he swings from branches (or the tyres fixed to them). Whole movements of trunk and limbs are involved in this play, but the change of role may involve fine muscles of hand and feet as he balances on the trapeze or strums a guitar like his favourite pop star. Girls, too, will assume any role they wish, whether man or woman in reality. There are female police, female robbers and, of course, Wonder Woman, but in fantasy the sex of the model is not important.

Intellectual benefits. Dramatic play is also an effective way for children to acquire permanent logic and mental structures. Complicated and expensive materials are not required for the 'logicomathematical materials' project mentioned. Children can work just as well with household and factory junk: a variety of inexpensive materials, e.g. plastic tubes, puzzles, blocks, Cuisenaire rods and transportation toys. Children lay the basis for learning through differentiated body movement integrated with speech–auditory systems as well as through dramatic play with these collected and prepared materials and forces.

Given this wealth of materials to play with, the children discover them using all of their senses. In the freedom of play with the confidence to lightly try one thing and then another, children find vitally personal interests and satisfactions. It is the process of the child's actions with forces and materials, and the continuing need to think about these actions, that leads the child to truly learn.

Emotional and social benefits. Role playing by the children themselves or by using people dolls enables them to enact many family experiences. Experiences of love, fear and discipline sometimes need partial resolution in play. Role play always involves a give and take, a trying out of another's ideas and a dynamic relationship with peers. Such play promotes solid social values, namely sensitivity, cooperation, self-esteem, emotional maturity, curiosity, optimism and gaiety.

Domestic Play

Domestic play can be described as dramatic, imaginary play, manipulative play, or creative play, as it embodies aspects of each of these. In domestic play we can include bakery and cookery, real and imaginary, home play, with household activities such as sweeping, dusting, mealtimes, shopping, use of telephones, doll bathing, washing dolls' clothes, pegging out, ironing, sewing, dressing up, and play with dolls and puppets.

The Home Corner

Ideally, enough space to create a two or three 'room' set apart from through traffic is best. At times when great interest is centred on this activity, the space could be extended to accommodate more children. A variety of materials should be stored in cupboards near at hand. There is danger of over-stimulation if too many materials are out at one time. Furniture such as a bed, table and chairs, sink, oven and refrigerator should be provided, all child-sized, so that the children can actually use them as they play out the daily function of family life. Washing and cleaning equipment extend the house play. A cardboard or wooden box can become a washing machine or dryer. Kitchen utensils, including pots, pans and plastic dishes, with a mirror, armchair (or rocking chair) and a telephone are useful. Parents, teachers or nursery nurses can make some of the equipment themselves. Some nursery nurses do woodwork as part of their training course, and some colleges also offer short courses for nursery staff. This enables staff to furnish their nursery at very little cost, which is a major advantage as play furniture is so expensive. Both boys and girls should be encouraged to join in house play, and adults must not encourage sex-role stereotyping by excluding boys from the activity.

Benefits of play in the home corner

Physical. Acting out housekeeping activities provides plenty of opportunity for large and small muscle development, as floors are swept, washed, furniture dusted and polished where appropriate, windows and mirrors cleaned, bed linen washed and put out to dry, bed(s) made, and meal prepared. Dressing-up clothes can be kept in the home corner, so that working clothes (dungarees, aprons, overalls) can be donned. Outdoor clothes, including uniforms, high-heeled shoes, coats, jackets, dresses, shoes, hats and jewellery also have a place, and if possible a full-length mirror is more exciting. Dressing up helps manual dexterity in real-life dressing.

Intellectual. Concepts related to housekeeping and occupational roles are clarified in domestic play. There are opportunities for scientific observations and learning concepts related to water, and the changes which take place as they add detergent or see it change into ice or steam. Mathematical principles come into play as children classify and arrange dishes according to colour, shape and size. Water is measured in jugs, cups and pots. Groceries are packed onto shelves or put in cupboards according to contents, shape or size. There are many opportunities for language development, as the children talk to each other in their assumed roles. The refrigerator can become the washing machine, as the Mother does the family washing. Daddy prepares hamburgers and steaks for the barbecue in the garden. Problems arising from each situation are solved as they arise.

Emotional. As the child engages in imaginative play, tries different roles, and gains competence in many situations, his self-concept improves. He can role play his parents, brothers, and sisters, become a milkman, postman, policeman or family doctor. He gains some idea of how adults work at home and outside, and experi-

ments with many different kinds of relationships. Problems such as preparation for a family outing are solved without panic or anxiety, and this sense of mastery over people and events increases his self-confidence.

Social. The home corner is ideal for social development, as the family members converse, talking about their jobs or school experiences. The baby begins to cry and has to be put in the pram and taken out to the garden. Mother and Father tell the childen about the new car or the birthday party arrangements. During this time, nursery staff often become privy to many real-life family secrets, so discretion must be exercised, although with troubled children this can give a useful insight into the source of their problems. Telephone conversations may range from the mundane call to arrange babysitting to the fantastical coded messages devised to mislead the secret agent who has bugged the phone.

Preparation of Food

This involves baking, cookery and the exciting experience of food/meals preparation by the children themselves. Some nurseries have a cookery area apart from the home corner, others incorporate it in the 'kitchen'. Either way, safety factors are most important when an oven, as a table top type, or full cooker is used. It must be placed next to a wall, with socket and flex hidden behind it to avoid any child tripping over the flex or upsetting pans on the cooker. The adult must stay beside the cooker, and in front of the cookery tables throughout the activity, to ensure constant supervision. Precautions as to cutting vegetables and hot liquids should be discussed with the children. Cleanliness of table tops and utensils must be ensured beforehand, and all the children (and adults) involved should wash their hands, so that children appreciate prevention of infection. Small groups with an adult supervising each is the best arrangement. Planning is also very important, and the children can help with this, as grouping items and equipment helps them with classifying. Wooden cutting boards should be used to protect table tops, and real knives must be sharp enough to cut finely. Plastic bowls, measuring jugs, wooden spoons and whisks are necessary. Cooking pots and casserole dishes can be obtained in clear non-breakable glass, which makes the cookery part more interesting for the children as they see the colour and consistency change. All food experiences should be based on good nutritional values, as children become accustomed to enjoying foods which are good for them, even though at first they may object if they are used to a diet of junk food. Involvement in the preparation is the incentive, and even a snack of buttered toast becomes exciting! Despite the inclusion of subjects like nutrition and menu planning in nursery nurse training schemes, too often they do not venture beyond sweet or starchy foods like sponge cakes and toffee. There are many meals which involve all the nutrients in vegetables, fruit, first class protein in milk, eggs and cheese, and sufficient fibre. Soup made with potatoes, onions, carrots, lentils and barley is an excellent idea for cold days, and baked potatoes with fillings of grated cheese or coleslaw are popular and very nutritious. Milk puddings, which may be refused at home, suddenly become 'great!' to the young chef who prepares it. Some fast food can also be very nutritious – hamburgers made from beef mince served with onions in a bun are tasty and chilli made with mince and beans is also a good choice if a full meal is required.

Benefits of food preparation activities

Physical. Apart from the benefit of nutritional food, the process of preparation has many physical benefits for children. Cutting, chopping and sprinkling all require hand–eye coordination; grinding peanuts takes a lot of energy; while patting the mince into hamburgers uses other muscles and different pressure. Scrubbing potatoes involves hand and finger control, while cracking an egg requires both coordination and judgement as to the amount of force necessary. Squeezing an orange with a hand squeezer involves strength and large muscles of the arm with small muscles of hand and fingers. As mixtures are beaten by one child with a spoon and another with an electric mixer to compare the speeds, the change in colour and consistency can be observed. If there is a nursery garden, children can pick the vegetables they have seeded; if not, a visit to a farm or garden centre helps them to realize that there is a lot of physical effort involved in food production, apart from its preparation for eating.

Intellectual. The sensory experiences involved in food preparation provide very good learning opportunities. They see variety in shape, colour, size, texture and consistency. They hear grating, cracking, beating and pouring, while their taste buds are stimulated as they smell the flavourings and spices, and sample their mixture to test the amount of salt or sugar required. Touch experiences include softness, smoothness, stickiness and lumpiness. Vocabulary is increased as they describe the appearance of long green beans, fat green broad beans, red kidney (why so-called?) beans, and yellow haricot beans contrasted with carrots, diced turnip, green broccoli, lettuce and cucumber. Food preparation gives children the opportunity to go through processes from beginning to end, thus gaining an understanding of sequencing, which is essential for reading. They observe that the pancake mixture gets thicker as they add more flour and smoother as they stir. Each piece of equipment has a name related to its function which helps them to relate the two, while following a recipe with figures and symbols helps to establish the relationship between these and abstracts. Figure–ground relations are enhanced as the child sees the egg against the mixture of flour and water. Mathematical experiences involve counting the number of eggs, measuring in fractions as in a half or quarter pound of flour, comparing other measures like teaspoons and tablespoons and noting the difference in volume of flour in a bowl as they remove some or add some. They learn how to measure weights of butter and cheese, and come to realize that time of cooking and temperature of oven also require measurement. Scientific principles involved relate to observation of similarities and differences between food items, both before cooking and afterwards, e.g. jelly making is dependent on the heat of the water added to the gelatin, which dissolves, then sets in mould; solids change to liquids as butter is heated and sliced apples cooked; sugar dissolves out of sight in water but flour and water make a mixture; before corn is popped it looks like little orange coloured seeds, and after heating in a large covered pan or in a popping machine with a little oil (which could be produced from corn as well), they become large air-filled puffs – what magic! Some foods look different between ripening, e.g. the green tomato becomes red, the yellow banana has changed from green. Concepts are learned, as they see that apples, oranges and tomatoes are round, but differ in size, texture and taste. Continual questioning to himself, the adults or other children helps to express the problems and leads the child to make predictions, such as: Will I have enough mixture to fill all the patty tins? How high will my buns rise? Will there be enough custard for everyone in this pan? Will brown eggs taste different from white eggs? Reasoning also comes from his calculations: one spoonful of pancake mixture fills one patty tin, so there should be 12 pancakes after baking. Use of plain and self-raising flour and yeast shows that raising agents can make bread and rolls twice their original size. The most startling change is seen in the dough before and after baking.

Emotional. Food preparation is great fun, so enjoyment is the principal benefit, but the ability to provide even a snack for himself and others gives a feeling of achievement. Provision of food is one of the main functions of parents, and the child feels important and even protective towards those who will eat his finished product, much as he interprets his parents' reaction to him. Praise for the good taste of his food endorses his self-esteem and helps develop a positive self-concept.

Social. The planning, method and clearing away of this activity makes it a communal experience. Removing fresh peas from pods is even more fun when the rest of your group join in a contest to see who has the most; taking turns to whisk the eggs or beat the cake mixture, and preparing coleslaw ingredients as a group make interaction inevitable. It may be that in these happy, chatty little groups the child who is usually shy and unsure of herself will be able to share in the glory of her group's efforts, while the boastful, unpopular child will have to share the success of his group. Other communal activities like singing, rhymes and fingerplays can arise out of food preparation, and the children begin to talk of 'us', 'we', 'ours', instead of 'me', 'mine' and 'I'. Books on this theme include *Little Gingerbread Boy, Gingerbread Man, The Big Pancake* and McDonald Starters *Bread, Cake and Biscuits* and *Who Wants to Cook*? An excellent selection can be found in E. Matterson's *This Little Puffin.*

A film on children and dough, available from Concord Films Council, is useful to nursery nurses and playgroup workers.

Recipes

Bread or bread rolls. Combine 2 teaspoons of sugar with 1 ounce of yeast. Blend in 1 pint of milk (warmed to 37°C), 1 teaspoon salt. Rub 4 ounces of fat into 2 ounces of flour. Knead together all the ingredients. Put the dough into the bowl and sprinkle with flour to keep it from sticking to the clean towel used to cover the bowl. Place in a warm area, such as on top of a medium heated cooker. Allow the dough to rise until it has doubled in size. Knock down dough

Table 7.3   Record of play activities

Category of play	Date	Time
Names of children involved		
Space used for play		

Time children concentrated
    Longest
    Shortest		

Equipment and materials used most frequently		
Equipment and materials never used		
Materials used for improvisation		
Materials used in a stereotyped way		
Materials used destructively or aggressively		
Regulations made by children in course of play		
Rules broken by the children		
Reason for participation		
Reason for intervention		
Reason for initiation		
Emotional		
Social		
Language		
Mathematical		
Scientific		
Physical		
Manipulative		
Problem solving		
Motivation		
Drama role playing		
Concentration		
Curiosity		

gently. Put it on a clean lightly floured board or table and knead until it becomes smooth. Soon it will feel elastic – if not, a little more flour should be added. It should be pliable enough to be rolled over on itself, sides folded into middle and pressed down again. Repeat this three or four times. Place into a greased loaf tin for a bread loaf.

For bread rolls, shape the dough into small rolls and place on a greased baking sheet. Return them to the warm place until they double in size again, then bake at 450°F for about 20 minutes.

Strong flour for bread making can be obtained from health food shops.

Recording Play Activities

Recording play is not the same as reporting play. The former involves constant observation at various times of play, under the guidelines given in Table 7.3. Reporting can be in the form of an essay on an experience witnessed during play.

8

The Child and the Nursery

The Nursery Environment

Nurseries should endeavour to be environments with scope for exploration and discovery. This can be achieved by careful planning and arrangement of furnishings and equipment. The physical arrangement of the rooms and buildings is very important in creating an atmosphere free of confusion to allow the children to take as much responsibility as possible for themselves, and to reduce the need for adult interference.

Physical Environment

The playroom

This should be set up with materials and equipment convenient to the space allotted for the activity. The floor block corner should have its own cupboard and space, so the children building will not be disturbed by other children moving around the room. Often the cupboard set out at right angles to the wall will make a boundary to keep the play within a specific area. This area must be large enough that children can put away the blocks without meticulously piling them, otherwise it is unreasonable to ask nursery children to tidy up after themselves. Trains and large trucks set out on a shelf will provide ideas for imaginative play.

The dramatic play centre should be set up in a bright part of the room. If it contains cupboards or a sink or cooker unit, these may be set out to provide the wall. If not, a simple fence or the use of the regular playroom cupboards will define the area.

Easels should be set up in a space free from traffic. Provision of simple aprons which the children can put on themselves, with the paint jars set out conveniently for them, will reduce the need for adult interference. Since spills occasionally occur, the floor should be well protected with a plastic sheet or newspapers.

Painting can always be available by using table and floor space as well. The creative materials and small equipment such as individual boxes of blocks, peg boards and puzzles will be set out on an open shelf where children can readily see what is available. The tables where children play with this material should be arranged conveniently around this shelf, leaving enough space by the shelf for the children to move about freely. This shelf need not necessarily be flat against the wall, as it can often be placed out in the room to make a natural boundary for some other activity. Water and sand trays can be kept to one side of the room on plastic sheets, with sufficient room for the children to stand around them as they play. If a table is set up for a special activity such as dough, clay, finger painting or Plasticine, it can be placed as a centre of its own.

The library corner, with book racks as partitions, should be as far away from the activities as possible to ensure peace and quiet for those who want to enjoy pleasant read. Musical corners, Science/Nature corners and seasonal or interest displays can be set up behind the library partitions. Wallboards and windows provide space for treasured artistic objects to be displayed. Special paints can be used for glass if desired.

Decorating

Green is said to be a restful colour, but yellow, which looks bright and clean, may be preferred. The walls should preferably be covered in matt paint or non-gloss, washable wallpaper. Brilliant glossy painted walls can be a source of irritation to those who spend most of their time in the nursery, and should be avoided. Lighting must be adequate to avoid strain and the floor should be covered with a comfortable, hard-wearing, washable cord carpet in a dark colour. Curtains give a 'homely' look to a nursery, and could be of heavy cotton in a toning colour.

Equipment and furnishings

These must be safe, firmly fixed, sturdy and capable of withstanding rough and tumble. Paint must be non-toxic, and any splintering or sharp-edged tables avoided to prevent accidents.

Cloakroom

This should be set up convenient to the outside doors, to avoid carrying mud and snow through the building. A hallway or basement can often be utilized for this purpose, but if it is necessary to have the cloakroom in the playroom, it should be placed so that the children can go to it directly from outside, rather than wandering through the playroom to reach it. Hangers should be provided for coats and racks for boots or wellingtons. A drying cupboard is essential for drying out thick coats, jackets and footwear.

Toilets

These should be set up with child-sized sinks and lavatories. Towel, comb and toothbrush racks are not hygienic, as these items may come into contact and so spread infection. Paper towels (soft enough for faces) are preferable. Toothbrushes and beakers should be sterilized before they are stacked away, as should combs and brushes. Mirrors at child height should be available, but not behind sinks, as is the usual custom, in case of accidents.

Dining room

As pre-school children cannot sit still for very long, the dining room routine can be arranged to give them some opportunity for moving around during the meal. A central serving table can be arranged where the child goes to collect his meal and to which he returns if he wants more, and for dessert. After this little excursion to the serving table, he returns to his meal with renewed interest. If the children are served by the adult at their table, they could carry their plates around to him/her for servings, rather than sit at their place to be served. Some nursery staff may feel happier if the children remain seated throughout the meal, but the needs of the children must come first, and meal times should be enjoyable experiences.

Sleeping/rest room

Some children may require a midday rest if they have had an early start. Folding cots can be provided, but they should have at least 18 in (45 cm) between them when set up. If there is insufficient space for a separate rest room, the playroom can be darkened and ventilated while the children have lunch. When they return, it is a quiet restful place suggesting sleep.

Other Factors

Apart from the physical environment, an atmosphere free from tensions (which can be created by adults who are unhappy), is essential. Children can only gain emotional stability and learn about relationships through what they see in adults who care for them. If their parents are constantly feuding, the children may feel insecure and show this in aggressive behaviour. Teamwork, with each person aware of the importance of their own part in the team, is conducive to a pleasant friendly atmosphere in which children gain most from their experiences in play.

Health education can easily be carried out in a modern nursery with all facilities; it may not be so easy when a home lacks a water supply which is hot and always on tap. Here the nursery staff have to compensate for the deficiencies of the home and the inabilities of the parents. Simple hygienic practices like washing hands after using the toilet and before meals, keeping hair and clothes clean and tidy, careful disposal of tissues, can all be taught by example and in doll play.

Planning The Child's Day

The day-care programme should provide the child with plenty of opportunities for freedom of choice of activities in line with his own interests and needs. The programme should also ensure that the child is able to enjoy a good deal of expressive outdoor play and interesting excursions. A well balanced programme is essential to provide opportunities for:

1 individual and social activities,

2 creativity and conformity to established procedures,
3 self-reliance and acceptance of adult support, help and guidance,
4 new challenges in the nursery and on interesting trips as well as for the tranquil and comfortable periods spent in familiar day-care activities. Even time to be alone is important.

A good nursery programme should supplement the care a child receives at home and help to promote and sustain harmony in the relationships he has with his family, playmates and nursery staff. The core of the programme for the young child in day care is play, balanced by regular times allotted for routines such as washing, lunch, snacks and a rest period. Play periods should provide opportunities for finding new interests, for extending experiences and developing new skills. In regular routine activities, the children will require adult supervision and guidance as individuals until they are familiar with the procedures and capable of self-direction when general adult supervision should be sufficient. While a daily routine provides security, flexibility is essential so that excursions such as picnics, swimming instruction at the local pool, visits to places of special interest may be arranged. It is useful to have an open activity like a slide ready to start the day as children come in. Some children may be very sleepy if they have had an early start – a mid-morning nap may have to be arranged for them.

When children start at 7.30 a.m., breakfast is usually provided for them and this should include porridge or cereal, boiled or scrambled egg and fingers of toast with a drink of milk or hot chocolate. Any meal time must be regarded as a social occasion, but lunchtime is usually more suited to this as children will be wide awake and not as cold and hungry as they are in the early morning. One member of staff should be available to deal solely with the children and parents as they arrive, to hear any problems, such as the arrival of a new baby, daddy out of a job, mother going into hospital, which could affect the child's behaviour that day.

Structured and free play have a part in the daily programme but, as stated before, all play situations require planning beforehand if the child is to benefit from all that play can offer. Activities such as storytelling may be enjoyed as a 'winding down' period after boisterous play, before lunch. However, the story should be timed if the children are not to be frustrated by having to wash for lunch before it is over. All members of staff should be aware of the programme and who is involved in which activity to ensure that they do not intrude on each other and spoil a carefully nurtured atmosphere.

Children can help to prepare for lunch and enjoy helping themselves with a cafeteria-type arrangement. Some nursery units with small groups prefer the children to sit at table for the whole meal and be served by the adult, as they feel this lends more opportunity for a 'family' occasion. Conversation can still proceed once the children have their food but freedom to move about is very important for some children. Flexibility and attention to individual needs should determine the pattern. Lunchtime can be a time when the child learns how to share attention, how to help others, develop his language skills, and gain self-confidence through recounting the morning's events. All aspects of development can be promoted and parents will enjoy an exciting account of even routine parts of the daily programme.

A Framework Of Child Study

Please discuss this framework with your Officer in Charge or your Nursery Teacher before beginning your Child Study.

1 *Name and age of child.* (As this is confidential, use only the child's first name.) Reason for your choice.
2 *The family.* Home environment. Parents. Position in family and any details of siblings. It would be useful to know if there were any early difficulties, whether milestones were normal, whether there were any separations, accidents, traumatic events? Include any other relevant information that you are allowed to give.
3 *Physical development.* Appearance of child: any abnormalities? If possible include a history of the child's physical development, e.g. when did the child sit up, crawl, teethe, begin to walk, say his first words? Are height and weight normal? Coordination of hand and eye? Control of large and small muscles? Is the child over-active/underactive for age? Eating and sleeping aspects? Illness?
4 *Entry to day nursery or nursery school/class.* At what age? Can you describe the mother's and child's reactions and find out about the settling-in period?

5 *Social development*. Attitudes to adults: strange and known. Attitudes to other children. Proportion of time spent in solitary/parallel/group play. Role in group: special friends?

6 *Intellectual development*. Language development. Attitude to stories and books. Does the child play with sorting and grading toys, jigsaws? How long is the child's concentration span? Is he creative? What sort of questions does the child ask? Watch his/her play with sand, water, blocks, and any other material that interests the child: what does the child seem to be learning? How confident is the child? *Back up your work with relevant observations please.*

7 *Emotional development*. How dependent is the child? How does he show aggression and how often? (Watch him with adults, other children, toys and materials.) Does the child have any fears? (Parents may know.) Is he/she anxious, insecure? How is this shown? Is he/she easily frustrated, moody? Describe expressions of affection (to adults, other children, toys, pets). Describe any make-believe play.

8 *Conclusion*. Summarize what you have learnt about this child in the course of your child study, describing your own feelings about this child, and about your relationship.

This study is designed to help you look closely at one particular child, and it is hoped that by the time you have completed the study you will have a good picture of that child's all-round development.

The study will take some weeks; carry a notebook with you so that you can jot down notes and observations. Give yourself plenty of time to write up your work.

Points when Observing the Child at Play

1 Ask your teacher nursery officer whether you may have time for making observations.

2 Sit a little way from the group you choose and jot down notes. These should later be rewritten. State the names and ages of the children in the group, and the material/equipment. Write down the length of time of your observations, and note length of time each child stays. Try to describe:

a physical aspect – how children handle materials, move, etc.;

b emotional and social aspect – report conversation, monologues, quarrels, friendly gestures, what benefits children gain from this play;

c intellectual aspect – what learning, questions, reasoning, discovery?

Observations on a Baby of 3–5 + Months Old

1 *Posture and large movements*. How does the baby react when:

a he is pulled into a sitting position,

b he is placed facing down,

c he is held standing with feet on a hard surface?

2 *Vision and fine movements*. How does he respond to:

a a nearby human face,

b a mobile or dangling toy,

c his own hands,

d his feeding bottle?

3 *Hearing and speech*. How does he react to:

a a loud, sudden noise,

b his Mother's (or Mother-substitute's) voice,

c a spoon rattled in a cup, or a bell rung (out of his sight)?

4 *Social behaviour and play*. How does he respond:

a when he is being fed,

b when you are preparing his bath,

c when he is being bathed,

d when he is being nursed, cuddled, played with?

Observations on a Child 6–9 Months Old

1 *Posture and large movements*. How does he react when:

a lying flat on his back,

b you grasp his hands,

c you hold him sitting up,

d you hold him standing with feet on a hard surface,

e you place him prone on his front?

f Can he sit alone – for how long?

g Can he turn his head and look round when sitting?

h Can he roll over – from front to back, from back to front?

2 *Vision and fine movements*. What is his response when:

a you attract his attention,

b you move around the room,

c you place a toy about 6 inches from him,

d a toy falls and he can still see it,

e a toy falls outside his visual field?

f Do his eyes focus in unison?

3 *Hearing and speech.* What happens when:
a he hears Mother/Mother-substitute's voice from across the room,
b something annoys him,
c you imitate the sounds he makes? What sounds does he make?

4 *Social behaviour and play.* What does he do:
a when a toy is placed out of reach,
b when he picks up a toy (one hand, two hands?),
c when he has picked up a toy,
d when you offer him a rattle,
e when a stranger approaches him,
f when being fed,
g when being bathed?

Observations of a Child of 9 Months to 1 Year +

1 *Posture and large movements*
a How long can he sit on the floor?
b Can he lean forward to pick up a toy without losing his balance?
c Can he progress over the floor? Describe in what way.
d Can he pull himself up to stand?
e Can he lower himself?

2 *Vision and fine movements*
a How acutely does he watch objects, people, happenings?
b What does he do when offered a small toy?
c What does he do if a toy with a pull string is placed near him?
d What does he do when he drops a toy over the edge of the chair or pram?
e Does he point at objects?

3 *Hearing and speech*
a Describe his babbling. What sounds does he make?
b How does he communicate?
c Does he respond to 'no' and 'bye-bye'?
d How does he react to a loud bang?
e Does he imitate sounds you make?

4 *Social behaviour and play*
a What does he do when you give him a rusk?
b Describe him at a meal time. What does he enjoy?
c How does he express annoyance?
d Put a toy half hidden from him, and describe what he does. Now hide it completely and describe the result.
e How does he react to other children of his age?

f Does he show affection?
g Does he play? How?

The Child's Discovery of Life and Science

Many of the ostensibly simple and commonplace phenomena which occur in nature and science are a source of wonderment and discovery to young children. The elements: rain, snow, mist, changes of season; how plants and animals grow; the nature of heat and cold; all provide opportunities for discovery, observation and wonder. Adults working with children need to make use of the innate curiosity of young children: to help them see these wonders around them; to bring into the nursery objects such as seeds that will further their interests; and to take the children where possible on visits to broaden their experience and interests. The adult capitalizes on the interests expressed by the children to help lead them in an awareness of the natural things around them. They share the thrill of watching and wondering with the children. Opportunities for them to experience the excitement of discovery are provided, as children are encouraged to find out for themselves. Science and nature topics can develop from whatever occurs in the woods, on a walk or in the playground or playroom. The adult may not know all the answers to the numerous questions the children will put, but a trip to the library looking for books on specific subjects will help children realize the fund of knowledge to be found in books.

Animals in the Nursery

Children have an opportunity to become familiar with an animal if it lives in the nursery for a while. There is time to watch, to handle, to feed, to care for and come to understand it. With such close acquaintance, real liking, interest and companionship have a chance to develop.

Birds

Even nurseries and homes in inner city areas have pigeons, blue tits, sparrows, robins and starlings which children can watch and imitate. They can observe differences in feeding, walking, flying and song. Feeding stations will attract more birds and bring them close enough for the children to observe. When new birds are seen, the child can look them up in the bird book with the teacher's help. A half coconut suspended from a circle of wood which acts as a shelter can be hung from a window or a pole in the playground. Closer inspection is possible if a square, wooden box containing seeds or crumbs can be attached to the window. Blue tits are fun to observe as they hang upside down to nibble at a pack of peanuts (in their shells) in their own net bag. These packs can be bought at a pet shop and if they are attached to a pole near the window the children can see their feeding habits. Canaries and budgies require exacting care and can contract pneumonia, and therefore they are not suitable pets for children. Parrots and budgerigars are also unsuitable as they can spread a disease known as psittacosis.

Frogs

The complete life cycle can be shown in an aquarium from egg to tadpole to frog. The frogs' eggs, usually found in ponds in February or March, are a mass of sticky jelly full of little black dots – the frog spawn. The eggs become tadpoles which like to feed on leaves and vegetables, or baby-food spinach. Adult frogs like to feed on flies which they catch with the help of a long tongue fastened to the front of the mouth, which uncoils to snap up the fly. Both tadpoles and frogs need to be fed daily. It is interesting for children to watch the rapid growth of tadpoles; a few are more easily observed than a great many. Frogs need both land and water in the aquarium as they are *amphibian* animals – a lovely word which some children will manage to pronounce and remember!

Setting up an aquarium

An aquarium can be used not only for observation of the frog's life cyle but also to house goldfish, minnows, newts and snails. Usually the pet shop will advise on the correct size of tank. If tropical fish are to be kept an electrical supply will be required for heating, and the tank must be placed carefully so that children can see all the exotic colours and shapes without the danger of spillage or interference in the electric supply.

1 Wash the aquarium with salt solution (salt in water). Rub some salt on the glass. Rinse with clean water.

2 Wash the sand, stir it with a ruler. Keep washing it until the water is clean.
3 Put the clean sand into the tank. Smooth it out so that it is deeper at the back.
4 Put a piece of paper on the sand. Pour the water on.
5 Bring the roots of the water plants (mosses and ferns) to the sand. Plant them near the back of the tank.
6 Lay a large sheet of paper on top of the water. Pour more water on the paper. Fill the tank nearly to the top, then take the paper out.
7 Cover the tank with a piece of glass or metal. Let the tank stand for a day or two.
8 Leave the fish in its jar. Float the jar in the tank for an hour or two. Empty the fish into the tank.
9 Shake a little food (ants' eggs or daphnia) on the water every 2 or 3 days. Too much food is as bad as too little. Fish and other animals breathe out carbon dioxide, and the plants need this carbon dioxide to grow. As the plants grow they give off oxygen which animals must have to live, so each helps the other and nature stays in balance. This is called the carbon dioxide-oxygen cycle. When there is the right number of plants, the correct amount of light and water and the right number of fish, the aquarium is said to be balanced.

Problems.

1 Green water and green scum on the glass mean that the tank is getting too much light.
2 If the water turns a milky colour, it means either that there are too many fish and not enough plants in the aquarium, or that there is too much food in the water.
3 If the water smells, there may be dead snails or fish or too much food in the water. The tank should be washed out.
4 If the upper (dorsal) fin is down flat on the fish's back, the fish may be sick. It should be taken out and put into water which has half an aspirin in it, or some salt, and left there until it appears well again.
5 If there are white spots (fungus) on the fins or tail the fish should be put into another tank and one or two drops of iodine added.

Do's.

1 Always put the fish into water of the same temperature.
2 Always let the fresh water stand for at least 24 hours before you add the fish.

Figure 8.1   Caring for animals can help children learn selflessness and compassion.

3 Only feed fish three times a week, and only with a small quantity of food.
4 Give them a little raw meat (or small worms) every second week.
5 Always store the tank with water in it and the top on. A dried out tank usually leaks when it is used again.
6 Rewash the sand. It can be used over and over again.
7 The aquarium should be kept full of water.

Don'ts.
1 Don't clean a tank with hot water.
2 Don't carry a tank when it is more than one quarter full of water.
3 Don't change the water unless it is absolutely necessary.
4 Don't overcrowd the fish – there should only be one inch of fish for every gallon of water (usually two or three).
5 Don't put the tank in the sunlight. Indirect light is better.

Guinea pigs

These can be bought at a pet shop and kept in a wire cage that is rustproof. Newspaper should be placed under the cage and replaced each morning. The doors of the cage should be tight fitting and the animals kept at room temperature. Guinea pigs will not climb or jump, they are safe for children to handle, gentle (will not bite), squeak, and like to be cuddled. They also eat large quantities of food: fruit, vegetables or

rabbit pellets and water. A wooden house can be constructed with a detachable runway so that the pet can be transported out of the school at weekends. The roof can be hinged so that the house can be cleaned. This type of house and runway gives the guinea pig space for exercise and a place to hide and sleep. The fence round the runway does not need to be more than 8 inches (20 cm) high because guinea pigs do not climb or jump. As they drink large quantities of water, guinea pigs urinate heavily and the hutch needs to be cleaned out at least twice a week.

Hamsters

Hamsters can be bought at a pet shop, kept in a wire, rustproof cage with newpaper placed underneath which is replaced each morning. Hamsters are adept at escaping through small holes so the cage should be escape proof. They should not be in a temperature below 60°F and, as they are nocturnal, they sleep most of the day. They are rodents with two pairs of gnawing teeth and feed on seeds, grain, vegetables and fresh water.

Gerbils

Gerbils are mainly active during the day so they make good pets for children. If a couple are bought, the children should be able to find the numerous homes required for their offspring but as they are social animals it is best to keep two, ideally two females, who will live together quite happily.

Gerbils should be kept indoors and can be housed in an old fish tank or plastic aquarium which measures at least 60 × 30 × 30 cm with a fine wire mesh lid. This tank should be filled with a mixture of garden peat, sand and straw which will allow the gerbils to burrow underground and make a nest as they do in the wild. Nesting materials can be provided in the form of paper towels or wood shavings. The cage should not be placed in direct sunlight.

Water is best supplied in a drip feed bottle and food should consist of sunflower seeds, wheat, oats, maize and barley with fresh fruit and vegetables. Gnawing blocks should be placed in the tank to allow the gerbils to wear down their incisor teeth which can become overgrown. As gerbils urinate infrequently (they are desert animals) the tank need only be cleaned out every 3–4 weeks. Gerbils should be handled regularly at least once a day, and should be picked up carefully in cupped hands. Children should be told that if they frighten any animal it will scratch in panic as it tries to escape.

Dogs

Dogs and cats are family pets, but it is better to delay buying them until the children are 4–5 years old since they can spread infection and cause problems with babies and toddlers. Small and middle-sized dogs are often chosen as large dogs are expensive to feed and take up too much space in a small house or flat. Very small dogs can be too delicate for the rough and tumble of family life. If a female is chosen she should be spayed or neutered to prevent her producing unwanted puppies. It is best to buy a puppy from a reputable breeder, and it should be at least 8 weeks old and fully weaned. Many puppies need worming at 8 weeks, so a vet should be consulted for advice on this and any vaccinations which may be required. Puppies need four meals a day at 8 weeks and the number of meals decreases as the amount they eat increases. At 4 months, three meals a day are enough; at 8 months, two meals a day; and at between 12 and 18 months the puppy is usually ready to start adult feeding once a day.

House training. This should be started as soon as the dog comes home. The puppy's need to urinate and defecate should be anticipated so that he can be taken outside. When he does this on his own, he should be praised. Unfortunately some dogs have *Toxocara* larva infection and produce faeces containing worm eggs. Children can contract the disease if they eat dirt or play in an area which has been contaminated by infected dog faeces. This disease is rare, but many people object strongly to fouling of pavements, parks and public areas and in some states of America there are special dog lavatories which are an attempt to hygienically dispose of dog faeces. Until these are part of the environment in the UK, dog owners must ensure that their dog's faeces are removed from areas where children play, and that the dog is wormed regularly by a vet. .

The dog should have its own kennel outside or a basket in the kitchen for sleeping. Parents who are considering the purchase of a dog should remember its need for exercise and ensure that someone will always be willing to take the dog out! Dogs should be kept away from babies as they may lick them and infection may be passed on. Crawling babies should be kept away from dog food bowls, and leftover baby food should not be given to dogs as this often encourages them to join in at meal times. Dogs should continually be checked for fleas, parasites and skin disorders and a vet consulted if these occur.

Cats

Cats tend to be more independent and less demanding than dogs. They should be bought when they are between 8 and 12 weeks of age when they are weaned and starting to eat solid food. At first they should have four meals a day, two of cereals and milk and two of meat, fish or egg. As they grow older this can be reduced to two larger meals each day. The kitten should have a health check by a vet and relevant vaccinations arranged. Cats should be neutered before they are 6 months old and so prevent unwanted litters. A dirt tray should be provided for them and young kittens will scratch in this before they defecate. They can soon be encouraged to dig in the garden outside. A cat bed, scratch board and cat door for access are essentials.

If there is a baby in the house, cats must be carefully watched as they like sleeping in warm places and could easily settle on a baby's face in a cot or pram and cause suffocation. A cat net must be used and it should be firm enough to prevent cats from scratching holes in it.

Plants

Living plants in the garden can be watched with the teacher helping the children to be aware of changes. Garden weeds can be watched as they produce flowers and seeds, e.g. dandelion 'clocks'. Trees and shrubs can be watched through the stages of early buds, bursting buds, leaves, flowers and fruit (if any). Evergreens can be watched and characteristics of needles, new growth and cones examined. A small garden plot where children can plant, water and watch their own seeds or bulbs develop is fascinating, particularly if they grow lettuces, onions, potatoes and carrots and are able to eat the results of their labours. A real digging hole can help the children discover the qualities of soil through feeling, handling and lifting.

Indoor plants

Growing plants inside the nursery gives the children an opportunity for close observation of changes and growth. A magnifying glass in the science corner makes it easy for the children to see the small details.

General potting instructions. Soil mixture can be used for most plants. Two parts garden loam to one part peat moss or potting fibre can be bought in larger stores.

1 Cover the hole in the bottom of a flower pot with pieces of broken pottery or a stone.
2 Place a thin layer of pebbles or broken pottery in the bottom of the pot to a depth of ½ inch (1.5 cm).
3 Add a piece of charcoal to maintain the sweetness of the water and soil.
4 Half fill the pot with soil.
5 Place the plant in the pot and add soil to a depth of ½ inch (1.5 cm) below the top of the rim. Firm the soil around the roots so that maximum contact has been made.
6 Add water and place the pot in a shaded area for 2 or 3 days.

Seeds

Beans (broad beans) and peas. Each child could grow his own bean or pea plant and the exercise becomes more enjoyable as they vie with each other to see how fast the roots and stem of their plant grows. Fortunately they do sprout and grow quickly so children are not left wondering if the seed will ever grow. The bean or pea should be placed in a glass jar between a piece of blotted paper (rolled round to fit inside) and the jar. There should be a little water in the glass to keep the blotter moist. If placed in a warm cupboard they will sprout more quickly. Some can be planted in soil on a shallow tray to show how quickly they grow in comparison.

Grass and oats. These grow very rapidly in soil (about a week), or in sponge or sand. If grass and oats seeds are planted before Easter in individual pots or containers they can be used as 'nests' for Easter eggs.

Mustard and cress seeds. These are great fun as they grow quickly on blotting paper, felt squares, cottonwool or lint (not pink). When they have grown sufficiently, the children can have cress sandwiches or use the cress as an addition to salads and baked potatoes.

Grapefruit, orange and lemon seeds. These should be rolled in newspaper and moistened, then sealed in wax paper or plastic to prevent evaporation and placed in a warm spot. The package should be opened every week to check moisture and the seedlings houseplanted into pots when the roots are 1 inch (2.5 cm) long.

The *dispersal and transportation* of seeds by wind, water and animals should be demonstrated by a collection of each type made on walks. Sycamore and ash seeds have natural 'wings' for their dispersal by wind, burrs of thistles or into flowers. They stick to the woolly coats of sheep and others, and are carried knowingly or otherwise by humans on nature treks. Those carried by water have to be in a natural container that will float unless they are seeds of ferns, mosses and bullrushes which will grow in swampy ground.

Rooting mediums are usually sand, soil mixture or water. If sand is used, it should be sterilized beforehand. Water is quite effective and when cuttings are placed in a glass container the children can observe the root development. Plants which root best in water include ivy, coleus, pussywillow, geranium, wandering sailor, begonia and African violet (the leaf of this should be kept out of the water by inserting it through a cardboard circle). A little charcoal keeps the water sweet.

Carrot tops. About ½ inch (1.5 cm) should be cut from the top of the carrot. The mature leaves are removed and the slice put into a shallow dish of water. The children will enjoy watching the development of the green feathery leaves.

Bulbs

Narcissus bulbs. These are best placed on stones in water about November, in order to produce January blooms. They should be left in a cool, dark place until the roots develop. Alternatively, the bulb can be planted in 2½ inches (6.25 cm) of soil with the pointed end upwards. General planting instructions should be followed. The bulbs should be placed in the dark at 45–50 °F for 2 months to allow root development, watered sparingly and brought into full light gradually. Watering can be increased as the leaves grow, but the soil should *never* be saturated.

Tulip bulbs. These should be planted so that points are 1 inch below soil surface level. Directions given above should be followed. October planting is recommended for January blooms.

Hyacinth bulbs. These should have points *above* the soil surface. They should be kept cool and dark for 3 months, brought into sunlight when the flower stock is 3 inches high (7.5 cm), and watered sparingly until the leaves appear.

Daffodils. These may be planted with pointed ends extending above soil surface in both soil or peat moss. They should be kept cool for 2 months and the procedure given above followed. After blooming is over, the daffodil bulbs can be restored to full vigour in a year's time by planting outdoors.

Natural Events and Materials

Whenever children express an interest in any of the everyday things around them, the teacher nursery nurse will make the most of the opportunity to guide the child to explore further. Occasionally the teacher nursery nurse may arrange for an experiment to demonstrate a point, e.g. the 'skin' on the water's surface which supports a needle or pin and provides a rink for the water-skater insect, but this is always done in an informal way. The following points can be developed to encourage an enquiring attitude towards basic scientific knowledge.

Water

Experiments to discover some of the properties of water:

1 Some things will float – which? Cork, stone, paper, empty tins, yoghurt cartons and full tins can all be tried.
2 Water runs downhill – holes or low areas in the play yard, streams on slopes, rain runs down the window.
3 Some things absorb water – try blotter, linoleum, sand, concrete (paint with water on different surfaces).
4 Water evaporates – water disappears from a shallow pan, steam disappears from a kettle.

5 Water dissolves some things – try salt, sand, ice, flour.
6 Water freezes and expands. Fill a jar with water and put the top on tightly. Place the jar on a window ledge overnight to freeze. Similarly, leave out a full milk bottle with a cardboard stopper. Try freezing water with salt or anti-freeze in it. Take a tray of ice cubes out of the refrigerator to melt.
7 Water condenses on a cold jug of water, and on glass placed over a plant. Where does it come from?

Rain, mist and storms

What causes cloud? Observe kinds of clouds. Observe the rain on the window; drops running together. Observe the effect of the wind in rain. Observe streamlets on slopes.

Look for a rainbow.

Watch patterns of lightning – what is it? What is thunder? Why don't we hear it right after seeing lightning?

Imitate rain and thunder sounds; soft and loud noises.

Link with rhymes, songs, activity games: 'Singing in the Rain' 'Raindrops are falling on my head', 'Somewhere over the rainbow', 'Pitter, pitter patter goes the falling rain', 'Rain, rain go away'.

Snow, ice and frost

What causes snow? Observe snowflake patterns under a microscope.

Note the lightness of fresh snow and its heaviness after a few days. Observe what happens to a bowl of snow taken indoors. Put a thermometer in it and watch. Then put the melted snow outside to see if it turns into snow again.

Observe icicles. Observe them dripping on a warm day. Bring one down to the children's level and tie it where they can really see it. Breathe on the window on a cold day, then observe the condensation or frost designs on the window. Use a thermometer to check the temperature of ice.

Sun

Place a thermometer in the sun and then in the shade. Make shadows with leaf, flower, etc. Note shadows of the building. Note how the shades change during the day. Use a prism to see what happens in the sun.

Wind

Demonstrate that wind is movement of the air by fanning with a paper. Watch streamers in the water. Blow bubbles in the breeze.

Watch how the wind turns a pinwheel and a model windmill, and explain simply how these are used in flour mills in Holland.

Listen to the sound of gentle and strong winds. Imitate them.

Notice wind in trees, smoke, a fluttering scarf, leaves, papers, Watch dandelion seeds carried by the wind. Fly a kite. Wet your finger to feel which way the wind is blowing. Feel the wind push you on a windy day.

Magnifying glass

A few of these are useful in the science corner for close observation of leaf patterns, parts of flowers, stones and other objects of interest.

Magnets

Discover magnetic and non-magnetic substances by experimenting with a variety of materials: iron filings, pins, needles, plastic and wooden beads. Exercise care to ensure that needles and pins do not cause harm.

Sound

We are surrounded by a sea of sound, and there is not a moment of the day when we cannot hear some sound. Experiment with reproducing and creating sound. Encourage children to listen for sounds of high and low pitch on a musical instrument.

Feel vibrating drums and vibrating strings on the autoharp. Produce sounds by tapping on different objects such as wood, metal and plastic. Listen, then imitate sounds in nature and mechanical sounds.

Exploration of Natural Haunts

Visits to woods, the seashore or a pond enable children to observe creatures in their natural surroundings. Each adult should have a small group only, as this means more attention can be given to the children's discoveries as they look, listen, smell and feel in the open air. There may be logs to turn over to see what is underneath, a stream or a pond in which to search for minnows or frog spawn, branches to swing on, grass to

run in, sounds to hear, insects to watch crawling and birds to watch flying, fragrances to enjoy, soft moss or leaves to roll in. Jars and baskets should be taken to gather all the objects to bring home. Leaves, cones, seeds, feathers, bark and pieces of sheep's wool will all have a place in the science corner. A visit to a farm or a zoo helps children to see familiar and unfamiliar animals in their natural or simulated habitat and gives them an idea of relative sizes (not always clear in picture books).

On a farm the children can watch the processes involved in milk production, see how cereals begin as plants and possibly how butter and cheese are produced. Extension of vocabulary results from naming animals and comprehension increases as they see the difference between rough and smooth hides, big and little, large, tall, hungry, greedy animals. New smells, sights and sounds heighten the senses and walking in fresh air makes the child alert and able to derive maximum benefit from the outing. If the children live near a field, seasonal changes can be observed in hedgerows where numerous insects, worms, wild flowers and weeds flourish.

A visit to the seaside

Preparations for the visit (similar points can be made on visits to the zoo, farm or park) should include a story or perhaps a discussion of a television programme or film strip about sea animals or birds. A seaside word book could be kept if the children are learning to read and the adult should plan beforehand how the visit will be used to expand comprehension as well as vocabulary. There should be groups of four or five children with each adult for maximum individual benefit.

Physical benefits. Suitable clothing should be chosen and parents of children on a nursery visit should be asked beforehand to dress the child sensibly for the outing. A light cotton teeshirt and shorts with swimming trunks for boys, cotton dresses and swimsuits for girls. The youngest children may want to sleep or rest if they have had an early rise, so cushions and rugs can be brought for them. A minibus is often used for an outing of this kind and some seats can be used for small chidren who want to sleep. Quiet games such as guessing types of cars or names of animals can be used to prevent boredom or restlessness. Desire for noise can be channelled into singing. Each child can be given a paper bag to hold his own rubbish to prevent too much mess. If the journey lasts longer then 30–40 minutes a stop will have to be made for toilet usage, unless the bus has a toilet. All these factors will enable the children to benefit from the journey as well as the seaside.

Picnic meals can be prepared with the children's help. Sandwiches should contain nutritious items such as cheese (proteins, vitamins A and D, calcium, phosphorus), tomatoes (vitamins A and C) and watercress (vitamin C). Potato crisps, an apple or orange with a portion of nuts and raisins are also nutritionally beneficial and enjoyable. Drinks of milk and orange juice taken after food should help to eliminate the desire for fizzy drinks which may make some children sick. Dry biscuits are also useful to prevent sickness. At the seaside the children can run, hop, skip, jump and play in the sand, benefiting from exercise in the fresh air and if possible sunshine.

Exploration of rock pools with an adult can help balance and small muscle control as the children collect shells and seaweed. Water and sand play take on a new meaning as they venture into the cold sea water, play at chasing the waves, and notice the difference between the cold, wet sand under the water and the warm, dry sand of the beach which clings to their wet feet, legs, arms and body. Filling and emptying sand-buckets and building sandcastles helps hand–eye coordination. When they return home the poem about 'Sand between the toes' is greeted with glee as they recall the sensation and perhaps the difficulty parents had removing it in the bath! Most beaches have a wide expanse and the feeling of space for unrestricted movement delights those children who come from cramped houses.

Sand-between-the-toes

I went down to the shouting sea,
Taking Christopher down with me,
For Nurse had given us sixpence each —
And down we went to the beach.

We had sand in the eyes and the ears and the nose,
And sand in the hair, and sand-between-the-toes.
Whenever a good nor'-wester blows,
Christopher is certain of
Sand-between-the-toes.

The sea was galloping grey and white;
Christopher clutched his sixpence tight;
We clambered over the humping sand —
And Christopher held my hand.

We had sand in the eyes and the ears and the nose,
And sand in the hair, and sand between-the-toes.
Whenever a good nor'-wester blows,
Christopher is certain of
Sand-between-the-toes.

There was a roaring in the sky;
The sea-gulls cried as they blew by,
We tried to talk, but had to shout —
Nobody else was out.

When we got home we had sand in the hair,
In the eyes and the ears and everywhere;
Whenever a good nor'-wester blows,
Christopher is found with
Sand-between-the-toes.

*From *When We Were Very Young* by A.A. Milne. (Reprinted by permission of Methuen Children's Books.)

Intellectual benefits. The child learns about contrasting environments as he travels on the bus to the seaside. His senses of sight, smell, touch, taste and hearing are developed as he lies on the sand or sits in the water, listens to the sea and the gulls, notices the different shapes, colours and sizes of shells and rocks. New words and new meanings of words will accompany his discoveries as he finds tiny animals that live in the sand or on rocks and in pools, observes the birds' nests and the visits made by food-bearing parents to baby fledglings, and admires the natural patterns made by the sea on the sand, which he will then try to imitate. He may ask questions about how birds fly, how fish live in water, how ships stay upright in water and other wondrous matters which can probably be explained more fully when they return to the nursery and the science corner to discover for themselves which things float.

Social benefits. The children enjoy group activities on the bus and games on the sand. They learn in simple ways how to share, to admire other children's handiwork, and to rely on them for company and support as they venture into the water with the adults' supervision.

Emotional benefits. The child is able to overcome any fears he may have about bus travel or the sea water. Splashing about in the water, demolishing (his own!) sandcastles, and running about without restriction all help as release of tension and frustration. Pounding sand into shapes and kicking a beachball around provide an acceptable outlet for anger and aggression. Positive enjoyment and fun in such an amenable environment can literally cause him to jump for joy.

After the visit the children will be happily tired and ready to enjoy a good night's sleep, looking forward to returning to the nursery to talk and laugh for many days to come about their exciting adventures at the seaside.

Treasures for the nature corner

These may be found on country walks or by turning out cupboards. Examples of these are pine cones, acorns, chestnuts, seeds, seed pods, shells, cocoons, birds' nests, berries, leaves, postcards, pictures of animals and birds, and magnets.

Poisonous Plants

The discovery of wild flowers, different trees and plants is an exciting part of visits to parks and woods. However, a number of wild flowers and hedgerow plants have poisonous leaves, berries or seeds and it is important that children can recognize these to avoid mishaps and fatalities.

Parents and others responsible for children should make themselves familiar with poisonous plants and thumb through coloured reference books which can be purchased quite cheaply. Their knowledge, passed on to children, may save lives.

Project On Discovery Of The Environment

Where possible, and with the cooperation of placement staff, nursery nurses should link their college theory to practice. In a module based on the above theme, nursery nurses can use their own observation and books available in the college library to discover and identify trees, plants, flowers and other growing things in the environment of the college and the placement. They can then introduce the theme into the nursery, with a discovery/nature table to which children can be encouraged to contribute, and by taking small groups of children (as allowed) on walks in the park, or just around the area.

Children can be encouraged to utilize their full senses on these exploratory walks, and bring their treasures back to share with others in the class. After the 'nature' part of the project, other aspects of the environment can be discovered, as outlined here. Students may be fortunate to be in a placement near a building site, in which case item 4 on the programme (Table 8.2) becomes more meaningful. Mortar can be mixed, using cement powder, sand and water. Books on almost every topic here can be made by the nursery nurse, and she can gauge their success when she introduces them to the children in the nursery.

Local police, nurses and firemen are usually very obliging when asked to visit the nursery, and their visits serve to remove any fear the children may have of uniformed adults which could be useful if the children ever needed their help.

Table 8.1 Poisonous plants and fungi

Apple pips	Contain elements of prussic acid. If eaten in large quantities they can be fatal. Refer to hospital.
Black bryony	Very common in hedgerows and twines round other plants. Clusters of bright scarlet berries it produces are deadly poisonous. *Urgent referral to hospital.*
Daffodil	Bulbs can cause nausea and vomiting if ingested. Refer to doctor.
Deadly nightshade	This has shiny black berries like blackcurrants, which attract children, but even two or three can be fatal if ingested. *Urgent referral to hospital.*
Hemlock	The leaves of this look like parsley and the seeds resemble a cooking herb. The hollow stalks make 'peashooters', but these can be dangerous and should be avoided.
Monkshood	The most dangerous British plant. The roots resemble horseradish, but they contain aconite, a deadly poison. *Urgent referral to hospital.*
Laburnum	The pods hang down very temptingly from the trees, but they contain brown seeds which cause burning in the mouth, vomiting, diarrhoea, irregular pulse and respiration, possibly convulsions and death. The child should be made to vomit. *Urgent referral to hospital.*
Laurel	Ingestion can cause vomiting, convulsions, slow pulse, low blood pressure. *Urgent referral to hospital.*
Lupin	Ingestion can cause paralysis, depressed respiration and convulsions. *Urgent referral to hospital.*
Mushrooms	Wild mushrooms must never be eaten until an expert opinion is obtained as to their nature. When a suspect mushroom has been eaten, a sample of the same mushroom should be taken with the child to hospital.
Rhododendron	Poisonous and can cause vomiting, convulsions, lowered blood pressure and paralysis. *Urgent referral to hospital.*
Rhubarb	The leaves contain oxalic acid, which can cause vomiting, diarrhoea, haemorrhages. Refer to hospital.
Yew	This tree is often seen in churchyards. It has brilliant red berries containing seeds which are fatal if eaten. *Urgent referral to hospital.*

Table 8.2

Teaching programme in college	Assignments
1 Introduction to second half of module. Values and benefits to the child of discovery and learning about local environment. Log books. Book list.	1 Revision of developmental aspects and effects of stimuli provided by natural and man-made environments. Books used in nursery.
2 Types of environment. Walks around the area of the placement for observations of buildings, road.	2 Help in arranging walks for children around the area of the placement to observe buildings and roads.
3 Visit to a farm.	3 Help in planning visit to a farm or in 'bringing the farm to the classroom' if a visit is impossible.
4 Looking at buildings, sizes, shapes, functions, materials used. Mixing 'mortar'.	4 Activities planned and carried out relating to buildings, materials, and mixing mortar, sand, etc.
5 Houses – types. Compare with animal 'houses'. Water, gas, electricity supplies. Book to be made.	5 Implement theme of houses in practical play. Help arrange walks to observe different types of housing in the area.
6 Shops – types. Games for children – relating workers to shops, shopping lists. Video.	6 Activities arranged by student relating to shops – developed as a theme. Help in planning shopping trip with small group of children.
7 Schools – sizes, functions, numbers in area. Modes of travel to school. Public transport.	7 Developing theme of 'schools'. Modes of transport. Help in arranging bus trip.
8 Visits of police, nurse, fire service– how to arrange, prepare and follow-up. 'People in our Community'.	8 Assist in planning visits of community personnel as opposite. Preparation and follow-up.
9 Roads – types, road signs, road safety. Names of roads (streets, lanes).	9 Develop theme of roads – language, pre-numeracy ideas.
10 Water supplies and rubbish disposal.	10 Discovery of nursery's supply of water. If possible help with visit to reservoir or refuse tip.

Teaching road safety also comes as a natural part of the discovery walks, and if children learn it in this way they will come to observe safety rules automatically, which could protect them at some stage when they cross roads on their own.

Assignments will be given by the College Tutor but it is hoped that these will be seen as examples of what the student might be doing and that she is encouraged to gain maximum experience in the various stages.

9

The Role of the Nursery Nurse

The nursery nursing qualification is NNEB (England), i.e. National Nursery Examination Board, and SNNB (Scottish Nursery Nurses' Board) in Scotland.

As a nursery nurse, on completion of her training, is qualified in child care for babies and young children up to 7 years (8 years in Scotland), it follows that the scope for employment in areas where child care is involved, is very wide (Table 9.1).

The role of the nursery nurse in society should be encouraged and seen as invaluable, regardless of any economic climate or trend.

Nursery teachers in some areas are now working as Educational Home Visitors. They visit families who may have problems and require help in learning to play with their children. The family may live in a rural area without access to nursery school, or the children may have special needs. Nursery nurses may be employed to assist nursery teachers in this task.

Table 9.1 Employment options for nursery nurses

1 *Local Education Authority Schools*
Nursery schools
Infant and primary schools
Special schools
Day nurseries/nursery/child centres

2 *Local Social Services Facilities*
Day nurseries
Residential care
Home visiting
Childminding

3 *Hospitals*
Maternity units
Special care baby units
Children's wards
Special hospitals

4 *Private Sector*
Nanny
Private schools
Holiday industry
Crèches (e.g. colleges, hospitals, industry)
Working abroad

Obviously, maturity is required in this work, as it involves confidentiality.

Working as a Nursery Nurse

When applying for a job and completing an application form, remember that this is the first representative of you that the prospective employer will see. Always add any personal experience you have had during your training, such as a placement with special needs children, any voluntary work, babysitting, and any particular skills and interests, like playing the guitar or aerobics. Your reasons for wanting the post should also be given. Make sure you understand details of the job, including hours, time off, salary, but obviously you need to find out first about the establishment, the staff, hierarchy (i.e. Officer in Charge, Senior Nursery Officer, Third in Charge, Student Supervisor, Nursery assistants and ancillaries), any rules and regulations which affect the children and staff, number of children, how they are grouped, daily timetable and shiftworking.

Local Education Authority Schools

The Department of Education and Science (and Scottish Education Department) recognizes the NNEB and SNNB certificates for employment in education.

Nursery schools and nursery classes. Here, the nursery nurse will be a Nursery Assistant working alongside and assisting the nursery teacher. While the teacher retains overall responsibility, the nursery nurse participates in planning and carrying out the programme of activities, taking groups of children for story-telling and outdoor activities.

Primary schools. Nursery nurses are more frequently employed today in primary classes with children of 5–7 years (8 years in Scotland), where they participate in all aspects of the primary school programme.

Special schools. Nursery nurses are greatly in demand here. Children in these schools may have physical disabilities or learning difficulties.

Family centres. These may be run jointly by local education and social service departments and effectively combine both nursery school and day-care provision under one roof. Open all day and also during the school holidays, these centres provide for the children of working parents and offer both flexibility and continuity in their programme. The centre requires good accommodation and staffing, and nursery nurses will work closely with teachers and social services staff as a team.

Local Social Service Facilities

The NNEB/SNBB is also recognised for employment by the DHSS.

Day nurseries/Children's centres. These are run and staffed by nursery nurses known as Nursery Officers. Here, under fives are cared for all day when it is not possible for them to remain at home. Staff are involved in shiftwork and children of all ages are mixed together. The success of each nursery depends greatly upon the training and experience of the nursery nurses.

Hospitals

Maternity units. Nursery nurses are often employed to assist midwives in looking after newly delivered mothers and their babies. Work here involves caring for babies and helping mothers with breast or bottle feeding. There is a certain amount of routine work – bathing, weighing, preparing feeds – and shift duty, but the nursery nurse may find satisfaction in the care of newborn babies.

Special care baby units. These are intensive care units for babies who need constant 24-hour-a-day care and supervision. The babies will (usually) be in incubators and be premature, postmature, undernourished or ill. Nursery nurses will form part of a very close team of

parents, paediatric nurses, general nurses, midwives and paediatricians.

Children's wards. When children are ill in hospital they require even more mothering, attention and opportunity for play than they do when at home. The nursery nurse has a valuable role here, encouraging feeding and drinking, helping with bathing and dressing, and most importantly, providing play facilities for sick children.

Private Sector

Nanny. Many nursery nurses are now choosing to work in the private family situation as a nanny. Often, the mother is working, or the child may have special needs which are best met by a nanny.

There are a number of good agencies, many of whom advertise in the local press and journals such as *Nursery World* and *The Lady*, and some nursery nurses prefer to register with these, rather than reply to an advertising employer directly. Before paying a registration fee it is wise to find out whether the agency will obtain a job which will be better than one you can obtain for yourself. Sometimes employers who register with agencies have to agree to certain conditions laid down by the agency, which prevents discrepancies between what is promised at interview and the reality when the employment begins. Whether using an agency or not, it is most important that conditions of work such as hours of duty, time off, salary, personal conveniences (own quarters, use of car, etc.) should be made clear on both sides by the drawing up of a contract, which must be signed by employer(s) and employee. The period of notice should also be specified, to ensure that pay is given in lieu of notice when the family moves away or terminates the employment for any other reason. This also gives the employers time to find another nanny if the nanny wishes to terminate employment. A trained nursery nurse should command a good salary, and if she 'lives in', as is most usual, an amount will be deducted, or taken into consideration, when salary is determined. There is no point in accepting the same salary as an untrained nanny would be offered, and the nursery nurse should check with other nannies and agencies before agreement is reached. If any housekeeping duties are required (beyond the reasonable duties concerned with cleaning and care of the child's or children's rooms, clothes and provision of meals), an enhanced salary should be offered.

Where the nanny is required to look after a newborn baby from birth onwards, experience during training in a maternity hospital or even in a private family with young babies (and this type of practical placement is now part of some college courses) will now prove useful. Care of a new baby is very tiring, particularly if the baby wakes frequently during the night, and off-duty time becomes essential if the nanny is to remain in peak form. The off-duty times should be decided upon before employment begins. It is not ideal for the nanny to have to dress and feed baby and/or children before she can leave for her 'day off'. In some places there are now groups of nannies who arrange to meet regularly to discuss problems or just exchange news, which is a useful safety valve for those who feel homesick or lonely. 'Nannies need Nannies' is one such group, and support from friends in similar situations is always valuable. One problem that nannies face is emotional involvement with the baby or child in their care. This is not harmful, but if a nanny becomes too attached she may find it very difficult to move on, even when it is right for her to do so. Another problem can arise from these attachments in that the natural mother may come to resent the affection shown by the child towards the nanny. This calls for considerable maturity from the nanny, who should try to appreciate parent's feelings for their child.

Private schools. Private nurseries and schools are often keen to employ nursery nurses in some capacity. Duties and responsibilities will vary according to the establishment.

Holiday industry. Holiday companies who run cruises or holiday camps offer programmes for children while allowing the parents to relax in a variety of settings. Hence, there are job opportunities here for trained nursery nurses.

Crèches. Rather like day nurseries, these are facilities for baby and child care situated in the work place, e.g. factory, hospital, university.

Working abroad. The British nanny has an outstanding reputation and work abroad is frequently available. The opportunity to learn another language and appreciate a different culture is often regarded as an additional attraction to the job.

The United States and Canada are popular for nannying posts, but a work permit and visa must be obtained before accepting a job. This is often difficult to obtain. For European posts, it is wise to have some basic knowledge of the language. Arrangements should also be made for a 'trial period' and return fare if the post proves unsatisfactory.

Before taking up a post, nursery nurses should ensure

(a) that they have a contract, giving clear details of working hours, time off, exact duties (these should relate only to the care of child/children, their clothes nursery equipment and meals), and salary.

(b) that they have a work permit/visa for posts in the United States, Canada and European countries.

10

The Prevention of Accidents and First Aid

Prevention of Accidents

Accidents cause more deaths in children aged 1–14 years than any other factor. Road accidents involving motor vehicles are the most common, but of all the accidental deaths which occur in the home, fire is the major cause.

Factors which contribute to accidents can be described as human or environmental. *Human factors* include:

1 ignorance, sometimes culpable, as in the case of a nursery nurse who could make herself familiar with safety precautions and neglects to do so;
2 carelessness and lack of observation, sometimes due to fatigue or worry which are often predisposing factors to accidents;
3 illness, which affects alertness;
4 influence of drugs or alcohol – many mothers nowadays take tranquillizers which can influence their accident proneness;
5 disobedience of safety regulations which are often clearly displayed and explained to staff.

Environmental factors include:

1 siting of buildings and outdoor play areas, e.g. proximity to main roads and traffic can increase the risk of road accidents;
2 lack of gates or doors to prevent children wandering out of the room or building;
3 internal arrangements in the home or the nursery, e.g. playroom next to cooking area, kitchen or bathroom;
4 lack of gates at the top of a flight of stairs;
5 kitchen, bathrooms and bedrooms unsafe;
6 furniture, cots, beds, bedding, fixed toys, windows, heaters, play equipment;
7 clothing, footwear;
8 cleaning and cooking equipment, safe storage of sharp knives and scissors.

It would take a whole book to explain all the precautions which can be taken to prevent accidents so we can only consider some of the most common ones here.

Choking and Suffocation (or Asphyxia)

This can be avoided if care is taken in the choice of bedding initially, and careful attention paid to putting a baby or child to bed. It is important that the cot stands firmly as the child could slip to one side and suffocate if the cot is unbalanced. It should preferably not have bars, but if it has bars the space between them should not exceed 3 inches (7.5 cm) to prevent the child poking his head through: subsequent struggling could cause asphyxiation.

If the mattress is plastic it should be covered firmly to prevent the child's face coming into contact with plastic which can cause suffocation. The mattress should fill the cot when made up, to ensure that the baby cannot become wedged between the mattress and the cot. Pillows are not necessary for children under 1 year of age, and after that a safety pillow should be used. Blankets should be light, but without loops and fringes which the child could play with, pull over his head, or trap his fingers in and entangle round his face. Similarly, open weave nylon cardigans and those with ribbons or cords threaded through should be avoided, as they could catch on a knob on the cot or pram and cause strangulation as they pull tight around the baby's neck. It can also endanger the blood supply to the baby's fingers, if they become wound tightly through holes in nylon material.

Large, fluffy toys should never be allowed in the cot or in the child's bed. Mobiles should not be hung too close to the baby's face, and soft balls are best kept away from the cot. Wrapping

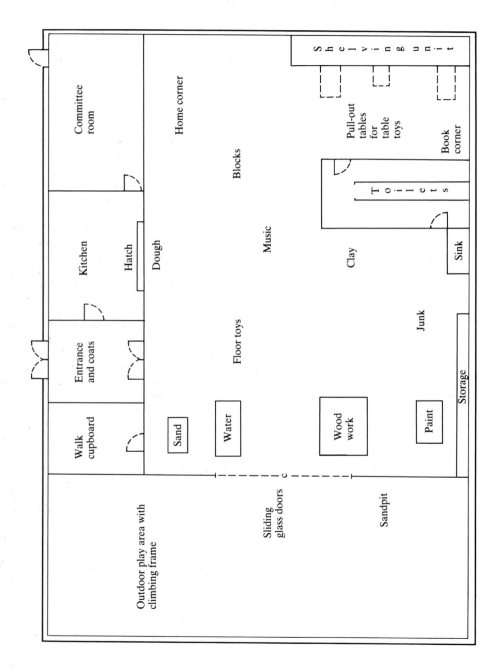

Figure 10.1   Orderly layout of the nursery helps to prevent accidents.

the baby firmly in a shawl before putting him into the cot not only prevents suffocation but increases his feelings of security. Some older babies kick off the blankets, so sleeping suits may be used, or bags (designed to prevent the possibility of suffocation). If the sleeping bag is too big, with the possibility that the baby could snuggle down too far, a rolled-up sheet or towel should be put at the bottom of the bag.

It is thought better to place the baby on his stomach or side rather than on his back, so that any milk which dribbles from his mouth will not run back down his throat and choke him. However, most normal babies move their heads to a comfortable breathing position whichever way they are placed. Parents are advised not to have the baby in bed with them in case they fall asleep and the baby is 'overlaid' by one of them and is suffocated. Care must also be taken in feeding practices to avoid the danger of suffocation. Babies should never be left on their own with a feeding bottle propped up against their mouths while lying in their cots or prams. Not only can they inhale vomitus but the milk itself can pass into the Eustachian tube which leads from the throat to the middle ear.

Small items such as beads, eyes of toys, coins and even peanuts can all cause choking when they are taken into the baby's mouth, which is fairly common in babies under 1 year, as the mouth is the organ of discovery for them. Dummies should not be attached by a long cord or ribbon to the baby's clothing.

If cats are kept as pets and allowed to roam near where baby is sleeping, a cat net must be placed over the cot or pram to prevent the cat falling or jumping into it and resting on the baby's face. Obviously, when the baby is sleeping indoors, pets should be kept out of the room.

Plastic bags, which are used to pack everything from food to nappies these days, are extremely dangerous if left lying around. Young children can easily pull them over their heads when playing, and due to the large number of cases of suffocation which have resulted, many bags carry written warnings of the danger, and in many instances have ventilation holes. The inner sleeves of records left around by teenagers can have the same harmful effect on small children as plastic bags.

Falling Accidents

These are common both inside the home and nursery and without. Children rarely fall from climbing frames, though onlooking adults often fear they will, but they seem to know just how far they can safely go! However if the frame is unstable, slippery or has splinters or nails protruding, and a number of children are playing on it at the same time, they could fall from it. It is best to place climbing frames on grass rather than concrete if possible, to soften the fall if it does occur. Garden tools should not be left around. The same precaution should apply to swings and roundabouts. As young children will try to climb walls, trees and anything which can be climbed, adult supervision in outdoor play is essential. Restrainers may be used for those babies who try to climb out of their prams, but these must be short bands and really firm to prevent risk of strangulation.

Indoors, chairs and furniture should not be placed near windows or near taller pieces. Windows should not be left open without safety catches. All furniture should also be steady to reduce the risk of falls. Children who have just learnt to walk often stumble and fall, so it is sensible not to have loose rugs, highly polished floors and large toys lying around in case they hurt themselves. A non-slip mat should be used in the bath. Where there are steps leading into the house or room, children should be taught how to climb up and down without falling, and strong gates should be placed at the top and bottom of stairways as exploratory crawlers can often fall when their mothers are not around. Obviously constant supervision is not always feasible, so children should be taught to crawl downstairs backwards to help prevent falls. Stools and small chairs should not be in the bathroom as the child could climb up and fall into the bath, which can be dangerous even when empty. Horizontal stair banisters can be very dangerous as children will attempt to climb them, so they should be boarded over. There should be no space left under the banisters for the child to fall through. Balconies are a feature of many blocks of flats, and the door leading to the balcony should be kept locked to prevent access by children.

Babies should never be left on a table top or beside a sink top in the middle of bathing, as they easily roll off. Bouncing cradles used by young babies must not be placed on a table or worktop either. Most baby high chairs have restrainers, and this should be used to prevent any possibility of the child falling out.

Burns and Electric Shock

Open fires are not too common nowadays, but when they are a feature of a living room a fine mesh guard, with a top, strong enough to resist knocking over and broad enough to cover the whole fireplace must be firmly secured in place. Fine mesh is important to prevent children poking sticks through it into the fire. Electric fires also require fireguards, even the one- or two-bar kind, which are usually sold with inadequate guard grills. Crawling babies can reach free-standing electric heaters and put their hands through the bars, so every gas and electric heater should have a safety guard (this is a legal requirement for children under 12 years) preferably with a cover on top and fixed to the wall, to prevent children throwing flammable items over it. The tops of safety guards should never be covered with wet clothes and other items for drying, and clothes racks should not be propped up against the guard. Electric flexes should be carefully placed where no-one can trip over them, and never under carpets. Crawling babies and young children can bite electric flexes. Worn or frayed flexes should be replaced immediately. Paraffin heaters are not a good idea, as the portable variety can be knocked over and even when fixed these are considered a health risk by some doctors, particularly to children with susceptibility to respiratory conditions. Convector heaters rarely cause burns but storage heaters and radiators which become very hot should be guarded to prevent burns. Electric heaters should not be placed close to furniture or drying clothes. The old saying 'a burnt child fears the fire' should never be interpreted in practice as severe burns can cause permanant scarring and even death in young babies. Fires usually cause most danger by inhalation of smoke and of course severe shock. Mirrors should not be placed on walls above fires, as clothing may catch fire. Portable electric heaters should never be used in bathrooms or children's bedrooms and fixed models should be high up on the wall where children cannot reach them. The bathroom light switch should preferably be of the pull cord type.

In the kitchen or cookery corner, children should not be allowed near hot ovens or hotplates. While some mothers often have to work in the kitchen with young children around them, it is best if they can be kept in another play area or even in a playpen in the kitchen. When cooking with hot fat or oil, great care must be taken to see that the child is not within danger distance. Chip pan fires are very common, and one of the causes may be that the pan is too full. When a chip pan fire does occur, a wet cloth or the pan lid can be used to cover it before it spreads, but no attempt should be made to try and remove it from one place to another, as burns to the face and hair could result. Where kitchen windows are situated above the cooker or heater, it is best not to have curtains which extend beyond the sides and bottom of the window frame. A kitchen blind which covers only the glass is much safer here.

The television set and other household appliances should always be unplugged when not in use, and before the family go to bed. The back of the television set should never be removed, and the ventilation holes should always be left uncovered. Faults in wiring and sockets which are overloaded (e.g. where two or three items are plugged into one socket) can cause fires and electric shock and should be avoided. Children find electric plug sockets ideal for sticking fingers and other small objects into and it is a pity that house designers still place sockets at floor level. Dummy plugs and safety sockets are now widely used and these prevent the child from poking implements into the openings when the sockets are not in use. Some 4- and 5-year-old children are able to turn on television sets without any difficulty, but where a child has a fascination for plugs and sockets it may be wise to organize the furniture to prevent access. Every November in Britain large numbers of children are exposed to fire hazards as they celebrate Guy Fawkes on 5 November with fireworks and bonfires. All shops which sell fireworks now have to give copies of the *Fireworks Code* to children who buy them. Television adverts also carry warnings and children are told only to use fireworks if an adult is at hand, not to go near those which appear to be 'duds' in case they explode in the child's face, and to keep clear of bonfires. Fortunately, many parents are now holding safe firework displays for neighbourhood children, so casualties have decreased recently. Camping holidays can also be marred by outdoor fires caused by unsteady or leaking paraffin stoves, and these should be guarded with great care. Children should never have access to matches or lighters inside tents. Aerosol cans and flammable liquids should never be thrown into bonfires.

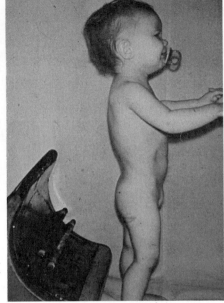

Figure 10.2   Four ways in which burns can occur.

Matches are often the cause of fires when young children experience the excitement of creating light by striking a match. Some people believe that children should be taught how to use matches correctly to prevent the novelty aspect but it is risky to leave matches or lighters in the hands of young children unless they are supervised. Non-flammable clothing has been widely used for children's pyjamas and nightdresses and this has helped to prevent a number of cases of burning. Nylon nightgowns with wide hems should be avoided as they can be a fire hazard even when the child is standing next to an electric fire, as can nightclothes made of flimsy cotton. All children's nightdresses and dressing gowns made in the UK have to conform to safety regulations and be treated if necessary to make them non-flammable, but care should be taken with those imported from other countries where these rules do not apply.

Electric blankets should be switched off before the child gets into bed, and should never be used where a child wets the bed. Gas and electric installations must never be adjusted, except by experts. Petrol should never be kept in plastic containers as it seeps through. Metal containers with petrol in should only be stored in the garage, never in the house. The family 'rubbish dump' of old papers, magazines and comics should not be under the stairs.

When decorating, polystyrene ceiling tiles should not be used as they give off poisonous fumes when they catch fire.

A fire extinguisher or fire blanket is useful, and should be kept in an easily accessible place.

Scalding

These accidents usually occur in the kitchen area too. Handles of pans on the cooker should always be turned inwards to prevent children reaching up and pulling the contents over themselves. Safety guards can be fitted over the top of the cooker. Kettles containing boiling water should be kept way out of reach and not carried over a child's head to the table. The flex leading from the socket to the kettle should be short to prevent the risk of the child pulling it. Children should be carefully watched when the teapot and cups of hot tea are on the table in case they pull the tablecloth and pour the hot liquids over them. Tablecloths which can be pulled off by a child should not be used, and hot drinks should be placed away from the edge of the table. Mugs, which have a broader base than tea-cups, are safer as they cannot be knocked over so easily, and adults should not carry hot drinks over a child's head. When filling a bath for a child, cold water should be put in first to prevent scalding and the temperature of the water should be tested with the adult's elbow. It should not exceed 90 °F.

If worktops are fitted to both sides of the cooker, there is no need to carry hot pans across the kitchen. The cooker should not be near a door or have cupboards fitted above it, as a child running across through a door or reaching up to get something from the cupboard may knock over a pan on the cooker. The kettle flex should be short and out of reach, to prevent the child from reaching it. Kettles which have automatic switches which turn off the current when the water is boiled are safer, since steam from a boiling kettle can cause serious scalds. The danger of scalding persists for half an hour after the water in the kettle or teapot has boiled.

Poisoning

Of all poisoning in children of up to 14 years who are admitted to hospital, 65% are caused by medicinal products. Unfortunately many numbers of families store a considerable number of pills, medicines and lotions after their prescribed course of treatment is over. Some pills also resemble children's sweets, hence their eagerness to taste them when they find a treasure trove. Nowadays, most pills are packed in child-proof containers but these tops are not always replaced correctly by the adult and many young children can open these with ease! Many mothers keep aspirin (which can be fatal to a young child) and tranquillizers in their handbags and take them in front of the children, which is not a good idea. Some types of antidiarrhoeal medicines are also harmful, and iron tablets are very toxic and require urgent hospital treatment. All used medication should be discarded after use and medicine cupboards must not only be placed above child height, but preferably kept locked. Cigarettes, too, can poison and should not be left on tables at child height. Cosmetics should be kept out of the reach of young children to whom a dressing table with a colourful array of jars and bottles represents a veritable Aladdin's cave. Nail varnish contains acetone, which is toxic, so should be locked away after use. In this age group 35% of poisoning cases are due to ingestion of common household items, 4% of these to petroleum products like lighter fuel, petrol and paraffin and, 5% to corrosive substances such as bleaches, drain cleaners which contain caustic soda and paint removers. Matches are dangerous only if a large quantity is taken, as in DIY putty. Of poisoning cases in children, 19% include ingestion of other non-medicinal substances which contain alcohol, dry-cleaning fluids which contain carbon tetrachloride or trichlorethylene, marker inks, lavatory blocks used in the bowl for deodorizing, dry cell batteries which contain mercuric chloride, paraquat (a weedkiller which is lethal if ingested) and lead. Disinfectants and household cleaners and weedkillers should be kept in childproof containers, not in lemonade bottles, and placed not under the kitchen sink where many toddlers like to explore but in a locked cupboard in the garage. In children of 1–14 years, 7% of cases relates to poisonous foodstuffs, including a number of plants, berries, flower seeds and leaves, all of which can be discovered by children during play in the garden or on walks to the park (see Table 8.1, p. 258).

Laurel leaves are deadly as are laburnum and lupin seeds. The berries of belladonna (or deadly nightshade) which look like blackcurrants, and daffodil bulbs which look like onions, are also poisonous. Common garden plants like rhododendrons and sweet pea are poisonous and, when ingested, require urgent hospital treatment. The leaves of rhubarb plants contain oxalic acid which can cause serious illness, and the wood, bark and seeds of yew trees (often found in public parks and gardens) are all poisonous and ingestion again requires urgent medical aid.

A large number of fungi are particularly poisonous and children should always be warned never to eat any plant which resembles a mushroom as this could well be the deadly *Amanita*. It is important for adults caring for children to be aware themselves of poisonous species of plants, and a small handbook illustrating these in colour should be found in every nursery.

Non-poisonous items

These include ballpen contents, pencils (the 'lead' in these is graphite, not lead), soaps, playdough, play putty, felt-tipped pens, crayons, bubble bath soaps, caps for toy pistols and candles.

Panic may ensue when a child bites a mercury thermometer, which is why under the tongue methods should not be used with children under 4 years who require temperature taking, but the only danger is if the glass cuts the mouth, since the small amount of mercury present is not harmful even if swallowed.

Dangers Around the Home, Nursery and Garden

Check toys and dolls with loose buttons or glass eyes which can be removed and swallowed by a child. Put all tiny ornaments, pins, needles and scissors away from little hands.

Stair carpet should be firmly fitted, and any holes or frayed parts should be promptly repaired. Toys and other objects should not be left lying around.

Garden gates should have a childproof catch.

Never run the car engine when the garage door is closed.

DIY enthusiasts should not allow children to be close at hand when they are sawing, sanding or spraying.

Small children on swings should always be supervised.

Ladders used indoors or out must have secure bases, fixed in firm footings.

Any animal excreta in gardens should be removed or dug well in, as certain worms (*Toxocara canis*) found in dogs' excrement can cause blindness if ingested by children.

Ponds and paddling pools should be completely and securely covered over when not in use, and usage restricted to times when an adult is present.

Cuts (Lacerations)

Accidents with glass, which can cause severe cuts and bleeding are very common and necessitate hospital treatment for some 7000 children in the UK every year. Many are caused by toddlers, who may be unsteady on their feet, falling through French windows or glass panels in doors, and older children who may rush around in rough play or crash through glass doors on their bikes. Ordinary glass is easily broken, and sharp, jagged pieces can cut like daggers. Glass doors are not a good idea in homes and nurseries with young children, and where they are present, the glass must be of the safety type. This is specially toughened and, like wired glass, it resists damage, so it is safer. Glass in lower parts of doors and full length should be covered with board, or covered in coloured strips to make it easily seen. Frosted or patterned glass is not safety glass just because it seems thicker than ordinary glass.

Children should not be asked to carry lemonade or milk bottles in case they drop them and fall onto the pieces. Sharp knives and tools should not be left about, and children should be taught to use scissors safely. All toys and play equipment must be constantly checked for sharp edges and protruding points. Children who wear glasses should be given plastic lenses, which are unbreakable, if possible.

Safety when Travelling with Children

Now that many parents take their children to school or shopping in the family car, it is essential that safety factors are observed. Ensure that the child in his pram, high chair or push chair has restraints to prevent him falling out. 'Reins' should be used to control toddlers when they are taken for walks in case they run out into the road. Carry-cots must be safe (see Choice of equipment) and, in the car, carrycots must be firmly fixed in with straps on the back seat, and the shelf above the seat should not contain any objects that could fall on the baby's face – this includes cushions! Cars should be fitted with childproof locks and children should always sit in the back of the car. Young children should be placed in specially designed safety seats attached to the back seat and which carry the British Standard safety mark (Kitemark). In no circumstances should a child be allowed to play about unrestrained or stand on the back seat of the car in case he is thrown about. If no children's safety seats are fixed in the car, the child will be safer in the front seat with an adult seat belt adjusted to fit him as far as possible. Motorists are usually advised never to sit children in the front seat of the car, but it can be

necessary if the alternative means unrestricted freedom and injury in the case of an accident with the child in the back seat of the car. Mothers carrying young babies are advised never to travel in the front seat of the car as the baby may be fatally injured if he is thrown forward in an accident, or trapped between the mother's body and the door or windscreen.

Children should never be allowed to wave their hands (or worse still put their heads) out of windows.)

Children should never be left in a closed car in hot weather, as they can easily overheat. When taking clothes home from the dry cleaners, ensure that the windows are open sufficiently to overcome the possible fumes from them. Cars should always be locked when in the garage or driveway, in case children want to be like Daddy or Mummy and take the handbrake off as a first move! Care must be taken when reversing the car to ensure that no children are behind.

Bikes, sometimes expensive models, are still the favourite Christmas present for many children, but the careful parent will ensure that the brakes, lights, tyres and reflectors are in good working order before use. If children are allowed to ride their bikes in the neighbourhood, they must learn road safety rules as it applies to cyclists. It is better if they can confine their cycling to waste land, as main roads are usually dangerous, and older people will be annoyed at bikes taking up all the space on pavements.

Road Safety

This is best demonstrated by example, rather than teaching as drill without understanding. Children should be taught the Green Cross code by example, and encouraged never to cross the road without thinking about it, as most accidents occur when they dash out in excitement. It is best if all children under the age of 10 years are forbidden to cross main roads without an adult.

1 Show the child how to cross the road, look to one side, then the other, listen (for sounds of cars, lorries and motor bikes approaching) and keep looking and listening as you cross the road.
2 Tell children always to wait for the lollipop man or woman and to use pedestrian crossings when available. At 5 years old he may be able to recognize the green and red man and explain what the signs and traffic lights mean.
3 Warn children never to dash out from behind

Figure 10.3   Child safety in the car.

a parked car and not to run in case he trips and falls.

4 Show children how to be extra careful on foggy days. Mothers should be asked to dress their children in light-coloured clothes with luminous armbands for dark mornings and afternoons.

Tufty Clubs, organized by the Royal Society for Prevention of Accidents (ROSPA) have books, kits and speakers who will visit play-groups and nurseries and provide help to mothers of young children to promote road safety. A local policeman may be invited to the nursery, and apart from learning about road safety, the children will quickly learn that they can approach him when in trouble or when they are 'lost'.

Drowning

Water holds great attraction for young children, whether in the bath, paddling pool or pond, and as they can drown in very little water, stringent precautions must be taken.

Some parents have a rain water trough in the garden, and if the child can climb into this, it should be removed or securely covered up.

Babies and toddlers should never be left in the bath while the adult goes off to answer the door-bell or tidy the bedroom, since this could be dangerous. The child should be lifted out, covered with a bath towel, and carried along.

Paddling in the garden pond or at the seaside must always be supervised by an adult. At the seaside, children should wear inflatable arm-bands or rings, and they must never be allowed to play by themselves with inflatable mattresses or dinghies, in case they float out to sea.

Children should be taught to swim as early as possible – classes for babies of weeks old are now held in a number of public swimming baths, at times when few swimmers are present. Mothers are usually amazed when the instructor tells them to throw the baby into the water, but this is not a cruel or silly suggestion, since babies of a few weeks have a safety reflex which enables them to roll onto their backs and float. Having no fear of the water, they are able to learn how to swim without difficulty. When older children learn to swim, it is not a good idea to push them in, as this sometimes makes them so afraid that they will refuse to go near the swimming baths again.

Children who are keen on water sports like sailing and canoeing must have proper instruc-tion, and should always wear life jackets when on boats and canoes. As with all sports equip-ment, life jackets should carry the British Stan-dards Kitemark on the label. It is also useful for children to learn life-saving skills, and courses in this are often mounted locally by the Royal Life Saving Society or the Royal Society for the Prevention of Accidents (addresses in Appen-dix). In any country where winter weather involves frozen lakes and ponds, children must always be taught the dangers of attempting to walk on thin ice, and rescue skills, in case the danger befalls any of their companions.

Aims and General Principles Of First Aid

First Aid is temporary treatment given in cases of accident, sudden illness or emergency pend-ing the arrival of the doctor, or the removal of the patient to hospital. The priorities are:

1 to keep the person alive,
2 to prevent his condition getting worse,
3 to promote his recovery.

The responsibility of the first aider is to:

1 assess the situation,
2 arrive at a diagnosis,
3 give immediate and adequate treatment bear-ing in mind that some conditions will require more urgent treatment than others,
4 to arrange appropriate transportation.

Assessment and initial reaction

1 Be calm, take charge, give the child con-fidence by talking to him and reassuring him.
2 Get others to help – ask someone to go for a person in charge and to send for ambulance, police, fire service or other help.
3 Stay with the child until medical aid or a senior person arrives.
4 Give emergency help while you are wait-ing – Check the safety of the child and yourself, remove the source of danger, e.g. fire, elec-tricity, fumes, *then* check the child's breathing, any bleeding, whether he is conscious.

Aids to Diagnosis

The history is important, e.g. one child might

say 'he slipped' while another will report 'he fell and banged his head on the wall'. Try to find out as much as you can about what actually happened.

Signs are what the first aider can see, i.e. pallor (paleness of skin), cyanosis (blue/purple colouring of skin), evidence of poisoning (whiteness or blueness of lips).

Symptoms are complained of by the patient: 'I feel cold', 'my head hurts'.

Give the essential treatment:

1 *a* Emergency resuscitation.
  b Control bleeding.
  c Treat shock.
2 Prevent the condition from becoming worse – cover wounds, immobilize or support injured limb if fracture is suspected.
3 Promote recovery by reassurance, move as little as possible, handle gently and protect from cold.

If a senior person decides it is necessary, a doctor or ambulance will be summoned. A brief written report should go with the child and the person who accompanies him to hospital. Parents must be informed, without causing undue alarm or upset.

Summary of essentials

Act quickly, quietly and methodically. Give priority to most urgent conditions. Remember:

1 Breathing
2 Bleeding
3 Shock

Do not attempt too much.
Do not allow other children to crowd round.
Do not remove clothing unnecessarily.
Do not give anything by mouth to anyone who is unconscious, has a suspected internal injury or who is likely to need an anaesthetic.

Contents of a First Aid Box

There should be a fully equipped, easily accessible (to adults) first aid box in every classroom/area of nursery/home. Recommendations as to contents may differ in regions but in general, the following items should be included. The number depends on the size of the group.

1 Triangular bandages (for support of sprained, strained or fractured limbs and to hold dressings in place on hand, foot and head where there are no roller bandages).
2 Adhesive plasters of various sizes to cover minor cuts and prevent infection, some waterproof.
3 Savlon lotion or cream to apply on minor cuts and abrasions after cleaning to prevent infection.
4 Cottonwool swabs (for cleansing) or cottonwool roll.
5 Gauze dressings (in sterile packs) for application to wounds to prevent infection.
6 Elastoplast strapping to hold dressings in place.
7 Roller bandages – 1 inch, 2 inches, 3 inches wide to hold dressings in place and keep wound covered.
8 One pair of tweezers to remove splinters.
9 One pair of surgical scissors.
10 Sterile eye pads (to cover and protect eye after entry of foreign body which cannot be easily removed, or after blow to the eye).
11 Small plastic bowls for holding lotions, swabs or for nose bleeds.
12 Disposable kidney dishes or bowls for vomitus.
13 Paper tissues (for application to area of pressure in haemorrhage, cleansing, etc.).

General principles should be applied in all cases apart from detailed treatment of specific cases as given below

Shock

Children who require first aid should always be treated for shock as it is usually a result of all accidents, however mild. The severity of shock depends upon the nature and extent of the injury. Shock causes a lack of blood supply to internal organs which can affect vital functions.

Major causes of shock are:

1 *Severe bleeding*:
  a external, from an artery or deep wound,
  b internal, e.g. into the abdomen, the chest cavity or the tissues surrounding broken bones.
2 *Loss of plasma* from the circulation caused by burns or crush injuries.
3 *Heart failure* – acute heart attacks.
4 *Acute abdominal* emergencies.
5 *Loss of body fluid* – recurrent vomiting or severe diarrhoea.

Signs and symptoms of shock:

1 The child will become very pale.
2 His skin is cold and clammy with profuse sweating.
3 He may feel faint or giddy.
4 He may feel sick and may vomit.
5 He may complain of thirst.
6 He may be very anxious.
7 Consciousness may be clouded.
8 Pulse rate increases, pulse feels weak and thready.
9 Breathing is shallow and rapid.

Treatment of shock:

1 Place the child in recovery position unless fractures or serious injury are present.
2 Loosen clothing at the neck, chest and waist.
3 Make sure the child has a clear airway.
4 Do not overheat the child with blankets as this draws blood from vital organs to the skin.
5 Do not give the child anything to drink or eat.
6 Do not give any alcohol (e.g. brandy) or any drugs (e.g. aspirin).

The 'Recovery' Position

It can be dangerous for an unconscious child to lie on his back since the tongue may fall back and block the throat, or vomit in the mouth could be inhaled. In both cases the child could stop breathing, so if he is still breathing but unconscious he must be placed in the recovery position.

Turn the child halfway over onto his front, with the underneath arm behind and the upper arm bent in front. Bend the upper leg so that it is at right angles to the trunk. Turn the face toward the ground with the neck back so that the tongue falls forward and the child can breathe.

If the child has fractures or internal injuries, don't move him unless it is essential.

Never leave an unconscious child alone as he may stop breathing or choke.

Cuts (Lacerations) with Bleeding

If a child has cut his hand, arm or leg on a knife, pair of scissors, broken glass or jagged tin, or perhaps suffered a puncture wound with a sharp-pointed instrument, the profuse bleeding will probably frighten him and the other children nearby. However, the bleeding may stop of its own accord – often the blood clots to form a plug. Application of firm pressure to the area is usually sufficient to stop the bleeding.

Treatment

1 Reassure the child and have him sit down. Ask another adult to occupy the other children, to prevent panic.
2 If the bleeding is severe, pressure should be applied over a dressing for 5–15 minutes, and medical aid obtained urgently.
3 Treat the child for shock.
4 If the wound is dirty it should be cleansed with Savlon lotion, but do not disturb the clot or bleeding may recur.
5 Apply sterile dressing quickly and bandage firmly in position.
6 Raise the limb to relieve pain and prevent further bleeding (but not if it is fractured).
7 A ring pad may be necessary if there are fragments of glass in the wound.
8 If the cut is minor, an adhesive plaster may be all that is required.

Fainting

Treatment

1 Check if the child suffers from diabetes or epilepsy and, if so, apply treatment accordingly.
2 If a child has a simple faint, he may have complained of nausea or dizziness. He will then suddenly collapse and his pulse rate will be slower.
3 The child appears pale and clammy.
4 Do not lift the child up or attempt to sit him down. Collapse is simply the natural way for the brain, temporarily deprived of blood and oxygen, to recover.
5 Make sure the child is left lying flat for at least half an hour after he recovers.
6 Loosen his clothing and provide a cool air current if possible. Prevent other children from crowding round.
7 When the child has recovered, he can be given sips of water. Reassure and comfort him.

Concussion

Whenever a child becomes unconscious after a fall, e.g. from a climbing frame, concussion must always be considered as a complication. Concussion literally means 'a shaking of the brain' and can have serious effects if untreated. Never attempt to pick the child up or carry him indoors as this could lead to further problems. *Do not panic.*

1 Check if the child is unconscious (this may only last a short time) and his limbs move freely.
2 Check if the child is a known epileptic (he may have had a fit) and call medical aid if he is unconscious.
3 If the child is still unconscious after 3 minutes, he should be taken to hospital immediately.
4 Place the child in recovery position.
5 In cases of suspected concussion, the child may have to remain overnight in hospital for observation.
6 Parents should be informed as soon as possible in order that they can accompany the child to hospital and help relieve any panic and distress he may feel.
7 On return to consciousness the child may vomit, so the adult should prepare for this by sending for a container and towels.
8 The child should never be lifted indoors but should be made as comfortable as possible until the ambulance or doctor arrives.
9 If the child regains consciousness very quickly he may want to resume play but this should not be allowed. He should lie down until he has been seen by a doctor.
10 Reassure and comfort the child.

Burns

Burns are caused by dry heat. Small burns are not serious but can be very painful. Extensive burns can be extremely dangerous as they cause loss of essential fluid from the body and death may occur unless the child is transported to hospital quickly for plasma transfusions. If in any doubt as to the severity of the burn, obtain medical aid.

Treatment of minor burns (less than 2.5 cm or 1 inch square)

1 Allow cold tap water to run gently over the area or immerse the burnt part to reduce heat in the skin.
2 Cover with a sterile dressing and bandage to exclude the air and prevent friction. *Do not prick blisters.*
3 Reassure and comfort the child.

Treatment of extensive burns

1 Gently remove any watches, bracelets, rings, shoes or other constricting articles from the injured area before it begins to swell.
2 *Never remove any clothing which is sticking to burnt skin.*
3 Keep the child in a flat position.
4 Cover the injured areas with a sterile dressing or a clean non-fluffy cloth.
5 Keep the child warm, but not hot.
6 Treat for shock.
7 Obtain medical aid immediately, or instruct others to do so.
8 Reassure and comfort the child.

Do not apply ointments, lotions, pastes, powder, oils or grease to burnt areas. If the child's clothing is on fire, make him lie down on the floor to stop the flames reaching his face. Cover him with a wool rug or blanket to smother the flames.

Nose Bleeding

Nose bleeding is rarely serious, but the sight of blood may frighten the child.

Treatment

1 Reassure and comfort the child, support him in a sitting position with his head slightly forward and provide a bowl and tissues, and a towel round the child's neck for protection.
2 If possible the seat should be near a window or a cool current of air.
3 Firmly pinch the soft part of his nose for a few minutes (the child will open his mouth to breathe).
4 Loosen the clothing about his neck and chest.
5 A cold compress (some folded tissues soaked in cold water) can be applied over his nose.
6 Do not tell the child to blow his nose in case this disturbs the blood clot.
7 If the bleeding does not stop, or recurs, medical aid must be obtained.
8 Never let a child put his head back as the blood could cause choking or make him sick.
9 Treat for shock.

Electric Shock

Treatment

1 Do not touch the child directly or with any

object which will conduct electricity.

2 Turn off the electricity supply or remove the child from the source using a dry broom handle or dry rope. Never allow wet objects or anything metallic to come into contact with the electrocuted person or youself as the current will pass through even quicker. If nothing else, grasp the child's loose dry clothing and pull. Ensure that you do not endanger yourself.

3 If breathing and heartbeat have stopped, begin resuscitation immediately.

4 Get medical aid urgently, or instruct others to do so.

5 If the child is conscious, ensure a clear away and treat as for shock (p. 272).

6 If the child is unconscious but breathing normally, place him in the recovery position (p. 273).

7 When medical aid arrives, pass on all information about the duration of electrical contact.

Scalds

Scalds are caused by wet heat such as boiling water, steam, hot oil or tar. Treatment is the same as for burns.

Scalds of mouth or throat may occur if a child drinks hot water from the spout of a kettle, and soup and other drinks can also cause scalding if they are too hot. This can be very serious as the tissues within the throat swell and may interfere with breathing. In this case:

1 Arrange for removal to hospital.

2 Lay the child down in the recovery position.

Table 10.1   First aid of common household poisons

Glue	Certain types, mainly used for sticking parts of models, are only harmful if inhaled in large quantities (glue sniffing), but can be an irritant if swallowed or accidentally squirted into the eye.
Alcohol	May cause intoxication. Refer to hospital, unless only a small amount taken.
Aspirin	If more than the prescribed dose is taken, refer to hospital.
Bleaches	May be corrosive, so refer to hospital.
Batteries	Contain toxic substances. Refer to hospital.
Bubble bath foams	Detergents, may cause vomiting. Refer to doctor.
Candles	Not likely to cause symptoms, as they are made of paraffin and beeswax.
Crayons	Usually non-toxic.
Cigarettes	Usually cause vomiting. Refer to hospital if more than one has been eaten, as nicotine is poisonous.
Contraceptive pills	Not usually harmful, but refer to doctor if in doubt.
Detergents	May irritate the stomach lining and cause vomiting. Refer to doctor.
Domestos and other drain cleaners	Caustic alkalis, cause burns of the mouth, pharynx and oesophagus. *Urgent hospital treatment* required.
Dry-cleaning fluid	Often contains carbon tetrachloride or trichlorethylene, which are both poisonous. Fumes of these may cause vomiting. Refer to hospital.
Iron tablets	Extremely dangerous for young children. Refer to hospital.
Lavatory blocks	Contain toxic substances. Refer to hospital.
Lead	Whether ingested from sucking lead paint or inhaled while burning lead batteries, requires *urgent hospital treatment*.
Lighter fuel	Toxic – refer to hospital.
Matches	Usually not harmful, but if eaten in large amounts can cause sore throat and vomiting, so refer to doctor.
Marker pens	May be poisonous, so refer to hospital.
Nail varnish or nail varnish remover	May contain acetone, so refer to hospital.
Paints	If old or red may contain lead, so refer to hospital.
Paint strippers	Usually strong alkalis, which can cause burns of mouth, pharynx and oesophagus. *Urgent referral to hospital.*
Paraquat and other weedkillers	Lethal – *urgent referral to hospital.*
Petrol	Dangerous if ingested. Refer to hospital.
Playdough	Harmless.
Putty	Dangerous if ingested. Refer to hospital.
Soaps	May cause vomiting. Not serious, but refer to doctor if in doubt.
Thermometers	Dangerous only if the broken glass cuts the mouth. The small amount of mercury present is not harmful, even if swallowed. Refer to doctor if in doubt.

3 If breathing is failing, give artificial respiration.
4 If conscious treat for shock, reassure and comfort the child.

Poisoning

1 Act quickly.
2 If unconscious, arrange removal to hospital with utmost speed together with any clues as to what the poison may be – such as tablets, empty bottles or vomited material.
3 If the child is conscious, find out which poison he has taken.
4 If the poison causes burning of the lips, mouth or tongue, send the child quickly to hospital.
5 *DO NOT INDUCE VOMITING.*
a Paraffin or other petroleum products, furniture polish, insecticides or paint thinner can be inhaled into the lungs through vomiting and they can do more harm.
b Strong acid or caustic preparations may further damage the throat and oesophagus which may already be severely damaged.
c If the child is unconscious or convulsing he may inhale vomited material.
d Any salt given to induce vomiting will create serious electrolyte disturbance.
6 Inform the parents (if the child is not at home).
7 Save any samples of vomited material in a container for inspection at hospital.
8 In hospital, the nurse or doctor may give the child spirit of ipececuanha to induce vomiting.
9 Lean the child over basin while vomiting to prevent him from inhaling vomit.
10 Reassure and comfort the child as vomiting is distressing for him.
11 Dilute the poison by giving the child two or three glasses of lemonade, milk or water.
12 Send him quickly to hospital.

Gas poisoning

1 Turn off the gas.
2 Open the windows.
3 Get the child out of the gas-filled room. The adult should cover his nose and mouth with a wet cloth, crawl into the gas-filled room and drag the child out.
4 Loosen tight clothing, especially at the neck.
5 Keep the patient warm.

6 Begin artificial respiration.
7 Send for medical aid or remove to hospital.

Asphyxia

Asphyxia results from deficiency of oxygen and may be due to obstruction of the air passages by:

1 the tongue having fallen back,
2 pressure of a foreign body,
3 blood clot,
4 vomitus,
5 swelling of the glottis due to scalding, corrosive poisoning or a sting,
6 strangulation,
7 inhalation of coal gas,
8 drowning,
9 electric shock,
10 lightning,
11 sun and heatstroke.

General treatment of asphyxia

1 If possible remove the obstacle and allow a free passage of air – pull tongue to one side.
2 Loosen tight clothing at the neck.
3 Treat for shock.

Apply artificial respiration if necessary.

Artificial respiration mouth-to-mouth or mouth-to-nose

No delay.

1 Quickly ensure that there is nothing in the mouth to obstruct breathing.
2 Pull the jaw forward by one hand placed under it, at the same time arching the neck backwards; this will pull the tongue forwards and allow air to get in.
3 Squeeze the nose tightly by the fingers of the opposite hand.
4 Place the mouth firmly against the victim's mouth and blow.
5 Whilst blowing watch for expansion of the person's chest. If the chest does not expand, the neck must be arched further backwards by the hand under the jaw.
6 When the child's chest is seen to expand fully, take away your mouth from the child's, and take a normal deep breath, at the same time watching the child's chest contract.
7 When the child's chest has finished contracting place the mouth against the child's and blow

again, watching for expansion of the child's chest.

8 Go on doing this rhythmically 12–15 times a minutes.

> mouth to mouth–blow–take away–deep breath–mouth to mouth–blow–take away–deep breath

Carry on until medical help arrives. Other adults present can help in relays, as artificial respiration is very exhausting.

With a baby, it is easier to breathe into the mouth and nose at the same time. If after several breaths given mouth to mouth the child is still very pale or a blue/grey colour (cyanosed), the heart may have stopped. If you think the heart has stopped, give heart massage as well as mouth-to-mouth resuscitation.

Heart massage

1 Lay the child on his back on the floor. Kneel beside him.
2 Press on the lower half of the child's breast-bone (sternum). Use moderate pressure for a young child and even less for a baby. Press about once every second, quicker for a baby.
3 The child will not start breathing until after the heart has started beating, so, after pressing five times, stop the heart massage and give a breath by mouth-to-mouth resuscitation. If there is another person with you, get them to do the breathing while you do the heart massage, stopping every 5 seconds to let the other person fill up the child's lungs.
4 Once the heart has started beating, keep on with mouth-to-mouth resuscitation until the breathing starts again.
5 Gently place the child in the recovery position.

Stings

Wasp and bee stings

These are extremely painful, and multiple stings can make a child really ill.

1 Reassure the child to allay shock and anxiety and prevent panic.
2 If the sting is visible, remove it with tweezers to allow an outlet for the poison.
3 Bathe in undiluted Milton or Savlon solution to prevent infection.
4 If the skin becomes red and swollen, obtain medical advice.

5 If the child is known to be allergic, give him such medication as he may carry with him for this purpose.
6 If he has a history of allergies and has no medication with him obtain medical care immediately to prevent him developing breathing difficulties.
7 Calamine (Caladryl) lotion or cream may be applied to ease the pain.
8 Treat for shock.

Insect stings

These may be trivial and forgotten but within 24 hours the face or limbs may swell to alarming proportions.

1 Bathe with warm water.
2 Apply Caladryl lotion or cream.
3 If the discomfort persists, refer the child to a doctor who will order antihistamine drugs by mouth.

Sting in throat

This could be serious due to swelling which could affect breathing.

Treatment

1 Give ice to suck.
2 Reassure and comfort the child.
3 Take the child to a doctor or hospital.

Bites

Dog and cat bites

1 Reassure and comfort the child.
2 Wash the area of the bite with soap and water.
3 Hold under running water (comfortably warm if possible) for 2 or 3 minutes if not already bleeding profusely.
4 Apply clean (preferably sterile) dressing if bleeding.
5 Doctor should be informed.

Snake bites

Non-poisonous. No fang marks are present, at most a semi-circle of tooth marks.

1 Calm and reassure the child.
2 Treat as for dog and cat bites.

Poisonous. The adder is the only poisonous

British snake. It is rarely fatal, but can make small children very ill.

1 Act quickly but calmly. Reassure the child.
2 Local pain may be intense and swelling increases rapidly.
3 Inform senior person or call another adult to help.
4 Call an ambulance and transfer the child quickly to hospital.
5 Keep the child as quiet as possible while transporting him. Keep reassuring him that he will recover.

Foreign bodies

In the eye
1 Prevent the child from rubbing his eye.
2 To remove a small particle, pull the upper lid down over the lower lid and release several times, but not if it significantly increases local pain.
3 If necessary lay the child flat with a towel under his head, tip the head toward the affected side and gently pour warm water over the eyeball.
4 If a particle or pain remains, gently place a clean folded tissue over the eye.
5 Obtain medical help and inform his parents.
6 Reassure and comfort the child.

In the ear
1 If the foreign body cannot be easily removed, obtain medical help immediately.
2 Never try to remove a foreign body, such as beads or beans which cannot easily be removed, with forceps.
3 Reassure and comfort the child.

In the nose
1 Do not try to remove foreign body.
2 Tell the child to breathe through his mouth.
3 Obtain medical help.
4 Reassure and comfort the child.

Swallowing foreign bodies. Pins, coins and buttons may be swallowed but are usually evacuated in the natural way.

1 Reassure and calm the child.
2 Inform parents without causing undue alarm.
3 Medical help should be obtained.
4 Do not give anything by mouth.

Choking

Do not panic.
1 If a child chokes on food or other objects and stops breathing, turn him face downward over your knees or hold him upside down and forcefully hit his back with the heel of the hand between the shoulder blades in an effort to dislodge the object.
2 If this does not dislodge the obstruction, it may be necessary to do the abdominal thrust:
a Sit the child on your lap or stand the child in front of you and place one arm around the abdomen. Clench your fist and place it thumb inwards in the centre of the upper abdomen. Support the back with your other hand.
b Press your clenched fist into the abdomen with a quick upward and inward movement. Repeat up to four times as necessary; each thrust must be hard enough to dislodge the obstruction by itself.
3 If the child is unconscious:
a Turn him onto his back with the head in the Open Airway position. (With one hand under the child's neck and the other on his forehead, tilt the head back then transfer your hand from the neck and push the chin upwards. The tilted jaw will lift the tongue forward to clear the airway.)
b Kneel astride the child's thighs so that you can apply pressure at the correct mid-abdominal position.
c Place the heel of one hand in the centre of the child's upper abdomen, keeping fingers clear of the abdomen.
d With both arms straight, press into the abdomen with a quick inward and forward thrust. Repeat up to four times as necessary; each thrust should be hard enough to dislodge the obstruction.
4 If he can breathe readily even though coughing, the above is unnecessary.
5 If he does not breathe after the attempt to dislodge the object, apply mouth-to-mouth resuscitation.
6 Obtain medical aid, inform parents and get the child to hospital, but stay with him.
7 Reassure and comfort the child when he has recovered.

Babies.
1 Lay the baby's head downwards with the chest and abdomen lying along your forearm and use your arm to support the head and chest.

2 Slap the baby smartly between the shoulders up to four times.

3 If this does not dislodge the obstruction, it may be necessary to perform the abdominal thrust as follows:

a Place the infant on a firm surface with the head in the Open Airway position (see above).

b Place the first two fingers of one hand on the upper abdomen, between the navel and the breastbone, and press with a quick forward and downward movement. Repeat up to four times as necessary; each thrust must be hard enough to dislodge the obstruction.

Take great care when removing an obstruction from the mouth of an infant. Only put your finger in the mouth if you can see the obstruction and there is no danger of pushing it further down the throat.

Appendix I – Sample Examination Paper and Multiple Choice Questions

Sample Examination Paper on Health and Development

Time allowed : 2 hours

SECTION A

Attempt *all* questions

1 List *four* benefits of sound sleep to a 4 year old child. (2)
2 State *five* causes of accidents in the nursery. (5)
3 Describe briefly the treatment of sore buttocks. (4)
4 Outline *five* factors to be considered when planning for the convalescence of a 6 year old girl. (5)
5 Describe the first aid treatment for a child who is bleeding from a severe cut on his forearm. (5)
6 Explain briefly how constipation may be prevented in a 3 year old child. (3)
7 Outline *five* important factors in the promotion of dental health. (4)
8 State when the following developments usually take place:

(a) use of whole hand in palmar grasp;
(b) turns in response to hearing familiar sounds;
(c) picks up toy from floor without falling;
(d) holds cup with both hands. (2)

SECTION B

Attempt *one* question

10 (a) State *six* advantages of breast feeding to the baby. (6)
(b) List *four* functions of Vitamin A and name *four* good sources of this vitamin. (4)

(c) List the signs and symptoms of rickets. (5)
11 (a) Describe the principles of weaning. (10)
(b) State *two* reasons for weaning. (2)
(c) List the constituents of a well-balanced diet. (3)

SECTION C

Attempt *one* question

12 (a) List the signs and symptoms of mumps. (3)
(b) Describe the body defences against infection. (12)
13 (a) Describe the signs and symptoms of whooping cough and state *four* possible complications. (9)
(b) Describe *six* ways in which infection is spread. (6)

SECTION D

Attempt *one* question

14 Describe fully how an outing to the seaside on a warm sunny day aids the all round development of the child. (15)
15 (a) Explain fully how a child's health and well-being may be influenced by the wearing of suitable clothing and footwear. (12)
(b) Describe briefly the role of the Health Visitor. (3)

Multiple Choice Questions

A Child Development and Child Health (0–3 years)

Tick *one* item only

1 The newborn baby's actions are

a reversed

   b reflex
   c voluntary

2 At one month old, a baby

   a cannot see at all
   b shuts eyes tightly in presence of any
      direct light shone at it within 1–2
      inches
   c notices dangling toy in line of vision at
      6–8 inches.

3 The baby's neck muscles are sufficiently
developed to enable him to hold his head
up at

   a 3 weeks
   b 6 months
   c 3 months

4 Sudden loud noises cause a baby of 3
months

   a to be quiet
   b distress
   c to gurgle with pleasure

5 A baby first responds to his mother's face
at

   a 6 months
   b 1 year
   c 4 weeks

6 Until the age of 15 months, all activity is
centred round

   a the eyes
   b the mouth
   c the feet

7 Usually a child can crawl and/or stand
with support at

   a 6 months
   b 3 months
   c 10 months

8 Nowadays babies are weaned onto mixed
feeds at

   a 3 days
   b 18 months
   c 3 months

9 The first food to be introduced other than
milk should be

   a cereals such as Farex
   b egg yolk
   c beef broth

10 Giving a baby more than its feed produces

   a a healthy, bouncing baby
   b a fat baby who will have problems
      crawling
   c a taller child and adult

11 Orange juice is given to milk-fed babies
because

   a they like the taste
   b it contains Vitamin C which is lacking
      in milk
   c it is easier to prepare than a milk feed

12 Iron is necessary for babies because

   a it prevents them from getting rickets
   b it helps their teeth to grow
   c it prevents anaemia

13 Iron is given to babies

   a in tablets or injections
   b in egg yolk and strained liver
   c in malt rusks

14 Vitamin D is found in milk, eggs and
butter and is necessary

   a to develop the child's intelligence
   b to help bones and teeth to grow
   c to make baby's hair shiny

15 A child can put one brick on top of the
other at

   a 1 month
   b 15 months
   c 3 months

16 The mother should begin to speak to the
child at

   a 2 years
   b 9 months
   c at birth

17 A cup can be introduced to the child at

   a 5 years
   b 1 month
   c 6 months

18 Repeating syllables in strings, e.g. mam-mam, dad-dad is typical of a child of

  a 3 weeks
  b 2 years
  c 9 months

19 Toilet training should begin

  a at birth
  b about 15–18 months
  c not before 3 years

20 When a child of 15 months drops a toy purposely

  a he should be smacked
  b he should be asked to pick it up
  c the adult should pick it up

21 If a child of 18 months uses his left hand

  a he should be smacked
  b he should be taught to use the right hand
  c he should be left to use the preferred hand

22 A child of 18 months should not be given

  a thick pencil and paper
  b a picture book
  c fine crayons and sharp-pointed scissors

23 Wheeled toys are suitable for a child of

  a 6 months
  b 18 months — 2 years
  c 5 years

24 A child is able to build a tower of seven cubes and form a 'train' at

  a 9 months
  b 18 months
  c 2½ years

25 Temper tantrums in 2–2½ year olds

  a are a sign of bad temper and the child should be smacked
  b are a normal part of development
  c should be ignored and affection withdrawn

26 A vocabulary of 200 words, use of pronouns I, me, you, questioning What? Where? is normal for a child of

  a 12 months
  b 2½ years
  c 18 months

27 A child of 2½ years can

  a use a spoon for eating
  b dress himself completely
  c recite 2 dozen nursery rhymes

28 Copying circles, imitating a cross, copying V, H, T is typical of a child of

  a 1 year
  b 15 months
  c 3 years

29 A 3 year old will usually represent a man as

  a a circle with either legs or arms attached
  b two circles, neck and arms
  c a square

30 How many months after conception are the main parts of the body formed in the uterus?

  a 3 months
  b 6 months
  c 12 months

Answers

1	b	11	b	21	c
2	b	12	c	22	c
3	c	13	b	23	b
4	b	14	b	24	c
5	c	15	b	25	b
6	b	16	c	26	b
7	c	17	c	27	a
8	c	18	c	28	c
9	b	19	b	29	a
10	b	20	b	30	a

B Children with Special Needs

Tick *one* item only

1 ''Learning difficulties'' is now used to describe

  a children previously described as mentally handicapped
  b children with cerebral palsy
  c children with clefts of lip and palate

2 Down's syndrome

 a is due to brain damage
 b means that children are born with an extra finger
 c is due to 47 chromosomes instead of 46

3 Mothers are described as 'carriers' of haemophilia

 a as they often cut their fingers
 b one of their X chromosomes is affected and may pass to their son/sons.
 c the father cannot pass on any harmful conditions to his sons.

4 Cystic fibrosis is carried on a recessive gene:

 a if one parent has the gene, all the offspring will have the condition
 b it will not be seen in the children unless both parents carry the gene, and pass it on
 c only boys get the condition

5 Spina bifida

 a is caused by a defect in the neural tube while the child is developing in the uterus
 b is always accompanied by hydrocephalus
 c cannot be diagnosed until after birth

6 Cerebral palsy

 a is congenital, due to brain damage before or during birth
 b is hereditary, based on a recessive gene
 c means that all children affected have severe learning difficulties

7 Maternal rubella in the first 16 weeks of pregnancy

 a always causes spontaneous abortion
 b is a mild infection which is easily treated with no after effects
 c may cause deafness, blindness and congenital heart conditions in the baby

8 Pre-conceptual genetic counselling

 a is performed when the baby is 1 month
 b tells women over 35 not to conceive
 c checks family histories to determine presence of any recessive or dominant genes, and chromosome abnormalities before conception

9 Infection in the upper respiratory tract (nose and mouth) may cause otitis media

 a because children lick beads and put them in their ears
 b because the Eustachian tube links the middle ear to the back of the throat
 c because ear wax becomes infected and moves into the middle ear

10 "Glue ear"

 a is common during junk play when children stick things in their ears
 b arises when the Eustachian tube does not work properly and otitis media causes secretion of a discharge
 c refers to babies born with one ear fully attached to the side of the head.

11 Grommets

 a are gnomes in Norwegian mythology
 b are tiny drainage tubes placed inside the ear to treat glue ear
 c replace the ossicles in a deaf child

12 Birth anoxia

 a is the oxygen given to the mother during birth
 b is a lack of oxygen at birth, which may cause hearing impairment in babies
 c means that the baby's lungs are damaged

13 Hearing impaired children

 a never have any problems in speech/language development
 b speak sooner than other children
 c require early referral to speech therapy to prevent adverse effects of inability to verbalize

14 Deaf or partially hearing children

 a can only understand if the teacher/nursery nurse shouts as loud as possible
 b are never very intelligent
 c can be helped with a combination of hearing aids, sign language and lip-reading.

15 Congenital cataracts

 a mean that the baby will be permanently blind

b   are caused by the midwife slapping the baby

c   can be removed and contact lens fitted to give the baby normal sight

16   Nystagmus

a   means that the baby cannot sleep at night

b   relates to faulty nervous control, and causes eyes to be wobbly and shaky

c   is a type of blindness

17   Squints

a   can never be corrected

b   arise because of weakness in eye muscles and can be corrected through surgery

c   always accompany short sightedness

18   Partially sighted children

a   can only learn to read through using Braille texts

b   have any sight enhanced through Keeler spectacles and large print television/ computer programs

c   will never be able to read and write

19   Children have special needs if they

a   live in a bungalow

b   live in overcrowded, damp, high-rise flats

c   are not given 50p each day to spend on sweets

20   Children of Asian origin

a   are all lazy and should be sent back to Asia

b   need help in adjusting to a culture which may be different from home

c   are always exceptionally bright.

Answers

1	a	11	b
2	c	12	b
3	b	13	c
4	b	14	c
5	a	15	c
6	a	16	b
7	c	17	b
8	c	18	b
9	b	19	b
10	b	20	b

C   Play

Tick *one* item only

1   During the first 6 months

a   babies cannot play

b   mobiles and rattles aid listening and eye movements

c   a large fluffy toy provides comfort

2   Teething rings and plastic bath toys

a   should not be used until the baby is 1 year old

b   promote exploratory play using the mouth

c   may harm the baby's gums

3   Play with nesting cubes and beakers

a   prepares for manual dexterity and hand eye coordination

b   should not be provided until 2 years of age

c   teaches the baby tidy habits

4   Domestic equipment, such as wooden spoons and pan lids

a   provides enjoyment for the baby in banging and rattling

b   should never be given to children as play things

c   is the forerunner of play in the Wendy house

5   Jingles used in finger play (This little 'piggy', 'Pat a cake')

a   make children interested in guinea pigs and baking

b   develop the child's interest in his fingers which are to become an important part of manipulative play

c   bear no relation to real life, and should be avoided

6   Between 12 and 18 months

a   hammer pegs should be avoided in case the child hurts himself

b   only girls should be given soft toys

c   push and pull toys on wheels help in walking

7   Before 3 years of age

a   children should be kept away from a climbing frame in case they fall

b   a slide with steps at the back provides delight for children 18 months–2 years

c   trampolines are dangerous

8 Posting boxes with square and circle cut outs
  a should only be used for 4 year old children
  b begin recognition of shape and enable the child to gain confidence in achievement
  c cost too much money

9 Dress-up clothes and housekeeping toys
  a prepare children for adulthood
  b allow children from 2 years onwards to enjoy make believe play
  c are not suitable for boys

10 Development of skills in dressing and undressing
  a are unnecessary, as most parents will do this for their children
  b can be promoted through use of formboards or dolls made by nursery nurses which have laces, zips, buttons and belts for practice
  c should not be attempted until children are 7 years old

11 Auditory materials for shaking and rattling
  a can be made quite simply with used tins containing rice, peas, lentils, baking beans, for a variety of sounds
  b should never be made from edible items, in view of the famine in Ethiopia
  c are only of use if bought in an Early Learning Centre where experts know how to make them educational

12 Books and storytelling
  a are not necessary until the child is 4 years old and knows not to tear the pages of books
  b story telling can begin from the earliest days, as the mother talks to the baby, and cloth, washable books are enjoyed by children from 12 months on
  c have been replaced by TV

13 Wooden jigsaw puzzles can be made in grades of simplicity
  a two or three main pieces for 2½–3 year olds helps recognition of shape, and is a pre-number activity
  b are not appreciated in nursery, where most children will put the pieces in their mouths
  c do not help manual dexterity

14 Painting materials
  a only create mess and ruin children's clothes
  b provide enjoyment just in covering the paper with paint and encourage a sense of 'mastery'
  c are useless unless the children have white paper

15 Sorting items by colour, size and shape
  a is a useful play activity for 4 year olds, as acquisition of skills needed in number and reading are furthered
  b means buying a proper 'sorting' set from Galt's
  c is boring, and time should be spent in learning to count

16 Play is
  a a pleasant way for nursery children to spend their time
  b a medium in which children learn about themselves, their environment, and gain self confidence to progress to formal learning
  c a waste of time, since 3 year olds can learn to read without all these 'pre-reading' activities

17 When children play with water
  a they are preparing for the future when they will have to wash dishes
  b they are acquiring the concepts of "wet", floating, sinking, solutions, as well as gaining pleasure
  c there should only be 2 items in the water to prevent mess.

18 Adult intervention in play
  a should be well timed, and can enhance the play experience by skilful questioning, labelling and explanation
  b should never be allowed as it restricts the freedom of children
  c is necessary to keep the nursery tidy

19 Books and other play materials
  a are of little use, unless they are "educational"
  b should be chosen to match children's ages, stages, interests and needs
  c should all be laid out every day so that children have freedom of choice

20 When setting out play equipment

    a the nursery nurse should choose one 'new' activity each day and ensure that there is no clutter to hindrance the children moving from one activity to another

    b a book corner should always be set up next to the Wendy house.

    c the children should be asked which activity they want before equipment is set up

Answers

1	b	**11**	a
2	b	**12**	b
3	a	**13**	a
4	a	**14**	b
5	b	**15**	a
6	c	**16**	b
7	b	**17**	b
8	b	**18**	a
9	b	**19**	b
10	b	**20**	a

Appendix II – Helping Agencies and Their Addresses

United Kingdom

Action Research for Crippled Children
Vincent House
North Parade
Horsham
West Sussex RH12 2DA

Association of Breastfeeding Mothers
131 Mayow Road
Sydenham
London SE26 4HZ

Advisory Centre for Education
18 Victoria Park Square
London E2 9PB
01–980 4596

Association for all Speech Impaired
Children
347 Central Market
London EC1A 9NH
01–236 6487

Association of British Adoption and
Fostering Agencies
4 Southampton Row
London WC1B 4AA
01–242 8951

Association for Improvements
in Maternity Services (AIMS)
19 Broomfield Crescent
Leeds LS6 3DD
0532 751911

Association for Spina Bifida and
Hydrocephalus
Tavistock House North
Tavistock Square
London WC 1H 9HJ
01–388 1382

Asthma Research Council
12 Pembridge Square
London W2 4EH
01–229 1149

British Agencies for Adoption and
Fostering
11 Southwark Street
London SE1 1RQ
01–407 8800

British Association for Early
Childhood Education
140 Tabernacle Street
London EC2A 4SD
01–250 1768

British Diabetic Association
10 Queen Anne Street
London W1M OBD
01–323 1531

British Epilepsy Association
Crowthorne House
New Wokingham Road
Wokingham
Berks RG11 3AY
0344 773122

British Institute for the Mentally
Handicapped
Wolverhampton Road
Kidderminster DY10 3PP
0562 850251

British Migraine Association
Ottermead Lane
Ottershaw, Surrey KT16 OBJ
093–287 3242

British Polio Fellowship
West End Road
Ruislip, Middx HA4 6LP
08956 75155

British Pregnancy Advisory Service
(BPAS)
Austy Manor
Wootton Wawen
Solihull B15 6DA
05642 3225

British Red Cross Society
9 Grosvenor Crescent
London SW1X 7EJ
01–235 5454

British Rheumatism and Arthritis
Association
6 Grosvenor Crescent
London SW1X 7ER
01–235 0902

Brook Advisory Centre (Family
planning)
223 Tottenham Court Road
London W1P 9AE
01–580 2991

Cancer Information Association
Gloucester Green
Oxford OX1 2EQ
0865 725223

Chest and Heart Association
Tavistock House, North
Tavistock Square
London WC1H 9JE
01–387 3012

Child Poverty Action Group
1 Macklin Street
London WC2 5NH
01–405 5942

Children's Chest Circle
Tavistock House North
Tavistock Square
London WC1H 9JE
01–387 3012

Church of England Children's Society
Old Town Hall
Kennington Road
London SE11 4QD
01–735 2441

Coeliac Society
PO Box 181
London NW2 2QY
01–459 2440

The Compassionate Friends
(support for bereaved parents)
25 Kingsdown Parade
Bristol BS6 5UE
0272 47316

Cystic Fibrosis Research Trust
5 Blyth Road
Bromley BR1 3RS
01–464 7211

Deaf/Blind Rubella Children
61 Senneleys Park Road
Northfield, Birmingham
021–475 1392

Disabled Living Foundation
346 Kensington High Street
London W14 8NS
01–602 2491

Down's Children Association
Quinborne Community Care
Ridgeacre Road
Quinton
Birmingham B32 2TW
021–427 1374

Dr Barnardo's
Tanner's Lane
Barkingside, Essex
01–550 8822

Dyslexia Institute
133 Gresham Road
Staines
Middlesex TW18 2AJ
81 59498

Family Fund
PO Box 50
York

Family Planning Association
27 Margaret Street
London W1N 7RJ
01–636 7866

Family Planning Information
Service
27/35 Mortimer Street
London W1N 7RJ
01–636 7866

Family Service Units
207 Old Marylebone Road
London NW1 5QP
01–402 5175

Family Welfare Association
501/505 Kingsland Road
Dalston
London E8 4AU
01–254 6251

Foundation for the Study of
Infant Deaths (Cot deaths)
15 Belgrave Square
London SW1X 8PF
01–235 1721

Gingerbread (Association for one
parent families)
35 Wellington Street
London WC2E 7BN
01–240 0953

Haemophilia Society
16 Trinity Street
London SE1 1DE
01–407 1010

Health Education Council
78 New Oxford Street
London WC1A 1AH
01–631 0930

Hyperactive Children
Support Group
59 Meadowside
Angmering BN16 4BV
09062 6172

Invalid Children's Aid Association
126 Buckingham Palace
London SW1W 9BR
01–730 9891

Kith and Kids
6 Grosvenor Road
London N10
01–883 8762

La Lèche League
BM3424
London WC1N 3XX
01-242 1278

Leukaemia Society
45 Craigmore Avenue
Bournemouth, Hants
0202 37459

MENCAP (Royal Society for Mentally
Handicapped)
123 Golden Lane
London EC1Y ORT
01–253 9433

Migraine Trust
45 Great Ormond Street
London WC1N 3HD
01–278 2676

MIND (National Association of
Mental Health)
22 Harley Street
London W1N 2ED
01–637 0741

Miscarriage Association
18 Stoneybrook Close
West Bretton
Wakefield
West Yorkshire WF4 4TP
092 485 515

Montessori Training Organisation
26 Lyndhurst Gardens
London NW3

Muscular Dystrophy Group of Great
Britain
35 Macaulay Road
London SW4 OQP
01–720 8055

National Association for Blind–Deaf
and Rubella Handicapped Children
164 Cromwell Lane
Coventry CV4 8AP
0203 23308

National Association of Certificated
Nursery Nurses
162 Langdale Road
Thornton Heath
Surrey CR4 7PR

National Association for the Childless
318 Summer Lane
Birmingham B19 3RL

National Association for Foster Care
Francis House
Francis Street
London SW1P IDE
01–828 6266

National Association for Gifted
Children
1 South Audley Street
London W1Y 6JS
01–499 1188

National Association for Maternal and
Child Welfare
1 South Audley Street
London W1Y 6JS
01–491 2772

National Association for Mental
Health (MIND)
22 Harley Street
London W1N 2ED
01–637 0741

National Association for Spina Bifida
and Hydrocephalus
Tavistock House North
Tavistock Square
London WC1
01–388 1382

National Association for the Welfare
of Children in Hospital
Argyle House
29–31 Euston Road
London W1 2SD

National Childbirth Trust
9 Queensborough Terrace
London W2 3TB
01–229 9319

National Children's Bureau
8 Wakeley Street
London EC1V 7QE
01–278 9441

National Children's Homes
85 Highbury Park
London N5 1UD
01–226 2033

National Childminding Association
8 Mason's Hill
Bromley
Kent BR2 9EY
01–464 6164

National Council for One-Parent
Families
255 Kentish Town Road
London NW5 2LX
01–267 1361

National Deaf Children's Society
45 Hereford Road
London W2 5AH
01–229 9272

National Eczema Society
Tavistock House, North
Tavistock Square
London WC1H 9BR
01–388 4097

National Marriage Guidance Council
Little Church Street
Rugby CV21 3AP
0788 73241

National Nursery Examination Board
(NNEB)
Argyle House, 3rd Floor
29–31 Euston Road
London NW1 2SD
01–837 5458

National Schizophrenia Fellowship
78 Victoria Road
Surbiton KT6 6JT
01–390 3651

National Society for Autistic Children
1A Golders Green Road
London NW11 8EA
01–458 4375

National Society for Epileptics
Chalfont St Peter
Bucks Sl9 ORJ
02407 3991

National Society for Mentally
Handicapped Children
17 Pembridge Square
London W2
01–229 8941

National Society for the Prevention of
Cruelty to Children
67 Saffron Hill
London EC1N 8RS
01–242 1626

Parents Anonymous: see local
directories or telephone
01–668 4805 (24 hour service)

Patients' Association
11 Dartmouth Street
London SW1
01–222 4992

Pregnancy Advisory Service
27 Fitzroy Square
London W1P 5HH
01–387 3057

Pre-School Playgroups Association
61–63 Kings Cross Road
London WC1X 9LL
01–833 0991

Professional Association of Nursery
Nurses
99 Friar Gate
Derby DE1 1EZ
0332–372 3377

Royal National Institute for Disability
and Rehabilitation (REHAB)
25 Mortimer Street
London W1N 8AB
01–637 5400

Royal National Institute for the Blind
224 Great Portland St
London W1N 6AA
01–388 1266

Royal National Institute for the Deaf
105 Gower Street
London WC1E 6AH
01–387 8033

Royal Scottish Society for Prevention
of Cruelty to Children
41 Polwarth Terrace
Edinburgh EH11 1NL

Royal Society for the Prevention of
Accidents
The Priory, Queensway
Birmingham B4 6BS
021–233 2641

Safety in Playgrounds Action Group
85 Dalston Drive
Manchester M20 OLQ

St John Ambulance Association
1 Grosvenor Crescent
London SW1X 7EF
01–235 5231

The Samaritans
17 Uxbridge Road
Slough SL1 1SN
0752 32713

Save the Children Fund
17 Grove Lane
London SE5 8RD
01–703 5400

Scottish Association for the Deaf
Moray House College
Holyrood Road
Edinburgh

Scottish Cot Death Trust
Royal Hospital for Sick Children
Yorkhill
Glasgow

Scottish Council on Disability
Princes House
Shandwick Place
Edinburgh

Scottish Council for Spastics
22 Corstorphine Road
Edinburgh EH12 6HP

Scottish Council for Single Parents
13 Gayfield Square
Edinburgh EH1 3NX

Scottish Down's Syndrome
Association
54 Shandwick Place
Edinburgh EH2 4RT

Scottish Society for Autistic Children
12 Picardy Place
Edinburgh EH1 3JT

Scottish Society for the Mentally
Handicapped
13, Elmbank Street
Glasgow G2 4PB

Scottish Spina Bifida Association
190 Queensferry Road
Edinburgh EH4 2DW

Sickle Cell Society
c/o Brent Community Health Council
16 High Street
Harlesden
London NW10 4LX
01–451 3293

Spastic Society
12 Park Crescent
London W1N 4EQ
01–636 5020

Spinal Injuries Association
5 Crowndale Road
London NW1
01–388 6840

Stillbirth and Perinatal Death
Association
51a Christchurch Hall
London NW3 1JY
01–794 4601

Toy Libraries Association
68 Church Way
London NW1 1LT
01–387 9592

Voluntary Council for Handicapped
Children
8 Wakley Street
London EC1
01–278 9441

Republic of Ireland

Association for Parents and Friends of
Mentally Handicapped Children
St Michael's House
Willowfield Park
Dublin 14
Dublin 987033

Association for the Welfare of
Children in Hospital
11 Hyde Park
Dalkey
Co Dublin
Dublin 801628

Asthma Society of Ireland
33 St Kevin's Road
Dublin 8
Dublin 757233

Children First
8 Savall Park Crescent
Dalkey
Co Dublin
Dublin 853200

Down's Syndrome Association of
Ireland
PO Box 1045
Ballsbridge
Dublin 4
Dublin 882612

Dyslexia Association of Ireland
31 Stillorgan Park
Blackrock
Co Dublin
Dublin 888463 (mornings)
696758 (afternoons)

Family Planning Service
67 Pembroke Road
Dublin 4
Dublin 681108

Irish Red Cross Society
16 Merrion Square
Dublin 2
Dublin 765135

Irish Society for Autistic Children
19 Lower Leeson Street
Dublin 2
Dublin 764420

Irish Society for the Prevention of
Cruelty to Children
20 Molesworth Street
Dublin 2
Dublin 761293, 760452

Irish Sudden Infant Death Association
34 Sycamore Road
Meadowbrook
Dundrum
Dublin 14
Dublin 983112, 986245

National Association for the Deaf
25 Lower Leeson Street
Dublin 2
Dublin 763118

National League of the Blind of
Ireland
35 Gardiner Place
Dublin 1
Dublin 742792, 745827

Index